FORGOTTEN RELIGIONS

FORGOTTEN RELIGIONS

(INCLUDING SOME LIVING PRIMITIVE RELIGIONS)

Edited By

VERGILIUS T. A. FERM

Essay Index Reprint Series

BOOKS FOR LIBRARIES PRESS
FREEPORT, NEW YORK

INTERNATIONAL STANDARD BOOK NUMBER:

0-8369-1922-X

LIBRARY OF CONGRESS CATALOG CARD NUMBER:

70-128240

PRINTED IN THE UNITED STATES OF AMERICA

EDITOR'S PREFACE

TWO FACTORS lie at the very basis of man's religious response. Without them he would never be religious; with them, he is always potentially religious—whatever his station in life, whatever his culture or environment.

In the first place, it is the most natural thing in the world to be religious because man is psychologically conditioned or equipped for that kind of response. As a psycho-physical organism he has the ability to adapt himself, to adjust himself to whatever comes within his reach and ken. His sensations, his whole bodily responses, his mental reactions are so many instruments by means of which he gets on in his world. He is fundamentally an adjusting organism. Without this ability, he would have perished long ago. To see ahead, to forearm himself, to prepare, to guess what is coming—these are also of the frame of his nature as an adaptive being. He differs from the animals in the superb way in which he holds together so much of his experience and then uses it to further his way for more, to anticipate events and to prepare to cope with them. Man not only concerns himself with the immediate, with the things close by; he reaches out to experiences unborn, to distances beyond his measure both in time and space, There are horizons in his world and, at times, these claim as much of his attention as the things which are in focus only in his immediate surroundings.

Man, in other words, is biologically equipped to pay attention to shadows, to perspectives far beyond his grasp. It is this psychological ability and its expression by thought, by word or deed, that characterizes the religious response. The religious man always takes hold of things that reach out beyond his heres-and-nows, things which seem to hold sway in wider spheres of existence. The ability to react to just such wider environments constitutes the first basic factor of the kind of response called "religious" and makes it normal, widespread and natural.

Older students of psychology, comparative religions and anthro pology looked for some specific psychological cause as ground for man's tendency toward religious interests and behavior. They spoke now of a "religious instinct", now of a "religious *a priori*", now of a "religious feeling", or, in theological language, of the universal spark of divinity in every soul. They explained the origin of that response as due to some particular emotion, such as fear or dread, a feeling of awe or a sense of the *mysterium tremendum*. Or, they defined it as the kind of response which supersedes attempts at coercion (magic) when nature does not respond to specific techniques and therefore must be entreated and courted. Or, they have invented more or less elaborate theories to explain it as due to man's projections of his own powers into an otherwise recalcitrant nature or to read into that nature spirits akin to himself and his fellowmen, spirits which may help or harm.

All these theories are entirely too artificial either by way of elaboration or over-specialization. The simple principle of adaptation to environment seems altogether sufficient—once it is clear how far a journey the mind of man can take into a larger world. In memories he takes just such long journeys into his yesterdays; in anticipations he travels far beyond his bodily limitations; his dreams carry him across the borders of his every-day associations; his mind continually transcends his own bodily confinement and makes him aware of things far beyond the farthest hill or beyond the line of his most remote visible horizon. This characteristic of mind—at the level of the human—impels him to make adjustments and the religious response is just that type of reaction which apprehends even though it may not comprehend the larger world.

A second factor is always present to the religious person. He finds his world to be the kind that evokes just such a response. It is a world which makes inadequate a myopic perspective. The world is strange and baffling; it holds to itself so many secrets; its behavior is not fully understood, no matter how much that understanding may seem to increase. It is a world that has to be reckoned with, one that disturbs any complacency; it is something Big and Powerful and man is so helplessly small and impotent by comparison. His own little life hangs so much in delicate balance in the face of forces over which there is no assured control. The world, in short, is the kind that *stimulates* the response which is characteristically religious.

These two factors are the grounds of the genuinely religious attitudes, be man a member of a primitive society or in a kind of culture which may be called "civilization." They promote and continue to sustain that kind of attitude toward life and the world which is more than plain living, more than making a way through life, more than the doing of good works or of enjoying the companionship of others. The religious man is aware of something more than the routine of naked existence and responds to that awareness. He has taken into his purview a slice of his environment bigger than himself and larger than his work-a-day world; and he is peculiarly adapted psychologically to react to that larger environment.

How he reacts is another question. He may be afraid. He may feel a sense of wonder. He may shout his approval and thanksgiving or he may curse. He may nourish hopes of a better tomorrow in some further extension of existence or of some more recompensing habitation. The *expressions* he gives depend upon the social and cultural environment into which he was born and reared.

The actual religious response is not the same as the possession of a religion. A man who himself *is* religious is possessed of an active experience. "A religion", on the other hand, is that body of beliefs and practices pertaining to that larger world, set by his family, his clan, his tribe, to which he is expected by his group to respond.

Religions become stereotyped affairs of men—codes of behavior held to be favorable and beneficial. Religions are frozen habit-patterns of society. Those who are made members must submit to certain prescribed and traditional mores; and then they are expected to "get religious" about them. Initiation ceremonies and rituals and techniques in general are the natural modes of self-perpetuation of a solidified religion; and institutions arise as a natural protection against its dissolution. Religious ideologies tend to become the guardian rationalizations to establish firmly the assumed sanctity of the prevailing mores.

It is becoming increasingly clear that religions reflect culture and environment in which they are set. Religious leaders, like all leaders, can only lead when the culture is caught up with their vision; but even they reflect their day, its thoughts and ways, its patterns. They may infuse new life into the old bones, re-set the focus or vision of those to whom leadership is given; but they must not be too far removed from the particular frame of social and cultural reference if their leadership is to be accepted. The disciples soon become a second generation and soon freeze visions into moulds acceptable to their own mores; and then the priests come readily along to wield the stick of power to hold the group into line by threats and promises. The priests are many. The prophets, few.

Ancient civilizations have had their appropriate religions. When they die their religions go with them or are so transformed so as better to suit the succeeding type of culture. Religions and civilizations both have their youth, their adult-life and old age. A host of factors make for their birth and their death: the flow of populations, new discoveries, geographical changes; wars and cross-cultural fertilizations. Religions die; but not the religious response itself. Modern religious man is no stranger to his remote religious ancestors because the same psychological conditions operate to promote the characteristic religious response to a world that is still just as baffling in its power and extent. Accumulated knowledge only pushes the frontiers of mystery still farther back and the world grows in its dimensions. The range of vision becomes infinitely larger and gives birth in expanding cultures to newer religions. Our own age is just beginning to reconstruct for itself religions which promise to be more adequate to the wider vistas of an expanding Universe of physical and cultural experience.

It is characteristic for peoples to regard their religions as hallowed by a special kind of providence, employing the specific devices of claims of revelation and election. Westerners are certain that the God of the Universe has selected their historical lineage as the special vehicle by which ultimate disclosures have been granted. The great Hebrew tradition is a marked example; and the Christians who followed in its foot-steps carried on. Easterners are just as earnest in a similar although not identical claim. Neither group has, as yet, been made fully aware of the possibility that perhaps other religions—coming out of other by-gone civilizations—now "forgotten," too, may have grounds for a fair measure to some such claim, however dim. Only recently is the information being acquired as to the character of the religions which undergirded man's long evolving religious history. The curtain is still only partially drawn—sufficient only for a glimpse of how well other civilizations were possessed by religions which served their day, religions, too, which give witness, however vague at times, to the highest outreaches of man's spirit and the kind of world which produces that spirit.

A student of the Old Norse religion makes this point in the essay in this volume and may well speak for some others. There are, he says, "just as great bottomless profundities in Norse religion as in any other. It is only the strangeness that needs to be overcome; and the setting need never be taken too literally." And another scholar writing of the religion of ancient Egypt is convinced of the lofty spiritual quality of ancient man when he affirms (also in this book) that it "is hard to find in any ancient literature as much evidence of a moral consciousness as in such writings as the 'Admonitions of an Egyptian Sage', the 'Eloquent Peasant', the 'Precepts of Ptah-Hotep', the 'Life of 'Rekhmara' ".

This book is an attempt to bring together expressions of the faiths of men who belong to civilizations far remote from that of our own—to show something of the splendor, the glory and the grace of peoples who have preceded us and are now forgotten, together with some of those now living whose pathways are isolated from our own immediate traditions. Many of them show forth ideas and manners which may, in some respects, not only compare favorably with those of our day but even surpass some of the twisted aberrations of our own cultural history. It is the hope that this book may serve to overcome the patronizing mode of traditional historians and apologists who, when they look back and across to strange cultures, dismiss these ancient religions with the scornful remark that they are "heathen" and "pagan" and would see in them only a black contrast to the whiteness of a modern and lofty civilization (forgetting that our own cultural history even up to our present-day—the continuing episodes of man's inhumanity to man—contains pages as dark as the blackest of blacks). The true historian no longer patronizes as he searches the past. He sympathetically unfolds for us the drama of by-gone yesterdays and is making the old cultures appear almost in a new light by reason of his unprejudiced reporting and evaluations.

We must remember that ancient religions, indeed, express the highest in the limited circumstances of existing cultural experiences. And, if we believe in a Spirit at the heart of things, brooding upon the sons of men, we must seek to find evidences of that Spirit expressing Itself even in cultures now so strange to us. The men of yesterday belong to the same family of humanity as we.

ix

Many monographs have been published relating to the character of these forgotten and remote religions, by students who are specialists in some highly specialized field. Most of these monographs are too technical and narrow in scope for a layman's understanding and not easily accessible for the general reader. This book is an attempt to bring together the "highlights" of these old religions, some of which, though ancient, are much alive to-day. A forgotten religion may well include those which to us as laymen are quite unknown because we forgot to remember that primitive religions still exist on our own very planet, neighbors to a modern twentieth-century civilization.

It has been the plan to present these essays in a manner and content which would teach scholars something but also, at the same time, engage the interest of the average reader curious enough to make an exploration in such a subject. Each contributor, a specialist in his field, was given full latitude to express himself in his own way and to select and arrange his material. The editor asked only for reasonable clarity of expression and an exposition of the principal tenets and practices of the religions, their history and chief characteristics—all in terms of the latest information that is now accumulating rapidly in the far-flung world of research in cultural studies. To these contributors the editor offers not only his thanks but, it is hoped, the thanks of the readers of this book, the reading of which is bound to open up vistas of surprising dimensions when they realize how many and how rich are the centuries which lie far back of our own and how deeply lie the roots of man's religious history in the soil of forgotten ages.

Some readers of this book may wonder at the absence of a number of qualified forgotten religions not appearing among these essays. A volume of modest size can hardly be all-inclusive. It can, however, be somewhat representative. It was difficult, for example, to make choices among the many kinds of Indian religions—even among the great varieties on our own continent. On this question, as on others similar to it, the editor was guided by the counsel of some experts on the subject. The ones selected were chosen because of their complexity, their importance, their appeal to general interest, and their peculiar contribution to a representative viewpoint. Attempts were made to include other forgotten religions but without success. The Celtic religion, for example, it was learned, is such an exceedingly narrow field and those who have done research work upon it are no longer among the living and what is now known is quite unreliable. So also, the so-called Pelasgian religion of the aboriginal Greeks remains still in the deepest shadows of our ignorance. Much is now being done in the study of the ancient Maya culture; but, in the report of one expert, so complex an affair is the Maya religion that no satisfactory account can, at this time, even be attempted since the data acquired from sculptural representations of deities are far from clear for a reliable interpretation.

The interested reader, however, will, if he scans carefully the index to this book, find references to other forgotten religions tucked away in the expositions of the major topics.

The editor expresses his appreciation of the continuing confidence and encouragement given him in this and other undertakings by Dr. D. D. Runes, president of The Philosophical Library and to The College of Wooster for a sabbatical year in which this and other literary projects were brought to completion.

VERGILIUS FERM

Wooster, Ohio

TABLE OF CONTENTS

CONTENTS

LIST OF CONTRIBUTORS

VERGILIUS FERM

PHYLLIS ACKERMAN

SAMUEL ALFRED BROWNE MERCER

SAMUEL NOAH KRAMER

A. LEO OPPENHEIM

HANS GUSTAV GÜTERBOCK

THEODOR H. GASTER

GEORGE EMMANUEL MYLONAS

CHARLES ALEXANDER ROBINSON, JR.

IRACH J. S. TARAPOREWALA

MURRAY FOWLER

LI AN-CHE

A. P. ELKIN

JULIAN H. STEWARD

MIRCEA ELIADE

MARGARET LANTIS

LELAND CLIFTON WYMAN

MISCHA TITIEV

THE DAWN OF RELIGIONS

Phyllis Ackerman (Mrs. Arthur U. Pope) was born in Oakland, California, in 1893. She holds three degrees from the University of California, B.L. (1914), M.A. (1915) and Ph.D. (1917).

One of her early professional assignments was to become asso ciate director of the California Art Museum, San Francisco, 1923-24. Her studies in art history brought to her the conviction early that it is important in that field to understand the undergirding religious history. Especially in her study of identification of the sources of West Asiatic textiles of the early Christian centuries did she see how deeply involved are the religious subjects and symbols which form the corpus of ornament—a subject which she found virtually neglected in iconography and the studies in the field of religion. This drove her back to sources far beyond her expectations—to unravel the meanings of the late syncretistic cults required a knowledge of sources far back, even to palaeolithic cultures. Working on this phase of her research, she has developed an iconographic index with full cross-references of some six thousand entries and has cooperated in developing an analytic drawing-file—a joint-work of the Asia Institute.

She is now professor in the field of iconography and textiles in the School for Asiatic Studies, the Asia Institute in New York (since 1944). Many of her works deal with tapestries of various celebrated collections, some with Persian art, ritual-bronzes of early China— monographs, articles and books. She lectures extensively in museums not only in this country but abroad, particularly in England, France and Russia. In 1935 she was awarded the Order of Elmi, first class, a Persian decoration.

Editor

THE DAWN OF RELIGIONS

PHYLLIS ACKERMAN

WHAT WERE man's first adumbrations of religion? Two main answers to this question have been offered, "Animism" and "Dynamism", both derived chiefly from studies amongst existing retarded peoples. According to Animists, primitive man imbued objects and elements in his world with "spirits", activating forces imagined as having more or less consciousness and character. These could be either benevolent—producing, for instance, plant growth, or multiplying fish; or malevolent—causing such disasters as storms, accidents, diseases. Dynamists, on the contrary, think that antecedent to the assumption of multiple, distributed "spirits", there was current a logically prior notion of power or force as such, conceived as disseminated, but also more or less concentrated in various kinds of specific foci. This conception of an undefined but widely decisive Power corresponds to the *"mana"* of Melanesia, the *"ton"* of the Dakotas; and similar conceptions are found among other retarded peoples, with a variety of names. In Akkadian literature this Power is represented by the Rays which all gods had and one god might steal from another, thereby depriving the victim of his supernatural functions. The hypothesis of belief in such a dispersed Power explains, moreover, various prehistoric cultural phenomena, as well as a wide range of persisting mythic, cultic and folkloristic factors.

Thus the use of ferrous earth in burials, beginning in the late palaeolithic period,[1] is most comprehensible as implying confidence that redness possessed a reanimating force. Uses of red earths by modern "primitives", and folklore references show an identification of the red earth with blood. Numerous blood rites involve the assumption that supernatural power of high potency is present in blood[2]; myths like the episode in the Ugaritic epic, of the revival of the slain Ba'al by burying him in the blood slaughtered comrades[3]

3

show that in the blood is the life (cf. *Gen.* 9:4; *Lev.* 17:11), to such an extent that its use in burial can restore life. Hence the hypothesis of a belief in a life Power being operative in late palaeolithic practices is reasonably verified. But since the Power sought was correlated with life, this earliest proto-religion might better be called, not "Dynamism", but "Vitalism".

The Vitalistic hypothesis also explains other late palaeolithic cultural phenomena, which further strengthens the hypothesis. Thus, bovine figures in the non-habitation cave of the Three Brothers at Tuc d'Audoubert[4] indicate almost beyond question bovine rites; but the bull, and to a lesser extent the cow, have a long subsequent history as embodiments or symbols of vital force attaining supernatural character. Other remains in the same cave-complex indicate phallic rites, and in various historical cults—most notoriously, the Phoenician—sex experience has been conceived as a manifestation of a religiously interpreted Power. The pregnant woman represented by late palaeolithic figurines are about to create life,[5] thus demonstrating their possession of a high degree of vital Power.

In general, foci of the Power fall into seven classes. First are differentia between life and death: e.g., blood (early man must often have died by hemorrhage); redness (the ruddiness of health contrasted with the pallor of death); breath; warmth. The importance of breath in the late palaeolithic proto-religion is attested by the Grimaldi burial, with a neat furrow of red earth leading to each nostril,[6] and another in front of the mouth. The implied direct association of breath and blood is found in both early Chinese thinking,[7] and in the Navajo religion.[8] Whether there was a palaeolithic fire-cult (corresponding to warmth as a recognized corollary of life Force) cannot be determined.

Second are *sine qua non* of life. Man must early have become all too familiar with death by hunger and thirst. The meat animals, especially in a hunting economy, give life—one source of the importance of bovines. The tremendous emphasis on shells, most conspicuous in the palaeolithic period in the shell burials, but also expressed by the popularity then of shell ornaments, may well have been due to their water-associations. And the famous East Gravettian all-over angular meander pattern engraved on a bone, found at Predmost,[9] is the first known appearance of a design that later represents water.

4

Third, the life-giver is obviously greatly endowed with the life Force, hence the representation, not only of pregnant females, but also of the vulva, as in the numerous small clay "apples" in the non-habitation cave of Montespan.[10] Here are remote forerunners of the *Genesis* myth of Eve offering Adam the apple; "Eve" means "life".

Fourth, vitalistic foci may demonstrate the presence of the Power by their own strength, another source of the bull's enduring significance, but also of the persisting symbolic use of such inedible powerful animals as the great felines.

Fifth, the Power is made manifest by the direct vitalizing efficacy of the focus. Rites connected with the phallos (and phalloi are quite numerous in varying forms in late Palaeolithic materials) [11] were probably based not on the recognition of its procreative function, since the participation of the male in conception is understood only in rather developed cultures, but rather on its relation to the orgasmic stimulation. This evaluation is explicitly attested later in non-procreative sex practices in various cults, such as the Phoenician.

A sixth major class of vitalistic foci consists of resurrection manifestations. Deciduous plants come in this category: "dead" in winter, "revivified" in spring; and late Palaeolithic bone engravings depict deciduous branches,[12] as well as a four-petalled blossom.[13] The snake "reborn" from its own slough is another, and engravings of serpents are fairly numerous at this time.[14] All these, and other, similar natural phenomena have been understood as showing the presence of a vitalistic Power which is so strong that death itself is overcome.

A seventh type of vitalistic symbol (not noted, however, in any Palaeolithic remains) demonstrates its Power by survival: notably evergreen trees which persist through adverse winter conditions. The Egyptian cultic stylized tree, the *"djed"* column, is an explicit representation of this idea since *"djed"* means "endurance."

Almost all the late Palaeolithic remains explicable only as proto-religious, find simple, inherently probable and reciprocally consistent explanations (the most effective test, outside the range of laboratory sciences, for any hypothesis) as expressions of the vitalistic Power, save one group, the most strikingly non-utilitarian of all. These are the Magdalenian carved stag-horn rods.[15] Since they are quite numerous and have been recovered at somewhat scattered

5

sites, they could not have been insignificant individual productions, especially as they all (or perhaps almost all) bear a recurrent ornamental repertoire, though in varying compositions. Persistent factors in the designs are S-scrolls (the earliest known examples of spiral ornament) ; a pair or two pairs of circles, each with a small center disk; an egg, radiant on one side; often a crescent; occasionally a star. The star and crescent give a clue to the curious egg with exaggerated rays on one long side: night is giving way to dawn in the sky and the egg is the rising sun, which often appears ovoid as it passes the horizon, and can have, at that moment, just such well-defined rays. Are the S-scrolls, then, clouds? Possibly; but later the S is a common water stylization. The paired circles with center-disk would seem to remain a mystery.

Here an Egyptian (Elephantine) myth-complex,[16] recognized as prehistoric and very ancient, provides striking coincidences. The sun first rose out of a wonderful island in the Nile (identified by the Elephantine priests with Elephantie itself), and the sun-egg was made from the mud of the Nile bed. But there, also, was a double cavern shaped like a pair of breasts, and the Nile flowed from these. The Nile, however (like many, if not all sacred rivers originally—compare the Ganges) is the earthly continuation of the Milky Way. This sky-river is a river of milk, first because it is white, second because, descending as rain, it nourishes sprouting plants as milk nourishes young animals; therefore it appropriately flows from a pair of breasts. It was certainly out of this celestial river that the sun-egg came, and it was made by Khnemu (an extremely ancient god), the Creator, who himself was also the primeval watery abyss; and in the Akkadian Creation myth (*"Enuma elish . . ."*),[17] the primeval watery abyss (Apsu) is the husband of the Milky Way (*"tamtu"*, *"Tiamat"*). The typical complex on the stag-horn rods, the sun-egg associated with the water-scrolls, the paired circles as breasts with emphatic nipples, the relation to the night sky as indicated by crescent moon and stars, is rendered intelligible by the parallel of the very ancient prehistoric mythic complex.

Historians of religion dependent on nineteenth-century German theories have refused to consider the possibility of astronomical elements in early religions, but a line of French historians indebted to the French historian Biot, continued to explore and expound the probability of early astronomical religious factors, culminating in

6

the notable work of de Saussure.[18] Meanwhile the brilliant, if eccentric, O'Neill[19] had extended the thesis to world mythology, with less scholarly rigor but with penetrating imagination, and comprehensive, if sometimes unsystematic, erudition. The German prejudice against admitting astronomical elements in early religion and religious iconography was, and is, due to their exclusive absorption in the comparatively late Babylonian solar-planetary astronomy. The astronomy which the Biot-de Saussure school of cultural historians has traced to far earlier origins is concerned primarily with the circumpolar system. O'Neill gave more recognition, in addition, to the Milky Way. Reaction against the German dogmatic rejection of early astronomical factors has strengthened in the last few years,[20] but recognition of the Biot-de Saussure contribution is still insufficient, and O'Neill—who has to be very critically used but is none-the-less suggestive and stimulating—is quite neglected.

That the Milky Way should have been the first feature of the night sky to attract man's attention accords with internal probability. It is large, obvious, always visible in clear weather in the north temperate zone where these developments took place. Moreover, Milky Way observations could have had practical value, for by means of simple estimates based on accumulated experience, which would provide allowances for the season, both direction and time, which were both determined by looking at the sun during the day, can be crudely calculated at night from the position of the Milky Way.

The next advance in practical stellar observations, which de Saussure emphasizes, is the recognition of the relation between the heliacal rising of two constellations at the opposite ends of the Milky Way, and the two equinoxes. Fixing the equinox dates became important with the introduction of agriculture, especially the determination of the Vernal equinox. Quite likely, then, this observation was a Neolithic advance. Orion is the modern formulation of one of these constellations, the Heart of Scorpio of the other. The two constellations appear in widely diffused myths personated as contrasted brothers, or complementary twins, or paired opponents.[21] Retarded peoples, notably in Oceania, still use thus calendrically these heliacal risings.

The recognition of the circumpolar system seems to have been the next step, and Ursa Major to have been the first constellation

7

isolated out of the complex. This advance provided a more accurate basis for the calculation of direction and time at night, and also for the equinoxial calculations. About 4000 B.C. Polaris was zeta Ursae Maioris (Mizar), which would explain the strong, and persistingly strong emphasis on this constellation, if the observations were established during that period. Moreover, in certain mythologies the Polar divinity is directly connected with that constellation. Thus in Chinese mythology, which contains many very early features, despite the Confucian destruction of prior mythological records, Shang-ti rides in the Chariot, which is one designation for Ursa Maior, comparable to our "Charles' Wain."

In various cosmologies the polaris center was marked by a mountain (amongst other emblems); this is often a two-peaked mountain, occasionally a pair of mountains. It would seem that the more ancient idea of breasts as the source of the Milky Sky stream had been magnified to landscape proportions, the emphasis on duality corresponding to the two streams of the Milky Way, owing to the visible hiatus in the white band, though that does not, of course, occur actually in the middle. Thus El (*"the* God"), in the Ugaritic epic, lives at the "source of the two rivers, at the fountains of the two deeps."[22] The cosmic mountain was sometimes square, with its sides corresponding to the cardinal points—a pyramid, hence the importance of this form in Egypt, China and elsewhere; and each side was sometimes (as on Mount Meru) a different color, corresponding to the hue assigned to each direction.[23] These color-systems vary from culture to culture, or even within the same culture. In other instances (as in Navajo mythology, for example) there may also be a mountain at each cardinal point, making five in all.

But mountains were not normal objects of veneration in neolithic or pre-neolithic cultural conditions. They are an impediment to both the hunter and the herdsman, to the tiller are waste land. Mountains are, on the contrary, important to metallurgists as the repository of ores.[24] This industry was being initiated in the early fourth millennium when Polaris was zeta Ursae Maioris. Similarly, the "hero" of the standardized, widespread Flood myth, rescuing a nucleus of living beings to repopulate the earth is a mountain—Ararat, in the *Genesis* form of the tale which is most familiar to us. It has been calculated that the first flood occurred about 4000 B.C.

8

This succession of advances in pre-solar, pre-planetary astronomy is paralleled by the opening divine genealogy in the Akkadian Creation myth (*"Enuma elish . . ."*). In the first cosmogonic phase nothing exists but a couple, Apsu, and Tiamat, also called "Mother Hubur". "Apsu" means the "abyss"; Tiamat, which is the same as *"tamtu"*, the common noun for the Milky Way, is sometimes called "Form" Tiamat,[25] and Mother Hubur means Mother River; the Milky Way is thus conceived as a formed body of water in the sky in contrast to the formless abyss and both are personalized, as female and male, respectively.

The nature of these personations is indicated only indirectly. Apsu has a *"mummu"*, which means his own creative utterance or life-force,[26] and this also is personated. When, in a subsequent contest, this Mummu is conquered, he is led away by a nose-rope.[27] The suggestion in this detail that these "personations" were rather zoomorphic than anthropomorphic, and bovine, is borne out by a simple Berber Creation myth in which the original procreative couple are bovine, and the female, a wild cow, is called "Thamuatz",[28] which is essentially a variant of "Tiamat". A people with a bovine dairy industry would tend to equate the Milky Way with their milk-animal, but Thamuatz, and quite likely therefore her remote antecedent, Tiamat, is a *wild* cow, a pre-bovine-domestication source for the type. "The wild cow" is also the peculiar name of a net which Ninurta—a complex sky-god—uses as one of his weapons.[29] But in various other contexts the Milky Way is envisaged as a great net. This would explain the designation "Wild Cow" for a sky-divinity's net, on the principle—fundamental in early symbolism—that things equal to the same thing equal one another.

Tiamat is thus in essence the same as the Egyptian sky-goddess, Nut, a cow with the Milky Way on her belly. Thus old Power emblems were re-used as figures for astral elements in later astro-cosmological religions. But Nut was also a woman, one of a large class of cow-woman goddesses (Hathor, Isis, Ishtar, etc.) ; and similarly, Tiamat's family was anthropomorphic as well as zoomorphic, for when, in the *"Enuma elish . . ."*, Apsu thanks his Mummu for advising him how to destroy Nudimmud, Apsu lifts the Mummu on his knees and caresses him[30]; he has already spoken of his Mummu as "bringing him into a good mood."[31]

Dr. Oppenheim, considering this passage, has suggested that the

Mummu was a dwarf of the Bes type.[32] But an extensive comparative study of Bes types[33] indicates that the figure originated as a phallos-personation, corresponding to the widespread notion, and designation of the phallos as the "Little Man"[34]; and the phallos is so depicted, for example, on some Maori gods, the "Little Man" being an exact miniature replica of the god himself.[35] This identification of the Mummu as the phallos-personation explains the whole *"Enuma elish . . ."* episode: Apsu's summons to his Mummu to "come to me", to "bring me into good mood"; then when the scheme has been worked out, Apsu's lifting his Mummu up on his lap and caressing him, and "The neck of Mummu he embraced."[36] Mummu who addresses Apsu as "My Father", is Apsu's phallos-personation; Apsu induced an onanistic revery in order to dream up his magic scheme for dealing with his rebellious son; and when he had thought it out, he fulfilled his satisfaction, "clasping the neck" of his Mummu, and caressing it. "Mummu" is interpreted by later Babylonians as meaning "Creative Utterance", or "life-force",[37] and this "utterance" with "life-force" would, therefore, be the semen.

But semen appears elsewhere as a generative force and is evoked, for that purpose, onanistically. Thus in the Egyptian parallel cosmogony, this is explicit, and here it is the phallic personality himself who speaks, Khepri, whose name comes from the root *"khoper"*, "to become, to be formed"—a designation determined, it would seem, by the erection image; and the father of Khepri is, like the father of Mummu, the Abyss—"Apsu". Khepri speaks:

"The Master of Everything saith after his forming:
" 'I am he who was formed as Khepri.
" 'When I had formed, then the forms were formed.
" 'All the forms were formed after my forming.
" 'Numerous are the forms from that which proceeded
    from my mouth.' "

. . . . . .

" 'I founded in my own heart' "

. . . . . .

" 'I am he who copulated with my fist, (as Apsu clasped
    the neck of his Mummu)
" 'I excited (or felt) pleasure in my shadow,
" 'Semen resulted out of my mouth.

" 'What I ejected was Shu (Atmosphere, but from a
  root meaning "to spit") ,

" 'What I spat out was Tefnet (Moisture, from another
  root "to spit") ,

" 'My father the Abyss sent them.' "[38]

. . . . . .

Exciting pleasure in the "shadow" refers to the fact that the phallic "Little Man", or Bes type, is commonly drawn with legs bowed in such wise as to create a void pattern of a glans; and Dr. Oppenheim suggests[39] that one of the undeciphered lines concerning Mummu speaks of his legs as "too short to run"—which would recall this feature.

The line "I founded in my own heart," or, as elsewhere translated, "I worked a charm upon my own heart",[40] is explained in the *Brihad-Aranyaka Upanishad,* where Varuna (the sky—the watery abyss—Apsu) is under discussion:

". . . Varuna—on what is he based?"

"On water."

"And on what is water based?"

"On semen."

"And on what is semen based?"

"On the heart. Therefore they say of a son who is just like his father (the phallic Little Man is the son who is the replica of his 'Father') , 'He is slipped out of his heart, as it were. He is built out of his heart.' For on the heart alone semen is based."[41] The erected phallos is thus in some wise an externalization of the heart; but we still locate love, including sexual love, in the heart. All this means that in one branch of this astral cosmogony the Milky Way was regarded as the creative semen of the Sky-god.

After Nudimmud had slain Apsu, he wrapped up his *mummu* and laid it crosswise in relation to his body,[42] an interesting burial rite, which also suggests that the anthropomorphic Apsu was figured as priapine.

Thus another of the ancient vitalistic Power emblems, the phallos, is fitted into the astro-cosmological system, and its Power function is still understood, not primarily as generative, but as orgasmic, and when generative, only onanistically, not bisexually.

Apsu and Tiamat give birth to twins, Lahmu and Lahamu, and in other texts these seem to be serpents.[43] In symbolism, the snake

11

and water or the river are repeatedly interchangeable, because both form a rippling line; and that these first children of Tiamat were only synonyms of herself, another symbol for the bipartite Heavens River or Milky Way, is indicated by a considerable repertoire of serpent-Milky Way identifications in mythology.

As Dr. Oppenheim has pointed out,[44] these serpentine synonyms of Tiamat do not play any considerable part in the subsequent story, nor do they take a place in the family line. Instead, Tiamat gives birth to another pair of twins "more highly developed than they". These second twins, in short, represent an advance over the rudimentary astronomy of the Milky Way observations, which would mean that they personate the pair of constellations at the ends of the Milky Way, important for the relation between their heliacal rising and the equinoxes. They are called "Anshar" and "Kishar", which mean "High" and "Low" "host". Kishar appears, in another text, as one of seven guardians of the house of Ereshkigal, who was the constellation Hydra,[45] suggesting that Kishar was Orion or part thereof, or near thereunto. The House of Ereshkigal was in the land of the dead, and Orion when first observed was, judging from the widespread mythological characterizations of its personations, the Autumn constellation, herald of winter, season of death. The land of the dead was in the netherworld, hence the emphasis on "below". That Anshar and Kishar were constellational seems also to be the explanation for the repeated emphasis, in the *"Enuma elish . . ."*, on their equality, as members of the same class, with the next two generations of the divine succession,[46] Anu, and Ea or Nudimmud, who can for more definite reasons be identified as astral, and are described in the *"Enuma elish . . ."* as going "Whirling through the 'Heavenly Mansions' "[47]—an excellent poetic description of constellational movement.

"Anu", the name of Anshar and Kishar's son, who was "an equal of his parents",[48] derives from *"an"* "high", and in Sumerian the same sign stands for *"an"* and for *"dingir"*, which means "shining", "bright", and also is used for "god", as such. Anu is in the "yoke of the wagon star"[49]—i.e., is part of the constellation which we call Ursa Maior. In short, this bright, high object, which is not only a god, but is the very type of the gods, is Polaris of *c.* 4000 B.C., the next stage in astro-religious development.

Apsu, Tiamat, Lahmu, Lahamu, Anshar, and Kishar appear

hereafter only incidentally in subordinate rôles. Anu remains important but is relegated to the highest Heaven and scarcely functions. His son, Nudimmud (or Enki or Ea) continues, on the other hand, to be a major god.

Ea establishes himself on the Apsu—which no longer means the husband of Tiamat, but has its literal significance, "the watery deep", and his name is written with the ideogram "Enki", which means "Lord of the Watery Deep". He is commonly shown holding a vase out of which flow two streams in opposite directions. Thus like El he lives at the source of the Two Deeps. But this means that he, too, was in the center of the Milky Way, whence it is conceived as flowing off in the opposite directions as a pair of rivers; for while the hiatus in the Milky Way as we see it is not in the center, iconography stylizes by regularizing natural fact. In short, Nudimmud was another Polaris, and his "birth" is equivalent to identifying another star (alpha Draconis-Thuban) that had come to supplant zeta Ursae Maioris; and this is specifically indicated in the *"Enuma elish . . ."* text: "Anu created a *replica of himself*, Nudimmud."[50] Anu then has to be removed from the dominant position of the pantheon, but without robbing him of his honors.

Another text about Ea confirms indirectly this temporal succession of Ea, for it describes Ea as the begetter of a group of craft gods, and specifically the patron of metal-workers (creating goldsmiths, smiths and jewellers), and also the originator of priestly ritual.[51] That is to say, he was the Polaris of the fully evolved Bronze Age, *c.* 3000 B.C.

Nudimmud, as Dr. Oppenheim has made clear, supplants Apsu as the mate of Tiamat,[52] and this accords with the astro-religious interpretation of one relation between Polaris and the Milky Way, which is indicated in a variety of other sources. Not only is Polaris male and the Milky Way female, but the polaric center is marked by a phallos, while the Milky Way, conceived as encircling the earth, with an aperture at the Pole (the stylization, again, of the visible hiatus) is thought of as defining a cosmic uterus and kteis, in which the phallos is inserted. This is otherwise stated, in a large number of works of art from the third millennium on, as a jar, similar in shape to the supposed outline of the Milky Way or the cosmic uterus, holding a phallic tree, e.g. cypress. The female as a jar is a widespread and obvious symbol. It is noteworthy that it was not Anu who mated with Tiamat, but Nudimmud; that is, this notion of a sex complementation between Polaris and the galaxy began only in the early Bronze Age.

Eventually in the *"Enuma elish . . ."* Tiamat in her turn is slain, and her hide is slit in two and stretched across the heavens. The description of its disposition is a bit confused,[53] but a careful analysis indicates with reasonable probability that it was used to mark the celestial equator and meridian. The Milky Way is a rough equivalent of the equator and meridian when it lies, respectively, east-west, and north-south; hence the use of Tiamat's hide (or body) to define the imaginary lines. The equator-meridian cross (Four Quarters motive) is the most frequent seal-type in about the second quarter of the third millennium B.C. It would be likely to be most conspicuous when the conception was novel, and this dating about accords with the chronology indicated by the *"Enuma elish . . ."* sequence of events.

The Milky Way ceases to be important, for practical purposes, when the celestial equator and meridian are "measured", so Tiamat can be thus obliterated, and Nudimmud now mates, not with a galaxy-goddess, but with Damkina, Lady of the Earth. This is a very familiar stage in cosmogony, represented in Greek mythology by Ouranos and Ge as the great cosmically procreative couple; and in Chinese thinking by Heaven as *yang* and Earth as the complementary *yin*. Since in the West the Four Quarters idea is novel and consequently conspicuous about 2700 to 2500 B.C., and the mating of Nudimmud and Damkina follows the fixing of the Quarters, the *yang-yin* cosmology might presumably have moved out to China shortly after that, which coincides with the period of the introduction into northwest China of the painted pottery, recognized to be derived from the West.

This correspondence between the successive generations in the early divine genealogy of the *"Enuma elish . . ."* and the successive stages in the development of astronomical observation (for compass, clock and calendrical utility), and of a resultant astro-cosmological pantheon, means that the mythological history of the universe was really a history of Man's conceptions of the main factors in the universe.

Meanwhile, Anshar and Kishar cooperate with Anu, and then with Nudimmud, and this continued interest in the pair of constel-

Fig. 1. Front of quiver, bronze repousse, Surkh-dum, Luristan, *c.* 1000 B.C. Metropolitan Museum of Art. *Hypothetical interpretation:* (zones numbered from top to bottom): (1) illegible; (2) procession of antelopes, curving backs and horns suggesting Milky Way water-undulation, animal on right reverted to mark cardinal-point "pole" (celestial west); (3) Polaric twins, doubled like two-peaked mountain, etc., alternation bull-personation summarized in headdresses, arms making Milky Way water-zigzag; on left, controlling pair of Polaric trees; on right, Milky Way bovine; on ground, stars; (4) Polaric "Little Man", arms with loin-forelegs making Milky Way zigzag, controlling both Milky Way lions and antelopes (latter forming *"omega"*, another Milky Way figure); (5) Polaric god with arms forming (angular) ring of *"phi"*, holding head (as often), which is North Star, and linked with Orion- and Scorpio-heart-Twins, arms making Milky Way zigzag; celestial east Twin making half-*phi* with arm; celestial west Twin holding West "pole" tree; (6) Milky Way animal procession with stars and below, band of stars as synonym; (7) Milky Way winged antelopes making Milky Way zigzag with forelegs touching Polaric tree.

15

lations which mark the equinoxes by their heliacal rising, along with Polaris, is also expressed iconographically. In one striking form of visual presentation the Polaris figure is based on the circumpolaric symbol of a ring (the rotating constellations) transfixed by a stick—Polaris as marked by a "menhir", which is also phallic. Abstractly this makes a *phi*[54]—a highly simplified indication of a standing man; illustratively it makes an affronted man with arms akimbo. (Fig. 1) This is a usual Bes pose, Bes being a phallic personation. The phallic significance is made explicit in some types by defining in the void between the bowed legs a glans, this void-pattern being what is referred to in the Egyptian cosmogonic text, as the "shadow". The bowed legs, evidently originally introduced to effect this "shadow" glans, represent an elaboration of the basic *"phi"* pose into a "figure eight" pose, such as characterizes the Sasanian King when he is ceremonially enthroned,[55] and the King assumes the attitude thus of the Polaric god because the King has his authority as surrogate of the Great God who was, in the first case, the Polaric personation. But the *"phi"* pose more commonly does not include the "shadow" glans, and it is used for many other Polaric personalities besides the Bes type, amongst them Osyris.

The Twins are often conceived as two half-men, hence as two half-*phi*: as such, they each stand on one foot and have one hand on hip, forming half the ring. (Fig. 2) These figures are developed, singly or together, in a great variety of ways. (Fig. 1) Thus the pair may wrestle, or otherwise contest with each other, indicating the "conflict" which accounts for their alternation in the night sky. Sometimes they stand directly on either side of Polaris and hold hands with him, their arms making the zig-zag line which is an ancient water symbol that had for centuries been used to sketch the Milky Way.[56] In an interesting Sargonid seal-type they stand together, each on one foot, the other foot twisted to outline the void glans as the Polaris marker.[57] This twisting of a foot to complete the outline of a void-glans explains a recurrent problem, both textual and iconographic, of divinities with twisted feet.[58]

When zeta Ursae Maioris was Polaris, alpha and iota Draconis lay on either side of the pole path and were called the "pivots of the pole".[59] The main triad of Polaris and the twin terminal constellations is, therefore, sometimes supplemented by these secondary twins, inserted between the older and more important twins

16

Fig. 2. Chinese Orion divinity, *cire-perdu* cast bronze, 16th century, writer's collection. An androgynous person posed as a "half-*phi*", standing on one leg, on one of the Milky Way lions couchant, the other leg and corresponding arm each making the half-ring of the "*phi*". In this hand is held the brush which is carried by the Taoist genius of Union, associated with the East and Spring, and *yang*, while in the other he holds above his head a small box also associated with the ancient Egyptian Orion, representing Canopus—and in Chinese thinking, *yin*. His tigrine nose and eyes, found also on Chinese gods of the Chou period, his small bull-horns and his claws as hands and feet (recalling Lahmu as Orion—*v.* n. 58) are relics of ancient West Asiatic antecedent personations.

and the pole.[60] This makes a pentad, and five is a sympathetic number to this system since it refers also to the four quarters and the center.

The foregoing outline of the development of proto- and early religions is reached by the hypothetical method developed in interpretive (as distinct from descriptive, and experimental) sciences. The correlation of a great range of varied but mutually relevant phenomena suggests a principle, or set of related principles of explanation. The formulation of this explanation—whether it be the molecular theory, or the theory of genes, or this vitalistic and astro-calendrical theory of the origins of religions—is an act of creative insight involving imagination and thus at its inception is subjective. The second step, whether it be in physics, biology or cultural history, is to test the hypothesis by the maximum number and variety of possible applications. The physicist, and to some extent the biologist, can at this point use more or less controlled tests in laboratory experiments. The cultural historian can compensate for the impossibility, in his domain, of such controlled tests by the greater richness of the material in which he can find relevant instances: archaeological (iconographic), mythological, folkloristic (including superstition). In proportion as the tests confirm the hypothesis, the interpretation becomes objective and ceases to be merely hypothetical.

The method, at least as applied to this particular cultural-historical realm, involves two premises: that concepts frequently long antedate their first known documentary recording; and diffusionism. In the same ratio that the testing of the hypothesis substantiates the interpretation, it provides support for these premises.

This vitalistic and astro-cosmological account of proto- and early religion, though it directly counters the usual description current just now of the history of West Asiatic mythologies and religions, has been forecast in respect of the early importance of astronomy, quite independently, and on quite different grounds:

"In this mythical world of the Chalcolithic, fertility myths were superimposed on still older astral myths." "That astral myths go back to the beginnings of human myth-making has become increasingly recognized by anthropologists."[61]

This starkly affirmative, because necesarily so brief, summary of one central line of development of the initial vitalistic interpreta-

18

tion of the universe and experience, followed by a logical succession of astral myths, though it is sustained by an extensive and intricately interrelated structure of confirming applications, is offered here thus apparently dogmatically, as an hypothesis, for others to test by world mythology, iconography, symbolism, folklore and superstition—not forgetting the persistent or revived early elements to be detected in Gnostic syncretisms, *and* in the religions of retarded cultures.

NOTES

1. (Re Palaeolithic red burials) D. A. Mackenzie, *Ancient Man in Britain* (London-Glasgow, 1932) pp. 19-20. 28-29; G.-H. Luquet, *L'Art et la Religion des Hommes Fossiles* (Paris, 1926) pp. 182-7; H. Peake—H. J. Fleure, *Hunters and Artists* (Oxford, 1927) p. 94; C. F. J. Hawkes, *The Prehistoric Foundations of Europe* (London, 1940) p. 38; G. Renard, *Life and Work in Prehistoric Times* (London, 1929) pp. 91, 175; L. C. Goodrich, *A Short History of the Chinese People* (New York, 1943) p. 2; (Neolithic) I. Schnell, "Prehistoric Finds from the Island World of the Far East," *Bulletin of the Museum of Far Eastern Art*, IV (Stockholm, 1932) pp. 37-38; (Chalcolithic) R. Ghirshman, *Fouilles de Sialk* (Paris, 1938) pp. 11, 27, 43; (Bronze Age) Hawkes, *op cit.*, pp. 220-1, 225, 234; S. Umehara, *Selected Ancient Treasures Found at Anyang, Yin Sites* (Kyoto, 1940) Pl. XXVIII; W. C. White, *Tombs of Old Lo-yang* (Shanghai, 1934) pp. 10, 23; C. W. Bishop, *Origin of the Far Eastern Civilizations* (Washington, 1942) p. 45; J. G. Anderson, "Symbolism in the Prehistoric Painted Ceramics of China," *Bulletin of the Museum of Far Eastern Art*, I (Stockholm, 1926) pp. 59, 67; A. Woodward, Collection from the Channel Islands of California," *Indian Notes*, IV (1927), p. 66. Cf. also E. Mackay, *The Indus Civilization* (London, 1935) p. 167; Mackenzie, *Myths of China and Japan* (London, s.d.) p. 161.

2. Lucien Lévy-Bruhl, *Primitives and the Supernatural* (New York, 1935) Chapter IX; *"Enuma elish . . ."* IV, 18; A. Heidel, *The Babylonian Genesis* (Chicago, 1942) p. 27, and n. 73; Numbers, 19; Hebrews, 12-14, 19-24; Li Ki, Chapter IX—*Liyun* (*Wisdom of the East*, XXVII, or Lin Yutang, *The Wisdom of Confucius* (1938) pp. 231, 232; also Li Ki, IV, IV, I, 11 (*Sacred Books of the East*, XXVII, p. 298); XVIII, II, II, 33 (*ibid.*, pp. 169-170); cf. H. G. Creel, *The Birth of China* (New York, 1937) p. 201; *The Writings of Kwang-Sze*, XXVIII, III, VI, 10 (*Sacred Books of the East*, XL, p. 164) ; Firdausi, *Shahnama*, V, 7, v. 55 (A. G. and E. Warner (Trans.), I (London, 1905) p. 164); J. E. Harrison, *Ancient Art and Ritual* (New York, 1913) p. 64; *idem, Prolegomena to the Study*

of Greek Religion (Cambridge, 1922) pp. 12, 125; Mackenzie, *Myths of China . . .*, p. 38.

3. W. F. Albright, *Archaeology and the Religion of Israel* (Baltimore, 1942) pp. 77, 85.

4. Peake-Fleure, *op. cit.*, pp. 82-83, Fig. 44; H. F. Cleland, *Our Primitive Ancestors* (Garden City, 1928) pp. 39-41; R. O. Sawtell—I. Treat, *Primitive Hearths of the Pyrenees* (London—New York, 1927) pp. 25-27, 94-95. For other indications of Palaeolithic bull-rites see; Luquet, *op. cit.*, p. 214 (Eyzies bone engravings), or R. de Saint-Périer, *L'Art Préhistorique* (Paris, 1932) Pl. XLVII (bottom), No. 8; Luquet, *op. cit.*, pp. 213-214 (Chancelade bone engraving); H. G. Spearing, *The Childhood of Art* (London, 1930) p. 50 ("bâton de commandement"); Luquet, *op. cit.*, p. 182 (Barma Grande burial with head on bovine femur).

5. See H. F. Osborn, *Men of the Old Stone Age* (New York, 1916) p. 321; and discussion in Albright, *From the Stone Age to Christianity* (Baltimore, 1940) p. 92.

6. Luquet, *op. cit.*, p. 185; and cf. apparent representations of animals' breath in late Palaeolithic bone engravings, *ibid*, pp. 92, 93, Fig. 67.

7. Li Ki, IX, III, 20 (*Sacred Books of the East*, XXVII, p. 444).

8. The writer is indebted for this information to Miss Mary C. Wheelwright; and cf. *idem, Hail Chant and Water Chant* (Santa Fe, 1946) p. 125.

9. de Saint-Périer, *op. cit.*, Pl.

10. Sawtell-Treat, *op. cit.*, p. 243.

11. Luquet, *op. cit.*, pp. 126, 156, 164; Spearing, *op. cit.*, pp. 50-51; Sawtell-Treat, *op. cit.*, p. 119; de Saint Périer, *op. cit.*, Pl. LII, Fig. 2; Mackenzie, *Myths of Crete and Pre-Hellenic Europe* (London, s.d.) p. 30.

12. Luquet, *op. cit.*, pp. 22-23; p. 62, Fig. 41; de Saint Périer, *op. cit.*, Pl. LIX, Fig. 5.

13. de Saint Périer, *op. cit.*, Pl. III, Fig. 5.

14. Luquet, *op. cit.*, pp. 142-143, 155-156.

15. Luquet, *op cit.*, p. 60; S. Reinach, *Répertoire de l'Art Quaténaire* (Paris, 1913) pp. 23, 136; de Saint Périer, *op. cit.*, p. 63, Pl. LVII, Figs. 7, 8.

16. L. Spence, *Myths and Legends, Ancient Egypt* (Boston, s.d.) pp. 153-155.

17. Heidel, *op. cit.*, p. 8.

18. L. de Saussure, "La Cosmologie Religieuse en Chine, dans l'Iran et chez les Prophètes Hébreux," *Actes du Congrès Internationsal d'Histoire des Religions* (Paris, 1923, 1925), II, pp. 79-92; *idem, Les Origines de l'Astronomie Chinoise* (Paris, 1930).

19. J. O'Neill, *The Night of the Gods* (London, I, 1893; II, 1897).

20. Cf., e.g., Albright, *op. cit.*, pp. 11, 180, n. 15; or *vide infra*.

21. The constellation "announcing" summer is a pacific personality, that "announcing" winter a ruder, sometimes a violent personality. Thus one may be an agriculturist, the other is commonly a hunter or herdsman; the one may be a musician, the other is typically a warrior. One of many typical characterizations is: ". . . Jabal . . . was the father of such as dwell in tents, and *have* cattle. And his brother's name was Jubal: he was the father of all such as handle the harp and organ." (*Gen.* 4, 20, 21.) (Cf. Amphion and Zethos) When the observation was first made (according to de Saussure, prior to the 24th century B.C.), Orion "announced" winter, hence this constellation is commonly personated by the shepherd, hunter, warrior, or "hero" type. The chief story about the pair has to explain the disappearance of one from the sky, and hence one usually kills the other. When complete, the story must also account for the return of that constellation to the sky, hence includes the resurrection of the personage, and should then recount the "death" of the other. The Ugaritic epic (C. H. Gordon, *The Loves and Wars of Baal and Anat* [Princeton, 1943] pp. 5-11) gives the complete cycle: the death of Ba'al, his resurrection, the destruction of Mot. "Mot", "Death" is an unusually explicit name for the winter constellation personality. Scorpio is also associated with fire, and Antares is the Fire Star, because Scorpio was originally the spring constellation, and in spring the great fire-festival was (and is) held, to help the birth of the new spring sun and the return of the hot season by "sympathetic" magic. For the same reason, the Scorpio personality is quite often a "red" god. But the attributes and identifications have sometimes become confused, because in the course of time the relations have been reversed, Orion becoming the spring, Scorpio the winter personality. The subject requires a monograph.

22. Gordon, *op. cit.,* p. 7.

23. This subject also requires a monograph, and the references are innumerable. For one typical early summary see: E. C. Sachau, *Alberuni's India* (London, 1914) I, pp. 247-250. In Canaanite mythology it is Mount Saphon, in Greek, Olympus (which is two-peaked): in the Dionysiac cult, Mount Nysa. Ararat is another double mountain with an ancient and complex religious history (cf. N. Marr—J. Smirnov, *Les Vichaps* [Leningrad, 1931] p. 94). For another summary discussion see: M. J. LaGrange, "L'Innocence et le Péché," *Revue Biblique,* VI (1897), pp. 375-376.

24. The connection between the double cosmic mountain and metal is explicit in Zech. 6.1.

25. I.4: S. H. Langdon, *Semitic Mythology* (Boston, 1931) p. 92. Heidel, *op. cit.,* p. 8, arbitrarily changes the Akkadian word (his n. 9) in order to make the passage read "Mother Tiamat". A. L. Oppenheim, "Mesopotamian Mythology," I, *Orientalia,* 16, 2, N. S. (1947), p. 208, accepts this change without comment. A female divinity of similar sig-

nificance, MAAt, "law, order, regularity", appears in the primeval stage of the parallel Egyptian Creation myth, when Khepri rises out of the watery abyss: see Spence, *op. cit.,* p. 13.

26. Langdon, *op. cit.,* pp. 109, 290.

27. I. 72: Heidel, *op. cit.,* p. 10.

28. L. Frobenius—D. C. Fox, *African Genesis* (New York, 1937) pp. 61-67; and *v.* n. 38.

29. Langdon, *op. cit.,* p. 128.

30. *"Enuma elish . . ."* I, 53, 54: Heidel, *op. cit.,* p. 10.

31. Oppenheim, *op. cit.,* p. 212, n. 4. Heidel (*op. cit.,* p. 4) translates it: "who rejoicest my heart" (l. 31)—and concerning "heart", *v. infra.*

32. *Loc. cit.*

33. In process, by the writer.

34. See, for a late literary development of the idea, Thomas Nash's "Merrie Ballad of . . . His Dildo".

35. *V.,* e.g., Peter Buck, "My People, the Maoris," *Asia,* XXXVIII (1938) p. 583, upper right.

36. Langdon, *op. cit.,* p. 292: Heidel, *op. cit.,* p. 10, 1. 53, reverses the relation ("Mummu embraced his [Apsu's] neck) —thereby defeating the esoteric meaning.

37. Langdon, *op. cit.,* p. 290.

38. W. M. Müller, *Egyptian Mythology* (London, s.d.) pp. 68-69. Khepri after recovering his potency creates man in a second semen ejection, but here the figure is changed from the idea of spitting out of the mouth, to weeping out of the eye:

"After I had united my members [obviously an awkward and somewhat incorrect translation for recovering potency, in some figure of speech] I wept over them. The origin of men was thus from my tears which came from my eye." It is interesting to find the same figure in Nash's account of his "youth" . . . "having but one eye"

"Wherein the rheum so fervently doth run
"The Stygian gulf can scarce the tears contain."

The primeval bull, who was the mate of Thamuatz in the Berber myth, similarly generates almost all the animals by spontaneous ejection of semen: *v.* n. 28; and in the Orphic emblematic writing, the phallos means "pallenetor", "universal generator": H. M. Westropp, *Primitive Symbolism* (s.p., s.d.) pp. 34-35.

39. *Loc. cit.*

40. Spence, *op. cit.,* p. 13.

41. R. E. Hume, *The Thirteen Principal Upanishads* (Oxford, 1931) p. 124. Cf. also the Sumerian idea that in ensemination the semen ("the bright water") reaches the woman's heart: *v.* S. N. Kramer, *Sumerian Mythology* (Philadelphia, 1944) pp. 45-47.

42. Oppenheim, *op. cit.*, p. 213; Heidel, *op. cit.*, p. 10, 1. 70, has, instead, "and locked him [Mummu] up"—which is meaningless for the esoteric significance.

43. At least, a *Lahmu* of the sea is a sea-serpent: Langdon, *op. cit.*, p. 291.

44. *Op. cit.*, pp. 208, 209.

45. Langdon, *op. cit.*, p. 164.

46. Emphasized by Oppenheim, *op. cit.*, p. 208.

47. *Ibid.*, p. 210; (Heidel, *op. cit.*, p. 9, 1, 24, has "moving (and) running about in the divine abode (?)"—which entirely loses the quality).

48. Oppenheim, *op. cit.*, p. 209 (Heidel, *op. cit.*, p. 8, 1. 14, has "the rival of his fathers"—which again blurs the significance).

49. Langdon, *op. cit.*, pp. 89, 93, 94.

50. Oppenheim, *op. cit.*, p. 209 (Heidel, *op. cit.*, p. 8, 1. 16 has "And Anu begot Nudimmud his image"—which again befogs the idea).

51. Langdon, *op. cit.*, p. 104.

52. *Op. cit.*, p. 210. So also Thamuatz mates with her son.

53. *"Enuma elish . . ."* IV, 137-145. Cf. *Job*, 38, 5-11.

54. On Spanish prehistoric (probably contemporary with Near Eastern Chalcolithic) painted pebbles; repeatedly illustrated, *v.* Cleland, *op. cit.*; but see especially Spanish rock paintings: H. Breuil—M. C. Burkitt, *Rock Paintings of Southern Andalusia* (Oxford, 1929) p. 5, Fig. 1, Series A, nos. 9, 11-13; and above all, Fig. 2, Series B, nos. 1, 2.

55. See, A. U. Pope (Ed.), *A Survey of Persian Art* (Oxford, 1938) IV, Pls. 203, 239.

56. See, e.g., a Mitanni seal from Kirkuk: H. Frankfort, *Cylinder Seals* (London, 1939) p. 184, Fig. 53; or, even more interesting, two seals of the Dynasty of Akkad (*ibid.*, Pls. XVII, *g;* XXI, *h*). In the first, the Twins, on one foot, contest with lions which, paired confronted or addorsed, are zoomorphic personations of the Milky Way; the semen which Khepri ejects as Atmosphere and Moisture is represented as a pair of confronted lions. The center god on the seal kneels in a gamma-cross ("swastika") position in order to indicate the rotation of the polaric constellation. On the second seal the Twins, again on one foot, control another pair of Twins whom they have turned upside down, anthropomorphic representations of the Milky Way, with their arms forming the rectangular U which defines the celestial equator with the terminal poles. Between, at the center of the Two Deeps, is Nudimmud (Ea), holding the jar with symmetrical flowing streams, the fountains of the Two Deeps. See also the Luristan bronze finial (Pope [Ed.], *op. cit.*, Pl. 40 B), where the Twins stand on the confronted Milky Way felines couchant. The hero holding confronted lions or bulls (often mis-called "Gilgamesh") is the anthropomorphic Polaris divinity controlling the rotation of the zoomor-

phically represented Milky Way. For another group of Polaris and the Twins holding hands with arms bent to make the River zigzag see a Pachacamac tapestry poncho: C. W. Mead, *Old Civilizations in Inca Land* (New York, 1942) p. 39, Fig. 17; and note the symmetrical pair of courtiers flanking the ceremonially enthroned Sasanian King on the silver plate found in Kazvin: M. Bahrami, "Some Objects Recently Discovered in Iran," *Bulletin of the Iranian Institute,* VI, 1-4, VII, 1 (Dec., 1946) p. 74, Fig. 5. In Navajo sand-paintings the outstretched zigzag arms of the god have the Milky Way drawn on them, making the reference explicit, as a chain of white lozenges—an angular water-guilloche.

57. Frankfort, *op. cit.,* p. 88, Fig. 29.

58. See, e.g., Harrison, *Prolegomena . . .,* p. 234, n. 2; and Langdon, *op. cit.,* p. 291, where Lahmu, from being the personation of one-half of the Milky Way, had evidently been specified as the terminal constellation, Orion—"calamity" because the constellation, when defined, of the violent winter season. Such transfers from one stage to another in religious development is common in the history of thinking and especially frequent and complex in the phases of the astro-cosmological religions. For other illustrations of divinities with "twisted feet" see: O. Wulff—W. F. Volbach, *Spätantike und Koptische Stoffe* (Berlin, 1926) p. 53, No. V. M. 9632, Pl. 63 (note breasts emphasized as a pair of disks with central dots, and cf. n. 16); *ibid.,* p. 69, No. J 6887, Pls. 24, 92, with the arms as a half gamma-cross (and in the aqueous landscape of the Milky Way river, with the constellational Twins together in a boat); *ibid.,* p. 67, No. J 4598, Pl. 22, with the arms alternately as the rectangular U, and as the half gamma-cross (and again in the Milky Way river aquatic setting); and note the emphatic navel, Polaris star being in various references the universe Ombilikos. Since the Erinyes are "clutch-footed", they must originally have been the Polaris constellation. But why three? Because there were three constellations, close together, in which Polaris was successively located (Ursa Maior, section of Draco, and Ursa Minor). Hence the Gorgonides (who, as Miss Harrison showed—*ibid.,* Chapter V, *passim*—were only another phase of the Erynes) lived on three islands close together, and had amongst them but one eye—Polaris itself—which passed from one to the other. Hence, too, they are depicted holding hands and all in the gamma-cross position. The Three Fates are another statement of the same idea, corresponding to the Wheel of Fortune—the circumpolar rotation, or the rotation of the polaric constellation (also, Buddhist Wheel of the Law).

59. O'Neill, *op. cit.,* I, p. 941.

60. B. Karlgren, "The Date of the Early Dong-so'n Culture," *Bulletin of the Museum of Far Eastern Art,* 14 (Stockholm, 1940) Pl. 19, Fig. 1; Pl. 20, Figs. 1, 3. 61. *V.* n. 20.

THE RELIGION OF ANCIENT EGYPT

Dr. Mercer was born in Bristol, England, in 1880. He has followed the academic life since he was graduated from Bishop Feild College, St. John's, Nfld., in 1900 with a B.Sc. degree. His bachelor of divinity degree came from Nashotah House, Wisconsin (1904); a C.E. from the University of Wisconsin (1905); a bachelor's degree from Harvard (1908); and a Ph.D. from the University of Munich (1910). He holds honorary doctor's degrees from Nashotah House, from Paris (Th.D., 1938) and from Kenyon College.

His teaching career began at Western Theological Seminary, Chicago, in 1910 and continued there until 1922; then followed a deanship at Bexley Hall in Gambier, Ohio, for one year; and then the deanship (1923-24) of Divinity at Trinity College (University of Toronto) in Toronto and professor of Semitic Languages and Egyptology until 1946 when he became professor emeritus.

Besides numerous articles in the fields of Egyptology and Semitics, Professor Mercer has published many books, among which are: "The Ethiopic Liturgy", Hale Lectures, 1915; "Egyptian Grammar", 1915; "Sumero-Babylonian Sign List", 1918; "Growth of Religious Ideas in Egypt", 1919; "Ethiopic Grammar", 1921; "Etudes sur les Origines de la Religion de l'Egypte", 1929; "Ethiopic Text of the Book of Ecclesiastes", 1931; "The Tell el-Amarna Tablets" (2 vols.), 1939; "Horus, Royal God of Egypt", 1942; "The Supremacy of Israel", Bohlen Lectures, 1945; "Sumero-Babylonian Year-Formulae", 1946; and "The Religion of Ancient Egypt", 1948.

He is well known as editor of such scholarly journals as: "The Journal of the Society of Oriental Research" and "The Anglican Theological Review" (founder and first editor). He is also editor of "Egyptian Religion" and of the section on Egyptology in the latest edition of Webster's New International Dictionary.

He is a member of many learned societies and has been decorated Officier de l'Instruction Publique (France) and by the Order of the Trinity (Abyssinia).

Editor

THE RELIGION OF ANCIENT EGYPT

SAMUEL ALFRED BROWNE MERCER

AS THE ancient Egyptians themselves left no systematic account of their religion, our knowledge of it is a modern reconstruction based upon a mass of myths and legends; poems, songs, hymns, and prayers; narratives, biographies, and other literary remains; as well as upon that which classical writers have handed down to us. And, even then, the finished work, at best, has to be but fragmentary and uncertain, the mere *a posteriori* reconstruction of a modern scholar, with his limited insight into ancient ways of religious thought. However, each fresh student of this ancient religion, if he is prudent, will attempt to profit by the mistakes of his predecessors. Thus, no doubt, he will avoid the extremes of those who, like certain Greeks and some moderns, would see in Egyptian religion the source of all wisdom; of those who would make the ancient Egyptians mere African barbarians; or of those who would see only solemnity and gloom in the religious life of the early inhabitants of the Valley of the Nile. There is sound reason to believe that the modern student of ancient Egyptian religious ideas will find that the ancient Egyptians were no more—perhaps less—logical in religious ideas than any other ancient or modern peoples; that while the human brain tends to fall readily into familiar rhythm, resulting in a certain continuity of religious thought, there was nevertheless an evolution of religious ideas throughout the centuries; and that while, in a sense, "Egypt never forgot" and scarcely ever discarded old religious beliefs, she did very often learn and adopt new ones.

The glaring inconsistencies and contradictory beliefs held all at one time by the ancient Egyptians are the cause of much of our trouble in attempting to reconstruct an account of their religious ideas. The modern student, moreover, has come to learn that the religion of ancient Egypt was never one—never in place nor in time

—for there were many cults at many places. Even at the height of ancient Egyptian culture, there existed side by side at least an official religion and a popular one. The Egyptologist also counts with the fact that no one modern classification, such as, for example, fetishism, animism, nature worship, henotheism, pantheism, monotheism can account for all the peculiarities of this religion, or religions, of ancient Egypt. In fact, it contained elements and aspects of all these; and withal it was symbolical and literal, mystical and pragmatic, conservative and syncretistic, and supremely contradictory and inconsistent at one and the same time.

The following brief outline of the religious ideas of ancient Egypt must avoid many an interesting problem as well as all details, and give as simply as possible the main features of a great religion which satisfied an extremely cultured people for a period of more than three thousand years, from about 3000 B.C. until in the reign of Justinian, 527-565, when the worship of Isis came to an end at Philae.

Animism, polytheism and anthropomorphism, more than any other theories, account pretty well for the ancient Egyptian idea of god. According to animism, all unusual, strange and incomprehensible things in nature were the abodes of beings which he called gods. Gods were good or evil; the evil ones were called demons. Gods were worshipped and propitiated; demons were abhorred and feared, sometimes propitiated. According to anthropomorphism, inanimate objects and even abstract ideas were personified, and then they as well as man and other living creatures could be deified and worshipped as gods. Thus polytheism is a good general designation of the religion of ancient Egypt. There was no limit to the process of personification and deification: stones, springs and rivers, plants and trees, hills and mountains, cities and districts, living creatures of all kinds and abstract ideas. Any one of these when personified and deified could be considered the external manifestation of a god and was worshipped as such. In case it was merely personified and considered the abode of a god it was not worshipped in itself; it was merely venerated, but it was the god dwelling in it who was worshipped.

Among the greatest Egyptian deities were those who were manifested by natural phenomena. Thus the sky (*nut*) became the goddess Nut; the earth (*geb*) became the god Geb; the sun was Rē, the Nile Hapi, fertility was Osiris, truth was Maāt. Then, deities could take the form of men or women or living creatures or inanimate objects. Sometimes they appeared in composite forms, such as a falcon-headed man (Horus), a lioness-headed woman (Sekhmet), but in whatever form they appeared they were given a human personality; that is, man made his gods in his own image and likeness, and endowed him with human attributes and characteristics. A deity was an enlarged human being, physically, mentally and morally. He was imperfect in every respect as man is. However, the Egyptians ascribed the best they knew to their gods. While the gods had the same attributes and characteristics as men, they had them in the superlative. A god was an enlarged human being, not capable of being seen at all times, but still visible. According to our idea of perfection, he was not perfect, but he was all that the Egyptian could imagine as appropriate to the greatest and most important of all classes of beings.

From a modern point of view, the Egyptian gods were anthropomorphic. They possessed man's characteristics, because the Egyptians could not conceive of anything better or higher. The gods in this world, at any rate, were mortal. Rē grew old and Osiris was slain. Orion enjoyed hunting, slaying, and eating other gods. The gods suffered, and took revenge. They were not omniscient, but were obliged to investigate in order to be informed. They were controlled by magic, and were obliged to use human agencies in the accomplishment of their tasks. In short, they were constituted as men, only endowed with superlative powers; for example, some of the gods had as many as seventy-seven ears and seventy-seven eyes. But of course this conception was due to the need of explaining how the gods could hear and see all men at all times.

Some gods were greater than others; but they became so largely because of the power and influence of their clients. Each community believed that *its* god was creator, sustainer, and preserver, all in one. But when the official priesthood tried to systematize theological thinking, the greatest god of the system became the creator. Thus at Heliopolis, Rē was creator; at Thebes, it was Amūn; and at Memphis, it was Ptah.

Perhaps the earliest indigenous god to reach country-wide importance was Set, whose cult center in historic times was Ombos. His chief fame consisted in his murder of Osiris and his antagonism

29

to Horus. He was a personification of the atmosphere, husband of Tefnut, and was usually represented as a man with the head of an animal of uncertain species. The sun was worshipped usually under the form of the god Rē, who was as a rule represented as a man with the head of a falcon surmounted by the solar-disc and *uraeus*-serpent. His earliest worshippers may have come from Western Asia. As there were other sun-gods, Rē represented the sun in full strength. His cult center was Heliopolis. Perhaps the most re-nowned of Egypt's gods was Osiris, judge and ruler of the dead, and supreme god of the funerary cult. He may have originally been a human leader who was deified and identified with fertility in the eastern Delta. He was usually represented in mummiform, wearing the *atef*-crown.

Besides these four, there were other great gods: Min, god of sexual reproduction, located at Coptos, and represented in ithy-phallic form; Thot, scribe of the gods and lord of wisdom and magic, located at Hermopolis, and appearing as a man with the head of an ibis; Anubis, patron of embalming and guardian of the tomb, at Cynopolis, a man with the head of a jackal; Ptah, divine artificer, with cult center at Memphis, depicted in the form of a primitive idol with legs not separated; Khnum, creator of the bodies of mankind and gods upon the potter's wheel, located at the First Cataract, and represented as a man with the head of a ram; Khonsu, moon-god of Thebes, a young man, crowned with lunar disc and crescent upon his head; Soker, a funerary god of Memphis, often identified with Osiris and Ptah, appearing as a mummified man with the head of a falcon; Sebek, a crocodile god of the Fayūm, depicted as a man with the head of a crocodile; Montu, a war god of Hermonthis, appearing as a man with falcon's head surmounted by a solar disc; Amūn-Rē, later national god of Egypt, at Thebes, and represented as a man wearing a cap surmounted by two tall plumes; and Aton, a personification of the disc of the sun, became state god during the reign of Ikhnaton, and appearing as a disc with projecting rays ending in human hands. Ikhnaton broke with the orthodox regime of Amun-Rē in Thebes and set up a new cult on the basis of an old idea at a new capital, Akhetaton, now called Tell el-Amarna. The theology of Ikhnaton's reform was expressed in a beautiful poem which has been compared with Psalm 104, in which the disc of the sun is represented as creator and sustainer of

THE RELIGION OF ANCIENT EGYPT

all things. It begins: "Thy dawning is beautiful in the horizon of the sky, O Living Aton, beginning of life." Ikhnaton was a religious genius, original and fanatical; not a monotheist, for he acknowledged the existence of other gods, himself included, but his emphasis upon beauty, truth, family love, reality in art and in life, his aversion to many of the old meaningless forms and symbols made his religion unique in Egypt.

Besides numerous minor gods and demons, there were many goddesses. Most important among them were: Isis, sister-wife of Osiris, and prototype of motherhood and of the faithful wife; Nephthys, wife of Set, and assistant of Isis in her attendance upon the slain Osiris; Hathor, an ancient sky-goddess, nurse of Horus and of the pharaohs, and goddess of love; Neith, the hunter-goddess of Lower Egypt; Mūt, wife of Amūn and vulture-goddess; Maāt, personification of truth and justice, and many others.

When Egypt became a world-empire, and came into contact with other peoples, she sometimes recognized their deities. The most important of these were: Baal or Bār, introduced into Egypt from Phoenicia, a war-god and god of the mountains and deserts; Astarte, a Syrian war-goddess and goddess of love; Resheph, a Syrian war-god and god of lightning, fire, and of the pestilence which follows in the train of war; Kedesh, a West Asiatic goddess of love and beauty, the divine harlot of the gods; Sutekh, a West Asiatic god and special deity of the Hyksos; Dedun, a Nubian war-god; Bes, patron of music and childbirth, a domestic deity probably of Sudanese origin; Meri, who came from Punt; etc.

Many animals, inanimate objects and abstract ideas were personified and deified. Thus, the Apis-bull of Memphis, the Mnevis of Heliopolis, the Buchis of Hermonthis, the Ram of Khnum, the Buck of Mendes, the evil serpent Apophis, the good one Wazit, the scorpion as Selket, the scarab-beetle as Rē, the falcon as Horus, the vulture as Mūt, the swallow as Isis, the crocodile of Sebek, the oxyrhynchus-fish of Behnesa, the dolphin at Mendes, the persea-tree of Rē, the ded-tree of Osiris, the lettuce of Min, the benben-stone of Heliopolis, the temple of Rameses III at Thebes, the royal crowns of the South and of the North, truth as Maāt, writing as Seshat, magic as Heka, and many others.

There were also cosmic and other nature deities, such as, Nun, the first great self-produced divine being, the boundless watery mass; Atum, who rose out of the primeval watery abyss; Nut, the sky personified as a goddess; Geb, the earth personified as a god; Shu, god of the air; Tefnut, female personification of dampness; Iāh, the moon-god; Hapi, the Nile personified; Stars, such as Orion, Sothis (Sirius), the Great Bear, the circumpolar stars; the Four Elements; the Four Winds; etc.

All pharaohs were considered divine, an idea which had its origin in the belief that gods ruled as kings of Egypt in prehistoric times, and that the earliest human kings were the actual offspring of the gods. And furthermore, the Egyptians believed that any man after death may be identified with a god. This is true especially according to the cult of Osiris, when the deceased human, commoner as well as king, could become an Osiris. From first to last in the history of ancient Egypt, the pharaoh was deified, but, except in rare cases by anticipation, he was not worshipped until after his death. Certain great men also, during the course of Egyptian history, because of their own worth, in their own right, and not because they were Osirianized by death, were deified long after their death and worshipped as gods. The most famous and greatest of them was the wise man Imhotep, priest, diplomat, physician, and architect of the great king Zoser of the Third Dynasty. Others were Amenophis, son of Hapu, wise man and architect; the vizir Isi; as well as certain persons drowned, especially in the Nile.

Although ancient Egyptians, so far as we know, never produced a system of philosophy, there was no lack of the kind of speculation about man and the world, which produces myths and legends and more or less systematized theologies; and so from time to time and at various centers, their theologians, in speculating about the gods, formulated and constructed certain theological systems, which we are now able to reconstruct. Thus, in the great religious cities of Heliopolis, Memphis, Hermopolis magna, Abydos, and Thebes, various systems of theological speculation were developed.

The priestly theologians of Heliopolis, perhaps before the rise of the dynasties, had already constructed at least two great companies of deities, the Great Ennead and the Little Ennead, a system of theology, which by the time of the Pyramid Texts* of the Fifth and Sixth Dynasties had gained the support of the king and his

---

* See footnote, p. 40.

high officials. According to the system of Heliopolis, Atum existed in the primeval watery abyss (Nun), whence he came forth. Then by onanism he created Shu and Tefnut, who gave rise to Geb and Nut; and these two in turn gave rise to Osiris and Isis, Set and Nephthys. Rē of Heliopolis was made head of this system.

The early theologians of Memphis constructed a similar system of theology, under the influence of the worship of Osiris, but with Ptah at its head; and the Ogdoad of Hermopolis, with Thot at its head, goes back for its origin to the very beginning of historic time. Then there were the systems of Abydos, Osirian in form; of Thebes, an amalgamation of Heliopolis and Hermopolis; and of Ikhnaton and his god Aton. There were also groups of gods, sevens, fives, and fours; there were triads; and there were pairs of gods, and families of gods.

At the same time throughout ancient Egypt two great systems of theological thought were operating side by side, and so far as popularity was concerned overshadowed all others. These were the cults of Rē and of Osiris, the two greatest of all Egyptian religions. They had many characteristics in common, as did all Egyptian cults, but they became so dominant and general that they truly constituted two religions. So great were these two theologies that there were very few, if any, cults which were not Osirian or solar, or both, in coloring and characteristics.

Long before the rise of the Heliopolitan school of theology, Osiris had achieved renown, first as a peaceful leader of a higher culture in the eastern Delta, then as powerful all over the Delta, the husband of Isis and father of the great war- and sun-god Horus; and then as conqueror of northern Upper Egypt with an important seat at Abydos. It was then that he came into conflict with Set, who slew him. Then, at last, it was that he gained his greatest renown, for though slain, he rose again from the dead, and became for his followers a god of the dead and of resurrection, joining that idea to his earlier attribute as a god of culture, of life, growth, earth, and vegetation, a god of the Nile and its inundation.

To the expansion and popularity of the cult of Osiris, Heliopolis and its theologians could not afford to remain indifferent, so attempts were made by that great school of theology to absorb the Osirian cult, but without success. On the contrary, Osiris entered Heliopolis, was adopted into the official Ennead as a great grand-

33

son of Rē, and became so powerful and indispensable that the whole system of Heliopolitan theology was manipulated in such a way as to include into its very essence the fundamental teaching of Osiris. Henceforth, during the whole history of ancient Egypt, the cult of Osiris overshadowed that of Rē, becoming the dominant feature of all Egyptian religion. But it was as champion and friend of the dead, and not as a member of the Heliopolitan Ennead, that he gained his eminence in Egyptian religion.

The theology of Rē was fundamentally solar and heavenly. Rē was a creator god and a king by nature. He, thus, became patron of the earthly king, and later his veritable father. When the king died, he went home to his father in heaven, and there he passed his time much as he did when on earth. Rē and his theology concerned themselves with the world, its origin, creation, and government; while Osiris and his doctrine were concerned with the problems of life, death, resurrection, and a righteous future. The liaison between the two was Horus, who was at one and the same time a sky, heaven, and sun-god, and also dutiful son and heir of Osiris.

The general outline of the career of both Osiris and Rē can be traced with probability down to the time of the Pyramid Texts, and thence with a fair amount of certainty to the very end of Egyptian religious history. The career of Osiris may be divided into two periods—the earlier one extending down to the Pyramid Texts, during which he was primarily a great leader and bringer of a higher culture; a peaceful political power, who united the Delta and northern Upper Egypt into one realm; the ideal husband and father; and, after his death and resurrection, a god of fertility, and also a god of the dead, of resurrection, and of a subterranean realm beyond the grave. The later period extended from the time of the Pyramid Texts until the end, when he was primarily god of all the dead, judge and king of the underworld.

The earliest worshippers of Rē in Egypt probably migrated, in prehistoric times, into the Nile Valley from without. They were an intellectual people, and were the first, so far as we know, to record their thoughts for future generations. In time, these ideas grew into a system of theology, philosophical in some simple respects, which has survived to our day in what we call the Pyramid Texts. The religion of these men was a sun-cult, learned and aristocratic, which in time became the state religion, and remained so, with varying vicissitudes from the Fifth Dynasty until the fall of the imperial city of Thebes in 663 B.C. It was a heaven-religion with a royal hereafter. With the expansion of the kingdom into an empire, beginning with the Eighteenth Dynasty, the idea furnished a strong reason for the universal character of sun-religion which now was becoming popular and powerful. However, there was a slight reaction against this in the Atonism of Ikhnaton, which, nevertheless, was only another form of sun-worship. Amūn-Rē declined, for a short time, and Aton increased, but one and both were sun-worship. With the quick restoration of Amūn-Rē, an age of personal piety set in, and also a gradual strengthening of the popular cult of Osiris, and Amūn-Rē became like Osiris the champion of the common man and of the distressed of whatever rank. However, this was arrested by priestly ambition, when the head of the cult became the head of the state, so that when the state fell at the hands of the Assyrians, the cult of the sun was struck a deathly blow. Thenceforth Osiris and his cycle were left without opposition.

Man was considered the offspring of the gods, and his nature presented many problems to the mind of the early Egyptian. In addition to the body, the Egyptian felt sure that many other elements went to make up the individual. There was the *ba* or soul, which could be seen at death when it left the body in the form of a human-headed bird. During life it was an intangible essence, associated with the breath, like the Greek ψυχή. Besides that there was the *ka*, a kind of ghostly double or genius or power, which was given to each person at birth. As long as a man was master of his *ka* he lived, but as soon as he died the *ka* began a separate existence, resembling the body to which it had been attached, and requiring food for its subsistence. Then there was the *ren* or name, which had a separate existence, and seemed to have been the underlying and permanent substance of all things. Besides these there were the *khu* or intelligence, the *ab* or heart (mind and will), the *sakhem* or ruling power of man, the *khaybet* or shadow, the *ikh* or glorified spirit, and the *sahu* or mummy. The most important of all these elements was the *ka*, which became the center of the cult of the dead, for to a man's *ka* all offerings were made, and those persons ordained to carry on offerings to the dead were called "servants of the *ka*."

This complicated psychology of the Egyptians, together with their emphasis upon death and the hereafter, has led many students to describe the Egyptians as a most sanguine and nervous people, exceedingly pessimistic and gloomy. But nothing could be farther from the truth. The literary remains of ancient Egypt and especially their monuments show them to have been an exceedingly happy and light-hearted people, who too often, perhaps, followed the ancient advice to "eat, drink, and be merry."

There was never an ancient people who insisted upon believing that "it is not death to die" with more emphasis than the Egyptians. The climate and atmosphere of Egypt both conspired to deepen this conviction, if they were not in reality the origin of the belief. Death came, but although the body became inert, it did not dissolve. It persisted and, like all other natural phenomena, was the abode of that which possessed life. Death consisted in a changed relationship between man's vital being and his body. The same body remained, as also did the same vital forces, but their natural relationship was changed.

In order further to insure the persistence of the body as a center of individual soul or spirit-manifestation, the greatest care was taken to preserve it. It was carefully embalmed and mummified and laid in a coffin, on its side, like a sleeper, and in the tomb were placed all utensils that a living person could possibly need, together with vessels for food and water, weapons and toilet articles. It was also customary to bury with the body of the deceased a number of little figures, called *ushabtiu,* whose duty was to answer for their client during the trial of judgment before the forty-two divine judges.

The most important ceremony connected with burial was the opening of the eyes, mouth, ears, and nose of the deceased. This ceremony guaranteed life to the body, and made it possible as the home of the *ba.* The realm of the dead according to the solar cult was situated in the east of the sky; that of the cult of Osiris was in a subterranean kingdom with its entrance in the west.

The eyes of the Egyptian were ever turned towards the future. There were his gods, there were those whom he had loved in the past, there were the fulfilment of all his ideals and aspirations, his hopes and desires. No individual ever thought and dreamed and lived in the future as did the ancient Egyptian. It was his great ideal. Nor did it render him unduly visionary and impractical. On the contrary it served as a stimulus to better living and higher thinking in this life. The condition of future bliss was present integrity,

and present human helpfulness and divine piety were the best
guarantee of the eternal favor of the gods.

After death came the judgment. The Egyptian scene of a future
judgment is so closely allied to Osirian ideas that its origin is usually
ascribed to that cult, although it was not unknown to Rē religion.
Judgment took place in the presence of Osiris, sitting upon his
throne. The deceased was led in by Anubis, with Isis and Nephthys
following. There were forty-two judges or assessors, in the presence
of whom the deceased denied forty-two misdeeds. A large pair of
balances was there with the heart of the deceased and the feather
of truth, one in each of the pans. Thot read and recorded the findings. A large composite creature was there also, prepared to devour
the deceased should he be found wanting. In case of justification
the deceased was permitted to proceed to the Fields of Aalu, where
he was received into the divine barque. To the Egyptian, the great,
real, desirable world was where the gods lived, and as gods and men
were so closely related, the natural outcome of things would be their
eternal association and companionship. It was not conceit or pre-
sumption, but a belief in the natural fitness of things. Immortality
was fraught with neither doubt nor questioning for the Egyptian; it
was a certainty, which needed no demonstration.

The most fundamental idea of worship in ancient Egypt connected itself with the person of the god-manifesting pharaoh. When
Rē receded to heaven a human king reigned as his son and heir.
The king then, as son and heir of Rē, represented the people before
the gods and the gods to the people. The king remained in Egypt
the only representative between gods and men. Even when the priesthood developed, and offerings were continually made to the gods on
behalf of mankind, the priests were not the mediators, for they
merely represented the king. Their offerings were made in the name
of the king. And this was so universally and consistently true in
Egypt that the phrase, "an offering which the king makes," came to
mean any and every offering. The priests offered sacrifices, approached the gods, mediated between man and god solely in the
name of the king. This was inevitable. For while in the earliest and
smallest communities the head of the tribe or family was naturally
the mediator and was the only one who ever acted in that capacity,
in later times when the families became clans, and clans developed
into national states, the king could no more offer all sacrifices and

37

appear personally in all cases of mediation. The result was that others were made mediators, that is, priests, and so an order of priests arose. These priests were substitutes of the king. Even when the priesthood seized the throne in the Twenty-first Dynasty, sacrifice remained the peculiar function of the pharaoh through his deputies, the priests.

In time the priesthood grew, and so different orders of priests arose. One was called the *kherheb,* consisting of priests who recited the sacred texts; another was called the *wab,* consisting of those who offered sacrifices. This latter was divided into classes, each one of which served for a quarter of a year. At the head of the different orders stood chief-priests, "servants of the god," there being usually one for each temple. Besides these and others, there were sub-priests, "openers" of the shrines, who also made offerings of incense and libations. The priests were often referred to as "divine fathers," and in time were granted semi-hereditary privileges and duties. They were very attentive to cleanliness, wore white linen, shaved their heads, abstained from fish and beans, and were probably circumcised. Many of them were pluralists, but received their living from temple revenues, stipends being paid in kind. From time to time priests became very powerful, being famed as chieftains and as great physicians. Thutmose III merged all the priesthoods of the country into one sacerdotal body, headed by the priests of Amūn-Rē. Women also held a kind of priestly rank, for many are called priestesses in the inscriptions, but it consisted chiefly in musical matters.

The Egyptian temple was modelled upon a common type. It was shut off from the street by lofty walls, adorned with religious and secular scenes. It was entered by a small gateway between two pylons, which led into a forecourt open to the sky. Then came the hypostyle with pylons, which was used for processions. Beyond this was the dark cella, or holy of holies, the dwelling place of the god, to which none but priests were admitted. Here was the image of the god. All around the cella were storehouses and sacristies. There was a shrine for the image of the god, provided with double doors of metal. Every morning the shrine was opened by a priest, who offered incense, purified the statue of the god, and presented food and flowers. Temple revenues were derived from endowments, offerings and fees, and they were also subsidized by the state.

The order of divine service was about the same all over the land.

The priests began by acts of purification, purifying themselves as well as the statues of the gods. Then offerings were made, which was followed by a procession of the gods. Music and dancing accompanied the various ceremonies, and the singing of hymns was a common feature.

Offerings consisted chiefly of animals and of vegetable material. On solemn occasions the eating of a specimen of the sacred animal at stated intervals took place, such as a bull at Memphis and a ram at Thebes. In early times the animals most frequently sacrificed were the gazelle, the antelope, and the wild goat.

Besides the official religion, there was a popular cult, mainly dominated by Osirian ideas, and hence associated with the dead. The masses were devoted to it. Tombs were built in the western desert, some of which were very elaborate. In the sepulchral chamber were furniture for the use of the deceased, rooms for the cult, and walls adorned with religious texts and pictures. The innermost chamber was a chapel, on the west side of which was an imitation door, through which the deceased passed to receive his offerings. In addition to the service of the cult of the dead, there was a form of domestic worship. Shrines were erected in the homes of the people, and ceremonies were performed in connection with birth and marriage as well as with death. There were also wayside shrines, and although the laity had no recognized part in the service of the god in the official temples, they were permitted to bring their offerings to the great altar on all occasions, and undoubtedly took their place in the temples on each festive occasion.

Feasts and festivals were quite common. There were festivals of fertility and harvest, and the great temple feasts, such as that of Amūn of Thebes. Each god had his own calendar of days on which there were great processions, and when elaborate offerings were made. The *sed*-festival was one of the most important. It was celebrated every thirty years, commemorating the deification of the king as Osiris. Sometimes as in the case of Rameses II this festival seems to have been repeated every three years after the thirtieth year. The feast of the New Year was also important, when gifts were exchanged, and given to the dead, and an illumination took place for the "glorification of the blessed." It was a kind of Feast of All Souls. The *wag*-feast took place on the eighteenth of the First month, and on its eve. There were many other feasts, such as, the *rekeh-*

feast, associated with Horus; the feast of Amenophis I in the Valley of the Kings, etc. The "Passion Play" of Osiris was performed as early as the time of Sesostris III, 1887-1850 B.C., and became so important that it was engraved in text and picture on the walls of the temples of Dendera, Edfu and Philae. Indeed, the Egyptian mysteries were the prototypes and originals followed and copied by the Greeks in the Eleusinian, Dionysian and Orphic mysteries as Pausanias, Diodorus Siculus, Plutarch, Iamblichus and others asserted.

Among a people who believed itself so closely related to the gods as the Egyptians did, magic was inevitable, for magic was primarily the power of the gods. Thus, Thot was called the master of sorcery, and Isis the mistress. By learning and understanding the power of the gods, the gods could be controlled. Even Rē himself was forced by magic to reveal his hidden name. The chief method of magic consisted in symbolic or imitative acts, verbal spells, and formulae from such literature as the Book of the Dead.* It became a

---

* The oldest collections of literature in the world, and still extant, are the Pyramid Texts. They were inscribed on the stone walls of five pyramids at Saqqareh during the later part of the Old Kingdom, 2400-2240 B.C., and had been compiled by priestly scholars from the most varied sources, some dating earlier than the beginning of the historic period, about 3000 B.C. Beginning with the Middle Kingdom, about 2000 B.C., it became customary to copy large portions of the Pyramid Texts on the sarchophagi of kings and nobles, many of which portions were changed and added to. These texts are now known as the Coffin Texts. Then as early as the Eighteenth Dynasty, which began in 1580 B.C., most of the religious literature of Ancient Egypt, including the Pyramid Texts and the Coffin Texts, was brought together, re-edited, changed, and added to, and painted on coffins and written on papyrus. This we call the Book of the Dead. The authors and compilers were many, their sources numerous. There are many extant copies, but no one copy contains all the chapters, which are about 200. The chapters are as independent as the various psalms in the Old Testament. The largest known copy is in the Turin Papyrus, which contains 165 chapters. The main subject of each chapter is the beatification of the deceased. The last recension of the Book of the Dead was made in the Twenty-sixth Dynasty, 663-525 B.C., and was still in use during the Ptolemaic, Greek, and Roman periods, even to the very end of Egyptian civilization. The native name of the Book of the Dead was "The Chapters of Coming Forth by Day."

perfectly legitimate practice within certain limitations, and was recognized officially. It is often difficult to know where magic ends and religion begins in Egyptian custom; even the gods were thought to rule the world by magic. But certain magical acts were considered illegal, such as making wax figures of a man to injure him, and were strictly forbidden.

In ancient Egypt prayer was the ordinary mode of communicating with the gods, and it rose to very great heights of perfection, as the following prayer of Ikhnaton shows: "I breathe the sweet breath which comes forth from thy mouth. I behold thy beauty every day. It is my desire that I may hear thy sweet voice, even the north wind, that my limbs may be rejuvenated with life through love of thee. Give me thy hands, holding thy spirit, that I may receive it and may live by it" (A. Weigall, *A Short History of Ancient Egypt* [London, 1934] p. 159). But, too often, instead of being considered the putting into practice by word and deed of a want, prayer was thought of as a means of inducing the gods to respond favorably. Polytheism encourages unscientific prayer. Indeed, the average modern conception of prayer, as a means of bringing about a change in the purpose of God, is a remnant of polytheism. One god may thwart the decision of another, and the suppliant could gamble on his favorite god's will and power to help. And that is where magic made its appeal. Among Egyptians, as always, the margin between prayer and magic is very narrow.

If the morals of a people may be defined by their conception of goodness, purity, faithfulness, truth, justice and by that of evil, impurity, faithlessness, falsehood, and injustice, the Egyptians would stand high morally among the peoples of the ancient past. Proof of that can be found abundantly in all their extant writings from the time of the Pyramid Texts, when, for example, justification was tested by truth, until the latest times when Osiris and Isis were exalted as the ideal father and mother, and when Set the murderer became a demon. During the time of the Middle Kingdom, beginning about 2000 B.C., a gospel of righteousness and justice was preached such as few periods in the history of any country have ever witnessed. It is hard to find in any ancient literature as much evidence of a moral consciousness as in such writings as the "Admonitions of an Egyptian Sage," the "Eloquent Peasant," the "Precepts of Ptah-Hotep," the "Life of Rekhmara." Little wonder that Professor Breasted found the "Dawn of Conscience" in this early literature of ancient Egypt. Nor was this power of making moral distinctions confined to any one period in the history of Egypt, as the Book of the Dead shows in its one hundred and twenty-fifth chapter, the famous so-called "Negative Confession."

A study of the customs and laws of the ancient Egyptians reveals many defects. Their idea of God as a rule was very anthropomorphic. Their gods were created and died; they married and suffered; they intrigued and were coerced. They accepted human sacrifices, and magic words could control them; they were local and national. The punishment for blasphemy was excessive. In family life, polygamy was permissible, concubinage was common; in social life, punishments were very severe, and slavery and forced labor were legal; and in international affairs, cruelty to captives was common.

On the other hand, it is quite clear that the Egyptians were devoted to their gods; and how sure they were of the love, righteousness, truth, and justice of the gods! The fundamental principle in family life was equality and love; in social relationships, justice and kindness were always admired and encouraged; in international affairs, the ideal was peaceful trade; and in personal life, goodness was at a premium.

In a sense Egyptian national life ended with Alexander's conquest of the country in 330 B.C. There are indications, however, that the conqueror intended, and his successors the Ptolemys saw to it, that Egyptian life and religion were encouraged to remain as far as possible as they were. The Greeks, with very few exceptions, always admired the Egyptians, and learned much from them. And so Alexander was far from desiring to annex Egypt. On the contrary he wanted to rule as an Egyptian pharaoh, and so he had himself accepted as son of the Egyptian state-god Amūn and was deified as all pharaohs before him; and when Ptolemy V, by the decree of the priests of Memphis, was proclaimed a god, he saw to it that the document was written *first* in the ancient sacred language, hieroglyphics, and *secondly* in the native Egyptian tongue and script of his own time, demotic, and *lastly* in Greek.

And so during the Ptolemaic period, the deities of Egypt remained the same, with the exception of Serapis, which, however, was merely a combination in Greek of Osiris and Apis. The great triad Osiris, Isis, and Horus (now called Harpocrates) was supreme,

42

but they as well as other native gods were sometimes called, in Greek, by their Greek equivalents. The Ptolemies were zealous in their observance of Egyptian religious customs and rites and devoted themselves to the building of many beautiful temples in all parts of the land.

When Egypt became a Roman province in 30 B.C., there was no essential change in religion and form of worship, except that some new deities were introduced from Rome, such as Jupiter Capitolinus and Roma, chiefly for the benefit and comfort of Roman officials and soldiers. The passion of Osiris and mysteries of Isis became very popular with the Romans, and many of the ancient temples were repaired, restored, and added to. Over the highways of the empire the religion of ancient Egypt spread north, south, east and west, even as far as France, the Rhineland and England; and although it was outlawed by decrees in 391 A.D., it lived on in beautiful Philae till the middle of the sixth century, during the time of Justinian; and only about a century after that in 642 the Arabs appeared and put an end to the Roman empire in Egypt.

BIBLIOGRAPHY

J. H. BREASTED, *Development of Religion and Thought in Ancient Egypt* (New York, 1912).

————, *The Dawn of Conscience* (New York, 1933).

E. A. W. BUDGE, *From Fetish to God in Ancient Egypt* (Oxford, 1934).

————, *The Gods of the Egyptians*, 2 Vols. (London, 1904).

A. ERMAN, *Die Religion der Aegypter* (Berlin, 1934).

S. A. B. MERCER, *Growth of Religious and Moral Ideas in Egypt* (Milwaukee, 1919).

————, *The Religion of Ancient Egypt* (London, 1948).

A. MORET, *The Nile and Egyptian Civilization* (London, 1927).

A. H. SHORTER, *An Introduction to Egyptian Religion* (New York, 1932).

J. VANDIER, *La Religion égyptienne* (Paris, 1944).

SUMERIAN RELIGION

Born in Russia in 1897, Dr. Kramer came to America in 1906. He studied in Philadelphia's School of Pedagogy, Temple University, Dropsie College and the University of Pennsylvania. In 1930 he was awarded the Ph.D. degree by the University of Pennsylvania for work in the fields of Archaeology and Semitics.

During the years 1930-1931, he was a member of excavating expeditions in Iraq. Then followed a series of important research projects: for ten years (1932-1942) he was a member of the Assyrian Dictionary Staff of the Oriental Institute of the University of Chicago; a Guggenheim fellow, 1937-1939; engaged in the project of copying Sumerian literary tablets in the Museum of the Ancient Orient in Istanbul, Turkey.

Since 1939 he has been studying and copying the Sumerian literary tablets in the University Museum at the University of Pennsylvania, first as research fellow, then as associate curator in the Babylonian section. During 1946 and 1947 he travelled in Turkey and Iraq for archaeological and epigraphic researches as annual professor of the American Schools of Oriental Research.

His present position is that of Clark research professor of Assyriology in the University of Pennsylvania and curator of the Tablet Collections in the University Museum.

His major works include: "Gilgamesh and the Huluppu Tree" (1938); "Lamentation over the Destruction of Ur" (1940); "Sumerian Literature" in the "Proceedings" of the American Philosophical Society (1942); "Sumerian Mythology" (1944); "Sumerian Literary Texts from Nippur" (1945); "Enki and Nihursag: A Sumerian Paradise Myth" (1945); "Gilgamesh and the Land of the Living" in the "Journal of Cuneiform Studies" (1947); and "Iraqi Excavations in the War Years" (1948).

Editor

SUMERIAN RELIGION

SAMUEL NOAH KRAMER

IN THE third millennium B. C., Sumer, the land corresponding roughly to the lower half of modern Iraq, was the seat of what was probably the predominant civilization in ancient Near East. Its most characteristic features were the existence of relatively large urban centers and—particularly in the second half of the millennium—the effective use of writing. Politically it consisted of a group of city-states, several of which were continuously vying for control of the land as a whole, and at times for that of its surrounding neighbors. Economically, it rested on an agricultural base which as a result of the application of successful irrigation techniques, provided a surplus sufficient to support large and varied groups of artisans and craftsmen, merchants and carriers, clerks and scribes, priests and temple officials, soldiers and court officials. Socially, it was characterized by the breakdown of the more primitive clan and tribal loyalties and the gradual emergence of local and national patriotisms. In the field of religion it witnessed the growth of highly complex temple cults together with the development of a polytheistic theology and mythology which to some extent became paradigmatic for the faith and creed of the entire ancient Near East. It is with certain aspects of the religious thought and practice of this Sumerian civilization that this essay will deal. First, however, it will be advisable to review briefly the historical background of third-millennium Sumer for a view of the ethnic threads woven into the seemingly homogeneous "Sumerian" cultural fabric of that period. The reader must bear in mind, however, that the days preceding the middle of the third millennium are "prehistoric" even for lower Mesopotamia; there are no written records to control our conclusions. The following sketch of the earliest history of the land which in the third millennium came to be known as Sumer is therefore to be taken as an hypothesis;

47

it is based largely on the interpretation of the mute archaeological finds in the light of the pattern of historical developments in other regions and later days. Nevertheless, and in spite of its highly over-simplified character, it may come closer to the truth than those hitherto suggested.

The first humans to settle in lower Mesopotamia were probably immigrants from southwestern Iran who arrived at the beginning of the fourth millennium B.C. In their new habitations they introduced the economic techniques, social mores, and religious beliefs and practices which characterized the "peasant-village" culture developed in their former homeland. Not long after the establishment of the first settlements by the Iranian immigrants, there is reason to believe that the Semites infiltrated into southern Mesopotamia both as peaceful immigrants and as warlike conquerors. It is probably largely as a result of the fusion of these two ethnic groups, the Iranians from the east and the Semites from the west, and the consequent cross fertilization of their cultures, that there came into being the first civilized *urban* state in lower Mesopotamia, the land that was later known as Sumer. As in the case of the later Sumerian state, it consisted, no doubt, of a number of cities between which there was continual strife for supremacy over the land as a whole. But now and again through the centuries relative unity and stability was achieved, at least for a brief interval. At such times, this Irano-Semitic power in which the Semitic element was probably predominant, must have succeeded in extending its influence over many of the surrounding districts, and developed what may well have been the first empire in the history of civilization.

Now part of the territory which this empire came to dominate both culturally and politically no doubt consisted of the more westerly parts of the Iranian plateau. It was in the course of these political activities and their accompanying military campaigns that the Irano-Semitic state of lower Mesopotamia first came in conflict with the Sumerians. For this primitive and probably nomadic people which may have erupted from Transcaucasia or Transcaspia, was pressing upon the districts of western Iran, the buffer state between the civilized Mesopotamian empire and the barbarians beyond, and these had to be defended at all costs. In their first encounters there is little doubt that the Irano-Semitic forces with their superior military technique, were more than a match for the Sumerian hordes. But in the long run, it was the mobile primitive Sumerians who had the advantage over their more civilized sedentary adversary. Over the years, as captive hostages in Mesopotamian cities, and as mercenaries in the Mesopotamian armies, the Sumerian warriors learned what they needed most of the more advanced military techniques of their captors and hirers. And probably some time toward the end of the fourth millennium, as the Irano-Semitic empire weakened and tottered, the Sumerians poured through the buffer states of western Iran and invaded Mesopotamia itself, where they took over as masters and conquerors.

The incursion of the Sumerian barbaric war-bands in the wake of the collapse of the earlier and more advanced Irano-Semitic civilization must have brought about an era of stagnation and regression in lower Mesopotamia. In the centuries spanning the end of the fourth millennium B.C. and the beginning of the third, it was the culturally immature and psychologically unstable Sumerian war lords with their highly individualistic and predatory dispositions who held sway over the sacked cities and burned villages of the vanquished empire. Moreover, these Sumerian invaders were themselves at first far from secure in their new Mesopotamian habitat. For not long after they had made themselves masters in the land, new nomadic hordes from the western desert, Semitic tribes known as Martu, poured into lower Mesopotamia. Under these circumstances it is hardly likely that the times immediately following the arrival of the Sumerian hordes were conducive to progress in the economic and technological fields, or to creative efforts in the field of art and architecture. Only in the oral literary field do we have reason to believe that there was a marked creative activity on the part of the illiterate court minstrels who improvised and composed their oral epic lays for the entertainment of their lords and masters.

It is the approximately two centuries following this era of stagnation and transition, of political change and ethnic adjustment, that probably proved to be most creative for the culture now generally known as Sumerian. In the course of the first quarter of the third millennium it would seem that the more stable elements of the Sumerian ruling caste, particularly the court and temple administrators and intellectuals came to the fore. A strong movement

49

for law and order developed in the land bringing with it an awakening of community spirit and patriotic pride. A rather extraordinary fruitful fusion, both ethnic and cultural, of the Sumerian conquerors with the vanquished but more civilized native population, brought about a creative spurt that was frought with significance not alone for Sumer—it is perhaps at this time that the name Sumer first came to be applied to lower Mesopotamia—but for Western Asia as a whole. It was during this cultural stage that architecture was developed to a new high level. This was the period that probably witnessed the first steps in the invention of the Sumerian system of writing, an event which proved to be the decisive factor in molding the Near East into a cultural unit in spite of its diverse and polyglot ethnic components. For the Sumerian system of writing in its later highly conventionalized form was borrowed by practically all the more cultured peoples of Western Asia. As a result, the study of the Sumerian language and literature became a major discipline in the narrowly restricted but highly influential "literate" circles of the ancient Near East.

It will now be clear that the so-called Sumerian civilization of the third millennium B.C.—it is designated "Sumerian" because the archaeological remains of its later stages, that is of the second half of the third millennium, are accompanied by inscriptions written in the Sumerian language—is actually a product of the cultural and biological fusion of at least three ethnic groups, the earliest Iranians whose ethnic and linguistic affiliations are at present altogether unknown, the Semites, and the Sumerians. Similarly it is obvious, the so-called Sumerian religion of the third millennium is not a homogeneous Sumerian development but contains elements taken over from the preceding Iranian and Semitic peoples. There is little doubt that many a deity in the "Sumerian" pantheon as known from the inscriptions, is actually non-Sumerian in origin, and at times even in name. However, since we are at present unable to distinguish its different ethnic components, the following sketch of Sumerian religion will treat it as if it were a homogeneous unit. Beginning with a brief description of the temple and its cult, our sketch will continue with an outline of some of the more significant theological tenets developed by the Sumerian thinkers, and conclude with a résumé of the contents of several of their more important extant myths.

What then did a temple in third-millennium Sumer look like? Fortunately several have been excavated in the course of the past few decades and we can perhaps do no better than describe briefly two of these: the "Painted Temple" from Uqair dating probably from the first quarter of the third millennium, and the Ekishnugal temple complex in the Biblical Ur of the Chaldees dating from the last quarter of the millennium.

Uqair is the modern name of an ancient ruin located about fifty miles south of Baghdad; the ancient name of the site is still unknown. The "Painted Temple" excavated at this site seems to consist of a central hall with an altar at one end and an offering table in the center. Two ranges of four subsidiary rooms each surrounded the central hall. The temple was built of bricks of modern shape on a terrace which in turn rested on a tall D-shaped platform. One stairway led from the platform to the terrace, and two symmetrically arranged stairways descended from the terrace to the bottom of the platform. The outer walls of the building consisted of alternating rows of buttresses and recesses and were painted white with a coat of gypsum paint. The inside walls of the temple were covered with frescoes; every surviving foot of its walls bore traces of color washes and painted ornament. The most common arrangement on these murals consisted of a band of plain color, usually some shade of red, forming a dado about one metre high all about the room. Above this was a painted band of geometrical ornament about thirty centimeters high. The upper parts of the walls were then decorated with scenes of human and animal figures painted on a plain white ground. Unfortunately, none of the human figures was recoverable above the waistline owing to the denudation of the mound.

Let us now see what a temple complex in one of the larger city centers of Sumer looked like in the last quarter of the third millennium. The city is Ur, one of the most important of Sumerian capitals, and the temple complex is known as the Ekishnugal dedicated to the city's tutelary deity, the moon-god Nanna. This enclosure measured about four hundred yards by two hundred yards, and it contained the ziggurat, a large number of temples, storehouses, magazines, courtyards, and dwelling places for the temple personnel. The complex has been only partially excavated. Its outstanding feature was the ziggurat, a rectangular tower whose base was some two hundred feet in length and a hundred and fifty feet in width;

its original height was about seventy feet. The whole is a solid mass of brick-work with a core of crude mud bricks and a "skin" of burned bricks set in bitumen. It rises in four irregular stages and is approached by three huge stairways. On its very top was a small shrine built entirely of blue enamelled bricks. The ziggurat stood on a high raised terrace surrounded by a double wall. Partly on this terrace and partly at its feet lay the large temple for the moon-god Nanna with a wide outer court surrounded by numerous store-chambers and offices. Not far from it was a temple dedicated to both Nanna and his wife Ningal; then came a building which may have been used as as "court house"; then the temple sacred to Ningal known as Giparku, which itself contained two separate temples as well as a host of private and storage rooms. All in all the Ekishnugal must have contained the outstanding group of buildings in ancient Ur.

Turning now to the cult practices in the temples of third-millennium Sumer, the reader is asked to bear in mind that our written sources for this period consist almost entirely of votive building documents and administrative lists; there are almost no religious texts from this millennium, that is, documents describing the varied and picturesque rites and ceremonies which must have been witnessed there throughout the year. We may take it for granted that in the major temple of each city there were offered daily sacrifices consisting of animal and vegetable foods, libations of water, wine, and beer, as well as the burning of incense. In addition there were, of course, the new moon feasts and other monthly celebrations. Finally there was the prolonged New Year celebration with its human and divine processions culminating in the hieros-gamos ceremony.

As for the priests in charge of the cult, we know little more than the names of several of the more important classes. Spiritual head of the temple is the high priest, the *en,* as he is known in Sumerian. He was chosen from time to time with special rites, and his selection was a significant public event. Under him were a number of priestly classes of which we know the names only, the *pashes,* the *lumah,* the *ishib.* In addition there was a large group of singers and musicians. Corresponding to the high priest was a high priestess in charge of groups of priestesses whose functions are unknown. In certain cults, particularly those connected with the Sumerian goddess Inanna, better known by her Semitic name Ishtar, there participated large numbers of eunuchs and perverts, hierodules, and other types of sacred prostitutes.

In addition to the priestly personnel involved in one way or another in the religious rites and ceremonies carried on in the temple, it must have housed a huge group of secular officials necessary to conduct its varied enterprises. The upkeep of a major temple in ancient Sumer must have required large revenues, and these were provided no doubt by gifts and endowments from the king and the ruling classes. In the course of the centuries the temple became one of the major landowners in the state; its serfs and employees in field and factory ran into the hundreds, perhaps thousands. Indeed it is not unlikely that the wealth and power of the priestly corporations brought them in conflict from time to time with the secular rulers, the kings and their appointed governors. By and large, it is true, of course, that the secular rulers were more than ready to follow the priestly line for the sake of peace and harmony. But even in the case of so theocratic a city-state as that of Lagash we find a priestly-minded reformer-king by the name of Urukagina revealing a rather unexpected state of affairs. According to his inscription which dates probably from the twenty-fourth century B.C., his predecessors had not hesitated to appropriate the rich fields of the gods—that is of the temple and priests—for their own use; they even used the "oxen of the gods" to plow their own fields. Obviously there were times when the palace-temple relations were by no means as smooth as our votive inscriptions and other priestly sources would have us believe.

In the matter of metaphysics and theology there is good reason to conclude that relatively early in the third millennium B.C. the Sumerians produced a group of thinkers and intellectuals who, within the narrow range of their limited and superficial scientific data, evolved and formulated a number of basic concepts which became more or less paradigmatic for the entire Near East. Moreover, since they were no doubt convinced that they were in possession of profound cosmic truths of utmost importance to their own conduct and that of their fellow-beings, these hoary theologians must have propagated them zealously and fervently by word of mouth in order to have them accepted as the official creed and universal faith of the land. In the course of these efforts they must have formulated many an argument and devised more than one proof for their support. But unfortunately there is little likelihood that we will ever recover the contents of these arguments and discussions, since the Sumerian scribes and men of letters failed to develop a written literary genre to serve as a vehicle for their expression and conservation. All that we can hope for is to dig out and piece together a few of the more basic theological concepts from the Sumerian votive and religious texts, particularly from the hymns and myths dating from the first half of the second millennium B.C. At the same time it will be well to bear in mind that these theological principles and metaphysical notions, important and significant as they may have seemed to the intellectuals and philosophers who evolved them, did not necessarily lead to any revolutionary changes in the temple cults. While they probably resulted in some significant alterations and adjustments, the temple ritual and priestly practices no doubt continued in their own special grooves and moved in accordance with the expected conservative rhythm.

Let us now examine several of the more fundamental Sumerian theological concepts. From as far back as our written records go, the Sumerian theologians assumed as axiomatic the existence of a pantheon consisting of a group of living beings, man-like in form, but superhuman and immortal, who though invisible to mortal eye, guide and control the cosmos in accordance with well laid plans and duly prescribed laws. Be it the great realms of heaven and earth, sea and air, be it the major astral bodies, sun, moon, and planet, be it such atmospheric forces as wind, storm, and tempest, or finally, to take the earth, be it such natural phenomena as river, mountain, and plain, or such cultural phenomena as city and state, dyke and ditch, field and farm, or even such implements as the pick-axe, brickmold, and plow—each was deemed to be under the charge of one or another anthropomorphic but superhuman being who guided its activities in accordance with established rules and regulations. Behind this axiomatic assumption of the Sumerian theologian no doubt lay a rational inference, for he could hardly have seen any of these huge human-like beings with his own eyes. Our theologian, reasoning from the known to the unknown, took his cue from human society as he knew it. He noted that all lands and cities, all palaces and temples, all fields and farms, in short all imaginable institutions and enterprises are tended and supervised, guided and controlled by living human beings; without them lands and cities become desolate, temples and palaces crumble, field and farm turn to

desert and wilderness. Surely therefore the cosmos and all its manifold phenomena must also be tended and supervised, guided and
controlled, by living beings in human form. But the cosmos being
far larger than the sum total of human habitations, and its organization being far more complex, these living beings must obviously be
far stronger and ever so much more effective than ordinary humans.
Above all they must be immortal; otherwise the cosmos would turn
to chaos upon their death and the world would come to an end,
alternatives which for obvious reasons did not recommend themselves to the Sumerian metaphysician. It was each of these invisible,
anthropomorphic, but at the same time superhuman and immortal
beings which the Sumerian designated by his word *dingir* and
which we translate by the word "god."

Moreover, just as the doctrine of the existence of a pantheon
developed from what may be termed a common sense approach to
the question "How is the cosmos run?" so, too, did the notions concerning its organization. In the first place, it seemed reasonable to
the Sumerian theologian to assume that the deities constituting the
pantheon were not all of the same importance or of equal rank. The
god in charge of the pick-axe or brickmold could hardly be expected
to compare with the deity in charge of the sun. Nor could the deity
in charge of dykes and ditches be expected to equal in rank the one
in charge of the earth as a whole. Then, too, on analogy with the
political organization of the human state it seemed not unreasonable
to assume that at the head of the pantheon was a deity recognized
by all the others as their king and ruler. The Sumerian pantheon
was therefore conceived as functioning as an assembly with a king
at its head; the most important groups in this assembly consisting of
seven gods who "decree the fates" and of fifty deities known as "the
great gods." But a more significant division set up by the Sumerian
theologians within their pantheon is that between creative and non-
creative deities, a notion arrived at as a result of their cosmological
views. For according to these, the basic components of the cosmos
are heaven and earth, sea and atmosphere; every other cosmic phenomenon could exist only within one or another of these realms.
Hence it seemed reasonable to infer that the deities in control of
heaven and earth, sea and air, were the creating gods and that one
or another of these four deities created every other cosmic entity in
accordance with plans originating with them.

55

As for the creation technique attributed to these deities, our Sumerian theologians developed a doctrine which became dogma throughout the Near East, the doctrine of the creative power of the divine word. All that the creating deity had to do, according to this doctrine, was to lay his plans and utter the word, and it came to be. No doubt this notion of the creative power of the divine word, too, was the result of a rational inference based on observation of human society. If a human king, it was reasoned, could achieve almost all he wanted merely by the word of his mouth, how much more so the immortal and superhuman creative deities in charge of the four realms of the universe.

Similarly the Sumerian theologians, again no doubt taking their cue from the human world about them, adduced a significant metaphysical inference in answer to the problem as to what keeps the cosmic entities and phenomena, once created, operating continuously and harmoniously, without conflict and confusion; this is the concept designated by the Sumerian word *me*, whose exact rendering is still uncertain. In general it would seem to denote a set of rules and regulations assigned to each cosmic entity and phenomenon for the very purpose of keeping it operating forever in accordance with the plans laid down by the deities creating it.

Before proceeding with a brief outline of the more important Sumerian myths, let us summarize some of the more obvious cosmogonic notions current in Sumer. First, according to these, was the primeval sea, probably thought to be eternal and uncreated. The primeval sea in some way engendered a united heaven and earth, probably in the shape of a mountain. Heaven and earth were conceived as solid elements. Between them, however, and somehow engendered by them, was the atmosphere whose main characteristics seem to be movement and expansion. Heaven and earth were thus separated from each other by the expanding element air. Air succeeded in producing the moon and the stars which may have been conceived as made of the same stuff as air. The sun was conceived as emanating from the moon, just as the latter emanated from air. After heaven and earth had been separated, plant, animal, and human life became possible on earth; all life seems to have been conceived as resulting from a union of air, earth, and water.

Transferred into theological language, the Sumerian cosmogonic concepts may be thus described. First was the goddess Nammu, the deity in control of the primeval sea; the name of her husband who must have shared her rule over the sea is still unknown. This goddess Nammu gave birth to An, the male heaven-god, and Ki, the earth-goddess. The union of An and Ki produced the air-god Enlil, who proceeded to separate the heaven-father An from the earth-mother Ki. Enlil, the air-god, now found himself living in utter darkness, with the sky, which may have been conceived by the Sumerians as made of pitch-dark lapis lazuli, forming the ceiling and walls of his house, and the surface of the earth, its floor. He therefore fashioned the moon, stars, and sun, and begot the moon-god Nanna who in turn begot the sun-god Utu. Also from the union of the air-god Enlil and the earth-mother Ki, vegetable and animal life was produced on earth with considerable help from the water-god Enki. Man, on the other hand, seems to be the product of the combined efforts of the goddess Nammu, the goddess known as Ninmah who may perhaps be identical with the earth-mother Ki, and the water-god Enki.

Turning finally to the Sumerian myths, the reader is asked to bear in mind two fundamental facts. In the first place, almost all our available mythological material is inscribed on tablets dating from the first half of the second millennium B.C. when Sumer was no longer a Sumerian but a Semitic state. There is good reason to believe that much of this mythology was current in third-millennium Sumer; just how much, however, is difficult to determine. Secondly, the reader must not confuse the Sumerian mythographers with the Sumerian metaphysicians and theologians; psychologically and temperamentally they were poles apart. The mythographers were scribes and poets whose main concern was the glorification and exaltation of the gods and their deeds. Unlike the metaphysicians and philosophers they were not interested in discovering cosmological and theological truths; they accepted the current theological tenets and practices without worrying about their origin and development. The aim of the myth makers was to compose a narrative poem in an effort to explain one or another of these tenets and practices in a manner that would be appealing, inspiring, and entertaining. They were not concerned with proofs and arguments directed to the intellect; their first interest was in telling a story that would appeal primarily to the emotions. Their literary tools, therefore, were not logic and reason, but imagination and fantasy. In telling their story, these poets did not hesitate to invent motives and incidents patterned on human action which could not possibly have any basis in reasonable and speculative thought, nor did they hesitate to adopt legendary and folkloristic motifs that had nothing to do with rational cosmological inquiry and inference. With these facts in mind, let us look briefly at the contents of several of the more significant Sumerian myths.

Our first myth may be entitled "Enlil and Ninlil: The Begetting of the Moon-god Nanna." The poem begins with passage descriptive of the ancient Sumerian city Nippur; Enlil, the air-god, is "its young man" while Ninlil, the air-goddess, is "its young woman." At the advice of her mother, the poem continues, Ninlil bathes in Nippur's river and walks along the river-bank. Enlil sees her and is attracted by her; he cohabits with her and she conceives the moongod Nanna. But for some obscure reason, Enlil is seized by the fifty great gods and is banished to the nether world. The faithful Ninlil follows him on his journey. As he comes to the gate of the city, Enlil instructs the "man of the gate" not to tell Ninlil of his whereabouts. When Ninlil comes up to the "man of the gate" and demands to know whither Enlil has gone, the latter seems to take the form of the "man of the gate", cohabits with her and impregnates her with the deity known as Nergal, the king of the nether world. He then proceeds on his journey and arrives at the river of the nether world, whither Ninlil follows him. Enlil now impersonates the "man of the river," cohabits with Ninlil, and impregnates her with another underworld deity known as Ninazu. He then comes to the ferryman, the "man of the boat" who is, no doubt, to ferry him across the river of the nether world. Here, too, Ninlil turns up, and the result is her impregnation with a third nether-world deity whose name is unfortunately destroyed in the text.

Our second myth may be entitled "Emesh and Enten: Enlil Chooses The Farmer-god." Enlil, the great and beneficent Sumerian god, the leader of the Sumerian pantheon during much of the third millennium, has set his mind to bring forth trees and grain and to establish abundance and prosperity in the land. For this purpose two cultural beings, Emesh and Enten, are created, and Enlil assigns to each specific duties. But a violent quarrel breaks out between the two brothers; not unlike the Biblical Cain and Abel they seem to vie with each other in the matter of bringing gifts to the

58

god responsible for their existence, in this case Enlil. Several arguments ensue, and Emesh challenges Enten's claim to the position of "farmer of the gods." And so they betake themselves to Enlil and each states his case. Enlil decides in favor of Enten, and Emesh accepts the decision without protest.

The major protagonists of our third myth are the water-god Enki and the goddess Ninhursag, who may perhaps be identical with the more original Ki, the earth-mother; it may be entitled "Enki and Ninhursag: A Sumerian 'Paradise' Myth." The poem begins with a eulogy of the land Dilmun, identified by some scholars with the Bahrein Islands in the Persian Gulf, and by others with a land in southwestern Iran. This Dilmun, according to our poem, is a place that is pure, clean, and bright. It is a land in which there is probably neither sickness nor death. It is a city which, by the command of Enki, is full of sweet water and of crop-bearing fields and farms. The main action begins when the water-god Enki impregnates the goddess Ninhursag, "the mother of the land" who, after nine days of pregnancy, gives birth, without pain and effort, to the goddess Ninmu. Enki then proceeds to impregnate his daughter Ninmu who gives birth to a goddess named Ninkurra; the latter, too, is impregnated by Enki and she gives birth to a goddess named Uttu. Enki is now evidently all set to impregnate his great-granddaughter Uttu, when Ninhursag, the great-grandmother, intervenes and seems to advise her not to cohabit with Enki until and unless he brings her a gift of cucumbers, apples (?) , and grapes. Enki obtains these from a gardener, brings them to Uttu, and the latter now joyfully receives his advances. But of this union no new goddess is born. Instead, Ninhursag seems to utilize Enki's semen in a way which leads to the sprouting of eight plants. And now Enki committed a sinful deed. He has his messenger, the two-faced god Isimud, pluck each of the eight plants for him, and he then ate them one by one. Angered by this act, Ninhursag utters a curse against Enki saying that until he dies she will not look upon him with the "eye of life." And as good as her word she immediately disappears. Whereupon Enki, no doubt, begins to pine away, and the Anunnaki, the great gods, sit in the dust. Enlil, the king of all the gods, seems unable to cope with the situation, when up speaks the fox saying that if properly rewarded he will bring Ninhursag back to the gods. His words prove to be no idle boast; in one way or another the fox succeeds in having Ninhursag return to the gods. She then seats the dying Enki by her vulva, and asks where he feels pain. Enki names an organ of his body which hurts him, and Ninhursag then informs him that she has caused a certain deity to be born for him, the implication being that the birth of the deity will result in the healing of the sick member. In this fashion eight deities are born for the eight parts of the body which pained Enki. The poem concludes with Enki decreeing the fate of each of the newborn deities.

Our next myth may be entitled "The Organization of the Earth and Its Cultural Processes." Its major protagonist is once again the god Enki, but it differs widely in tone and temper from the preceding myth; it aims to furnish a detailed account of the activities of Enki, the god of wisdom as well as of water, in organizing the earth and establishing law and order upon it. We first find Enki going to Sumer, then to its capital Ur, then to Meluhha, perhaps to be identified with the eastern coast of Africa; he blesses each of these localities in lofty language. He then turns to the Tigris and Euphrates rivers, fills them with sparkling water, and appoints a deity by the name of Enbilulu to take care of them. He next fills them with fishes and makes another deity, described as the "son of Kesh," responsible for them. He then sets up the rules for the sea and places the goddess Sirara in charge of it. He calls to the winds and appoints over them the god Ishkur. He turns next to the plow and yoke and places Enkimdu, "the man of dykes and ditches," in charge. He brings about the production of grain and plants in the fields, and places the goddess Ashnan in charge of them. He appoints the brick-god Kabta over the pick-axe and brickmold. He lays foundations and builds houses with the building implement *gugun* and puts them in charge of Mushadamma, the "great builder of Enlil." He fills the plain with plant and animal life and puts them under the care of Sumugan, "king of the mountain." He builds stables and sheepfolds, fills them with milk and fat, and puts the shepherd-god Dumuzi in charge of them. The appointment of Dumuzi does not mark the end of the poem, but unfortunately the text is destroyed from here on and we have no idea how the myth ended.

We conclude with another myth in which Enki plays a major rôle but one in which, in spite of his wisdom, he is outwitted by another deity, the goddess Inanna, "the Lady of Heaven," now more generally known under her Semitic name Ishtar. The myth, which may be entitled "Inanna and Enki: The Transfer of the Arts of Civilization from Eridu to Erech," tells the following story. Inanna, the tutelary deity of the ancient Sumerian city Erech, is eager to increase the welfare and prosperity of her city and to make it the center of Sumerian civilization. She therefore decides to go to Eridu where Enki, the Lord of Wisdom, who "knows the very heart of the gods," dwells in his watery abyss, the Abzu. For this Enki has under his charge all the divine decrees that are fundamental to civilization. And if she can obtain them, by fair means or foul, and bring them to her beloved city Erech, its glory and her own will, indeed, be unsurpassed. As she approaches the Abzu she is welcomed by Isimud, Enki's messenger, and a banquet is prepared for her and Enki. After their hearts had become happy with drink, Enki presents Inanna with the over one hundred divine sets of regulations which, superficially considered, formed the basis of the culture-pattern of Sumerian civilization. Among them were those referring to lordship, godship, the crown, the throne, the scepter, the shrine, shepherdship, kingship, the priestly offices, truth, descent into the nether world and ascent from it, the flood, music, eldership, heroship and power, enmity, straightforwardness, falsehood, goodness and justice, the craft of the carpenter, metal worker, scribe, smith, leather worker, mason, and basket-weaver, wisdom and understanding, purification, judgment and decision, musical instruments. Inanna is only too happy to accept the gifts offered her by the drunken Enki. She takes them, loads them on her "boat of heaven," and makes off for Erech with her precious cargo. But after the effects of the banquet had worn off, Enki noticed that the divine decrees were gone from their usual place. He turns to Isimud and the latter informs him that he, Enki himself, had presented them to his daughter Inanna. The upset Enki now rues his munificence and decides to prevent the "boat of heaven" from reaching Erech at all costs. There were seven stopping points between Eridu and Erech, and Enki dispatched his servant Isimud with a varied group of sea monsters to one after another of these seven places to seize the "boat of heaven." But each time he fails; Inanna and the boat are saved by her ever-present messenger Ninshubur. Finally, Inanna and her boat arrive safe and sound at Erech, where amidst jubilation and feasting on the part of its delighted inhabitants, she unloads the divine decrees one at a time.

BIBLIOGRAPHY

SAMUEL NOAH KRAMER, *Sumerian Mythology* in *Memoir* XXI of the American Philosophical Society (1944).

————, *Enki and Ninhursag: A Sumerian "Paradise" Myth.* Supplementary Study No. 1 of the *Bulletin* of the American Schools of Oriental Research (1945).

THORKILD JACOBSEN in *The Intellectual Adventure of Ancient Man* (University of Chicago Press, 1946).

ASSYRO-BABYLONIAN RELIGION

The special field of study and research in which Dr. A. Leo Oppenheim has been long engaged is that of Assyriology. Many articles on Akkadian lexicography, religion and technology have been contributed to the world of scholarship by him. His most recent articles (published during 1946-48) deal with the ancient Near East, with Mesopotamian mythology, appearing in the "Journal of Near Eastern Studies", in "Orientalia" and in the "Bulletin of the American Schools of Oriental Research."

When the present article was written, he was on absence-leave from his regular position in the Oriental Institute of the University of Chicago, at work upon an Assyrian Dictionary project. In the United States he has been a visiting lecturer at Johns Hopkins University, visiting professor for Assyriology at Dropsie College in Philadelphia and holds the position of associate professor of the History and Civilizations of the ancient Near East at the Asia Institute in New York.

He was born in Vienna, Austria, 1904. The doctor of philosophy degree was granted him by the University of Vienna.

Editor

ASSYRO-BABYLONIAN RELIGION

A. LEO OPPENHEIM

THE ENTRY of the Semitic ethnic element upon the Mesopotamian historical scene, held for countless centuries by Sumerian protagonists, was sudden and, politically, of far-reaching consequences. This event is directly linked to the unique personality of the first Semitic king, Sargon of Agade (or: Akkad), who ruled approximately in the 23rd Cent. B.C. With dramatic impact, he transformed the age-old pattern of political life in Mesopotamia; he changed an agglomeration of primeval city-states of essentially equal standing into an empire administered from a newly built city and reaching beyond the limits of Sumer.

In the domain of religious life and thought, the new element was slower in gaining importance and in evolving that complex "assemblage" of conceptual patterns, emotional attitudes with their correlated forms of expression, of institutions, etc., which we are to call here "A (ssyro-) B (abylonian) R (eligion)." Sprung from the Sumerian matrix, this religion was constantly faced with the problem of expressing the particular attitude towards life and the divine with which its followers were gifted, in forms and concepts not their own. During the intricate process of adjustment and reinterpretation, this religion was furthermore subjected, for more than two millennia, to ever-changing political, economic and social contingencies. The fluctuating influences of distinct local traditions, the steady shifting of emphasis, due to internal developments, add further complications, yielding in the end a picture of mosaic-like fragmentation.

The nature of the extant evidence but increases these difficulties. The literary sources, by far the more relevant, offer direct evidence in prayers, hymns, rituals, mythological texts and the various writings of the native theologians. Other texts bear indirect witness to

65

religious customs and concepts, such as the mass of historical inscriptions, political documents and the rich material which reflects legal transactions, administrative practices and the daily life of private persons.

Unfortunately, these sources fail, very often, to cover important aspects of the ABR, or remain mute for centuries and in crucial regions. The inevitable hazards of preservation, discovery, publication and interpretation leave us with a minute fraction of the original material which—even if more completely preserved—would still fail to answer many and the most important of our queries. Not only centuries and continents but also a different mental climate separate us from the culture which has blossomed into this religion.

In the realm of archaeology, the situation parallels in all respects the state of affairs just described. It often seems a hopeless task to put the mass of data into the correct relation, in a temporal, spatial, sociological, and evolutionary framework. To fill the most patent gaps one may either resort to the expedient of projecting all data on a given subject—if they also originate in different periods, regions and are valid only for a definite social stratum—upon one plane, or one may utilize similar concepts and trends in neighboring civilizations to supply missing links or the corroborative evidence of parallels. The first type of approach yields necessarily a confusing picture—mitigated as it were by the inherent traditionalism of religious institutions and modes of expression, the second, the heuristic value of which should not be denied, tends to blur the specific mood and the individual achievements of each of these civilizations.

In the following presentation, an effort is being made to give special consideration to three frames of reference: area, social stratification and internal development.

Assyria and Babylonia

Agriculture was, in Mesopotamia, the easternmost section of the "Fertile Crescent", the economic basis upon which alone the population could increase to that density which is a prerequisite of higher civilization. The religious attitude was therefore essentially one which is natural to farming folks woven into the rhythm of seasonal work with its accompanying moods and their traditional ritual expressions. Here, however, one should not fail to observe an important regional difference in the tenor of this attitude. Agricultural techniques divide Mesopotamia into two cultural provinces and it can be shown that this dichotomy underlies, to a great extent, all things Mesopotamian, accentuated as it was by differences in the ethnic background and the distinct cultural traditions of the two areas.

In upper Mesopotamia and in the hilly piedmont east of the Tigris, rain-agriculture was at home, while irrigation-agriculture was practiced on the alluvial soil along the lower course of both rivers, Tigris and Euphrates. In accordance with these technical differences, different patterns of thought developed with regard to the relation between man and the supernatural powers as well as to those between men.

While the farmer in the south trustingly expected the river to bring annually the life-giving water right up to his field, that of the northwestern regions had to depend upon the whims of the weather to save him from famine. He had to resort to prayers and magic to force the correct amount of rain, at the appropriate moment, from the grudging sky. Little there was to induce him to think of the world he was living in as permeated and governed by a harmonious, well-planned and "philanthropic" order as did the farmer in the southern village. The latter derived an added feeling of security from the fact that his god was actually residing, like a fatherly ruler, within his settlement. The relationship of this deity to the priest and/or ruler of the group were conceived as very intimate and patterned on basic human interrelations. The rain-agriculturist's god, however, was an irritable god, riding in the storm-clouds and ready to pour down the direly needed rain as well as devastating storm-floods. His permanent residence was often in distant mountain regions, while his shrines and altars were scattered throughout the farmland and villages. Here, the rain-maker is king as well as priest. Tense in mood, and, at times, hectic in expression, the relations between the group and the deity are emotionally more sincere (on both sides) and, above all, are not subjected to parochial limitations. This god might migrate with his worshippers in quest for better living conditions or in war.

Obviously, such extreme set-ups do not correspond normally to

67

reality. Hybrid forms, showing in varying degrees fusions and combinations of these two basic patterns, did, however, materialize all over Mesopotamia with the lines of cleavage running rather irregularly, but following, in a larger perspective, the geographical dispositions of the two techniques in agriculture as modified by subsequent political developments. Changes in environment, encroachments, coalescence of different groups, the spread of certain religious concepts and forms, make it difficult and often impossible to analyze the structure of a given unit. Moreover, many composite layers have developed which cover up this basic dichotomy.

The Pantheon

In the cities of southern Mesopotamia (Babylonia proper) we find as city-gods the most important figures of a populous pantheon which is the creation of Sumerian religiosity. These deities unite two functions in their person: they and their temples are the focal points of an elaborate annual cycle of ritualistic activities in which clergy and population join and which vary but little in their essential outlines from town to town. Yet, these deities were also included, according to their individual function and rank, in the super-urban religious life of the country. In Nippur, for instance, the old sacred city, never entangled in the struggles for ephemeral supremacy, stood the temple of Enlil (Ellil), a *"Weltgott"* figure. The patron-god of Larsa (southern Babylonia, also called Sumer) as well as that of Sippar (northern section: Akkad) was the sun-god Shamash who brought light and justice to all mankind. The wise moon-god Sîn (Nanna) journeyed over the nightly sky in his miraculously changing bark, revealing the future to all expert interpreters of his ways, yet his beloved residence was the "Temple of Joys" in "Ur of the Chaldees." The main female figure of the pantheon, Ishtar, was no exception. At home in Uruk, the biblical Erech, she was worshipped as Evening and Morning Star and wherever the most violent human emotions affect the very existence of mankind. Even the chthonic gods resided in mundane cities, such as Ea (Enki) in Eridu and Nergal in Kutha; the domain of the first were the subterranean primeval waters whence he brought the arts and crafts to man, the second ruled the shadows in the Nether World. The gods of the "second generation", those who lived in younger cities through the vicissitudes of their careers, ruled in Babylon: Marduk, son of Ea, and in Borsippa: Nabû (Nebo), son of Marduk.

The regions where agriculture depended on rain harbored divine figures of different types. There was the "heartland" of impetuous weathergods, armed with lightning forks and associated with the bull. Worshipped under many names and in many tongues throughout the "Fertile Crescent"—reaching into Asia Minor and, at times, even into Egypt—the weathergod had no city of his own in the irrigation area, though he was well-known there. Even in the vast rain-agriculture area, his temples were few. In this realm of village agricultures of neolithic descent, urban settlements were exceptional and occasioned only by outstanding local fertility of the soil (combined with fortunately timed river-irrigation), favorable location with respect to main trade-routes, and the existence of a sacred locality which attracted and interconnected widely scattered groups and thus favored the formation of religious or secular amphyctionic confederations gravitating towards the sanctuary and enhancing its political and religious importance. Such sacred and otherwise privileged places have been Assur on the Tigris (before it became the capital of an empire), Arbela in the piedmont hills of the Zagros-mountains (seat of a female deity) and the cities staggered along the Euphrates road to the Mediterranean such as Mari, Carkhemish, Harran, Aleppo. It should not be forgotten that the inevitable set-backs in a rain-agriculture society keep nomadic traditions alive with their proclivities for war, booty and commerce. Periodical pilgrimages to such sanctuaries are operative in fusing the groups together by providing collective religious experiences.

This was, for these very reasons, not only the homeland of the numerous Baals, but also that of gods who shared their names with their tribe. Above all and best known on account of its historic rôle is Assur, the god of the Assyrians whose high-priests, the kings of Assyria, ruled the ancient Near East for about one millennium. The Amorites, linguistically a group of western Semites, worshipped a "god of the Amorites" (Amurru) and rose to political importance when they penetrated southern Mesopotamia, some centuries after Sargon's empire, to act again as a "catalytic agent" by stimulating the growth of a territorial state in a world of city-states. The most prominent figure of the "Amorite intermezzo" was Hammurabi, king of Babylon. The Kassites, a group of mountaineers, worshipped the god Kassu when they invaded the lowlands to succumb to an intensive acculturation-process. They ruled Babylon for nearly half a millennium. These events are obviously typical; the inherent fragmentation-tendency of the city-state pattern in an irrigation agriculture can apparently only be overcome by the aggressive political concept of a priest-king who aspires world-domination for his god. Here Egypt shines forth as the outstanding exception.

Whenever a sanctuary town gained enough political and religious prestige, the inevitable sequel was the introduction of the ritual forms and techniques of the city-state religiosity with specialized and institutionalized priests, theological speculations and aspirations in order to integrate the native god into the alien pantheon, etc. The typical example is the Babylonization of Assur where a foreign religious tradition has been successfully superimposed upon as well as interwoven into a native one.

This enumeration of the foremost deities of the ABR has left some important figures of the pantheon without mention, quite apart from the mass of gods and goddesses recorded in the available literary sources. These texts mention a startling galaxy of divine figures, but only in relatively few hymns, prayers, etc., do we find enough detailed information to cause something like a typology of Mesopotamian deities to emerge. Seen from this point of view, we find world-gods (such as Anu, Ellil, Bêl) omnipotent but shadowy rulers who tend to recede into unapproachability, slightly misanthropic yet never quite losing contact with living religiosity. Their offspring populated the pantheon as war and storm-gods, temperamental bringers of fertility and victory, such as Ninurta, Ningirsu, Ilbaba, also Adad and his doublets. The deities with cosmic functions, the sun-god, moon-god and the goddess connected with the planet Venus, formed a well-defined group and so do the figures concerned with healing and death (Nergal, Gula). Some of the younger gods (Marduk, Nebo) assumed the position of mediators and intercessors which greatly increased their popularity. On the distaff-side, we have goddesses of the mother-type, often secondarily associated with male figures as consorts (Ninlil, Damkina, Baba, etc.) and the type which is rather *sui generis* in the Semitic Near East, Ishtar with her doublets. Labelled, as a rule, with the trite misnomer "Goddess of War and Sensual Love", it is exceedingly difficult to unravel the complex strains of thought and basic reli-

70

gious concepts which have been blended into this divine figure. Armed goddess of battle, temptress in the coarsest forms, splendid star, "Lady of Heaven", patron-goddess of Uruk—yet ubiquitously present in human and animal reproduction, Ishtar has successfully defied interpretation. What appears so incompatible to our mind as functions of the same deity constitutes probably the very nodal point of the complex: in the bloody melée, killing and being killed, man performed Ishtar's service and there she manifests herself just as wherever and whenever man or animal creates new life. In one of her many other aspects, Ishtar is linked to the cyclic phenomena of vegetal life as the loving sister of the god Tammûz who reflects in his sufferings, death and triumphal resurrection, the annual disappearance and rebirth of vegetation. The cult of which this god was the center, under many names, was dear and meaningful to the heart of agricultural societies all over the Near East; within Mesopotamia, however, a revealing phenomenon can be observed. In southern Mesopotamia this cult remained somewhat below the level of official religiosity; its documents are mostly written in a dialect of the Sumerian and little notice is taken of it outside this type of literature. Proceeding upstream, this religious substratum makes itself increasingly felt; from non-religious Assyrian texts we learn that the image of the dead Tammûz was, at an annual festival, set up, lying in state and surrounded by his mourning enthusiasts, and songs of love were sung in his praise which breathe an intimate lyrical poetry. Further westward, the expressions of communal mourning and joy grow even more hectic, and there the gods of the Tammûz-type vie in importance with those of the Baal-type.

When turning to the native priestly theologians for information concerning their pantheon, a different picture is presented. In elaborate and long lists of divine names—to be traced back nearly as far as the earliest intelligible epigraphic documents—they have amassed thousands of names. As zealous theologians, they busied themselves for many centuries in systematizing the status, rank and function of these gods into a hierarchic organization patterned on all kinds of human social relations. Gods were grouped in families, provided with servants and menials, or in clans with officials, etc. Where names were lacking, the pious scribes resorted to inventions.

Lastly, a still not fully explored source of information for the names of the gods should be mentioned. These are the countless theophoric personal names in Sumerian and Akkadian. They are, above all, a sensitive indicator of the fluctuations in popularity of a specific deity, of the local limitations of a cult and of the influx of foreign gods often indicative of invasions or infiltrations of alien people.

The Divine

The Mesopotamian concepts concerning that fundamental religious phenomenon: the Presence and Manifestation of the Divine, are difficult to investigate. One has to piece together what scattered information can be deducted from sources which only rarely allude to this subject matter. Two different forms of contact between the profane world and the realm of the Holy seem to have been known: a Presence which is inherent to and part of the very nature of certain objects, e.g., plants with meaningful qualities, stones of specific color, form or smell, and a Presence with which certain man-made objects can be endowed by magic means. These manufactured carriers of the Holy were either human-shaped, the images, or objects of specific forms which Assyriologists are wont to denote by the inadequate term "symbol".

As a rule, the Mesopotamian image does not depart from human forms and measurements, a fact which might be considered the sequel of a ritual tradition sporadically attested in monuments and literary documents according to which human beings, priests and priestesses, acted under certain circumstances—such as in the rite of the "Sacred Marriage"—for or as gods.

The above mentioned "symbols" are either likenesses of the heavenly bodies, such as the sun-disk, crescent, star, or weapons (maces, staffs, arrowhead, etc.), tools (plow, stylus, lamp, etc.) and objects which depict certain animals. Their sacredness was intimately linked to their form, and small replicas, used as charms, shared their divine quality to a certain extent. Apart from the fact that these symbols are, already in the early period, definitely connected with specific deities, little is known about the intriguing problem of the relation between these two kinds of objects of religious worship. During certain periods, a predominance of one or the other is noticeable in the iconography and the textual evidence, while, at others, the coexistence of image and "symbol" tended towards substitution.

72

It should be noted, that it was considered an indispensable prerequisite to transform images as well as "symbols" from dead and unclean matter into the proper seat for the Divine by means of a consecration which changed them into "living" things, ready for perception, sensations and even emotions.

The Temple

In parallelism with the twofold manifestations of the Presence—inherent and magically provoked—the Mesopotamians differentiated between localities which by virtue of their nature were endowed with the strange and uncanny phenomenon of divine presence, and those where the Holy could be made to dwell permanently. To the first kind belong mountain-tops, springs, certain rivers and other remarkable localities (e.g., bitumen-wells), also the fragrant shadow of a grove. Here again, the mentioned dichotomy of Mesopotamian religious concepts makes itself felt: the localities of the first type are preferred outside of the irrigation-province where the divinity lived, as a rule, in man-made sanctuaries. Nevertheless, certain of their features—such as the huge "mountain" of the temple-tower, the artificial groves and others—do seem to hearken back to a different past.

The preparation of a locality for the Presence is magic in character and includes purification-rites, protection against desecration, and the installation of an adequate and ritually correct carrier or seat: an image and/or a "symbol."

The emplacement of an old sanctuary was considered as especially sacred, new temples were built exactly upon the outlines of old and ruined ones. The rebuilding as well as the rather rare construction of new sanctuaries were linked by the priests to special divine wishes expressed by means of dreams, etc.

The main function of the temple was to shelter the image, to protect it from the impurities of the outside world and to make it live, eat, drink and act befitting its dignity and importance. In other words, to reside in its temple, surrounded by its servants, like a king in his palace.

None of the numerous images is preserved, but iconographic and literary evidence sheds some light on their appearance. The traditional features of form, apparel and appurtenances were carefully maintained in Babylonia where the clergy successfully refused modifications and innovations as they are quite frequently reported from Assyria where the king was also high priest and often instrumental in introducing new ideas into the religious statuary.

The images were made of costly wood, plated with the "divine" metal, gold, and provided with large and staring inset eyes. They were clad in sumptuous garments (exclusive for this purpose) and decked out with their characteristic insignia, such as jewel-studded miters and pectorals. Enthroned on a pedestal in the naos under which was a deep pit with clean sand, the image was often associated with its traditional "sacred" animal or its "symbol." It sometimes stood under a canopy or could be hidden by heavy curtains.

The cella itself was, in Babylonia, not accessible to the layman who could behold his god only from the court-yard through the monumentally decorated door of the naos and the two or more anterooms which often separated it from the court. In the sanctuaries of another type which seem to have been native outside Babylonia proper, the worshipper was allowed to enter and the image could not be seen from without the naos. The psychological and religious implications of these two different technical solutions of the problem arising from the meeting between man and deity, are obvious.

It seems important to point out here the mobility of the Babylonian image, especially with regard to indications that the images in the Assyrian culture-area lacked this ability. The image was transported, on human shoulders, on chariots or in special barques, in the temple-precinct, within the city, and outside of it. Within the sacred precinct, the statue was transferred into other chapels, such as the "Bedroom-Chapel" to perform the nuptials, into the "Grove" or into the court-yard where many important rituals were enacted in which participated clergy, king and population. Within the city, the image moved on biers or on chariots along the sacred circuit of the processional road marked out by street-altars, among the jubilation of the inhabitants. A major festival event was the departure and the arrival of the god on the occasion of his visit to the sanctuary of another god (always the visible expression of political dependency) or to an out-of-door sanctuary built for this very purpose. Into this sanctuary, the deity proceeded once a year, as an integral part of the New Year's Festival, accompanied by the population to participate there in rites that are likely to have included the dramatic enactment of characteristic mythological events in which the god played a decisive rôle. The various forms and degrees of participation in religious services and activities connected with all these dislocations of the image and their correlated emotional responses have certainly been a major factor in the integration of the community of worshippers.

The daily life of the image in its cella was patterned on that of the king in his palace. The few and late texts concerned with the duties of the priests, the fare to be prepared for the gods, the activities and prayers prescribed for daily or festival rituals, show a complicated and elaborate court-ceremonial from the awakening of the deity in the morning to the nightly closing of the doors of the sanctuary. Repasts were prepared in the temple kitchen and served two or three times a day together with numerous beverages, and even water for the washing of the fingers. It reveals the amount of searching religious thought at work in the establishing of the details of the ritual, that the food and drink was sometimes presented to the image with a solemn swinging or up-and-down motion, while, at other occasions, the repast was "consumed" behind the linen-curtain of a small tent erected for that purpose around the image and the sacrificial table. The actual consumption was thus considered a mystery not to be seen by human eyes. The custom of the Eastern Church to surround the altar with linen-curtains during the transubstantiation, shows impressively the survival of ritual forms.

It has to be borne in mind that—as the cuneiform religious texts repeatedly indicate—the deity actually "lived", that is: was kept potent, efficient and present, on its fare. Large amounts of food and drink, necessary for this purpose, had to be provided, stored, prepared and—after having been offered to the image—to be distributed among the personnel of the temple according to rank and status. The images had, furthermore, to be clad fittingly, scented with choice perfumes, fumigated with costly aromatic matter, and decked out with the jewelry appropriate to their dignity in design and value. The manufacturing or the acquisition of all this as well as of the sacred utensils for the needs of the ritual, and lastly, the decoration and maintenance of the sanctuary itself, required a trained and specialized staff of working, administrative and executive personnel in addition to the priests in attendance on the cult and those concerned with functions to be discussed presently.

From these few indications it follows that the temple organization was bound to grow into the foremost economic institution of the city-state with which the palace alone—and, as it were, only rather rarely in the course of history—could rival in importance. The relations between these two institutions and the domain of private economic activities, do not fall within the scope of this presentation although the temple's share did, at times and in places, overshadow the other factors.

Institutionalized priesthood and priests in still uncertain relation to the temple organization are connected in numerous ways with the religious and intellectual life of the country. Some were concerned with the treatment of the sick, therapeutically as well as prophylactically, using medical and magic procedures; others with the mediation of litigations utilizing, e.g., the awe of the Holy to establish the truth by means of oaths and ordeals. The interest of the temple in the maintenance of the cultural tradition is reflected in its endeavors to preserve social justice by regulating the system of measurements, reducing the rate of interest, and influencing the money-market by granting loans without interest in special cases. It induced the priests to evolve and develop methods of surveying, to establish and regulate the calendar, to observe, record and interpret astronomical phenomena. As theologians and scholars—both functions are difficult to keep apart—the priestly scribes collected, copied and commented upon the treasures of the religious literature as well as the text- and reference-books necessary to teach and study the Sumerian which was kept alive as a sacred and scholarly language. The training of priests specializing in divination-techniques of all kinds was considered of vital importance for the well-being and the security of the country.

The incomplete fragments of these scribal activities have been unearthed in many buried sanctuaries of the south, but they are all dwarfed in number and subject matter by the famous library of Assurbanipal, the last important Assyrian king. This is due again to the unique position of the Assyrian ruler who alone—as the high-priest of the national god—was able to break down the traditional particularism and zealous narrowmindedness of the scribes attached to local sanctuaries, and thus to plan and achieve a collection of all available cuneiform texts of religious, literary or scholarly interest. Without this library, our knowledge of the ABR would be much more restricted and incoherent.

The Common Man

The religion of the common man must not be passed over in silence, even in this succinct presentation. Although it left neither ruins of temples nor impressive literary documents, this social horizon has not altogether disappeared. Its traces are as rare as they are difficult to interpret and to evaluate. It seems that the common man was well aware of the divine spark which made him into a living being, or—to use Akkadian terms—of the fact that a transcendental phenomenon which he called "god-and-goddess" accompanied him through life endowing him with health, potency, peace of mind and what we may call success or even luck. The experience of the ego as subject of all emotions, the consciousness of being a unique individual (as to corporeal features and personality) and many other related psychological phenomena, such as e.g., the "inner voice", have found their somewhat hazy and very undogmatic expression in the strange concept of two or more divine companions of the individual. In spite of, or beside this tendency to personify the various aspects of this basic experience, there are indications that the spark divine was also thought of as being differentiated in quality as well as in quantity according to the social status of its carrier, and according to his individual "share" of this precious stuff. Courageously, the common man resigned himself to accept as much of "life", i.e., health, success, as some unknown power had allotted to him, apparently at his birth. When it was used up, his physical existence came to an end, and one may doubt whether the " (personal) god" of a common man was generally considered as having strength enough to "survive" that crisis for any length of time and to continue its existence in the Nether World or within the body of a child born into the family soon afterwards. The Nether World seems to have harbored only such privileged human beings as kings and priests whose "shares" were greater, qualitatively and/or quantitatively.

All these concepts remain below the level of the priestly or official religious life. Yet, man did hope against hope that magic practices could increase or strengthen his "share", he even approached, encouraged perhaps by the priests, certain deities of the pantheon, or put his trust upon charms, watched for signs and portents in the small world of his immediate surroundings for warning or encouragement. At bottom, however, his outlook was that of fatalistic resignation. There was no salvation. His religious experiences were collective and restricted to the extreme emotions of mourning and joy. Individual experiences were not considered valid in official Mesopotamian religiosity though there are some indications that, outside the Babylonian cultural province, charismatic phenomena have been more acceptable. Mesopotamia was not the land of individual revelation and personal salvation but that of portents and prodigies. The deity manifested its will by means of meaningful deviations from the normal which had to be interpreted by highly trained experts. These manifestations concern the king mainly and the country as a whole.

The only individual who could approach the deity in prayers, and expect an answer, was the king, according to the Assyrian concept of kingship which differs in essential points from the Babylonian. Endowed by birth and status with an extraordinary amount of that "divine" spark which endued his person with the supernatural awe-inspiring radiance of all beings and things divine, he had to live a life strictly regulated by ritual and moral obligations. He was personally responsible for their observance as well as for all his acts and works which had to conform to a definite pattern (his "good works" e.g., were the building, decoration and maintenance of the sanctuaries). His well-being, his success in war, the prosperity of his group—of which he was the only "real" personality—constituted the divine answer to his prayers and acts.

In contradistinction to the Religion of the Common Man without cult, priests or temples, we have here the Royal Religion with one adherent, the king, subjected to complicated obligations and duties, and enjoying unique privileges in his relation to the deity. It was up to the religious genius of a small nation in the westernmost section of the rain-agriculture area, called Palestine, to claim for every human being the responsibilities, obligations and privileges which in Assyria were restricted to the king and high priest. The ultimate success of this revolutionary movement relegated the

ASSYRO-BABYLONIAN RELIGION

Religion of the Common Man to the substratum of superstition and folklore which survives all revelations and reforms.

BIBLIOGRAPHY

No English book written within the last three decennia on Assyro-Babylonian Religion can be recommended. As more or less systematic and complete collections of data, those readers who can read Italian or French may use either GUISEPPE FURLANI *La religione Babilonese e Assire* (Bologna, 1928-29), 2 vols., or EDUOURD DHORME *Les religions de Babylonie et d'Assyrie* (Paris, 1945, Presses universitaires de France). Most of the articles published on this subject-matter in scholarly periodicals are too technical and narrow in scope to deserve mention in this context.

The interested reader will, however, be able to find some general and up-to-date information in such books as W. F. ALBRIGHT *From the Stone Age to Christianity* (Baltimore, 1940, The Johns Hopkins Press) and in the section "Mesopotamia" by THORKILD JACOBSEN in *The Intellectual Adventure of Ancient Man* by H. and H. A. FRANKFORT, JOHN A. WILSON, WILLIAM A. IRWIN (Chicago, 1946, The Chicago University Press).

HITTITE RELIGION

From 1935 to 1948 Dr. Güterbock was professor of Hittite studies in the Faculty of Languages at the University of Ankara in Turkey. Born in Berlin in 1908, he has pursued Semitic and Hittite philological studies in Berlin, Marburg and Leipzig, receiving his Ph.D. degree from the latter university in 1934. He did research-work on the cuneiform collections of the Vorderasiatische Abteilung of the Berlin Museum until 1935 and has taken part in the German excavations at Boghazköy in the summers of 1933 through 1935.

His researches, known to scholars who are specialists in the field, particularly in Hittitology, have appeared in such publications as "Zeitschrift für Assyriologie", "Archiv für Orientforschung", "Abhandlungen der Preussischen Akademie der Wissenschaften" with a doctor's thesis on "Die historische Tradition und ihre literarische Gestaltung bei Babyloniern und Hethitern"; he has edited cuneiform editions of Boghazköy tablets in the Berlin and Istanbul Museums and the seal impressions from Boghazköy and published other special monographs in Turkish, German and English.

Recently, Dr. Güterbock has been appointed visiting lecturer at Upsala University in Sweden.

Editor

HITTITE RELIGION

HANS GUSTAV GÜTERBOCK

Sources. The main sources of our knowledge of the Hittite religion are the thousands of religious texts contained in the royal
archives of the Hittite capital at Boghazköy. It is not accidental that
by far the largest number of all tablets found there are of the type
generally called "religious texts": this is a vivid manifestation of
the religious character of the Hittite kingship. Tablets have been
found at Boghazköy mainly in one of the temples and on the citadel.
But this does not mean that religious texts were kept in the "Temple Library", or political documents in the "Palace Archives"; on
the contrary, at both places there were found all kinds of texts,
which again shows that there was no distinction between what we
would call the religious and political functions of the king and
his court.

The extraordinary large number of religious fragments has
been, until now, rather an impediment than an advantage. Only
part of the texts have been published, and only a very small portion
translated. For any problem there may, therefore, exist some unpublished material besides the scores of texts already available but not
yet sufficiently investigated.

In spite of the overwhelming number of texts our sources are
limited in time as well as with regard to their contents. They all
belong to the two centuries of the New or Great Hittite Empire
(*c.* 1400-1200 B.C.) and, with few exceptions, cannot be ascribed
to a more exact date within this period. No development or history
of Hittite religion can, therefore, be traced. As to the contents of
the texts, it has to be kept in mind that they all have official character. Many of them deal with the religious performances and
duties of the king; the prayers found at Bogazköy are royal prayers
which, although they may reflect more general religious ideas of the

83

period and the people, cannot be regarded as direct evidence of the piety of the ordinary man. Nothing can be learned from the tablets about popular cults and religious customs. Even from the texts of magic which, according to their own words, are applicable to every man, only those are preserved which were included in the official archives.

To some extent this restricted picture can be supplemented from other sources, such as the earlier so-called Cappadocian tablets —documents of the Assyrian merchant colonies of the 19th century B.C.—, the Hittite hieroglyphic inscriptions which outlived the Empire by about 500 years, and archaeological finds. As we shall see, the Hittites took over many cultural elements from the earlier populations of Anatolia, which justifies our tracing back some of their religious conceptions through earlier periods.

Analogies drawn from Mesopotamian and Classical sources can be used only with the greatest caution. Together with the art of writing the Hittites took over some religious conceptions and practices from Babylonia; but one has to investigate in every single case how far the borrowing goes and what may be Hittite addition to or transformation of the Babylonian original. Some of the Anatolian deities known from Greek and Roman times may—and really do— go back to Hittite and even earlier periods; but here, too, one has to refrain from superficial comparisons.

The Gods. Hittite religion as reflected by the written documents shows a highly developed polytheistic system. It is clear that this was the result of a long development. Where do all those gods come from? Many of them belong to certain towns. We may assume, therefore, an early stage of local deities which might be compared with those of other countries. On the other hand, many of the gods and goddesses connected with certain places bear the same name, *e.g.,* the Weather God of the cities of Nerik, Samuha, etc. The question arises whether these were, originally, local gods or whether there was the conception of one Weather God worshipped here and there. The most likely answer is that all different Weather Gods were, in fact, primarily local deities who showed the common characteristic of bestowing fertility through rain, and whose names, therefore, were written with the Mesopotamian ideogram for Weather God when the Hittite priests learned to write cuneiform.

Other gods were distinct through their functions. Some of the systematization was reached by combining several deities in divine families. The conception of such families is attested in early times by small figures showing couples or triads, such as the discoid idols with two or three heads and, sometimes, a child, from Kültepe,[1] which can be ascribed only approximately to the period of about 2000 B.C., and the more elaborate lead figurines cast from moulds, which belong to the first half of the second millennium and show a couple of god and goddess, sometimes with a child.[2]

The deities worshipped by the Hittites can be ascribed to the various ethnic groups of the population of ancient Anatolia. We owe our knowledge of these peoples to the fact that the Hittites used to address some gods in their native tongue and that they wrote down the words spoken in such cases, adding the name of the language. These languages are[3]:

1. *Hattili, i.e.,* the tongue of the land of Hatti in central Anatolia, a language of agglutinative structure not yet thoroughly understood,[3a] which modern scholars call Hattic or Protohattic in distinction from the Indo-European language in which the normal texts are written, called Hittite today, *nesili,* Nesite (from the city of *Nesa*) by the Hittite scribes.

2. *Palaumnili,* the language of the land of *Palā* which, if correctly identified with Greek *Bla-ene,* is situated in Paphlagonia, north-west of the Hittite capital. It shows Indo-European characteristics and is, accordingly, related both to the official Hittite (Nesite) and to the following language.[4]

3. *Lūili,* the Indo-European tongue of the country of Lūya in southern and south-western Anatolia.

4. *Hurlili,* the language of the people called *Hurla* in Hittite, *Hurri* in an Akkadianized form, whence the modern designation of the language as Hurrian is drawn. It covered a large part of southeastern Anatolia, northern Syria and northern Mesopotamia. This language, the knowledge of which has made considerable progress in recent times,[5] is related neither to Semitic nor to Indo-European languages nor to any other idiom known from the ancient Near-East (except Urartean which was spoken around Lake Van in the first millennium B.C.).

Apart from actual quotations of hymns, prayers or incantations spoken in these languages the ritual texts mention singers singing (Proto-) Hattic, Luwian or Hurrian or belonging to the city of

Kanes. By observing the names of gods in whose cult such singers appear it is possible to ascribe these gods to certain ethnic groups. It has been noted that the gods for whom the singer of Kanes sings bear Hittite names, whereas the "Hittite" language is called "Nesite" elsewhere (see above). This inconsistency, however, should not be overrated. Although we do not know why the city of Kanes, the former center of the Assyrian colonies, near modern Kayseri, was a center for the singers concerned with the worship of Hittite gods, there is no reason why they should not have used the language called Nesite by the Hittites.

Starting from the data mentioned above and from an analysis of the languages concerned one has been able to determine for many divine names the ethnic group to which they belong. Others, however, cannot be ascribed to any one of them as yet and may belong to still other—perhaps older—languages of Anatolia. They have been termed appropriately "Asianic".[6]

A considerable number of divine names is written in Sumerian or Akkadian. Here, special caution is needed. It has to be investigated in every single case whether the name in question really indicates the name of a Mesopotamian deity or whether the Sumerian or Akkadian form is merely an ideographic rendering of a native name. Examples of both possibilities exist. Even worse, the same Mesopotamian name may be used in both ways. Ishtar, *e.g.*, the name of the famous goddess, stands very often as an ideogram for a local goddess who bears either the Hurrian name Shaushka or other names belonging to other languages; but there are rituals where she is addressed in Akkadian—the Hittite term being *Babilili* "Babylonian", which may be added to the list of foreign languages used in rituals given above. From the use of the Akkadian language it becomes clear that in these texts the Babylonian goddess herself is worshipped.

In this highly developed system of gods there can be found traces of previous stages such as the worship of mountains, rivers and sources, animals and fetishes. Mountain cults have been known in Anatolia through the ages. In Hittite texts, divine mountains which are considered either as independent gods or as satellites of the Weather God are mentioned, and both types are also represented in art. The fact that many personal names, especially those of Hittite kings such as Arnuvanda, Tuthaliya, Ammuna, are originally names of mountains, also points to the holiness of the mountains. Rivers and springs are mentioned as deities as well; they are goddesses, whereas the mountains are considered as male gods. Anthropomorphic representations of gods were known in Anatolia from the beginning of the second millennium. Besides the idols mentioned above there are representations of this kind on the "Cappadocian" seals of local style.[7] On the other hand, more primitive kinds of representations survived down to relatively late times. The reliefs adorning the front of the sphinx gate at Aladjahüyük, which belongs to the end of the New Empire, show the worship of the divine couple: here, the goddess is represented as a seated woman, the Weather God in the form of a bull. In lists of cult statues in the shrines of some small places in the Empire, not only bulls made of iron or other metals are mentioned as images of the Weather Gods of different towns, but even bull-shaped *rhyta* and some other kind of vessels of unknown form as well as simple stones represent the god. Most of these lists deal with reforms made by a certain king; some mention king Tuthaliya IV (*c.* 1250 B.C.) ; possibly all of them belong to him. The reforms involve, *e.g.*, the introduction of an iron bull instead of a simple stone. It is worth mentioning, however, that this kind of zoomorphic representation is restricted to the Weather God; no animal as image of any other god or goddess is ever mentioned. On a higher level of development the bull becomes the holy animal of the anthropomorphic god: two bulls may be attached to his chariot, and in the Late Hittite period the god is standing on the bull—just as Juppiter Dolichenus in Roman times. Holy animals of other deities are well known: the lion belongs to Ishtar and to the consort of the Weather God as well as to the Moon God, some of the Warrior Gods, etc.; the stag is the animal of the Tutelary God of the Fields. But here the animal never stands for the god himself. The stones just mentioned, called *huwasi* in Hittite, seem to be simple upright stones, just as the *baitylia* of later times. They may or may not bear some representations in relief, such as sun disks, crescents, and perhaps mountains. Sometimes imitations of such stones made of precious metals are mentioned. These *huwasi*-stones are not restricted to a single god. Besides them, other fetishes, such as mace-heads with representations in relief, appear in the texts as images of certain gods.[8]

It is clear that the primitive images which—as stated above—

seem to be found especially in small places, are to be considered as mere survivals and do not imply a general conception in Hittite times. Wherever gods are mentioned or addressed in religious texts they are clearly considered as anthropomorphic beings. But even as survivals these things are worth mentioning.

Of the gods and goddesses of the Hittite pantheon only the most important can be mentioned here.[9]

1. *The main god of the Hittites* is the *Weather God.* His Hittite name is always written with one of the ideograms of the Mesopotamian Adad, and its Hittite form, therefore, is still unknown, except for the fact that it ended in . . .*-una.*[10] In Protohattic he is called Taru, in Hurrian Teshub, in Luwain Datta. The hieroglyphic ideogram of the main god who probably corresponds to the Hittite Weather God is read Tarhunt.

His nature is not easy to describe. The conception of a supreme god who rules over rain and thunderstorm is, of course, very appropriate to a country like Anatolia, northern Syria and northern Mesopotamia where all life depends on the rains. In the theological system of the Hurrians, known to us through the Hittite version of the Kumarbi myths (see below), Teshub corresponds to the Greek Zeus as king of the gods. His Hittite counterpart, the "Weather God of Hatti" or "Weather God of Heaven" is the supreme king as well. He is the real king and owner of the Land of Hatti, who has only entrusted it to the mortal king.[11] There are many special forms of the Weather God which have been grouped[12] under two main aspects: one connected with nature like "WG of the Thunder", "WG of the Lightning", "WG of the Clouds", "WG of the Rain", "WG of the Meadows", etc., the other with political functions, like "WG of the Palace", "WG of the Head (of the King)", "WG of the Sceptre", "WG of the Army", "WG of Peace", etc. The question arises whether these are individual deities or only different manifestations of one and the same god. The second possibility would seem more likely, because the epithets listed above seem to express the manifold sides of a god of rain who, as king in heaven, protects the earthly king. But in enumerations of gods some of these special Weather Gods are listed side by side with one another, with the Weather Gods of different towns and with the "Weather God of Heaven". This leads to the conclusion that for the Hittite theologians every one of the special Weather Gods had become an individual divine personality.

As mentioned above, the Weather God's sacred animal is the bull, and according to an older conception he is a bull himself. The connection of a god of thunderstorm and rain with this animal, characterized through its force, its loud voice and its fertility, is easily understood. The bucranium as a common motif on the painted pottery of the so-called Tell Halaf ware, found in southeastern Anatolia and northern Mesopotamia in the fourth millennium, has correctly been interpreted as an early representation of the bull cult in the area of the later Hurrian god Teshub. In the tombs of Aladjahüyük in central Anatolia of the Early Bronze Age[13] bronze figures of bulls, stags and lions were found, *i.e.* of the three animals mentioned above as connected with deities. Although these figures seem not to be cult images but rather symbols mounted on staffs or the like in the way of standards, one has to connect them with religious conceptions in some way. The seals attest a much wider spread of the bull worship, but the northwestern part of the Near East, including Anatolia and the Hurri lands, has always been its center.[14] In Hurrian mythology Teshub has two bulls, called Sheri and Hurri "Day and Night", who probably were attached to his chariot. These two bulls were included in the Hittite pantheon as well.

The same is true of the holy mountains connected with the cult of the Weather God. The most famous are Mount Hazzi, the later Mons Casius at the seashore near the mouth of the Orontes, and Mount Namni whose location is still unknown: they belong originally to the Hurrian pantheon but were adopted by the Hittites. Other holy mountains are mentioned in connection with local Weather Gods.[15] Late Hittite reliefs of the Weather God and his consort stood on top of a hill dominating the plain of Islahiye, where they were worshipped by the local population until their removal to the Adana Museum.[16]

The Weather God's weapon is the mace according to the cuneiform texts as well as to the reliefs of the imperial period. The axe with which he is represented in Late Hittite art is restricted to some special Weather Gods in the time of the Empire and never takes the shape of a double axe.

2. *The Main Goddess.* She often even precedes her husband, the Weather God, in the ceremonial order of gods. Whether this reflects an older system of matriarchal character with a goddess as highest deity or not cannot be decided as yet. Whereas the equation of the Hurrian Teshub with the Hittite Weather God is complete, the same cannot be said of the Hurrian and the Hittite Main Goddess. Although it is said once in a prayer of queen Puduhepa[17] that she was called Sun-Goddess of Arinna in Hatti, Hebat in the "Land of the Cedar", *i.e.* Hurri, the two names not only occur side by side in rituals and offering lists, showing that two different deities are meant, but the Main Goddesses of the two people are evidently different in character as well. The Hittite Sun-Goddess of the town of Arinna is really a solar deity. This is shown first by a hymn[18] which can be traced back through another text, where the male Sun-God is addressed, to Akkadian Shamash hymns. The second evidence which counts more than this literary text under Akkadian influence comes from the mentioning of sun disks in her cult.[19] For the Hurrian Hebat, on the other hand, no evidence of solar character has been found so far. The lion as holy animal of the Main Goddess is attested, until now, for Hebat only. Corresponding to the numerous local Weather Gods there are some local Sun-Goddesses as their consorts[20] and Hebats of many places as well, some of the latter connected with mountains.

In Protohattic, the Sun-Goddess of Arinna is called Wurusemu; there is another name, Arinitti(ya), derived from the city name Arinna by an apparently Protohattic ending but used in a Hittite context.[21] Her Luwian name is not yet known.

The Sun-Goddess of Arinna is queen in heaven and queen of the Hatti lands; she is the supreme goddess of the state and protects the king in warfare.

3. *The family of the main couple.* As said above, some of the systematization of the Hittite pantheon was achieved by forming divine families. There are several traditions concerning the family of the main gods. In Hurrian, the son of Teshub and Hebat is called Sharrumma. In Hittite, the Weather Gods of the cities of Nerik and Zippalanda appear as sons of the Weather God of Hatti and the Sun-Goddess of Arinna; there is a daughter, Mezzulla, and a granddaughter, Zintuhi. Both names are Protohattic.[22] Whereas this family is well attested in cult texts and prayers, other relatives of

the Weather God are mentioned only in mythological texts. One ought not to go too far in equating the deities mentioned in such different traditions; for it is quite natural that the systematization reached by the Hittite theologians was not complete and that different conceptions existed side by side.[23]

4. *Sun-Gods.* Beside the Sun-Goddess of Arinna the Hittites knew of other solar deities, both male and female. There is a male Sun-God κατ' ἐξοχήν, sometimes called Sun-God of Heaven. His Hittite name is probably Istanu which seems to be of Protohattic origin.[24] As mentioned above, a great hymn addressed to him shows Akkadian literary influence. According to this and to other prayers the Sun-God, just as the Babylonian Shamash is the one who sees everything and therefore the supreme judge of men and beasts; his designation as shepherd, too, is borrowed from Babylonia. In the Hurrian pantheon, the sun-god Shimegi is male, too.

Just as there are different Weather Gods so there are different Sun-Gods. The Sun-Goddess of the Earth represents the sun during its course in the night; the fact that she is female shows clearly that she is a deity distinct from the Sun-God of Heaven. She is a chthonic deity who is invoked in the ritual of the dead. The "Sun-God in (or: of) the Water" may represent the sun rising from or reflected in the surface of the water. Other special Sun-Gods (listed by Laroche), too, are to be considered as distinct divine personalities rather than mere aspects of one and the same God.

5. *The Moon-God,* called Kasku in Protohattic, Kushah or Kushuh in Hurrian, Arma in Hittite and (probably also) in Luwian, plays no important rôle. His sacred animal is the lion which he shares with a number of other gods.

6. *Ishtar.* The great Babylonian goddess was known in Anatolia, too. Sometimes she is addressed in incantations in Akkadian (see above). Her Hurrian name is Shaushka, and of her more important places of worship Ninive is Hurrian; Lawazantiya (in Kizzuwatna) and Samuha are situated in the southeast of Anatolia and belong more or less to the Hurrian sphere, too. She is the goddess of love and sexual life, but also of warfare. The name "Ishtar of the Field" points to the battlefield and thus to her belligerent character. In this connection her sacred animal, the lion, and her weapon, the mace, may be mentioned. It has been shown that the name of the "Ishtar of the Field of the city of Samuha" was Lelwani[25]; but there

is another Hittite name of Ishtar ending in -*li*. Mention is made of many local "Ishtars", or, with other words, the Babylonian ideogram is used for a number of local goddesses who must have had their own names in one of the native languages of Anatolia.

The Hurrian Shaushka who is the sister of Teshub has a whole court of women attendants, the most important of whom are Ninatta and Kulitta. From a hymnic text[26] we learn that she had two kinds of hierodules, the "first" helping mankind in all things connected with love and matrimony, the "last" causing all kinds of trouble in the same field.

It is impossible to enumerate more gods separately here. Some can be taken together in groups, such as the *Warrior Gods:* the Babylonian Nergal with his counterparts, Sulinkatte in Protohattic, Shuwaliyatta in Hurrian; Babylonian Zababa = Protohattic Wurun-katte = Hurrian Ashtabi. Both have the lion as sacred animal. Yarri, "Lord of the Bow", also belongs to the group of warrior gods. Another group are the *Tutelary Gods,* written with the ideogram Lama, which in Akkadian stands for a goddess, Lamassu; in Hittite, however, this ideogram is used to write the name of male gods. There is a great number of different Lamas, of several cities as well as of the animals of the fields (Lama of the Field has the stag as his own sacred animal) , and of all kinds of attributes and actions of the king. A special tutelary god is called "Lama the Shield"; most probably he was represented by a shield. Some tutelary gods are known by name: Karzi, Hapantali(ya), Zithariya. These names are Proto-hattic; the second is furthermore attested by the personal name Habatali in the "Cappadocian" texts.[27]

After having dealt with the main deities, most of which are found in more than one of the Anatolian languages, we shall now glance at the different ethnic groups of gods. Here, again, we shall mention only the important names, referring to the complete list of Laroche for further details.

The main gods of the Hittite pantheon existed before the arrival of the Indo-Europeans. A considerable number of gods are *Protohattic.* The Weather God Taru, his consort Wurusemu, their daughter Mezzulla and grand-daughter Zintuhi; Istanu (Sun) and Kasku (Moon) ; the warriors Sulinkatte and Wurunkatte (both names containing *katte* "king") and the tutelary gods Karzi,

Hapantali and Zithari have already been mentioned. In addition we list here: the goddess Inar, appearing already among "Cappadocian" personal names[28]; Telepinu, son of the Weather God, who is known as the god who disappears; Hatepinu, his consort; Halmasuit, the deified throne, a goddess according to the feminine ending *-it*[29]; Kait "Grain", a goddess, translated into Hittite as Halki (the "Cappadocian" personal names Halkiya and Halkiasu[30] probably contain this Hittite divine name); Kattahha "The Queen"; Katahzipuri, a goddess whose Hittite name is Kamrusepa and who is known for helping the gods through her knowledge of witchcraft.

An interesting fact concerning the Protohattic gods has become clear through recent investigations[31]: they have two names, one "among mortals" (under which they appear in the texts), the other "among gods" (which is sometimes really a second name, sometimes rather an epithet).

The Indo-Europeans who spoke *Nesite* (our Hittite), *Luwian* and *Palaic* adopted the Protohattic and some other old deities, some of them with their original names, re-naming others in their own languages (since these languages are of mixed character, this does not mean that all the new names have Indo-European etymologies!). Thus, *e.g.*, Inar(a), Telepinu and others kept their Protohattic names in Hittite; Datta, the Luwian name of the Weather God, the name Santa which occurs in Luwian and is rendered by the Babylonian name Marduk in a parallel passage, and the name Tarhunt which occurs in Luwian context as well and probably is the name of the Weather God in the hieroglyphic inscriptions, seem to go back to some other substrative language. Ziparwā, the most important of the Palaic deities, bears a name which is certainly not Indo-European but may be Protohattic, just as the Protohattic goddess Katahzipuri is mentioned in Palaic texts as well. As examples of "translated" names we recall the Hittite name of the Weather God ending in . . .-*una*, Halki, the Hittite word for "Grain", and Kamrusepa for Katahzipuri, all mentioned above. The name Kamrusepa forms part of a whole group of Hittite feminine names ending in *sepa*,[32] many of which are derived from Hittite words. Other groups of names belonging to the languages of the new settlers are: feminines in *-sar(a)*, found in "Cappadocian" personal names already[33]; Hittite and Luwian derivatives in *-assi* from *nomina appellativa* and in *-assa* from names of parts of the body; ordinary nouns deified, like Aruna "Sea", Siwat "Day", etc.[34] Hannahanna, appearing already as a "Cappadocian" personal name,[35] the name of the Mother Goddess, is a reduplication of the Hittite word *hanna* "grandmother". Ilaliyantes (plural; nominative form reconstructed) is the Hittite participle of *ilaliya-* "to wish, desire"; in Palaic the same deities are called Ilaliyantikes, with a Palaic plural element *-ik-*.[36]

The *Hurrian* influence on the culture of the Hittite Empire is very strong. Religious texts dealing with Hurrian deities are very numerous. The main gods of the Hurrian pantheon have been mentioned above: the Weather God Teshub, his consort Hebat, their son Sharrumma, the Sun-God Shimegi, the Moon-God Kushuh; Shaushka = Ishtar, her attendants Ninatta and Kulitta; the bulls Sheri and Hurri, the mountains Namni and Hazzi and the warriors Shuwaliyatta and Ashtabi. Besides these, there is a great number of other gods and goddesses. Some are of Babylonian origin, their names being only slightly altered, *e.g.*, Nikkal from Sumerian Ningal, the consort of the Moon-God; Aya, mostly in the combination Aya(n)-Ekaldu(n), the wife of the Sun-God, not to be confounded with A'a, the transformed name of Ea, the Babylonian god of wisdom; deified Babylonian nouns like Hengallu from *hegallu* "abundance" and Hazzizzi from *hasisu* "wisdom". Aryan gods: Indra, Mitra, Varuna and the Nasatyas, are only mentioned in the treaty with Mitanni as gods of that kingdom and play no rôle in the religious texts; Agni is mentioned twice in Boghasköy, but the contexts are too fragmentary to prove his identity with the Indian Fire-God.

For a complete list of the Hurrian gods occurring in the Boghazköy texts we must refer to Laroche's work again. Much about Hurrian theology is learned from the myths concerning Kumarbi, "the father of the gods", where we find a whole system of several generations of gods built up under Mesopotamian influence. The conception of "Former Gods", evidently those of previous generations, who form a group of their own, belongs to the same system.[37]

A word must be said about the Anatolian gods of classical times with regard to their Hittite equivalents. That Juppiter Dolichenus is a survival of the Weather God has long been known.[38] For Kybele and Magna Mater we have to consider more than one old Anatolian correspondence. The goddess Kubaba, whose name corresponds to the Greek form Kybebe which appears besides Kybele, is primarily the queen of the city of Carchemish where she is mentioned in the Old Babylonian period and in the Late Hittite hieroglyphic inscriptions. One of the reliefs of that place shows a goddess seated on a lion, whose identity with the main goddess of the town is probable in itself although the slab bears no inscription.[39] In the "Cappadocian" tablets the name of the goddess occurs as Kubabat.[40] In Hittite texts, however, Kubaba plays no important rôle; here she is only mentioned as a minor goddess among Hurrian deities. Connection with the lion is given for two of the great goddesses: Hebat and Ishtar. The "Grandmother" Hannahanna, written with the ideogram of the Sumerian Mother-Goddess Nintud, may also be compared with Magna Mater. Since the texts of the royal archives give no evidence of popular worship, almost nothing is known about the existence, in Hittite times, of the rather orgiastic cult of the Great Goddess of Pessinus. Only one mould found in the Old Hittite level at Boghazköy bears witness to the existence of the type called Potnia Thērōn,[41] and of special interest in this connection is a passage stating that Hatepuna was represented "[like] a harlot" and had a harlot in the service of her shrine[42]; for she is the consort of Telipinu who, as the god who disappears, corresponds to Tammuz, Adonis and Attys. This is the only hint to this side of the Great Goddess in the official records. Of other gods, such as Tarhunt, Santa, Hebat, the names still lived in classical times.

The Cult. Our sources deal only with the official cult; nothing is known of how the ordinary man approached his gods. In the state, the worship of the gods is of the highest importance. The historical texts more than once mention the king's having to delay a campaign in order to perform his religious duties. If one reads the descriptions of the elaborate ritual feasts celebrated by the king, covering several days and sometimes including travels all around the shrines of the country, the special prescriptions which aim at keeping the king from contagion with anything ritually unclean,[43] the oracles which were consulted to investigate possible neglects of the cult and the prescriptions for the compensation of such neglects, one can hardly imagine how the Hittite kings found the time to do anything else. Festival rituals and oracle questions are the kinds of texts which form by far the greatest part of all Hittite tablets, and owing to their large number they have not yet been sufficiently studied.

Many names of religious feasts are mentioned in the texts. Some are named after the seasons of the year, others bear other names. Most are performed by the king or by the king and queen, some by the queen or a royal prince alone. A full list cannot be given here. It is possible, however, to sketch the course of a normal feast.[44]

After having purified himself and put on his robes and ornaments in a special building, the king, often accompanied by the queen, enters the courtyard of the temple where certain rites, such as hand-washing, etc., are performed. Then he enters the temple room proper, where he pours libations to the holy parts of the room such as the offering table, the hearth, the throne, the window and the door bolt. After he has seated himself, his royal insignia are brought in and put near him. The main part of the ceremony is a kind of meal: a table is brought into the room and put before the king, and to the accompaniment of music he breaks bread and drinks to the gods. The term used for this latter performance is difficult to understand. Verbally it means "the king drinks the god". This has been explained as "gives the god to drink" or "drinks in honor of the god" or even verbally in a mystical sense of drinking the god and so getting united with him. However that may be, it seems clear that the king is drinking wine or beer and this involves a libation of some kind. This ceremonial meal is ended by another hand-washing.

Besides the king and queen an audience is mentioned. The participants including different classes of officials are shown to their places by a herald, "the Bearer of the Staff". In some cases the texts speak of a "great assembly", evidently a greater number of people forming the audience of the feast. Parts of the meal are distributed among the audience.

Omina and Oracles. The omen literature of the Hittites is borrowed from Babylonia. Copies of Akkadian texts in the original language as well as Hittite versions of such texts have been found. Many kinds of omina, such as astrological or birth omina and others, are represented. Models of the liver which were used for the training of the haruspices and bore, for that purpose, inscriptions stating the meaning of the various shapes of different parts of the liver, were found at Boghazköy but are also taken over from Mesopotamia. As a whole the Hittite omen literature shows no original features.

Registers of questions investigated through oracles, however, are

typical of the Hittites and have been found in great number. The
system of questioning consisted in putting a question which could
be answered "yes" or "no". The procedure by which the answer
was secured—observation of the entrails of an animal or of the flight
of birds or throwing dice—and the result were registered together
with the question. If the questioning did not lead to a clear result
it was repeated; when one question was answered one proceeded to
the next.[45] How much the Hittite court depended on this way of
learning the will of the gods has already been stated in the preceding section. It is significant that two of the three Hittite texts found
until now in Atshana in northern Syria belong to this kind of texts.

Magic. Black magic was forbidden by the Law Code; it was one
of the few delicts which were punished by death. The extant texts
naturally deal with white magic only. Its main purpose was purification. Not only uncleanness in its proper sense, but illness, quarrel-
ing, the result of black magic, and similar things were cured by purification rites. The main procedures were symbolic cleansing like
washing, combing, putting on clean clothes, putting on some material which was thrown away afterwards and thought thus to remove the uncleanness, driving away an animal which carried it off,
or passing through a gate which retained it; another kind of performance consisted in symbolic acts working through analogy, accompanied by words in which this analogy was stated: *e.g.*, "as this
. . . disappears, so let the evil disappear". Other magic rites that
aim at forcing the gods to come, use magic paths made of honey
and other agreeable things.

Most of these procedures are common to all magic, and many of
them are found in Mesopotamia. In form, however, the Hittite
magical texts differ considerably from the Akkadian. Many of them
are ascribed to certain magicians who invented a certain procedure
and thus appear as a kind of author, and it is worth mentioning
that a considerable part of these men and women came from the
land of Kizzuwatna (Cilicia) where Hurrian influence was prevalent. Another difference in form between Hittite and Akkadian
magic is the following: whereas in Akkadian the incantation which
has a fixed literary form is given apart from the description of the
performances which accompany it, the Hittite magical texts are descriptions of the ritual, quoting the short words of incantation at
the phases of the performance to which they belong. The literary

pattern followed by these texts is this: "Thus speaks NN, the incantation-priest of the city X: If . . . (this and that is the case), I take (or: one takes) the following: . . ." Here, a list of the ingredients needed is given, after which the description of the different magical performances starts. With regard to the conception of the causes of evil there is an important difference between Hittite and Babylonian magic, too. In Hittite texts the evil is never imagined in the form of evil demons as it is in Babylonia. The cause of all troubles is "uncleanness", *paprātar*, or "sorcery", *alwanzātar*, the result of black magic. These are impersonal forces, not demons.[46]

Standard collections of incantations like the big canonical series of Babylonia are unknown to the Hittites. The fact, however, that several short rituals written for similar purposes either by the same or by different "authors" are sometimes united in one tablet, may be considered as a step toward systematization.

Prayers and Hymns. It has been stated above that no individual prayers of the ordinary pious are included in the royal archives. From this fact and by analogy with what has just been said about the lack of canonical series of incantations, it becomes clear that no Hittite counterpart of the Babylonian prayer literature has been found. Only some hymns to the Sun-God and Ishtar were taken over from Babylonia, both in the Akkadian original and in Hittite versions.

The prayers preserved in the royal archives are those of members of the royal family for special purposes. Best known are the so-called Plague Prayers of king Mursili II (c. 1350 B.C.), written on the occasion of a pestilence brought into the country by captives from his father's last Syrian campaign.[47] These are long compositions of the highest literary and religious quality. The disease is considered the result of divine wrath, the causes of which are investigated by different methods. Several causes are discovered: neglect of a certain sacrifice and two breaches of oaths by the king's father Suppiluliuma: one when he made himself king instead of his brother to whom he had sworn an oath; the second when he started war against the Egyptians with whom he had concluded a treaty some time before. It is significant for the Hittite conception of sin that Mursili confesses these sins of his father's as if they were his own, saying "The father's sin comes over his son". The request for ending the plague is based on two main arguments: one, it is true, is rather materialistic: if all die, there will be no one left to make the offerings necessary for the gods. The second, however, is based on the Hittite conception of confession: Man's relation to the gods is compared to that of a slave to his master. If a slave does some evil, his master may punish him as he likes; but if the slave confesses his fault, his master's heart will be calmed and he will, therefore, forgive him. In the same way the gods are asked to forgive, since Mursili has confessed his sin, or rather the sin committed by his father but accepted as his own by himself.[48]

Another prayer for the same occasion combines the plague prayer with a hymn to the Sun-Goddess of Arinna which, in turn, is influenced by a hymn to the male Sun-God and its Akkadian models.[49] In a similar way, parts of that Sun-hymn are included in a prayer of prince Kantuzzili.[50]

From other prayers we learn that the Hittites knew the idea of intercession. The divine children of the couple of the main gods, the Weather-God of Nerik and Mezzulla, and their grand-child Zintuhi are invoked and asked to intercede with their parents for the king and queen.[51]

Relations Between Men and Gods. The idea that the gods are the lords, men their slaves, which we found expressed in one of the Plague Prayers, is found elsewhere, too. "To (the god) . . . , my lord, speaks NN, thy slave" is the usual introduction of prayers.

A Hittite term for the special force through which the gods govern deserves mention. The Hittite word is *(parā) hand(and)ātar.* From a recently discovered duplicate to a well-known text[52] we learn the Babylonian equivalent of *handandātur:* Sumerian *nig.si.sá* = Akkadian *mīšaru.* This is the "order of justice" which, together with *kittu* "justice", rules the universe according to the Babylonian conception. The equation, of course, need not be complete. Hittite gods "show their *parā handātar*" which, accordingly, seems to be considered as a force belonging to the individual gods. Man can be *parā handanza* (participle) "guided in the just way"; such a man does not act in the way of ordinary mankind.[53]

Another term which is the abstract noun derived from "god", *siuniyātar,*[54] seems to have rather a broad meaning. When a god "shows" it, it seems to be a "divine power", similar to *parā handātar;* in a prayer it is said that "thy divinity is honored in the land of Hatti only"[55]; in the oracle texts, a certain "deity" is found out;

in descriptions of cult images, the same word seems to stand for "divine image".[56]

The gods could be influenced by vows. There are texts listing the vows made by the king or queen for different occasions. If, for example, the king recovers from illness, the gods are promised a life-size statue of his majesty made of precious metal, cult statues or other precious objects; if the city of Ankuwa is saved from fire, a silver model of the town will be given to the Weather God of Heaven. Even real estate is the object of such vows.[57]

Mortuary Rites. Burials have been found in excavations, both in the Old and New Hittite levels. In an edict of the Old Hittite king, Hattušili I, there is an allusion to his own burial.[58] In the New Empire, however, cremation was used besides burying. A deposit of urns has been found near Bogazköy. Fragments of an elaborate ritual for the cremation of the king or queen are preserved. From the tablet describing the performances of the second day we learn the following: Women go and extinguish the pyre with beer and wine; then they collect the remains of the bones from the ashes, drench them in perfumed oil in a silver vessel, wrap them in a linen cloth and put them on a chair. A table is put in front of that chair, and a funeral meal takes place in presence of the bones. Afterwards the bones are carried to a building called "Stone-House", where they are laid on a bed and a burning lamp is placed nearby. These ceremonies are accompanied by several offerings and magic rites which, after the deposition of the mortal remains in the Stone-House, go on for many days.[59]

The Stone-Houses—or, as we may call them now, mausoleums—are mentioned in other texts, too. From these we learn that such mausoleums owned land and had their own employees. They were considered taboo: eating the food of a Stone-House caused uncleanness, and the officials of these houses must not intermarry with other people.[60]

Myths. Mythological tales are sometimes included in magical texts. The purpose is to establish an analogy. In a ritual against some kind of paralysis, for example, it is told, how nature was paralysed (lit. "bound") by some evil force, how the news reached Kamrusepa, the goddess of witchcraft, and how she "loosened" everything that had been "bound"

One of the most famous Hittite myths is connected with a ritual in the same way: the myth of the God Who Disappeared. It is noteworthy that this myth is not connected with the cult—as one would expect from the comparison with Tammuz, Adonis or Attys—but with magic. Some fragments mention certain persons who aroused the wrath of the god, whose house is therefore afflicted by the catastrophe caused by his disappearance, and in whose behalf the ritual of appeasement is carried out. The name of the God Who Disappeared varies: in the best known fragment he is called Telipinu, but in other versions it is the Weather God who disappears, and in still another text the Sun-God.[61]

The fact that this myth was not handed down as a work of literature but included in ritual texts prevented its being fixed in one standard form. Considerable variation in details is the result. Disregarding these differences one may, however, outline the contents of the myth as follows:

The beginning of the myth is missing in all fragments. The first preserved part of the texts describes the god's wrath, aroused by the fault of a certain person (in some versions; we do not know whether this is true for all versions). In his angry mood he disappears, and as a consequence the waters dry up, vegetation dies, animals and human beings become sterile, and men and gods suffer from famine. The gods search for him, but in vain. His father (the Weather God in the Telipinu version, "the Father of the Weather God" in the Weather God myth) sends out the eagle, again without result. Hannahanna, the Mother-Goddess, then sends out the bee who finds the god hiding in his own town (Lihzina in one version, Hattusa in another) and sleeping. By stinging him she awakens him, but the only result is that his wrath increases. To appease him, one has to apply magic. The mention of Kamrusepa in one version, of Man in another, seems to indicate who is going to do it. The narrative is then interrupted by the description of the magic rites. After this ritual part of the text comes the end of the narrative dealing with the god's return and the restoration of life.

The resemblance of this story to those of Tammuz and Adonis has long been noticed. But there are significant differences. Besides the fact that the myth is not connected with a seasonal rite—as already stated—the narrative itself differs from those of the neighboring countries inasmuch as the god neither dies nor descends to the Nether World, but simply hides in his own town, and that his consort or lover plays no part in the story.

The connection of a myth with a certain festival was, however, not unknown to the Hittites. The myth of the dragon (or snake) Illuyanka has come down to us in the form of "the words of the *purulli* festival of the Weather God of Heaven", in two versions; the first, it is said, is not recited any more.[62] It may be outlined as follows:

In a first fight Illuyanka overcomes the Weather God who, then, asks for the help of the gods. The Protohattic goddess Inar helps him in the following way: she secures the assistance of a mortal, Hupasiya, by promising him her love. She invites Illuyanka to a feast at which he gets drunk and is bound by Hupasiya, so that the Weather God now has easy work in killing him. With the slaying of the dragon the main story is finished, but the text goes on to narrate the further adventures of Hupasiya after the pattern of the well-known fairy-tale of the mortal who married an immortal woman: Inar gives him a house to live in and tells him not to open the window. Of course he disobeys; when he opens the window in the absence of the goddess, he sees his own wife and son and longs for home. We may assume that he is punished either by death or at least by expulsion, but the end of the text is broken.

The second version is much more elaborate. Here, too, Illuyanka conquers the Weather God in a first fight and steals his heart and eyes. The Weather God then takes a mortal woman and has by her a son who, after having grown up, is going to marry the daughter of Illuyanka. His father advises him to ask for the stolen heart and eyes when entering his bride's house. This he does, thus restoring to his father his old strength. Thereupon the Weather God goes to fight Illuyanka again by the sea; his son (who has become a member of Illuyanka's family) is on the dragon's side and expressly asks his father not to spare him, whereupon the Weather God kills both Illuyanka and his own son.

This story has rightly been compared with one of the Greek versions of the Typhon myth, where Zeus, in a first fight, loses his sinews, which are recovered by Hermes and Aegipan with the help of the dragon's daughter. Here, too, Zeus, after having regained his strength, finally kills Typhon. The location of the final battle "by the sea" in the Hittite text, which stands there quite isolated, is better understood by this parallel; for Zeus is living on Mount Casius on the coast of North Syria, Typhon in the Corycian Cave on the Cilician coast.[63]

Telipinu and Inar belong to the Protohattic group of gods; the myths connected with them may be considered, therefore, as old Anatolian. Other myths were taken over from the Hurrians. Different from the Telipinu and Illuyanka tales which were written down in ritual texts, the myths borrowed from the Hurrians present themselves as real literary works. Quite a number of such Hurrian literary compositions are known in fragments[64]; the Babylonian Gilgamesh Epic which reached the Hittites through the Hurrians may also be mentioned in this connection. Here we shall only deal with two of them, which contain mythical tales in the proper sense, centering around the figure of the Hurrian god Kumarbi.[65]

One may be called Theogony—its original name is not preserved. It tells of three subsequent generations of gods who were kings in heaven: Alalu, Anu, Kumarbi. Of these, Anu is the Babylonian God of Heaven, and Alalu is mentioned in Mesopotamian god-lists as one of his "fathers". Kumarbi is the Hurrian name of a god equated with the Sumerian Enlil. Kumarbi emasculates Anu by biting his membrum, but spits it out when he is told that he has, by swallowing it, become pregnant with three mighty gods, one of whom is the Weather God. From the seed spat out by Kumarbi, Earth becomes pregnant. In the fragmentary continuation of the tablet it was, probably, told how she gave birth first to the Weather God (Teshub), then to two other deities. In a mutilated passage Teshub seems to fight some enemies, and from other texts we learn that he finally became king in Kumarbi's place.

This text may be compared with the Theogony of Hesiod: Anu "Heaven" = Uranos, Kumarbi = Kronos, Teshub = Zeus. As the Sumerian names Alalu and Anu show, these myths originally go back to Mesopotamia[66]; but a Sumerian or Akkadian model of our literary compositions has not been found. Perhaps the first who wrote these stories in the present form were the Hurrians. Between the Hurrians and the Greeks, the Phoenicians seem to have acted as intermediaries, since Hurrian influence was strong in Syria and similar tales are known from the work of Philo Byblius on Phoenician religion.

The second epic is called "Song of Ullikummi". Ullikummi is a monster of diorite stone begotten by Kumarbi in order to fight Teshub and the other gods. Ullikummi, who grows in the sea with enormous speed so that he reaches the sky, first conquers the gods near Mount Hazzi, the later Casius, and forces Teshub to give up kingship. With the help of Ea, the Babylonian god of wisdom and witchcraft, however, his force is broken, and in a new battle he is probably defeated by Teshub who thus establishes his rule finally.

This myth, too, seems to have influenced Greek mythology. In Hesiod's Theogony Zeus is attacked, after his victory over Kronos and the Titans, once more by the monster Typhon. What matters for the comparison is that both the Ullikummi and the Typhon episode take the same place in the order of events, and that in both versions the battle is located at Mount Casius. The fact that the Typhon story has also been compared with the Illuyanka myth does not weaken the argument; elements that appear in different Hittite and Hurrian myths can well have been combined by later mythographers.

It must be stressed that these myths are only Hittite versions of Hurrian originals. In fact they have little to do with Anatolian religion. What is of interest, however, is the fact that they spread so far, both in space and time. Why were the myths of the different generations of gods and the fights of the old gods against the young borrowed and refashioned by so many peoples? Probably the human experience of the antagonism between the old and the young generation, between the old and the new order is responsible for their appreciation.

These myths once more show how Anatolia was a link between East and West. In this short outline of Hittite religion we had more than once to look for Mesopotamian and classical parallels. But at the same time we hope that it has become clear that Hittite religion, in spite of its complexity and of the connections with the outside world, has a character of its own which keeps it apart from the religions of the neighboring regions.

HITTITE RELIGION

NOTES

1. Kemaleddin Karamete, in *Revue Hittite et Asianique*, Tome III (1934-36), pls. 5-8 and 10-11; Tome IV (1936-38), pls. 2-6; H. Th. Bossert, *Altanatolien* (Berlin, 1942), Nr. 328-347.

2. H. H. von der Osten, *The Alishar Hüyük, Seasons of 1930-32*, III (*Oriental Institute Publications* 30, Chicago, 1937), p. 346, fig. 269; Bossert, *l.c.*, Nr. 349-366.

3. F. Hrozny, *Uber die Völker und Sprachen des alten Chatti-Landes* (*Boghazköi-Studien* 5, Leipzig 1920); E. Forrer in *Zeitschrift der Deutschen Morgenländischen Gesellschaft* 76 (Neue Folge 1, 1922), pp. 174-269.

3a. E. Laroche, in *Revue d'Assyriologie* 41 (1947), pp. 67-98.

4. H. Otten in *Zeitschrift für Assyriologie* 48 (Neue Folge 14, 1944), pp. 119-145.

5. E. A. Speiser, *Introduction to Hurrian* (*Annual of the American Schools of Oriental Research* XX, New Haven, 1941).

6. A complete collection of the names of gods contained in Hittite texts, arranged ethnically, was published by E. Laroche, in *Revue Hittite et Asianique*, Tome VII, fasc. 46 (1946-47); published also as book: *Recherches sur les noms des dieux hittites* (Paris, 1947). References to this work are given hereafter under "Laroche" only.

7. The distinction of Mesopotamian and local styles in the seal impressions on the envelopes of "Cappadocian" tablets was first made by E. B. Reilly who never published his results. They have been communicated by E. Porada, in *Seal Impressions of Nuzi* (*Ann. Amer. Schools of Or. Res.* XXIV, New Haven, 1947), pp. 97-100.

8. H. G. Güterbock, in *Belleten* (Revue publiée par la Société d'Histoire Turque) VII (Ankara, 1943), pp. 295-317, and in *Orientalia*, Nova Series 15 (Rome, 1946), pp. 482-496, esp. 489 ff.

9. For a full list see Laroche's work quoted in note 6.

10. I do not agree with the scholars who consider *Hummuni, Hamani* as the Hittite name of the Weather God; for literature see Laroche, pp. 49, 109.

11. *Istanbul Arkeoloji Müzelerinde Bulunan Bogazköy Tabletlerinden Seçme Metinler*, Nr. 30, translated by Goetze, *Journal of Cuneiform Studies* I (New Haven, 1947) pp. 90-91.

12. Laroche, pp. 109-111.

13. R. O. Arik, *Les fouilles d'Alaca Höyük . . . 1935* (Ankara, 1937), pp. CCII-CCV, CCLXXI; H. Z. Kosay, *Ausgrabungen von Alaca Höyük . . . 1936* (Ankara, 1944), pp. 113, 121 f., 131 f.; Bossert, *Altanatolien*, Nr. 297-306.

14. M. O. Tosun in her Doctorate Thesis (Turkish), a German sum-

mary of which will appear in *Archiv für Orientforschung* 15.

15. Cf. the articles quoted in note 8.

16. Information of B. Landsberger who visited the place in 1947. One of the two reliefs in the Adana Museum: Bossert, *l.c.*, Nr. 958.

17. *Keilschrifturkunden aus Boghazköi* (abbr.: KUB) XXI, Nr. 27; A. Götze, *Kleinasien*, p. 129.

18. Hymn to the SG of Arinna: O. R. Gurney, in *Annals of Archaeology and Anthropology* 27 (Liverpool, 1940), pp. 10 f.; 22 ff.; hymn to the male SG: KUB XXXI 127, restored by new fragments published in the book quoted in note 52, Nr. 44.

19. F. Sommer, in *Zeitschrift für Assyriologie* 46 (Neue Folge 12, 1940), pp. 22, 34.

20. *Orientalia* 15, p. 493.

21. Laroche, p. 106; the same, in *Journal of Cuneiform Studies* I (New Haven, 1947), pp. 208-214.

22. Laroche, in *Journ. Cun. St.* I, p. 200, where the meaning "grandchild" is established for Protohattic *zintu*.

23. *Orientalia* 15, p. 487.

24. Laroche, in *Journ. Cun. St.* I, p. 198.

25. Laroche, p. 96.

26. KUB XXIV 7, translated by A. Götze, *Die Annalen des Mursilis* (*Mitteilungen der Vorderasiatisch-ägyptischen Gesellschaft* 38, Leipzig, 1933), p. 262 f.

27. F. Stephens, *Personal Names from Cuneiform Inscriptions of Cappadocia* (*Yale Oriental Series, Researches,* XIII, 1, New Haven, 1928), p. 39.

28. Stephens, *l.c.*, p. 49.

29. Laroche, *Journ. Cun. St.* I, p. 208 f.

30. Halkiya: Stephens, *l.c.*, p. 39; Halkiasu: G. Eisser and J. Lewy, *Die altassyrischen Rechtsurkunden vom Kültepe* (*Mitt. Vorderas. Ges.* 33 and 35, 3 [Leipzig, 1930 and 1935]), Nrs. 3; 189; 194, and other texts. Communication of Dr. Emin Bilgiç, Ankara.

31. Laroche, in *Journ. Cun. St.* I, pp. 187-216.

32. Laroche, p. 67 f.; the same, in *Revue Hittite et Asianique,* Tome VII, fasc. 45 (1945-46), pp. 3-11.

33. Laroche, p. 66 f.; *cf. e.g.,* Hasusar (Eisser-Lewy, *l.c.*, Nr. 36), Histahsusar, Niwahsusar, Supiahsusar (Stephens, *l.c.*, pp. 41; 59; 63). *Cf.* E. Bilgiç in a forthcoming article in *Archiv für Orientforschung* 15. I do not share the skepticism of F. Sommer (*Hethiter und Hethitisch* [Stuttgart, 1947], p. 86).

34. Laroche, pp. 68-77.

35. *Ha-na-ha-na* in an unpublished text. Communication of Dr. Emin Bilgiç, Ankara.

36. H. Otten, in *Zeitschrift für Assyriologie* 48, p. 128, note 19; Laroche, p. 71.

37. R. O. Gurney, in *Ann. Arch. Anthr.* 27, p. 81 f.

38. H. Demircioglu, *Der Gott auf dem Stier* (Berlin, 1939); A. H. Kan, *Juppiter Dolichenus* (Leiden, 1943).

39. L. Wooley, *Carchemish*, Part II (London, 1921), pl. B 19 a.

40. J. Lewy, *Die Kültepetexte aus der Sammlung Frida Hahn* (Leipzig, 1930), p. X.

41. *Mitteilungen der Deutschen Orient-Gesellschaft* 77 (Berlin, 1939), p. 25, fig. 27; Bossert, *Altanatolien*, Nr. 365.

42. C. G. von Brandenstein, *Hethitische Götter nach Bildbeschreibungen in Keilschrifttexten* (*Mitt. Vorderas. Ges.* 46, 2, Leipzig, 1943), pp. 8 f.; 83.

43. J. Friedrich, in *Mitteilungen der Altorientalischen Gesellschaft* IV (Leipzig, 1928-29), pp. 46-58.

44. A. Götze, *Kleinasien*, p. 155; J. Friedrich, in *Der Alte Orient* 25, 2 (Leipzig, 1925), pp. 5-9.

45. Specimen of an oracle text translated by F. Sommer, in *Die Ahhijava-Urkunden* (*Abhandlungen der Bayerischen Akademie der Wissenschaften*, Phil.-Hist. Kl., Neue Folge 6, Munich 1932), pp. 275-289. For divination in general see: A. Boissier, *Mantique babylonienne et mantique hittite* (Paris, 1935).

46. On Hittite magic in general see R. O. Gurney, in *Journal of the Royal Asiatic Society* (1941), pp. 56-61. Rituals translated: F. Sommer und H. Ehelolf, *Das heth. Ritual des Papanikrı von Komana* (*Boghazköi-Studien* 10, Leipzig, 1924); The Ritual of Anniwiyani in E. H. Sturtevant and G. Bechtel, *A Hittite Chrestomathy* (Philadelphia, 1935), pp. 106-126; J. Friedrich, in *Der Alte Orient* 25, 2, pp. 9-16; B. Schwartz, in *Journal of the American Oriental Society* 58 (1938), p. 334 ff.; L. Zuntz, in *Atti del Reale Istituto Veneto di Scienze Lettere ed Arti*, XCVI (1936-37), pp. 477-546; A. Goetze and E. H. Sturtevant, *The Hittite Ritual of Tunnawi* (*American Oriental Series* 14, New Haven, 1938).

47. A. Götze, in *Kleinasiatische Forschungen* I (Weimar, 1930), pp. 161-251.

48. Special literature on sin and confession quoted by G. Furlani in the chapter "Il peccato" of his *Religione degli Hittiti* (Bologna, 1936).

49. R. O. Gurney, in *Ann. Arch. Anthr.* 27, esp. pp. 8-12.

50. KUB XXX 10; cf. H. Otten's remarks on KUB XXXI 127 (KUB XXXI, p. VI).

51. KUB XXI 27.

52. *Ankara Arkeoloji Müzesinde Bulunan Bogazköy Tabletleri = Bogazköy-Tafeln im Archäologischen Museum zu Ankara* (Istanbul, 1948), Nr. 62, duplicating the Hattusili text, col. I 45 (A Götze, *Hattusilis* [*Mitt. Vor-*

deras. Ges. 29, 3, Leipzig, 1925], p. 10 f.; Sturtevant-Bechtel, *A Hittite Chrestomathy*, p. 66 f.). On the meaning of *p.h.* see Götze, *Hattusilis*, pp. 52-55.

53. Text of Hattusili (cf. preceding note), col. I 47-50.

54. H. Ehelolf, in *Zeitschrift für Assyriologie* 43 (Neue Folge 9, 1936), p. 179, with quotations of the texts used hereafter.

55. R. O. Gurney, in *Ann. Arch. Anthr.* 27, p. 18, line 9 f.

56. Von Brandenstein, *Heth. Götter* (cf. note 42), text 2.

57. KUB XV, Nrs. 1-30; cf. esp. Nr. 1 III 22 ff. (for Ankuwa) and Nr. 16 with the duplicates and additional fragments listed by A. Goetze in *Journ. Am. Or. Soc.* 61 (1941), p. 303 (for real estate).

58. F. Sommer und A. Falkenstein, *Die hethitisch-akkadische Bilingue des Hattusili I.* (*Abhandl. Bayer. Akad. Wiss.*, Neue Folge 16, 1938), p. 16 f., line 72 f.; pp. 197-200.

59. Texts in KUB XXX Nr. 15-24; section of first two days transl. by H. Otten, in *Zeitschr. für Ass.* 46 (Neue Folge 12, 1940), pp. 206-224, and in *Mitt. Dtsch. Orient-Ges.* 78 (1940), pp. 3-11; for archaeological material and comparison with Greece see K. Bittel, in *Mitt. Dtsch. Orient-Ges.* 78, pp. 12-28.

60. KUB XIII 8; *Keilschrifttexte aus Boghazköi* V (*Wissensch. Veröff. d. Dtsch. Orient-Ges.* 36, Leipzig, 1921), Nr. 2, col. I 7 f.

61. H. Otten, *Die Uberlieferungen des Telipinu-Mythus* (Mitt. Vorderas. Ges. 46, 1, Leipzig, 1942) ; Weather God version: Otten's "Fassung D" and "E"; Sun-God version: the so-called Yuzgat Tablet, last published by A. Götze, in *Verstreute Boghazköi-Texte* (Marburg, 1930), Nr. 58, with literature.

62. A. Götze, *Kleinasien*, p. 131 f. with note 1. I agree with Götze on the existence of two versions, based on line 3 f., in spite of R. Ranoszek's criticism (*Orientalistische Literaturzeitung* 41, 1938, col. 429) followed by J. Friedrich, *Hethitisches Elementarbuch* II (Heidelberg, 1946), pp. 51-53 and p. 76 f.

63. W. Porzig, in *Kleinasiatische Forschungen* I (1930), pp. 379-386.

64. Treated in the appendix of my *Kumarbi* (see following note).

65. H. G. Güterbock, *Kumarbi. Mythen vom churritischen Kronos* (Istanbuler Schriften 16, 1946). A short English version of these myths appeared in the *American Journal of Archaeology* L II (1948), pp. 123-134.

66. E. A. Speiser, in *Journ. Am. Or. Soc.* 62 (1942), pp. 98-102.

HITTITE RELIGION

BIBLIOGRAPHY

The best treatment of the Hittite religion is still A. Götze's chapter "Die religiösen Anschauungen" in his *Kleinasien* (Kulturgeschichte des Alten Orients, Handbuch der Altertumswissenschaft, Munich, 1933), pp. 122-160.

L. Delaporte, *Les Hittites* (Paris, 1936), has a chapter on "La religion," pp. 241-277.

A monography on Hittite religion was published by G. Furlani: *La Religione degli Hittiti* (Bologna, 1936). Its value is limited by the fact that the author could only use the sources available in translation at that time.

The latest treatment of Hittite religion was published by R. Dussaud in a volume containing also a study on Babylonian religion by Dhorme: E. Dhorme et R. Dussaud, *La religion de Babylonie et d'Assyrie; la religion des Hittites et des Hourrites, des Phéniciens et des Syriens* (Paris, 1945), pp. 331-388.

See also books and articles mentioned in the Notes.

THE RELIGION OF THE CANAANITES

Dr. Gaster is a professor of comparative religion at the Asia Institute, New York, and at the Dropsie College, Philadelphia. He is also lecturer in Semitic Civilizations at New York University and a visiting lecturer in Old Testament (summer of 1948) at the University of Chicago.

He holds a master's degree from the University of London and his doctor of philosophy degree from Columbia. Of British birth, he has for some twenty years been associated as a Fellow of the Royal Asiatic Society (F.R.A.S.).

An author of numerous studies in the literature and religion of the ancient Near East, he has contributed especially to the folkloristic and mythological intrepretation of the Canaanite texts discovered at Ras Shamra. The results of his researches have been published in "Folk-Lore"; "Religions"; "The Review of Religion"; "Studie Materiali di Storia delle Religione"; "Journal of the Royal Asiatic Society"; "Journal of the American Oriental Society"; "Journal of Near Eastern Studies"; "Journal of Biblical Literature"; "Orientalia"; "Archiv für Orientforschung"; "Archiv Orientalni"; "The Jewish Quarterly Review"; "Palestine Exploration Quarterly"; and many others.

Editor

THE RELIGION OF THE CANAANITES

THEODOR H. GASTER

SYNOPSIS

113

FORGOTTEN RELIGIONS

I. INTRODUCTION

1. The Religion of the ancient Canaanites has never wholly died out. Transformed and transfigured beyond recognition, several of its characteristic ideas and institutions survive in the culture of the modern world. This was the religion which the Children of Israel encountered when they entered the Promised Land, which they imitated in the outward forms of their cult and absorbed in their literature and popular lore. Refined in the crucible of their own genius, it is this religion that they have passed down to us in the legacy of the Old Testament. Canaanite religion is therefore of more than antiquarian interest; it is, in a sense, the rock whence we were hewn, the rude clay which the pliant hands of Destiny have moulded into such wondrous shapes.

2. Until a few years ago, little indeed was known about this religion, and that little was learned almost entirely at second hand. There were in the Old Testament sundry allusions to Canaanite beliefs and practices, but the evidence they provided was scarcely objective because they were couched in a deliberately censorious vein. They were murmurs rather than articulate voices. There were likewise several references to Canaanite gods and goddesses, and sometimes also to ritual implements and usages, in Egyptian and Mesopotamian texts and in the Tell el-Amarna letters and later Phoenician inscriptions, but these, too, were, for the most part, but mumbled names rather than clear-cut statements. Lastly, late Greek writers occasionally preserved scraps and tidbits of Canaanite mythology, some of which they professed to have derived from ancient and native sources; but these were so colored by their own ideas and so thickly coated with the veneer of Greek thought that it was difficult indeed to separate the genuine nucleus from the later accretions. We were, in fact, in much the same position as were students of Babylonian and Assyrian civilization before the decipherment of the cuneiform script. We saw through a glass darkly. It was like trying to reconstruct a man's personality from a few letters and scribblings and from the garbled gossip of neighbors, or like knowing his voice solely from a distant echo.[1]

3. Today, at long last, we see face to face. The Canaanites speak out for themselves, even though their mouths be still filled with dust. What has brought this about is a succession of remarkable dis-

114

coveries made, since 1928, at RAS SHAMRA ("Fennel Head"), an all but forgotten mound on the north coast of Syria, practically opposite the jutting promontory of the isle of Cyprus. Ras Shamra is the site of ancient UGARIT, a Canaanite city and seaport the heyday of which fell during the latter half of the second millennium B.C. In the ruins of that city—more specifically, of a local temple— there has been found a collection of clay tablets inscribed in the characters of an hitherto unknown cuneiform alphabet and in a language which may be described, loosely and approximately, as primitive Hebrew. Among other material which does not here concern us, these tablets include a series of long mythological poems and of shorter documents relating to the service of the sanctuary. Together they provide our first direct picture of Canaanite belief and practice in the age of the Biblical patriarchs—the centuries immediately preceding the advent of Israel upon the stage of history.[2]

Other epigraphic discoveries round out the picture. At Byblus, for example, recently deciphered Semitic inscriptions, written in a curious pictographic script, reveal knowledge of an Egyptianized sanctuary and cult which existed there in the fifteenth century B.C.[3] At Arslan Tash, on the Middle Euphrates, has been found our earliest known Canaanite magical text—an incantation against the child-stealing demon, dating to the eight century B.C.[4]; while the triumphal inscription of a certain King Aztwd (Astywandas?), discovered in recent months at Karatepe in Cilicia, adds to the register of known Canaanite deities.[5]

The information yielded by such epigraphic material is in turn supplemented and illustrated by that derived from the excavation and clearance of Canaanite sanctuaries and "high places" at such Syrian sites as Qutna (Mishrife) and Byblus and such Palestinian sites as Gezer, Megiddo, Lachish (Tell Duweir) and Bethshan (Beisan) and by the discovery there and elsewhere of cultic vessels and figurines and of plastic and pictorial representations of gods and goddesses and of mythological scenes.[6]

Moreover, the progress of Cultural Anthropology and of its sister disciplines, Comparative Religion and Comparative Folklore, has enabled us in many instances to construe and interpret the Canaanite material in the light of parallel phenomena found in other cultures, thereby recognizing several familiar patterns and motifs and clarifying much that would otherwise remain obscure.

4. In utilizing all of these resources, however, a considerable measure of caution must be exercised. We have, for instance, no right to assume that the mass of material now at our disposal necessarily adds up to a single consistent picture. Allowance must be made for differences in time and place, for local variations and peculiarities; and it cannot simply be taken for granted that every Canaanite everywhere recognized the sum total of deities revealed to us or that religious usage was uniform in all cities and villages. The title "Canaanite religion" is, in fact, a comprehensive term covering variety as well as similarity.

Then, too, a distinction must be drawn between literature and formal belief. Everyone knows that the medieval legends about the Virgin Mary or the rabbinic fancies (*midrashim*) about Old Testament characters possess no credal authority and that Dante's *Inferno* and Milton's *Paradise Lost* are not recitations of Christian dogma. By the same token, when we read the Ras Shamra poems we must realize that we are dealing with a literary treatment of the basic myths, characterized by all the embellishments of artistic fancy, and that they afford no automatic testimony to the manner in which the gods and goddesses were conceived in formal religious usage. That such literary traditions form a part of popular religious ideology is, of course, true, and for that reason they claim consideration in any general sketch of Canaanite religion; but the distinction between concepts entertained in popular lore and those canonized by formal religious doctrine is one which should not be overlooked. Unfortunately, it is at present impossible to draw the line, and in our description of Canaanite religion the popular and the formal have necessarily to be interfused. The bare fact, however, should at least be pointed out.

II. GENERAL CHARACTERISTICS

5. In order to understand the true character of Canaanite religion, it is necessary to bear in mind at the start the fact that it issued out of a world of thought and perception informed by concepts, categories and insights widely different from our own.[7]

To us religion is primarily the recognition of and appeal to a supreme universal Power. The Canaanites, however, like most primitive peoples, had no idea of a universe and hence none of a uni-

116

versal nature or of a single power which controlled it. To them, the world was a *multi*verse—a theater of disparate powers (usually personified) which undoubtedly came into contact with one another but which were not subsumed to a single over-all system. Accordingly when they wished to procure what we would describe as the "blessings of nature"—sunshine, rainfall, plenteous harvests or fecundity of man and beast—they could not address themselves, as does the modern worshipper, to a single supreme and cosmic godhead but had, instead, to fall back on one of two alternatives or, indeed, on both. Either (*a*) they could seek to persuade or coerce this or that particular power—the genius of sun, rain, or fecundity— or else (*b*) they could rely on their own concerted and duly regimented efforts. Canaanite religion consisted in the performance of these two techniques, sometimes as alternatives, sometimes in combination. On the one hand, it took the form of periodically establishing *rapport* with the various powers of nature in order to secure or render thanks for their beneficence; on the other, of periodically recruiting, under approved sanction, the total human effort considered necessary to satisfy the collective needs of the community without reliance on divine intervention. It was thus a fusion of two elements, viz., (*a*) worship and adoration, and (*b*) the routine execution of purely pragmatic techniques.

From this it follows that Canaanite religion was more of a public institution than of an individual experience. In its outward manifestations it was, in fact, barely distinguishable from the ordered regimen of society. Its headquarters were just as much a city-hall as an abode of deity. Its officers—the so-called "priests"—were just as much judges and physicians as sacristans and hierophants. Its rites were public exercises, and its "sacrifices" (*sit venia verbo!*) included taxes and levies, fines and imposts, no less than purely piacular or propitiatory offerings. In short, while it doubtless inspired feelings of individual piety and devotion, it was, in essence, an expression of communal economy. Sacred and secular were met together; church and state kissed each other.

6. The community whose interest was thus promoted was, however, more than a mere human society. In primitive thought, the basic collective unit is not the corporation of men and women living in a given place but the totality of all things to be found within it; not the family but the household, not the population

117

but the city; not, so to speak, the community of New Yorkers but New York itself, as a comprehensive and ideal concept. Religion, as a public institution, is directed towards the periodic revitalization of this entity, not merely of the men and women who form but one element of it.

7. Moreover, this entity is conceived to exist at one and the same time on two levels: the *punctual* and the *durative*. All that obtains in the immediate here and now is but the punctual realization of something which is in essence durative and sempiternal. The present generation of Americans, for example, is but the embodiment and immediate incarnation of an ideal America which embraces equally the past and the future; and it is immerged within that wider continuity even as a moment is immerged in time.

8. This conception—hitherto all but overlooked—is the basic clue to any adequate understanding of primitive religion, and not least to that of the Canaanites. Without it, we but stumble in darkness and fail to reach beyond description to real penetration. In the light of this conception, it is apparent that the periodic ceremonies of which we have been speaking necessarily possess a two-fold character: on the one hand, they are *presentations*—punctual and pragmatic performances designed to meet immediate needs; on the other, they are *representations*—portrayals of events and situations which take place simultaneously in ideal time. The punctual aspect is represented by *ritual*; the durative by *myth*. The two things are natural concomitants—the "close-up" and "long-shot" views of the same scene. Accordingly, when we read the Ras Shamra poems, we must be prepared to see in them, back of the inevitable literary veneer, a mythic projection of pragmatic ritual; and when we study the pragmatic rituals, we must recognize in them the punctual realization of ideal, mythic situations.[8]

9. The basic parallelism of punctual and durative comes out equally in the much-canvassed relationship between the king and the local god. Although, in the imagery of literary articulation and in the symbolism of cultic usage, the authority of the former is often represented as due to direct investiture by the latter or to the imbibing of special qualities along with the milk of a divine mother, the essential truth is that the king epitomizes the community in its punctual, and the local god in its corresponding durative aspect. King and local god are therefore correlatives; the former is but an

118

avatar of the latter. Accordingly, whatever the king does in punctual ritual is but a realization of what the local god is doing *eo ipso* on the ideal, transcendental level; and only in the light of this correspondence do both ritual and myth become fully intelligible.

When, for example, the myth relates that the god of the community's life and fertility—the Tammuz or Adonis type of deity—dies annually and is resurrected, as the symbol of the people's periodic eclipse and revitalization, we must expect to find in concomitant ritual some ceremony in which the king really or mimetically undergoes the same passion. Similarly, when the cult-myth of a seasonal festival recounts the victory of the god over a dragon and his consequent assumption of supreme power, we must expect to find in the ritual program of the occasion the performance of some corresponding sacred pantomime—such as is, indeed, by no means uncommon in modern European folk usage—wherein, on a punctual level, the king annually delivers his people by doing battle with the Evil One and is consequently acclaimed. So too, when the union of god and goddess appears as a dominant motif in the myth of such festivals, we must expect to find its punctual counterpart in the ritual "marriage" of king and chosen hierodule.

10. Equally important for a correct understanding of Canaanite religion is a realization of the fact that the superhuman beings which it recognized were not *gods* in the modern sense of the term. So to describe them is, indeed, to obscure their distinctive character by unloading upon it the accumulated mass of our own later concepts.

The Canaanites recognized two types of superhuman beings: *el* (plural: *elim* or *elohim*) and *baal* (plural: *bealim*).[9] *El* was *numen*—the personification of the power believed to dwell in any object or phenomenon which excited a reaction of *awe*, which gave a man "goose-flesh" or sent shivers up and down his spine.[10] Towering, majestic mountains were "mountains of *el;*" tall cedars were "cedars of *el;*" a resplendent throne was "a throne of *el;*" and the mighty wind which stirred the waters at the dawn of creation was "the breath of *elohim.*" In Arabic (a language cognate with Canaanite and Hebrew), a denominative verb formed from the word which is the equivalent of *el* denotes the sensation of numinous awe and wonder; while there is reason to believe that the term *el* itself originally meant "innate power." To the genus of *el*,

119

therefore, belonged not only such beings as might today be called gods (albeit in a restricted sense) but also ghosts, phantoms, spirits of the dead and demons—anything, in fact, which might be regarded as *awful* and as underlying the weird, eerie and uncanny. Plague and disaster were attributed to "the hand of the *elim*,"[11] just as among the Arabs they are considered to be due to the assault of a jinn. A man who was liable to ecstatic trauma and suprasensuous experiences was termed "a man of *elohim*;"[12] and when the witch of Endor conjured the spirit of Samuel from the netherworld, the wraiths which ascended were called *elohim*.[13]

Baal, on the other hand, was *genius*—the personification of that indwelling dynamic force which activated an object or phenomenon, gave it energy and determined its effectual and organic existence. In Semitic idiom, an eloquent man is "a *baal* of the tongue;" a husband who brings his wife to sexual fulfillment and, so to speak, "energizes" her womanhood, is termed her *baal;* one who "quickens" or cultivates soil is "a *baal* of the earth;" and these usages sufficiently explain the sense of the term when applied to a superhuman power. The phenomenon which the *baal* indwelt and energized might be the earth or the sky, the thunder or the rain; but it could also be the living community of men and beasts or, indeed, the total corporation of all actually or supposedly animate objects in a given place; and because they were thus so often regarded as personifications of the collective "self" of such places, the *bealim* of the Canaanites usually bore names signifying their attachment to specific localities—names which came later to be transferred, by metonymy, to the localities themselves, *e.g.*, Baal Hermon, Baal Hazor, Baal Zephon.

11. The two types tended, of course, to fuse and blend, every *baal* possessing, to a certain extent, the numinous quality of an *el*. As applied to our historical sources, therefore, the distinction between them is more schematic than real. Nevertheless, it is one which should be carefully borne in mind since it helps appreciably to account for the two variant attitudes or approaches which find expression in cultic practice.

The *el* is essentially a transcendental being, because the human individual is necessarily on the receiving end of its operations. The relationship of man to *el* is, therefore, that of patient to agent or of servant to master, and issues in *adoration* or *worship*. Less rigid,

120

on the other hand, is the nature of the *baal*. For while, to be sure, man can likewise be a mere recipient of the *baal's* activities, it is equally true that, as the energizing genius of a society or place, the *baal* can be but a projection of that whereof man is himself a part, wherein he lives and moves and has his being. In that case, the *baal* is necessarily immanent, and the relationship of human beings to him is one of immergence and communion rather than of subservience and communication. The movement is *out*ward rather than *up*ward; it is, *mutatis mutandis*, that of the individual American to "Uncle Sam" rather than of the average churchgoer to God.

Rites in which the superhuman being is regarded as an *el* will therefore take the form of submissive adoration and propitiation—the natural expression of awe; whereas those in which he is regarded as a *baal* will consist rather of pragmatic ceremonies in which he figures as a participant or as a mythic counterpart of the punctual celebrant.

III. THE PANTHEON

12. Having thus cleared the ideological ground, we may now proceed to a formal description of Canaanite belief and practice. We shall start with the pantheon, and would again remind the reader that this account is based perforce upon a combination of ritual and mythological material. The resultant synthesis is, therefore, to some extent artificial; but in the present state of our knowledge that cannot be helped. We do not yet possess adequate means of differentiating between the two.

13. In the "farthermost reaches of the north," at a point where the waters above the earth flow together with those beneath it, rose the great Mountain of Assembly on the summit of which the "gods" held session.[14] They were known collectively as "the numina" (*elim, bne elim*) or as "the holy ones," and were pictured after the manner of a human family or clan.[15] At their head was the patriarch El—the Numen *par excellence,* creator and sovereign of all that is. Nevertheless, despite his supreme authority, El interfered but little in the diurnal affairs of the world. He was what anthropologists call "a remote high god," somewhat like the Greek Kronos, who, while formally acknowledged in ritual and myth, was conceived in the rôle of a mild old gentleman delegating direct control

121

to his children and himself acting merely as general supervisor and final arbiter between them. True, he sometimes revealed himself to men in dreams,[16] but as a rule he was approached through other gods and goddesses. Conventionally, he was likened to a mighty bull, and "Bull" was one of his standard titles.

14. Practical dominion over the world was divided among three major powers, who correspond, more or less, to the Zeus, Poseidon and Hades of the Greeks.

The sky and the rains were in the hands of Baal—the "Energizer" *par excellence.* Baal was the epitome of all the *bealim,* just as was El of all the *elim.* It was upon the ministrations of Baal that the earth relied for its fertility; when he was absent from it, during the dry summer months, all life languished. In Arabic (and vestigially in Hebrew), the expression "land of Baal" denotes rain-watered soil. An alternative name for Baal was Hadad (or Hadd), "the Crasher," whereby he was designated as lord of the thunder. Two of his standard epithets were "Rider on the Clouds" and "Puissant." At the sound of his voice, mountains rocked, the earth shook, and all his enemies fled in terror to the creeks and crevices of the rocks. Like El and like most of his Near Eastern counterparts, Baal was popularly portrayed as a bull or steer. In reference to his Syrian provenience he was also known as Amurru, "the Westerner."

In actual cult, the mythological figure of Baal was identified in each locality with the peculiar *genius loci,* so that there were, theoretically, as many forms of Baal as there are of the Virgin Mary in Christianity.

The ocean, rivers, lakes and subterranean springs were under the control of Yam ("Sea"), also known as "Ruler of the Stream." Yam sought annually to gain possession of the earth by flooding it, but was invariably repelled by Baal, after a fierce battle. He seems to have been regarded as a hydra-like dragon and also to have borne the familiar name of Leviathan (literally, "Coiled One").[17]

The Nether-World and the barren places were the realm of Môt ("Death"), genius of aridity and lifelessness. In Arabic, sterile soil is called by the cognate term *mawat,* and in Hebrew, "Death" is used by metonymy as a name for the infernal regions.[18]

Alternative names for Môt, more popular in actual cult and attested especially in Egyptian sources, were Resheph, "the Ravager," and Hôron, "He of the Pit."[19] The former was regarded particularly as the demon of plague and pestilence, identical with the Mesopotamian Nergal, and is so mentioned in the Old Testament (Deut. 32.24; Hab. 3.5; Job 5.7). In an inscription of the 8th century B.C. from Karatepe in Cilicia,[20] he is styled "Resheph of birds," and in Job 5.7 the coterie (literally, "sons") of Resheph are described as winged beings.[21] This would suggest that popular lore sometimes conceived of him as a hideous vulture-like creature, somewhat analogous to the harpies of Greek mythology—an idea associated with gods of the Nether-World in many civilizations. Among the Phoenicians living in Cyprus he was identified with the Greek Apollo, in the latter's capacity of plague-god (cf. *Iliad* i, 44-52).[22]

As we shall see, the three-cornered contest of Baal, Yam and Môt for dominion over the earth forms the central theme of one of the mythological poems from Ras Shamra.

15. Besides these major powers, the Divine Assembly also included several personifications of natural phenomena.

Sun and Moon were deified as Shemesh and Yareah. The former, because he surveys all things, was regarded also as the god of justice, and in this capacity was attended by two ministrants named respectively Sedeq, "Right," and Mishor, "Equity."[23] The popularity of his cult is attested by such Old Testament place-names as Beth-Shemesh, "House of the Sun" (Jos. 15.10) and 'En Shemesh, "Spring of the Sun" (Jos. 15.7); while it has been held by some scholars that the heroic figure of Samson reflects, in large measure, the character of this solar deity.[24] In the Ras Shamra texts, his place is taken by a female counterpart called Shapash. This accords with the fact that in the South Arabian pantheon the sun is likewise regarded as a female deity; while in Hebrew, the common noun *shemesh* is of variable gender. Similarly too, the Hittite pantheon included a "sun-goddess of Arinna" besides the male solar deity.

Yareah, the moon-god, leaves his name in Jericho. His marriage to the goddess Nikkal (Sumerian Nin.Gal, "Queen") is the subject of one of the Ras Shamra poems.[25]

Two gods called Shahar and Shalem, "Dawn" and "Sunset," mentioned in a Ras Shamra text as sons of El, probably represent the equivalent of the Dioscuric twins Castor and Pollux, regarded

123

as deities of the morning and evening star. They are styled "the celestial ones," and bear the title of "princess"—the same as is customarily given to their Greek counterparts. Moreover, the story of their nativity appears to have formed the cult-myth of a festival celebrated in June, when the Heavenly Twins happen to be the regnant constellation.[26]

The same Ras Shamra text which mentions Shahar and Shalem also speaks of an offering to "Queen Shapash (the Sun) and to the stars;"[27] while another alludes to "the army of the sun and the host of the day" in connection with a ceremony performed on a rooftop.[28] This would seem to indicate worship of the heavenly bodies, and vividly recalls the denunciation of just this pagan practice by the Hebrew prophets (cf. Jer. 19.13; Zeph. 1.5).

Dagan ("Corn")—the Dagon of the Old Testament (Judges 16.23; I Sam. 5.2-7; I Chr. 10.10)—was the genius of the crops. He is attested as a West Semitic deity as early as c. 2500 B.C., and appears originally to have enjoyed greater prominence than was later assigned to him. In the Ras Shamra texts he is the father of Baal, and the older temple at that site, dating from the time of the Twelfth Egyptian Dynasty (2000-1785 B.C.), is dedicated to him. In Palestine, he had sanctuaries near Lachish and Eglon (Jos. 15.41) and in the region of Asher (Jos. 19.27).[29]

The pantheon also included a divine smith and handyman—counterpart of the Vedic Tvastri and the Greek Hephaestus. His name was Kôshar, "Adroit," and he was also known as Hasis, "Intelligent," and Hayin, "Deft." Kôshar fashioned and furnished the mansions of the gods and supplied them with weapons. Because, during the second millennium B.C., a great deal of Syrian and Palestinian ware was imported from the Aegean or fashioned upon Aegean models, his forge was popularly located in K-p-t-r—the Biblical Caphtor—which is either Crete or the island of Carpathos (modern Scarpanto). Similarly, during the days of Egyptian domination, he was commonly equated with the Egyptian potter-god Ptah, and his forge was therefore located at Memphis, seat of that deity.[30]

A Phoenician tradition preserved in Greek sources says that Kôshar was also the inventor of magical incantations and the first to "trick out words" in verse.[31] The basis of this tradition is the universal association of the notions "artisan" and "artist." The word *poet,* for example, means properly "maker, artificer;" and in Old Teutonic idiom a *minstrel* was called a "song-*smith.*" Similarly, the Sanskrit word for "to fabricate" is that employed for composing the verses of the Rig Veda; while the Hebrew and Syriac words for "to chant a dirge, sing" are related to the Arabic for "to forge like a smith." Moreover, in Canaanite itself, the term for "professional female musicians" was *kosharat.*

16. Nor was it only as males that the energies of the world were personified. The Canaanites realized clearly enough that certain functions might be attributed more appropriately to the operation of a Female Principle. Accordingly, the male deities were supplemented by three principal goddesses: Asherath, 'Ashtarth (Astarte) and 'Anath.[32]

These three goddesses correspond approximately to the Hera, Aphrodite and Artemis of the Greeks, and represented the three main aspects of womanhood. Asherath was the wife and mother, sedate and matronly mistress of the home and female head of the family. 'Ashtarth was the sweetheart and mistress, a glamorous and voluptuous embodiment of sexual passion and therefore also the genius of reproduction and of fecundity in general. 'Anath was the young girl, a beautiful and virginal creature, full of youthful zest and vigor and addicted especially to the thrills of battle and the excitement of the chase. Since, however, all of them were, *au fond,* but aspects of the same thing, they naturally shared several qualities and attributes in common, and were not infrequently confused with one another.

17. Asherath was the consort of the supreme god. In formal mythology, this was El, and it is with that deity that Asherath is associated in the Ras Shamra poems, where she also occasionally bears the name Elath, *i.e.,* "the Goddess" *par excellence.* In practical cult, however, El tended to be replaced by Baal, and it is accordingly with Baal that Asherath is most often paired in the purely ritual texts and in the Old Testament (II Kings 18.19; 23.4). In the latter capacity, she often assumes the name of Baalath, usually associated with that of a particular locality, *e.g.,* Baalath Gebal, "the female Baal of Byblus."[33] All of the gods were believed to be her children and to have been suckled at her breast.

Asherath was closely associated with the sea. Her regular title in the Ras Shamra texts is "Asherath of the Sea," and since the word Asherath can be taken to mean "she who walks," Professor W. F. Albright has suggested that this represents her original name and that she was primarily "she-who-walks-upon-the-sea."[34] Albright calls attention to the fact that Khidr (the Green One), the modern patron saint of the sea among the Arabs of Syria, is still called "he-who-walks-in-the-seas." A similar epithet, it may be added, is likewise applied to the Greek marine goddess Tethys in the Orphic Hymns (xxii 6).

> The association of the great mother-goddess with the sea has several parallels in ancient civilizations. The Hurrian Ishara, whose worship became widespread, is described in Mesopotamian texts as "Ishara of the deep,"[35] and is mentioned in a sacrificial tariff from Ras Shamra (I.13) beside Yam, god of the sea. 'Ashtarth, the counterpart of Asherath, is said in an Egyptian mythological text to "dwell in the ocean,"[36] and the principal centers of her cult were indeed located in coastal cities. The Aegean mother goddess is associated with the sea on lentoids found in the Idean cave and in the Chapel of Minos in Crete.[37] According to Homer (*Iliad* xiv 201), the "mother of the gods" was the marine goddess Tethys. Moreover, as Usener and Maas have shown, it is a sea-goddess of this type that really underlies the later Christian figure of Saint Pelagia (*i.e.*, "She of the Sea").[38]

18. Better attested than Asherath is 'Ashtarth (Astarte). Late Greek writers are unanimous that she was the personification of sexual passion and vigor, comparable to Aphrodite; and what we know of her Mesopotamian counterpart Ishtar tends to confirm them. Moreover, an Egyptian text associates her with 'Anath as one of "the two great goddesses who conceive but do not bear;"[39] and in the Old Testament (Deut. 7.13; 28.4, 18, 51) the choicest ewes are called "the *'ashtarths* of the flock"—an expression which doubtless harks back to the fecundity aspect of the goddess.

Like Ishtar, the goddess also had another function: she was the genius of warfare and combat. In the Ras Shamra poems, she appears but rarely, but always in this capacity. She helps Baal to

126

defeat his rival Yam, and she is twice invoked, in a standard com-minatory formula, to break the skull of an adversary.[40] Moreover, in the tomb of Thothmes IV (1425-1405 B.C.), that king is por-trayed standing martially in his chariot, and an accompanying in-scription likens his posture to that of 'Ashtarth.[41] Similarly, on a broken stele from Memphis, of the time of Mineptah (1234-1225 B.C.), she is portrayed holding shield and spear.[42]

The warlike character of the goddess is also attested in the Old Testament. In I Samuel 31.10 it is said that the Philistines de-posited the armor of the slain King Saul in the temple of 'Ashtarth. Now, the Philistines, not being Semites, could not very well have worshipped that goddess, and as a matter of fact, the parallel ac-count in I Chron. 10.10 substitutes the more neutral phrase "house *of their god*" for "house *of 'Ashtarth*." The significant thing is, how-ever, that when the Hebrew historian wished to convey to his Pales-tinian readers the idea that the Philistines had dedicated a trophy to the deity of war, he could find no better way of doing so than to say that they had placed it in the temple of 'Ashtarth!

The development of the goddess is not a little obscure. The most plausible view would seem to be that she was originally a *genius of irrigation* and thence evolved, by an association of ideas natural enough in an agricultural civilization, into a general spirit of fertility, exercising influence over all living beings. For (1) her name is to be connected in all likelihood with the Arabic verb *'athāra*, "to water," whence is in turn derived the technical term *'atharī* meaning "irrigated soil;"[43] (2) both the Mesopotamian Ishtar and the South Arabian 'A*th*tar are specifically associated with canals and waterways;[44] (3) the principal centers of her wor-ship were usually in the proximity of water, viz. in the coastal cities of Sidon, Tyre, Byblus and Ashkelon, or 'Ashtaroth (modern Tell Ashtarah) in the alluvial plateau of Bashan; (4) Eusebius expressly quotes a tradition that 'Ashtarth "came from the sea, from the watery element."[45]

In astral mythology, 'Ashtarth was identified with the planet Venus—an identification which was also made in respect of her Egyptian and Greek counterparts.

19. 'Anath is the best attested of all the Canaanite goddesses. In the mythological texts from Ras Shamra she is regularly styled "the Virgin"—reminiscent of Artemis' title *Parthenos*—and she is

the sister and helpmeet of Baal. It is she who mourns and searches for him when he is driven from the earth, who enlists the support of the Sun-goddess in retrieving him from the Nether-World, who accompanies him to Asherath when he seeks her intervention in securing El's consent to the building of a house for him, and who ultimately massacres the garrison of those who have meanwhile usurped his power. Moreover, another myth from the same site is concerned entirely with the manner in which 'Anath executes vengeance upon a mortal youth who has come into possession of a bow really designed for her.

In the ritual texts, the goddess is usually associated with Resheph—an association which recurs in Egyptian sources.

In Egyptian texts of the 18th Dynasty, 'Anath appears principally as a goddess of war. A stele in the British Museum depicts her holding shield and lance in her left hand and wielding a battle-ax in her right.[46] A statue found at Tanis describes her as the helper of Ramses II (1298-1232 B.C) in his campaigns, and she seems, indeed, to have been a special favorite of that monarch.[47] He is described as her "nursling;" his sword is called " 'Anath-is-victorious;" one of his daughters bears the name Daughter-of-'Anath; and even one of his dogs is called " 'Anath-is-protection." Similarly, in the 19th Dynasty Magical Papyrus Harris she is invoked in the incantation: "Stop! you wicked wolf! . . . Your foreleg is severed by Hershef after you have been slain by 'Anath!"[48]

In the Old Testament, 'Anath is known only in personal and geographical names. One of these, however, is particularly interesting. In Judges 3.31; 5.6, a hero renowned for his exploits against Philistine footpads is called Shamgar ben-'Anath. Seeing that Shamgar is a Hurrian (Horite) name, this style implies a remarkable religious syncretism, not unlike that which we actually find at Ras Shamra, where Semitic and Hurrian deities are mentioned side by side. Alternatively, the expression *ben-'Anath* ("son of 'Anath") may have been a popular expression for "warrior."

20. In addition to the gods and goddesses actually worshipped in the cult, the Ras Shamra texts also reveal the names of several who were mere figures of myth and who are nowhere mentioned in the ritual documents. To this category belong 'Ashtar, genius of artificial irrigation (cf. Arabic 'athari, "artificially irrigated soil"), who is represented as competing unsuccessfully with both Yam and

Baal for possession of the earth. To indicate his inferior status, he is depicted as a minor, perhaps even as a child.[49] To the same order also belong Baal's daughters, "Miss Soil" (Arsiya) and "Miss Dew" (Talliya), described as "attractive nymphs," and his messengers "Sir Vine" (Gephen) and "Sir Field" (Ugar) —all of them personifications of natural phenomena closely associated with the operations of Baal as genius of rainfall and fertility.

21. It would appear probable—though the evidence is as yet inconclusive—that the pantheon was conventionally subdivided into smaller groups. A ritual tariff from Ras Shamra (RS I) seems to distinguish clearly between "the family of El" and "the company of Baal" and another text (III K ii 7) speaks of "the companies of gods threefold." Moreover, in the Phoenician inscriptions from Zenjirli (8th cent. B.C.), Hadad, El, Shemesh and a certain Rakkab-el seem to form a standard group.[50]

22. The formal pantheon was supplemented by another important class of numinous beings: the dead. In the Ras Shamra texts, burial is described as "placing remains in the holes of the *elim*," which indicates clearly that the departed were considered to belong to the latter category. This may be illustrated from the fact, already mentioned, that when the witch of Endor conjures the spirit of Samuel from the Nether-World, the wraiths which ascend are likewise termed *elohim* (I Samuel 28.13). Furthermore, in a passage describing the duties which a son owes to his father, mention is made of "setting up his *ilib* in the sanctuary," and Professor Albright has suggested that this obscure word is really the equivalent of the two Hebrew terms *el*, "numen" and *ôb*, "ghost, revenant," the meaning being that a son is expected to erect a commemorative stele in honor of his father's spirit. If this interpretation be correct, it will afford further evidence that the dead were regarded as *elim*.

The more usual term for the denizens of the Nether-World was *Rephaim*—a term which occurs also in the Old Testament (Is. 14.9; 26.14; Ps. 88.11; Prov. 2.18; 9.18, etc.). Its precise meaning is unknown. The most probable suggestion is that it denotes "the inert, flaccid," in which case it will be exactly parallel to the Greek "weary ones" *(οἱ καμόντες)* used in the same sense.

22. An aura of numinosity also surrounded the person of the king. He was regarded as a nursling of the goddess Asherath, and when he became sick the prosperity and welfare of the land was

automatically imperilled. Both ideas are familiar to students of comparative religion. The belief that the king is suckled by a goddess reflects the fact that he possesses numinous and quasi-divine character; while the idea that his health is bound up with that of his people is inspired by the concept that he is but their punctual embodiment.

IV. RITUAL

23. We have little direct evidence concerning the nature of Canaanite ritual ceremonies. Certain details, however, may be recovered from indications in the Ras Shamra texts.

A document discovered in 1928 contains a form of sacrificial calendar for seven days and adds a special sacrifice of "two lambs" for the day of the new moon. Not impossibly, this is an order of service for the successive days of the week. The offering prescribed for the day of the new moon recalls that of "two young bullocks" ordained for the same occasion in the Pentateuchal code of the Israelites (Numbers 28.11).

The same text also mentions a ceremony performed on the rooftop apparently in honor of "the army of the sun and the host of the day," i.e., the heavenly bodies. This recalls the pagan practice denounced by Jeremiah (19.13) and Zephaniah (1.5).

24. Another text connects the nativity of the two gods Dawn and Sunset (*Shahar* and *Shalem*) with the performance of a ritual involving the trimming of vines and the seething of a kid in milk. Since the former operation takes place in June and the latter is expressly proscribed in the Israelitic legislation (Ex. 23.19; 34.26) in connection with the Festival of Firstfruits in the same month, and since, further, the Heavenly Twins are indeed the regnant constellation at that season, it would appear probable that this text was designed for the Canaanite prototype of the Israelitic Pentecost.

25. Of interest also is an obscure reference, in one of the ritual documents, to the king's "purifying himself" in the month of Teshrit (9:10-11); for this may be related to the common practice of instituting a ritual "lent" or period of purgation at the beginning of the year. The custom is paralleled in the New Year ceremonies of Babylon and in the Day of Atonement (or, Purgation: *Yôm hakippurim*) which preceded the autumnal Feast of Ingathering in

Israel, during the new year month of Tishri. It also possesses many analogies in the usages of primitive peoples.

26. Echoes of ritual are also preserved in the mythological poems. When Baal's temple is dedicated, for instance, the gods are said to be regaled at a lavish banquet where "oxen, sheep, fatlings, yearling calves and goats" are set before them. Since the myth projects an annual event and was designed originally as the counterpart of a ritual ceremony, this doubtless reflects the traditional institution of an annual *theoxenia,* or regalement of the gods, such as is paralleled in the *tâkultu,* or "collation" annually offered to the gods in Assyrian cultus. At the same time, it also recalls the ritual observed by the Israelites at the dedication of the Tabernacle (Numbers, chs. 6-7) .

Again, at the interment of Baal, an elaborate sacrifice is offered of seventy buffaloes, oxen, sheep, rams, mountain-goats and antelopes. Since "seventy" is merely a round number in Semitic idiom, this recalls the hecatombs offered at Homeric and later Greek funerals.

27. It is possible also to reconstruct some of the details of Canaanite ritual ceremonies from references in the Old Testament and from their survival in the cultic usages of Israel. Here Comparative Religion offers especially valuable aid since, on the strength of analogies in other cultures, we are able in many cases to isolate the earlier substratum from its later Israelitic historicization.

I Kings 18.23 ff., for example, describes the contest of Elijah with the prophets of Baal on the summit of Mount Carmel. The latter are said to have "leaped about the altar" and to have "cut themselves after their manner with knives and lances, till the blood gushed out upon them." The leaping dance, performed especially in connection with seasonal rituals, is paralleled not only by that of the Salii ("Leapers") which was carried out in the forum at Rome during the month of March, but also by numerous examples among other ancient peoples. Moreover, it is a constant element of Oriental funeral rites and would therefore have been peculiarly appropriate in ceremonies of mourning for the "dead" lord of fertility. The gashing with knives is attested by Lucian of Samosata, in the second century A.D., as a characteristic of the ceremonial mourning for Adonis performed annually at the Syrian sanctuary

131

in Hierapolis (Membij). It possesses analogies in the Phrygian mysteries of Attis and in other cults of the same type.

28. A number of Phoenician inscriptions make mention of a priestly officer called "the arouser of the god." In this title we have a further interesting glimpse of Canaanite ritual procedure. The "arouser of the god" was the priest charged with the duty of waking the god from sleep at break of dawn. Rites of this kind are attested in ancient and Roman Egypt, at the sanctuary of Dionysus in Delphi and in the temple of Yahweh in Jerusalem.

29. Another arresting feature of Canaanite ritual is revealed by the title *mtrh* borne by certain sacerdotal officials in late Punic inscriptions. The word means "bridegroom," and indicates that the official in question played the male rôle in a "sacred marriage" doubtless performed as a regular seasonal rite designed to promote fertility. The "brides" in such marriages were supplied out of the female personnel of the sanctuary; and it is this institution which led Israelitic prophets like Hosea to denounce Canaanite religious ceremonies as characterized by "prostitution."

30. Ancient and modern parallels suggest that several of the Israelitic festivals may have been but adaptations of traditional Canaanite usages. Thus, the complex of New Year, Day of Atonement and Feast of Ingathering, celebrated at the beginning of autumn, may well represent successive stages of a Canaanite seasonal festival patterned upon a model common throughout the ancient Near East and abundantly paralleled in modern folk customs. Its essential features would have been: (a) an initial period of mortification and lenten abstinence, symbolizing the eclipse of life at the close of the year; (b) a period of purgation and purification, designed to banish all noxious influences which might imperil the perpetuation and prosperity of the community; (c) a period of reinvigoration, during which the community collectively performs the techniques considered necessary to achieve life and well-being and especially to secure sunshine and rainfall; and (d) a period of restoration, symbolized by the formal reconfirmation of the king—as epitome of the corporate life—and his installation in a palace. On the mythic level, this last would have been represented as the reinstatement of the god in his temple; and this may explain why both of the temples of Yahweh at Jerusalem were, in fact, dedicated at

132

the Feast of Tabernacles. The last stage of the festival evidently coincided with the autumnal equinox; and it is noteworthy that, according to the Septuagint text, the song which Solomon is said to have sung at the consecration of the first temple, actually introduces a reference to the sun (I Kings 8.12) !

31. Similarly, the festival of Passover, celebrated in spring at the beginning of the barley harvest, probably represents an Israelitic adaptation and historicization of an older Canaanite institution. Its Hebrew name is *Pesah,* which derives from a verb meaning "to hop, leap." Although interpreted in the Biblical tradition as a reference to the fact that the angel of Yahweh *hopped over* the houses of the Israelites when he smote the first-born of Egypt, it is probable that this name really derived from the performance of a *leaping dance* such as characterizes harvest festivals in many parts of the world. The idea is that as high as the people leap, so high may the crops grow. So too, the abstention from leaven food, which is a dominant feature of the festival and which is said in the Biblical tradition to commemorate the fact that the Israelites had no time to bake their bread properly during their hurried exit from Egypt, probably reflects a widespread custom of abstaining from leaven food and intoxicants during the lenten period of mortification and austerity which invariably precedes the harvest.

32. If our reconstruction of Canaanite festivals is necessarily speculative, we are on safer ground as regards the sacrificial system, for this is amply documented both in the Ras Shamra texts and in later Phoenician inscriptions. It bears remarkable points of affinity with the Israelitic system described in the Pentateuch, showing that however late the literary redaction of that work may have been, the material it contains is often of genuine antiquity. Both sources, for example, mention the shelem, or "payment-offering" (wrongly rendered "peace offering" in the English Bible), the "wave-offering" (Hebrew *tenūphah*) and the "burnt-offering."

The materials used in sacrifice are also not without interest. The "fatted ox" occurs frequently, and there is also mention of doves, fowl, rams, birds, calves, and kids. A manna-like resin is probably indicated by the expression "blood of trees."

33. The temple, or headquarters of the cult, was known alternatively as "the great house, palace" (*hēkal*) or as "the house of the

god" (*bêth-el*) . Its precincts were regarded as sacred ground, and it would appear that aliens and refugees from vendettas enjoyed the right of sanctuary within it.

There is reason to believe that temples were sometimes designed to represent the world in miniature. The ceiling was identified with the sky, and the floor with the earth. Two columns at the entrance represented the pillars on which the heavens were believed to rest; and in the forecourt was an artificial lake suggestive of the cosmic ocean. (Features of this design, it should be noted, were incorporated in the structure of King Solomon's temple at Jerusalem.)

The temple staff consisted of priests (*kohanim*) , superintended by a "high priest," sacristans (*qedoshim*) ,[51] choristers (*sharim*) , doorkeepers, watchmen, barbers or branders, and such artisans as smiths, masons, builders, etc., charged with the maintenance of the sacred edifice. A "man of the gods"—perhaps a generic term for a sacerdotal official—is also mentioned, as well as female votaries known as "sacred women." The temple personnel subsisted on regular portions of the offerings, allotted to them in accordance with a fixed scale.

It would seem that some of the vestments of the Israelite high priest may have had their origin in earlier Canaanite usage. Thus, the bells on the hem of his robe may have been originally a device for forefending demons, while the mysterious Urim and Thummim may have been pebbles the casting of which by way of lots rendered negative and positive orders of the gods respectively.

In addition to formal temples, the Canaanites also performed their ritual ceremonies at open-air "high places." These are sometimes distinguished, as at Gezer, by alinements of dolmens or cromlechs—that is, of large unhewn stones topped by others set crosswise upon them. When arranged in a circle, these formed a kind of "stonehenge;" and it is probable that this is meant by the Biblical term *gilgal*, usually employed in connection with pagan rites.

Standing stones and pillars were likewise objects of veneration. So, too, in many instances, were trees and mountains. Indeed, the word for "hill" or "high rock" is a common designation for "god;" and the familiar Shaddai of the Old Testament, rendered "Almighty" in the English version, probably means "He of the Mountains."

V. MYTHS

34. The principal Canaanite myths which have come down to us in the Ras Shamra texts are: (1) the Myth of Baal; (2) the Myth of Aqhat; and (3) the Myth of the Gods Dawn and Sunset. All of these are incomplete, and all contain passages which have thus far defied elucidation. Nevertheless, the general drift of the narrative is in each case reasonably clear.

These myths were preserved as part of a sacred repertoire, and it is that fact which must condition their interpretation. Clothed as they are in genuinely poetic garb, they are none the less something more than mere literary *tours de force*. They belong essentially to the category of religious ritual, not to that of polite letters, and may best be regarded as the libretti of sacred dramas performed at seasonal festivals. That the more primitive meaning had often become forgotten by the time the texts reached their present form is no doubt true, and allowance must be made also for purely artistic elaboration; but for an understanding of their basic plots and the sequence of their several episodes, the ultimate ritual origin must be kept in mind.[52]

35. The Myth of Baal was evidently designed for the annual festival which marked the beginning of the rainy season in late September or early October. It is concerned with the manner in which Baal, genius of the rain, secured dominion over the earth.

The story opens, in the grey beginning of time, with El's award of sovereignty to Yam, genius of the sea and rivers. Baal, however, as genius of the sky and rainfall, contests this appointment, and engages Yam in a furious battle. With the aid of Koshar, the divine artisan, who supplies him with two wondrous weapons (evidently thunderbolts), he succeeds in defeating his antagonist.

However, Baal cannot yet assert his authority over the gods because, alone of them all, he has no palace. He therefore beseeches his sister 'Anath to intervene in the matter with the mother-goddess Asherath and to induce the latter to persuade her consort, the supreme god El, to grant permission for the required edifice to be built on the sacred Mountain of the North. 'Anath undertakes the mission, Asherath accedes to the request, and El finally gives the

135

necessary permission. Thereupon a magnificent palace is built and equipped by Koshar, and at its completion, all of the gods are regaled at a lavish repast.

Nevertheless, Baal's troubles are not yet over. Having subdued Yam, he now faces another rival—Môt, genius of the Nether World and the barren places. Môt is not content to remain confined in these unpleasant regions but aspires to usurp the position which Baal has but recently won for himself. To accomplish this purpose, he invites his rival to a banquet in the Nether World, knowing full well that anyone who tastes the food of that realm is automatically prevented from returning to earth—a motif familiar to us from the Greek legend of Persephone. Baal falls into the trap and is consequently held imprisoned. During his absence, all life languishes.

'Anath, disconsolate over the disappearance of her brother, reports the matter to El and Asherath. The latter's reaction, however, is simply that a substitute for Baal must now be appointed. 'Ashtar, the genius of artificial irrigation, is nominated, but it is found that he is physically too small to occupy the throne of Baal. He therefore contents himself with exercising a limited sway on earth without aspiring to Baal's heavenly honors.

At this juncture, 'Anath recruits the assistance of the sun-goddess Shapash, beseeching her, on one of her nightly journeys into the Nether World, to retrieve the inert body of Baal and bring it back with her to earth. Shapash complies, and 'Anath ceremonially inters the corpse on the Mountain of the North—a necessary preliminary to its resurrection.

After a time, Baal is indeed resurrected and engages Môt in mortal combat. Defeated, Môt is expelled from the earth and thrust into the Nether World. 'Anath then massacres the garrison which Môt had stationed in the palace of Baal, thus preparing the way for the latter's reinstatement. Baal announces that he is about to reveal his powers but a magnificent display of lightning flashes over the sacred Hill.

It is quite obvious that this myth allegorizes the alternation of the seasons in the Syro-Palestinian year. There is, however, more to the matter than this. The battle with the dragon, the consecration of a palace and the reinstatement of the divine king are, as we have seen, standard elements of the New Year festival throughout the ancient Near East. It is therefore equally clear that the poem mythologizes the punctual ritual of that occasion.

36. The Myth of Aqhat represents a more literary version of the seasonal cult-narrative.

Daniel, a king of the Haranamites, has no son. He therefore repairs to the temple of Baal and performs the rite of incubation, serving as an acolyte and sleeping in the sacred precincts in the hope of receiving the divine oracle in a dream. At the end of seven days he is assured by such a revelation that he will indeed have issue, and in due course a son, named Aqhat, is born to him.

One day, while Daniel is sitting outside his house, he espies the divine artisan Kôshar coming along the road carrying a consignment of bows which he is bringing from his forge in Memphis to the gods and goddesses on the Mountain of the North. Daniel invites him to partake of refreshment, and in return for this courtesy, Kôshar presents one of the bows to his host's son.

Now the trouble starts. The bow in question was that designed for 'Anath, goddess of warfare and the chase, who naturally feels outraged at the cavalier manner in which her sacred perquisite has been handed over to a mere mortal. She therefore encounters Aqhat and promises him wealth, immortality and even herself in exchange for the precious article. But Aqhat spurns these offers.

Thereupon 'Anath obtains permission from El to mete out condign punishment upon the impious youth, and to this end devises a cunning plot. Going again to Aqhat, she assures him that all is now forgiven and forgotten, and she invites him to betake himself to the region of Abelim, where she will instruct him in the arts of the chase. Aqhat readily complies. In the meanwhile, however, 'Anath has enlisted the cooperation of her henchman, Yatpan, to do Aqhat to death and thus recover the bow. The plot is that, while Aqhat is sitting down to a meal in the open air, and while birds of prey are hovering around him to get their pickings of the meet, 'Anath herself will fly among them carrying a sack in which her henchman will be concealed. At the critical moment, she will release him—history's first paratrooper!—and in the general melée caused by the birds, he will attack Aqhat and snatch the bow, subsequently being caught up again by the goddess.

All goes as planned—with one fatal difference. On the return flight Yatpan carelessly drops the bow into the sea. 'Anath now realizes that love's labor has been lost, and in a fit of remorse, vows to revive the slain Aqhat.

Meanwhile, Aqhat's sister notices that a strange drought has set in. In accordance with the common ancient superstition that the earth is rendered infertile by the shedding of blood upon it, she concludes that a murder must have been committed in the neighborhood. She is, however, as yet unaware of the identity of the victim. After she has reported the matter to her father Daniel, the two of them set out together on a tour of inspection, and while they are so engaged, learn that it is Aqhat who has been slain.

Suddenly, Aqhat's sister notices a flight of birds wheeling overhead. Thereupon Daniel prays to Baal, god of the weather, to break their wings so that they may fall at his feet, whereupon he rips open their gizzards in the hope of discovering the remains of his son. After two unsuccessful attempts, he indeed retrieves the fat and bone of Aqhat, and solemnly inters them—as a necessary prelude to eventual resurrection.

Aqhat's sister then determines on vengeance. Concealing a weapon beneath her skirts, she sets out to discover the murderer. By chance, her steps lead her to the very tent of Yatpan, who welcomes her cordially and offers her drink. She continues to drink with him, until eventually his tongue is loosened by wine and he boasts that "the hand which slew young Aqhat can slay foes by the thousands." Thereby he betrays himself as the assassin. But at this critical point, our text breaks off.

Although, at first blush, this would seem to be a purely literary story, the truth is that far more lies behind it. The tale of the brash young man who challenges the supremacy and authority of the goddess of the chase is but a Canaanite version of the familiar Classical myth of Orion; and with this there has here been blended the equally familiar myth of the dying and reviving lord of fertility whose annual discomfiture is regarded as the cause of the earth's bareness during the dry summer months. The reason for this fusion was that the constellation of Orion is actually absent from the evening sky during that period of the year. Accordingly, our story was, *au fond*, a seasonal myth designed to account for the summer drought. The importance attached to the bow is to be explained by the fact that in the ancient Near East the stars in which Classical astronomers saw the Hound of Orion were grouped differently to form the figure of a bow.

37. The Myth of the Gods Dawn and Sunset relates how El seduced two mortal women and begat the gods Dawn (Shahar) and Sunset (Shalem). Once they were born, he gave them to Asherath and 'Anath to suckle, thus affirming their divine status. He also threw open all the resources of heaven and earth for their subsequent sustenance.

The myth is associated with a ritual in which ceremonies were performed which elsewhere characterized the Israelitic Feast of Firstfruits (Pentecost) in June. Dawn and Sunset are therefore to be identified, in all likelihood, with the Dioscuric twins, gods of the morning and evening star, who, in their astral form, are the regnant constellation of that month. The myth is thus the cult-text designed for a seasonal festival.

38. Apart from the myths recounted in the Ras Shamra texts, the Canaanites doubtless possessed many others. Lucian of Samosata, for example, gives a vivid description of the myth of Adonis which formed the basis of summer ceremonies celebrated at Hierapolis (Membij). It is probable, however, that Adonis was merely another form of Baal, the Hebrew word *ādôn* meaning "lord." Accordingly, what Lucian saw and heard was but a local variant of the basic Baal myth. Similarly, when Greek writers relate that the Phoenicians knew a myth concerned with a primeval combat between the god Zas and the serpent Ophiōneus, they are but translating into Greek terms the Ras Shamra story of Baal's fight with Yam, *alias* Tannin.[53] Accordingly, because these later traditions evidently represent distortions of earlier material, we here forego any further discussion of them.

39. The foregoing account of Canaanite religion is necessarily no more than a general survey. Reasons of space preclude mention of several interesting features and details and confine us perforce to broad outline and analysis. Nevertheless, sufficient will have been said to make it clear that a knowledge of Canaanite religion is an indispensable prerequisite for the proper understanding of the Old Testament and the achievement of Israel and hence of the foundations of our own faith.

But it is not only as an ancillary to Biblical studies that the beliefs and practices of this ancient people are of interest and value. No less remarkable is the light which the newly-recovered Canaanite myths throw upon familiar legends of Greece and Rome and, indeed, upon folklore and story in general. The study of them is therefore as important for the classical scholar and the comparative mythologist as it is for the student of Scripture.

Above all, however, Canaanite religion possesses its own permanent values, and to dismiss it as a mere heathen abomination is to allow the bias and censure of its enemies to take the place of objective judgment. One light differeth from another in glory, and if the faith of Israel is the sun in the firmament of ancient religious thought, that of Canaan is none the less a shining star. Canaanite religion takes us back into a world of thought and feeling informed by concepts and insights which are none the less precious for having been overborne and overswept in the onrushing tide of history. Here is an approach to the world and its fashion which establishes an intimacy between man and nature such as a mechanical age is apt to obliterate; which validates human existence by making man a necessary agent in the continuous process of creation; which substitutes for the humiliation of dependence the proud status of a coworker with God. If its forms of expression are crude and its philosophy too immature to satisfy the requirements of a more refined metaphysic, that is only because it issues from the bright intuitions of the world's youth rather than from the clouded experience of its tired old age. Canaanite religion is assuredly one of the many mansions in the Father's house.

BIBLIOGRAPHY AND NOTES

1. Excellent summaries of the earlier material may be found in S. A. Cook's *The Religion of Ancient Palestine* (London, 1908), in the same writer's *The Religion of Ancient Palestine in the light of Archaeology* (London, 1930), and in E. A. Leslie's *Old Testament Religion in the light of its Canaanite Backgrounds* (New York, 1936). An authoritative guide to both the earlier and the more recently discovered sources is W. F. Albright's *Archaeology and the Religion of Israel* (Baltimore, 1942).

2. The Ras Shamra texts are collected in transliteration in C. H. Gordon's *Ugaritic Manual* (Rome, 1947), which also includes a grammar and glossary. There is no complete English rendering, and most of the trans-

lations previously offered are now antiquated. For a complete bibliography down to 1940, the reader may consult R. de Langhe's *Les Textes de Ras Shamra et leur rapports avec l'Ancient Testament* (Louvain, 1940).

3. Dhorme, SYRIA 25 (1946-48), 1-35. Deities mentioned include Isis, Thoth, Aten, Shu, Amon, Bes, Nefertum, Nun and Sutekh. There is also mention of *ephod* in the sense of an encased idol (cf. Judges 8.27) and of *tophet* in that of a sacred hearth (cf. II Kings 23.10; Jer. 7.31).

4. Gaster, ORIENTALIA 11 (1941).

5. Th. Bossert, and U. B. Alkum, *Karatepe. Second Preliminary Report.* Publications of the University of Istanbul, No. 340. (Istanbul, 1947.)

6. Cf. Cook, *Religion of Ancient Palestine . . . , passim;* H. Vincent, *Canaan* (Paris, 1907); M. Burrows, *What Mean These Stones?* (New Haven, 1941), 198-221.

7. Most of what here follows is presented at length and with full documentation in the writer's forthcoming work, *Thespis: Myth, Ritual and Drama in the Ancient Near East.*

8. Hitherto, the relation of myth to ritual has been obscured by too ready an acceptance of the view—sponsored especially by Robertson Smith —that the former is merely an offshoot of the latter—a mere *post hoc* explanation.

9. For the convenience of the reader, Canaanite terms are here given according to their more familiar Hebrew equivalents. *El,* for instance, was pronounced *ilu* among the Canaanites, and *ba'al* was pronounced *ba'lu.* This applies especially to the names of deities, where we write e.g., Asherath for the Canaanite Ashratu.

10. The concept of the numen is discussed in Rudolf Otto's classic monograph, *Das Heilige* (translated into English under the title: *The Idea of the Holy*).

11. RS 54:11-12. (References are to Gordon's *Ugaritic Manual.*)

12. Cf. Deut. 33.1; Jos. 14.6; I Sam. 2.27; 9.9-10; I Kings 3.1-31; I Chr. 23.14.

13. I Sam. 18.23.

14. Cf. Isaiah 14.14. In Hindu, Greek, Norse and other mythologies, the gods similarly live in the north.

15. They are called "family *(dar)* of the sons of El" in RS 2:17, 25-26. The usual name is "assembly of the *bne el".*

16. As in the Ugaritic Epic of Keret.

17. I*AB i.1 ff. Another name for him was *Tannin,* "Dragon."

18. Is. 28.11, 19; 38.18; Job 2.5; Pss. 6.6; 9.14; 107.18; Job 38.17.

19. On Resheph, see especially: Cook, *Religion* 112 ff.; Vincent REVUE BIBLIQUE (1938): 512 ff.; J. Leibovitch, "Quelques nouvelles representations du dieu Rechef," in ANN. d. SERVICE DES ANT. DE L'EGYPTE 39 (1939), 145 ff.; B. Grdseloff, *Les débuts du culte de Rechef en Egypte*

(Cairo, 1942). On Horon, cf. Albright, AMERICAN JOURNAL OF SEMITIC LANGUAGES 53 (1936), 1-12; BULLETIN OF THE AMERICAN SCHOOLS OF ORIENTAL RESEARCH 84: 7-12; E. Picard, SYRIA 17 (1936), 315-16. Six references to Horon in Egyptian texts are collected by Posener in JOURNAL OF NEAR EASTERN STUDIES 4 (1945), 240-42.

20. Cf. supra, n. 5.

21. EV, wrongly, "as the sparks fly upward"—through a traditional interpretation of *resheph* as "flame."

22. Cooke, *North Semitic Inscriptions* (Oxford, 1903), No. 30 (363 B.C.). The village of Arsuf near Jaffa was the Seleucid Apollonias.

23. These correspond to the Kettu and Mesharu of Mesopotamian mythology.

24. Cf. A. Smythe-Palmer, *The Samson-Saga* (London, 1913).

25. Gordon, BASOR 65 (1937), 29-33; Goetze, JBL 60 (1941), 353 f.; Aistleitner, ZDMG 93 (1939), 52-59.

26. The latest edition of this text is that by the present writer in JOURNAL OF THE AMERICAN ORIENTAL SOCIETY 66 (1946), 49-76.

27. Line 54.

28. RS 3: 50-53.

29. On Dagan, cf. H. Schmökel, *Der Gott Dagan* (Leipzig, 1928).

30. Cf. Ginsberg, ORIENTALIA 9 (1940), 39-44. Kôshar is the Chusor of Sanchuniathon.

31. This statement is made by Sanchuniathon.

32. On these goddesses, cf. E. Pilz, "Die weiblichen Gottheiten Kanaans," in ZDPV 47 (1924), 129-68; J. B. Pritchard, *Palestinian Figurines in relation to certain Goddesses known through Literature* (New Haven, 1943).

33. This goddess is mentioned both in the tenth century B.C. inscriptions from Byblus (Albright, JAOS 67 [1947], 153 ff.) and in the Tell el-Amarna letters. Hrozny finds mention of her also in the "Hittite" hieroglyphic inscriptions. She occurs also in the proto-alphabetic inscriptions from Serabit el-Khadim in the Sinai Peninsula.

34. *Archaeology and the Religion of Israel*, 77-78.

35. CT xxvi 42, i 9-10; II R 49:14; V R 46; 31b; Strassmaier, AV 8814; Dhorme, RB 8 (1911), 46. However, Mrs. E. Douglas van Buren suggests (AfO 12 [1937], 4) that *tamtum*, usually rendered "the deep," is here quite a different word meaning "struggle," and that the title therefore characterizes Ishara as goddess of battle.

36. Amherst papyrus; Spiegelberg, PSBA 24:41.

37. Nock, CLASSICAL REVIEW 39:174, fn. 1.

38. H. Usener, *Legenden der heiligen Pelagia* (Bonn, 1879); E. Maas,

"Aphrodite und die heilige Pelagia," in *Neue Jahrbücher f. d. Kl. Altertum* 25 (1910), 475 ff. Cf. also A. H. Krappe, *Balor with the Evil Eye* (New York, 1927), 77.

39. Pritchard, *op. cit.*

40. Krt C vi 55-56; III AB, D 7-8.

41. Carter-Newberry, *The Tomb of Thoutmosis IV* (London, 1904), pl. 10.

42. Pritchard, 68.

43. Wm. Robertson Smith, *Religion of the Semites*, ed. 3 (London, 1927), 99.

44. The Arabic word *'athur* means a canal or trench dug for purposes of irrigation.

45. *Praeparatio Evangelica* III ii 41.

46. Figured in H. Gressmann, *Altorientalische Bilder zum Alten Testament*, ed. 2 (1927), 270.

47. A. Montet, *Les nouvelles fouilles de Tanis* 1929-1932 (Paris, 1933), 126.

48. H. O. Lange, "Der magische Papyrus Harris," in *Det. Kgl. Danske Videnskabernes Selskab* 14.2 (Copenhagen, 1927), 28 ff.

49. When he is nominated to succeed Baal, he fails to qualify by being physically too small to occupy the vacant throne (I AB i 53-65). When he seeks to obtain the privileges which El has granted to Yam, his claim is rejected because he has no wife, *i.e.*, is still a minor (III AB.C).

50. Cooke, *North Semitic Inscriptions*, Nos. 61-62.

51. In the Old Testament *qedeshim* is the regular name for the sacred sodomites and *qedeshoth* for the sacred prostitutes of Canaanite cultus.

52. The presentation of the myths here offered is based on the writer's own reconstructions. These are presented in detail in his forthcoming work *Thespis*. Thus far, the study of these documents has been concentrated mainly on their philological exegesis. Consequently, little has been done to wrest a consecutive sense out of them, or to elucidate them in the light of comparative mythology and folklore.

53. Zas is simply a form of Zeus, and Ophioneus (also called Ophion) derives from Greek *ophis*, "serpent."

RELIGION IN PREHISTORIC GREECE

*Dr. Mylonas was born in Smyrna, Asia Minor, Turkey, in 1898.
His B.A. degree was awarded him by the International College,
Smyrna, in 1918; his Ph.D. by the University of Athens in 1927 and
a second doctorate by Johns Hopkins in 1929. He has studied in the
museums of Italy, France, England, America and the Orient. He has
attended the Universities of Munich, Berlin, the Sorbonne in Paris
and has taught in the Universities of Chicago, Illinois and, since
1933, at Washington University in St. Louis. At the latter institution he has been a professor of the history of art, archaeology, and
chairman of its department since 1937.*

*Professionally he has been connected with the Greek Interna-
tional College, with the American School of Classical Studies in
Athens and has assisted and directed in the work of excavations at
Olynthus, at Haghios Kosmos, at Eleusis, at Akropotamos, publishing many monographs and books dealing with the findings of these
expeditions. He is a member of a three-man board which grants
permission for all excavating done in Greece. During and after the
war he served on commissions for the relief and restoration of
Greece and has written extensively on the political situation in the
Balkans. He is a member of many academic fraternities.*

*As this book is being prepared for press he has returned for
another summer's work of unfinished excavations and study in
Greece.*

Editor

RELIGION IN PREHISTORIC GREECE

GEORGE EMMANUEL MYLONAS

ONE OF the outstanding achievements of prehistoric research in Greece, pioneered by Heinrich Schliemann, Christos Tsountas, and Sir Arthur Evans, was the proof that many a century of cultural activity lie beyond the days sung by Homer in his Iliad and Odyssey. Troy and Ithaca, Mycenae and the Labyrinth of Minos are but midway stations on a long road of achievement whose beginnings are lost in the haze of the Neolithic Age. The excavations which have been conducted in the last fifty years from Macedonia to Crete and from Leucas to Cyprus have revealed an almost unbroken record of man's activity in Greece throughout the Neolithic and the Bronze Ages, from about 5000 to 1100 B.C. In remains of settlements unearthed, in broken pottery pieced together, in discarded tools and weapons, in objects of art, in graves and their furniture we find the details of that record. In general the story revealed by the relics is very interesting, but it becomes brilliant when it deals with the Bronze Age culture of Crete, which has come to be known as Minoan (ca. 3000-1100 B.C.), and with the latter part of the Bronze Age culture of the Mainland of Greece that has come to be known as Mycenaean (ca. 1600-1100 B.C.) [1]

One of the chapters of this record, by no means the least interesting, deals with the religion of the Minoan-Mycenaean people of Greece. Our knowledge of that religion depends solely on the evidence obtainable from objects of art and from the remains of settlements brought to light by excavations. That evidence is neither as concrete and definite nor as complete and satisfying as that preserved in the writings of the ancient authors for the religious beliefs of Greece in the Classical Era, and, in addition, is subject to varied interpretation. As a result great caution should be exercised in its use and the fact should be recognized that at present it is only

147

possible to obtain a general picture of the basic beliefs of the prehistoric inhabitants of Greece, and even that should be considered as tentative and not final.

The earliest relics to which a religious significance has been attributed by some are female statuettes which characterize the Neolithic sites of Greece (ca. 5000-2800 B.C.) [2] Scholars, however, differ in their interpretation of these figurines and there are those who doubt their religious character. But they are unanimous in believing that a cave cult was developed early in the Prehistoric Era and that the earliest traces of that cult are to be found in Crete and in the cave of Amnisos, four miles to the east of Herakleion (Candia). In the center of that cave are still to be seen two isolated cylindrical stalagmites enclosed by a stone wall. There can be no doubt that these stalagmites formed the center of a cult, and the numerous vases discovered around them led Dr. Marinatos, its excavator, to conclude that in the cave of Amnisos was worshipped a "peaceful divinity" to whom were made offerings "of mild liquids, such as milk, honey or even wine." No idols of any kind were found in the site and this seems to indicate that in the cave of Amnisos we have an aniconic cult with the stalagmite accepted as the embodiment of the Divine Spirit. Homer tells us that the cave was sacred to the Goddess Eileithyia and modern research has proved that the Goddess Eileithyia belonged to and was venerated in the cave of Amnisos by the prehistoric people of Crete "from Neolithic down to Early Christian times." [3]

Other caves besides that of Amnisos were used as cult places. Of these most important are caves of Psychro, of Arkhalochori, of Mt. Ida, of Kamares, etc., and so with reason Crete has been called the "classic land of the cave cult." In the mainland of Greece thus far no caves have been excavated with remote prehistoric connections and a sure religious use; but that does not mean that such caves did not exist. I know at least two, one in the Argolid and another in Macedonia, in which a cult was held from the end of the Neolithic period down to classical times. It is difficult to determine how this cave cult originated, because of the paucity and the uncertainty of the material available. Perhaps it originated in the veneration of the dead buried in the caves in an older age; perhaps it was started as a domestic cult when the caves were used as habitations; the interior of caves with their fantastic decor of stalactites

Figure 1. Minoan Snake Goddess.
(Courtesy of the Museum of Fine Arts, Boston)

and stalagmites and their subdued, unearthly light perhaps provided the mystic, the awe-inspiring, the superhuman setting which appealed to primitive minds and apparently was required by primitive cults. The stalactites and stalagmites with their fantastic shapes must have excited the imagination of the people and made them see in their form the Spirits that filled their universe and controlled its destiny; certainly, the vast caves with their suspended roofs could have been considered as appropriate abodes of the divine Spirits. Whatever the reason for the beginning of the cave cult the fact remains that it forms one of the oldest religious practices of the prehistoric people of Greece.

As the centuries rolled on and by Middle Minoan times, mountain peaks and sacred groves were used for worship. Not very far from the Palace of Minos at Knossos and on one of the peaks of Mt. Juktas such a sanctuary was excavated by Sir Arthur Evans. A second important sanctuary was unearthed by the British School of Archaeology at Petsofa in Eastern Crete.[4] In both cases well-built walls support a terrace and surround an enclosure within which were found deep layers of ashes mixed with charcoal and filled with votive offerings, mainly figurines of men, women, and animals. The sure signs of burning found indicate that in those sanctuaries bonfires were lit and formed part of the cult, apparently of a Nature divinity.

Our knowledge of the peak sanctuaries is considerably increased by their many representations on gems and golden signet rings from Crete and Mycenae. In some instances the wall surrounding the sanctuary is represented (Figure 2A), but more often the sanctuary is indicated by a great stone portal, reminding the *trilithon* of the Megalithic monuments, over which spread the branches of a tree loaded with leaves and fruit. Very often a free standing column, a veritable baetyl, is represented between the door jambs of the portal, and it seems that the free standing column and the tree were indispensable elements of such sanctuaries. The place of the column could sometimes be taken by a mound or cairn. Such a cairn is depicted on a glass plaque from Mycenae approached by two "daemons" holding in readiness typical libation ewers, and apparently formed the central element in the great sanctuary of Mt. Lykaion in Arcadia. Two columns stood in front of the cairn on Mt. Lykaion even in historic times.[5]

Figure 2. Minoan-Mycenaean Religious Scenes and Symbols.
Copied from Sir Arthur Evans', *The Palace of Minos at Knossos.*

Sir Arthur Evans was the first to suggest that pillars and columns served as the temporary embodiment of a divinity, that "baetylic stones were always at hand as a material home for the spiritual being brought down into it by ritual." Indeed we have from Crete and Mycenae a good many representations of columns and pillars serving as cult objects, as the center of a cult. On a well-known cylinder seal from Mycenae, for example, we find a man standing between columns worshipping with raised hands. On two glass plaques, discovered by Tsountas in tombs of the lower town of Mycenae, we find a number of "daemons" pouring libations over free standing columns and pillars. On signet rings from Crete and Mycenae we have free standing columns whose sacred character is universally admitted. We can therefore conclude that such sacred columns and pillars served as the material home for the spiritual being, that sometimes they were even considered as the aniconic representation of a divinity; that pillar and column worship was prevalent in Minoan-Mycenaean times.[6]

To date no figurines have been discovered in the peak sanctuaries that could be construed as idols of the divinity worshipped there. This as well as the existence of the "baetyls" indicate that at the beginning and for centuries the cult of the mountain peaks was aniconic in character. As a matter of fact, in many respects the mountain cult parallels that held in caves; the imposing setting of the cave is matched by the grandeur of the mountain peak, and the stalagmites of the former are paralleled by the baetyls of the latter. The raising of hands in adoration, as seen in a number of votive figurines, the pouring of libations, the kindling of bonfires, and the offering of votive gifts apparently formed part of the ritual held in the peak sanctuaries.

Closely associated with the rites held in peak sanctuaries, and equally old, is the cult of the sacred tree. It is definitely proved that the Minoan-Mycenaean people believed that groves were haunted by the divine Spirits and their attendants, and that the sacred tree was the embodiment of a divinity, the divinity of vegetation. "The sacred tree might itself be regarded as permanently fitted with divine life as manifested by its fruit and foliage," writes Sir Arthur Evans. We have seen that sacred trees were almost always present in peak sanctuaries associated with the "baetyl", and, beginning with Middle Minoan times, trees—palms, cypress, pines, fig trees—and

152

even boughs were worshipped. Such sacred trees and boughs are represented on works of art placed between "horns of consecration", as the recipients of libations poured from sacrificial jugs by "daemons", and as the object of adoration by both men and women. Indeed the available evidence proves definitely that the tree cult was one of the most prominent cults of prehistoric Greece especially venerated by the country people.[7]

The people of the cities worshipped in shrines to be found in their dwellings and in the palaces of the ruling princes. Temples, in the common sense of the term, i.e., special buildings standing by themselves and serving as the abodes of the god or as the places for communal worship, were as a rule unknown to the prehistoric Greeks. The only exception to the rule is the shrine of Gournia which was not incorporated in the palace or in a house, and apparently served the entire village. The house sanctuaries as a rule contain but a single room and are very small in size. For instance, the shrine of the Double Axes in the Palace of Minos at Knossos, the latest shrine of Crete dating from the closing years of the Late Minoan period, is only 1.50 metres square; the main room of the sanctuary of Phaestos, the oldest house sanctuary thus far uncovered going back to Middle Minoan II times, measures only 3.65 x 2.60 metres. Larger in size and more impressive are the pillared rooms, found in practically every Cretan palace and known under that name because their main features are rectangular sometimes monolithic pillars set in the middle of the floor. Often the sign of the double axe is inscribed on the pillars, shallow basins for lustrations and libations are to be seen in some cases on the floor and near their base, and in one instance the stand which supported a double axe was found by the pillar. Apparently the pillared rooms were used for religious rites. But, as Sir Arthur Evans has pointed out, the pillared rooms were crypts over which were built columnar shrines. To date such shrines have not been uncovered, but they are represented on a fragmentary miniature fresco from Knossos and on the golden plaques from the IVth shaft grave of Mycenae. Their façades are divided vertically into three sections, of which the central is more spacious and more elevated, and are decorated with "horns of consecration."[8]

With the shrines must be grouped rectangular areas sunk below the level of the pavement and known as "lustral areas"; sometimes they are flanked by balustrades, and their floor is reached by broad descending stairways.[9] It is generally believed that these sunken areas were used for religious rites of an unknown nature. Their semi-subterranean character can, I believe, be explained only if we assume that a chthonic deity was venerated there. Altars were not uncommon in Minoan-Mycenaean times. Some of them were built within the palaces and houses and were considerable in size, but others were smaller and portable. Remains of built altars were found in the palaces of Knossos, Phaestos, and Haghia Triada, and complete examples are represented on the painted sarcophagus of Haghia Triada and on the ring of Minos. Portable altars are known from their many representations on objects of art, the most familiar of which is the relief of the Lions Gate at Mycenae.

The only architectural feature of the interior of the house shrines excavated thus far is a raised ledge or shelf on which were placed the idols and cult objects to be venerated. On the ledge of the shrine of the Double Axes, and on a floor of water-worn pebbles, were found still in their original position two pairs of "horns of consecration", made of white plaster over a core of clay, with round sockets for the insertion of the shafts of double axes, a miniature double axe of pale steatite, and five figurines of painted terracotta. In the past the "horns of consecration" were believed to be cult objects and fetishes, but it has been proved that they are mere stands on which were placed sacred objects. As time went on they were also developed into architectural ornaments used to indicate the sanctity of the structures they decorated. The origin of the "horns of consecration" is not certain, but it seems probable that they were developed out of the habit of memorializing a sacrifice by the nailing of the skull of the sacrificial animal on the sanctuary wall.[10]

Double axes were placed between the "horns of consecration" of the shrine. There can be no doubt that to the Minoan the "double axe" was as important a religious sign as is the cross to the Christian and the crescent to the Moslem (Figure 2F). Besides the double axe, as Sir Arthur Evans has proved, was considered as the aniconic image and the embodiment of the Minoan Divinity. Actual examples of the double axe in metal have been found in various shrines, small replicas were often used as votive offerings, and double axes are represented in cult scenes carved on signet rings. On the painted sarcophagus of Haghia Triada, on which a cult scene is certainly represented, double axes are mounted on high poles set into stepped stone bases and are crowned by birds. The evidence is ample and clear; the double axe was one of the most sacred cult objects of the Minoan-Mycenaean people. We may now note that the double axe is often represented with reduplicated edges and is covered with decorative motives. This reduplication has caused a good deal of speculation. Cook has seen in it the symbol of a joint cult of a God and a Goddess; Sir Arthur Evans has identified it with the divine pair, the Great Goddess of the Minoans and her male consort. But in view of the inferior position of the male God and his rather late introduction to the Minoan pantheon, such interpretations seem improbable. Perhaps we ought to see in the reduplication of the universal symbol of the Minoan religion two or more aspects of the same great divinity.[11]

Five terra-cotta figurines were found on the ledge of the shrine. Two of these—a man holding a bird in his extended hands and a female figurine—are votaries; the remaining three, with the part of the body below the waist in the form of a cylinder reducing the form to a bell-shaped type, must be considered as the idols of the shrine. The smaller two idols represent a female divinity with arms curving in front of the breasts; the larger, 22 cm. in height, and most important idol represents a Goddess with disproportionately long arms bent at the elbow and hands raised upwards with one palm stretched outwards and the other held in profile. The gesture can be interpreted as one of benediction. A bird, possibly a dove, is perched on the head of this idol. In the Shrine of Gournia a similar female bell-shaped idol of terra-cotta was found holding its raised arms in the same attitude of blessing. Instead of a bird a snake is represented passing over the left shoulder and encircling the waist of the statuette. Fragments of forearms entwined with snakes belonging to other statuettes were also found.[12] This will certainly prove that the snakes were the attribute of the Goddess worshipped in that shrine.

Our best example of the Minoan Snake Goddess rendered not as a bell-shaped form but as a woman richly dressed comes from a repository of the Palace of Knossos and dates from Middle Minoan times. It is made of faience and measures 34 cm. in height. From the top of the tall tiara which crowns the head of the Goddess emerges a spotted snake. Two more spotted snakes are entwined in her arms extended forward and downwards. The awe-inspiring spectacle of the writhing snakes is increased by the widely opened eyes of the Goddess. A second statuette in faience, found in the same repository and 29 cm. in height, represents either the Goddess or her votary holding two smaller snakes in her extended hands. An equally brilliant example of the Snake Goddess in gold and ivory this time is exhibited in the Boston Museum of Fine Arts (Figure 1). The provenience of this statuette, which stands only 16.1 cm in height, is unknown but Sir Arthur Evans believes it to have come from Knossos. The Goddess again holds two snakes in her hands, extended forward and downwards.[13]

Sir Arthur Evans and his followers maintain that the snake is the attribute of a chthonic divinity and that the Snake Goddess is the "Lady of the Dead" and consequently the Goddess of Fertility, since the realm of the dead to be found below the surface of the earth is fused by primitive people with the area from which plants grow up. Dr. Nilsson, however, has pointed out that statuettes of the Snake Goddess have not been found in cave or mountain sanctuaries, that the snake, as the guardian of the house, is the center of a domestic cult, that the snake must as a result be considered as the symbol of the Goddess of Domestic Cult.[14] In 1930 evidence proving the existence of a domestic snake cult was found in one of the private houses of Knossos. In a small room of this house and among other objects were discovered some tubular vases (26.5-29 cm. in height) bearing on their sides two pairs of cups symmetrically placed. Snakes, moulded in relief, were also placed on the sides as if they were ascending to the cups. It is evident that offerings, such as milk and honey, were placed in those cups for the snakes, and that the tubular vases served as the abode of the reptiles. With the tubular vases was also found a terra-cotta table standing on three legs the upper surface of which was divided into four compartments to accommodate four snakes drinking from a central bowl whose place is marked by a raised ring placed in the middle of the table. There can be no doubt that in the small room of that Knossian house the snake was venerated in a simple domestic cult as the "visible impersonation of the spirits of the household." That this cult was a very old one is proved by Early Minoan II (ca. 2500

156

B.C.) vase in the form of a woman with snakes coiled around her neck and passing over her shoulders.[15]

Sir Arthur Evans, however, has pointed out that the snakes held by the Snake Goddess are "vipers", to be hunted and exterminated, and these can have nothing in common with the harmless snakes cherished by households; that they represent a more deadly aspect of the Goddess, a chthonic aspect. This view, I believe, is corroborated by the evidence obtained at the sanctuary of Gournia. As we have seen above, that sanctuary is not associated with the palace nor with a private house, but, although wedged between other structures, it is independent of them and has its own approach from the public road. This fact, often forgotten, will exclude the conception of the snake as the "protector and guardian of the house." On the ledge of the shrine the idol of a Snake Goddess was found and on its floor, in their original position, a table of offerings surrounded by three, and the fragments of a fourth, bottomless tubular vases standing on their broad, hollow base and decorated by vertical handles and horns of consecration; on one of the specimens two snakes are moulded as if climbing toward its mouth. Sir Arthur Evans compares these vases to the tubular stands found in the snake room of the house of Knossos; but the lack of the offertory cups, their hollowed bottoms, and the fact that the Gournia examples were not found in a house shrine where a domestic cult was appropriate, would indicate that the Gournia specimens had a different function. They were used for libations poured through them and meant to percolate into the earth. Such libations were made to a chthonic deity, to the Snake Goddess as the Mistress of the Nether World whose idol was to be seen on the ledge. In the shrine of Asine, excavated by Professor Persson and his collaborators, with other things was found a jug standing on its mouth with the bottom missing "wedged between stones of the cult ledge."[16] That jug could serve no other purpose but to act as the channel through which libations were poured and allowed to flow into the earth; in other words, it served the same purpose as the tubular vases from Gournia. Furthermore, the existence of a cult in honor of a chthonic deity in the Palaces of Knossos is indicated by the so-called "lustral areas" discussed above. Thus we reach the conclusion that the Snake Goddess was both a chthonic deity, the Lady of the

157

Nether World, and in her milder aspect a benevolent deity, the Mistress of the Domestic cult. Sir Arthur Evans has published a statuette of a Goddess handling a snake which lacks the awe-inspiring air of the faience figure. That statuette must represent the Snake Goddess in her milder aspect as the patron deity of the domestic cult.[17]

A bird, perhaps a dove, is perched on the head of the largest idol from the Shrine of the Double Axes. Birds were often represented in Minoan-Mycenaean religious art. We have already noticed that the mounted double axes painted on the sarcophagus of Haghia Triada were crowned with birds, and we find birds flying to and from or perched upon shrines, columns, double axes, boughs, etc. These birds evidently were accepted as tokens of the visible presence of the Gods, as signs of divine epiphany.[18] However, it seems that the bird, perhaps the dove, was also the attribute of a Goddess, for otherwise we cannot explain the presence of terra-cotta votive offerings in the form of birds often found in shrines. From the Shrine of the Double Axes at Knossos we even have a votary who, in the words of Nilsson, is "holding out a bird as if to offer it." How can this bird, which apparently is being offered as a gift to the Goddess by a votary, be the token of the epiphany of a Goddess? The bird perched on the head of the idol is superfluous as a token of epiphany since the idol itself stands for the visible presence of the Goddess, but as an attribute it is essential. The idol from Knossos is not the only example of the Goddess with a bird. Two bell-shaped idols of the same Goddess were found in the house-shrine of Gazi excavated in 1936 by Dr. Marinatos; a single bird is perched on the conical head of Gazi idol No. 3, while two birds, on either side of horns of consecration, are perched on the head of idol No. 2. From the third shaft grave of Mycenae we have two gold leaves cut in the form of a nude female Goddess with a bird, perhaps a dove, perched on the head.[19] The existing evidence seems to indicate that the bird stood in general for the presence of the invisible divinity, but that it also served as an attribute of a Goddess. Sir Arthur has suggested that the bird, perhaps a dove, was the attribute of the Celestial Goddess; but I would like to modify that name and call her the Goddess of the Upper Regions, in contrast to the Goddess of the Nether Regions symbolized by the spotted snake.

The house-shrine of Gazi, dating from the closing years of the

Late Minoan Period, has also given us the bell-shaped statuette of another Goddess. Her attribute seems to be the cultivated poppy head (*Papaver Somniferum*), three specimens of which, in the form of pins, are attached on the broad band which the Goddess is wearing. The *Papaver Somniferum* is being cultivated today in Greece, as it was in the past, for its medicinal qualities. Even the Homeric heroes were familiar with these qualities, and so with reason Dr. Marinatos has called the idol: the "Goddess of Healing."[19a]

The votive offerings dedicated to these Goddesses were placed on tables made of clay or plaster and sometimes embedded on a raised dais to be found in front of the ledge on which stood the idols of the Goddess. In the shrines of Knossos and Gournia such tables were found *in situ,* but examples are known from the palaces of Mycenae and Tiryns, of Phaestos and Nirou Khani.[20] Libation tables were also found in the palace shrines proving that the Goddesses were also honored with libations, for which were used ewers with a globular body, a high swinging handle, and a pointed mouth.[21] Libations poured out of these ewers perhaps were offered to the Goddess of the Upper Regions while such poured through the tubular vases were offered to the Mistress of the Lower World. This seems to be indicated by the representation on the great golden ring from Tiryns; there we find the Goddess of the Upper Regions, accompanied by her attribute bird, seated on a stool and holding a "loving cup" which is to be filled by approaching "daemons" holding libation ewers.[22]

Animal sacrifices do not seem to have been prevalent in Minoan-Mycenaean times, and it is by no means certain which of the deities were honored by such sacrifices. We have but few representations of animals on sacrificial tables, and even fewer of skulls considered as memorials of the actual sacrifice. Our only definite example of an animal sacrifice on the sarcophagus of Haghia Triada seems to have been made in honor of a dead chieftain. Perhaps the place of animal sacrifices was taken by the imposing processions which the Minoans staged in honor of their Goddess and which are reflected in the palace frescoes. Sir Arthur Evans believes that even athletic sports, especially bull grappling events, were held in honor of the divinities. The double flute and the lyre provided the music necessary for the ritual and often a *Triton* shell was employed as a

159

trumpet for the invocation of the divine spirit. Long robes heavily embroidered and baggy skirts made of animal skins were the vestments worn by both men and women ministrants of the Minoan-Mycenaean deities.

The details regarding the religious rites held in house and palace shrines which we have gleaned from the relics unearthed are important and interesting, but equally interesting is the observation that the palace cults were instrumental in transforming the earlier aniconic beliefs into anthropomorphic conceptions. By Middle Minoan III this transformation had taken place and by the end of the sixteenth century anthropomorphic ideas had penetrated the other cults and especially those of the sacred tree and of the mountain sanctuaries. No idols have been found in those sanctuaries and the sacred tree and the baetyl to the end remained cult objects, the embodiments of the divinity. But under the influence of the palace cults the Minoan-Mycenaean people began to picture in the form of human beings the divinities of the tree and the mountain cults. This trend is reflected in the cult scenes engraved especially on signet rings. Thus we see the Goddess of the sacred tree in the guise of a mature woman seated under the spreading branches of that tree to receive the adoration of approaching votaries on the signet ring from the Acropolis of Mycenae (Figure 2J), and learn that the raising of the hands and the offerings of flowers was part of her ritual. From cult scenes engraved on other rings we learn that ecstatic, orgiastic dances and spirited songs formed another part of her ritual (Figure 2B) and that by such dances the Goddess was invoked to appear among her votaries. We can see the Goddess descending through the air in response to these invocations on a signet ring at Herakleion, on another found in tomb I at Isopata (Figure 2D), and on a signet ring of green jasper in the Copenhagen National Museum.[23]

A Goddess is represented on gems holding a spear and in company with wild animals. Often wild animals are placed on either side of her in a heraldic arrangement and sometimes she is represented with an animal grasped in either hand (Figure 2G). Scholars have recognized in her the "Goddess of Wild Life," the πότνια θηρῶν, of prehistoric times, the "Mistress of the Animals." Perhaps we should note that there is no evidence proving an animal cult among the Minoan-Mycenaean people. Animals, both real and imaginary such as griffins and sphinxes, are used as companions or guardians of divinities and shrines; bulls were apparently the favored sacrificial animals, and bull sports were the favorite events of the Minoans, but as far as our evidence to date goes neither the bull nor any other animal was venerated by them. Among the animals created by the imagination of the Minoan artist an important place is held by what we have called above the "daemons." These are indeed weird creatures with the body of a lion and a head sometimes resembling that of a lion and sometimes that of a horse (Figure 2 I). They possess long, mobile ears and their backs are covered with what seems to be a loose skin edged with bristles and dots and ending in a wasp-tail.[24] In spite of their almost hieratic poses they seem to be filled with the spirit of nature that survives in the satyrs of the Classical Age. They are represented standing erect and on their hind legs, approaching a Goddess with libation jugs, pouring out libations, acting as companions to the Goddess, and taking her place in heraldic designs. There can be no doubt that these creatures were considered as servants of the Goddess and ministrants of her cult. Perhaps they are the remnants of the old spirits with which primitive man filled his universe, spirits that have not attained Godship; benevolent daemons that haunt the sacred groves and the craggy mountains and can help the husbandman and the forester.

On a sealing from Knossos we find a Goddess holding a spear in her extended hand and standing on a conical mound; she is perhaps the Goddess of the peak sanctuaries[25] (Figure 2H). Two lions are seen on either side of the mound on which they have placed their front paws, while a man is standing in an attitude of adoration in front of the Goddess. The mound apparently stands for a mountain peak and we may call the divinity the "Goddess of the Mountains."

The spear held by the "Mistress of the Animals" and by the "Goddess of the Mountains" cannot be considered as the attribute of a war Goddess. From Mycenae we have a limestone tablet on which is painted a "War Goddess" holding an eight-shaped shield and venerated by two female votaries.[26] Finally we have a "Goddess of the Seas", the protectress of sea-faring people, portrayed as a

161

woman seated in a large ship in the ring of Mochlos (Figure 2E) and reposing among the waves on a sealing impression from the domestic quarters of the Palace of Knossos.[27]

It has become apparent by now that the Minoan-Mycenaean pantheon was dominated by female divinities. However, a male God was also venerated, although he may have been a later addition to the divine court. We have but a few representations of the male God and perhaps the most definite is that to be found on a gem from Kydonia (Canea). The God is standing between the "horns of consecration," a sure proof of his divinity, with arms folded over his breast. To his left stands a "daemon" holding a libation jug and to his right a winged goat (Figure 2C). It is apparent that in this composition we have the heraldic design used in the representation of the "Mistress of the Animals" and that our God is the counterpart of that Goddess, a veritable "Master of the Animals." This conception is strengthened by another lentoid gem from Kydonia on which our "Master of the Animals" is represented with hands extended and holding two lions standing on their hind legs. A male God is also represented on at least two signet rings; on the signet ring in the Ashmolean Museum he is a diminutive figure holding a spear, while on the ring from Knossos he is represented descending through the air in front of a peak sanctuary with a spear in his hand.[28] One could attribute the double axe to such a male God and consider it as his embodiment, because the double axe is often associated with the thunder God. However, in Minoan-Mycenaean representations the double axe is never seen in the hands of the male God; when it is not carried by votaries it is always associated with a Goddess. Even if we added to our list of male God representations the gold and ivory statuette of a boy, who according to Sir Arthur was a child God adoring the Mother Goddess, an interpretation by no means certain, still our examples will be few and will justify the conclusion that in the Minoan-Mycenaean religion the male God was of minor importance and served as the consort and satellite of the Goddess or even as her divine child.[29]

We may finally note that no evidence has yet been found proving the existence of a cult of the heavenly bodies in Minoan-Mycenaean times. The sun, the moon, and the sky are represented on works of art, but they form rather the natural setting within which a scene was placed; they may refer even to certain unknown to us myths and cosmogonic beliefs, but they do not indicate the existence of a cult of the sun or the moon.[30] Nor can we be certain of the existence of a cult of the dead. The Minoan-Mycenaean people buried their dead with great care, furnished the graves with gifts and furnishings, and built magnificent tombs for their chieftains. The altar discovered over the IVth shaft grave of Mycenae, the shrine-temple of Knossos, and the painting on the sarcophagus of Haghia Triada seem to indicate the existence of a hero cult in the Mainland of Greece and the emergence in Crete in Late Minoan times of the custom of extending divine honors to a departed ruler.[31] In the so-called ring of Nestor we may even have the proof that in Crete the conception of the Elysion began to be formulated.[32] Beyond these general notions, however, we cannot proceed, and we have no real evidence to prove the existence of a cult of the dead in prehistoric Greece.

Our survey of the prehistoric cults of Greece has shown that the Minoan-Mycenaean people worshipped a Goddess known by the name of Eileithyia, the Snake Goddess—patron of the Nether Regions, of fertility, and of the domestic cult—the Dove Goddess, the Goddess of Healing, the Goddess of the Tree Cult, the Mistress of the Animals and her companion, the Goddess of the Mountains, the Goddess of War, and the Goddess of the Seas. Whether all these Goddesses should be considered as one Great Goddess with different functions or a number of independent and separate divinities each characterized by a particular function remains still to be determined. Our authorities are divided in their opinions. Sir Arthur Evans believes that "we are in the presence of a largely Monotheistic cult in which the female form of divinity held the supreme place," that "we should treat the Goddess as essentially the same great Nature Goddess under various aspects—celestial with the dove, chthonic with the snake, etc." Dr. Nilsson, on the other hand, maintains that the available evidence and the stage of civilization reached by the Minoan-Mycenaean people will impose the belief in a plurality of Goddesses each with individual functions.[33] It seems to me that in Late Minoan times the people of Greece had reached such a high level of culture—indicated by their palaces, their paintings, their carvings, their script—that even monotheistic conceptions were not beyond their ability. Furthermore, the functions of the

various Goddesses are not definitely delineated and are characterized by a great deal of overlapping and fusion. Thus the Goddess
of the Sacred Tree can scarcely be differentiated from the Goddess
of the peak sanctuaries where a sacred tree was always present; the
Goddess of the household cult becomes one with the chthonic
deity; the "Goddess of the Mountains" with her spear and lion companions differs but little from the "Mistress of the Animals." It
seems to me that this overlapping and fusion can best be explained
by Sir Arthur's suggestion that the Minoan-Mycenaeans venerated
one Great Nature Goddess under various aspects. People worshipping one or the other Goddess representing this or that aspect of
the Divinity felt that they venerated at the same time the Great
Goddess herself. And I would like to think that the Double Axe was
the visual symbol of the ultimate union of the various aspects of the
Great Goddess in the same great divine being; so conceived and interpreted it becomes the universal emblem of the Minoan-Mycenaean religion.

No matter what view we may decide to adopt the fact will remain that the religion of the Prehistoric Greeks was a nature creed;
that the various aspects of Nature were pictured and worshipped in
the form of a female being to whom a male God was subordinated;
that it was a gay and optimistic creed carried out by brilliant pag-
eants, by singing and dancing, by the music of the flute and the lyre,
by impressive gestures and simple offerings; that it was not over-
burdened with somber conceptions of death and with visions of a
world of shadows but was based on an intimate relation of Goddess and worshipper. It was characterized by simplicity and lack of
fathomless theology. In that respect it differed strongly from the
contemporary religion of the Egyptians from whom the Minoans
borrowed so many cultural elements, and it reflected the mentality
and the temperament of the Aegean people. The details which we
can develop from their artifacts can give us but an incomplete outline of the beliefs of the prehistoric Greeks. When and if some day
it will prove possible to decipher the many tablets covered with an
unknown-to-us script which the Minoans have left behind, then we
shall be able to complete the picture of the religious beliefs of a
people who developed one of the most brilliant prehistoric cultures
of our world, and one of the most humane nature creeds known.
So humane, indeed, and so appealing were their beliefs that they

were developed into the foundation on which the Indo-European tribes, which flooded Greece in the latter half of the Bronze Age, based their own nature creed and their own mythology; a creed and a mythology that have delighted and inspired humanity for countless generations.

NOTES

1. Sir Arthur Evans, the founder of Cretan Archaeology, has developed the term Minoan from Minos, the royal title of the rulers of Knossos. It indicates the Bronze Age culture and period of Crete and is divided into three periods: Early Minoan (I-II-III) ca. 3000-2200 B.C., Middle Minoan (I-II-III) ca. 2200-1600 B.C., and Late Minoan (I-II-III) 1600-1100 B.C. The basic work on Cretan antiquities is Sir Arthur's monumental books *The Palace of Minos*, I-IV (London, 1922-37).

With the Prehistoric Age of Greeks the Pelasgi are intimately connected. To Herodotos as well as to the majority of the Classical Greeks, the Pelasgi seem to have been the aboriginal inhabitants of the Mainland of Greece who were displaced by the invading Indo-European tribes, who did not belong to the Indo-European homophyly, and whose character and identity had remained vague. The term "Pelasgian Religion" therefore applies to the vestiges of aboriginal religious practices which were preserved in the Mainland of Greece after its occupation by the Indo-European tribes about 2000 B.C. What those vestiges were, and how near they were to the Minoan religious conceptions are questions which in our present state of knowledge cannot be answered.

2. *The Palace of Minos*, I, 44-52 Figs. 11-13. G. E. Mylonas, *The Neolithic Settlement of Olynthos*, 59 note 16.

3. Sp. Marinatos, *Praktika* (1929) 95; (1930) 91; "The Cult of the Cretan Caves," *The Review of Religion* (1941) 129 ff.: Sir Arthur Evans, *The Earlier Religion of Greece*, 6 ff. *Odyssey*, XIX, 188. M. P. Nilsson, *The Minoan—Mycenaean Religion*, 54, 446 ff. Nilsson's work is a classic and fundamental for the study of the religions of Prehistoric Greece.

4. *Palace of Minos*, I, 151 ff., *Annual British School*, IX, 356 ff.

5. For the glass plaques see Chr. Tsountas, *Praktika* (1896) 29 ff. Sir Arthur Evans, *Mycenaean Tree and Pillar Cult*, Figs. 12-14. For Mt. Lykaion see G. E. Mylonas, "Lykaian Altar of Zeus," *Classical Studies in Honor of W. A. Oldfather* (1943) 122 ff.

6. Evans, *Tree and Pillar Cult*, Figs. 12-14, 24, 48, 53, 55. M. P. Nilsson, *op. cit.* (1927) 201 ff., *The Earlier Religion of Greece*, 13 ff.

7. Nilsson, *op. cit.*, 225 ff. *Tree and Pillar Cult*, 153 ff. *The Earlier Religion of Greece*, 13.

8. *Palace of Minos,* I, 146, 401, 436, etc.; " Tomb of the Double Axes". *Archaeologia,* LXV (1914) 64 ff. G. Karo, *Die Schachtgraeber von My-kenai,* Pl. XXVII, 26.

9. The largest to be found in the Palace of Knossos measures 2.50 m. square and 2 m. deep; *Palace of Minos,* I, 217, 406 ff. etc.

10. Nilsson, *op. cit.,* 140 ff. For the shrine and its contents see *Palace of Minos,* II, 335 ff.

11. A. B. Cook, *Zeus,* II (Cambridge, 1914), 537. *Palace of Minos,* IV Pt. II, 342. For the sarcophagus see Paribeni, "Il sarcofago dipinto di H. Triada," *Monumenti Antichi,* XIX, 1 ff.

12. For the Gournia shrine, see H. Boyd-Hawes and others, *Gournia,* 47 ff. and Plts. I, XI.

13. *Palace of Minos,* I, 500 ff., Figs. 359-362. *Amer. Journ. of Archaeology,* XIX (1915), 237 ff., Plts. I-XIX.

14. Nilsson, *op. cit.,* 278 ff. *Cf.* A. Persson, *The Religion of Greece in Prehistoric Times,* 50, where the snake is related to "fertility and the re-awakening of life in spring."

15. *Palace of Minos,* IV, 138 ff. and 159. *The Earlier Religion of Greece,* 25.

16. O. Froedin and A. W. Persson, *Asine* (1938), 298, Fig. 206. Nilsson, *op. cit.,* 76 ff., Figs. 3a-b. Zahn, in Kinch *Vroulia,* 27 ff.

17. *Palace of Minos,* IV, Figs. 149-151.

18. Nilsson, *op. cit.,* 285 ff. It is interesting to recall that in Christian iconography the Holy Ghost is pictured as a dove; apparently it is directly derived from the prehistoric use of the bird as the symbol of the divine epiphany.

19. Sp. Marinatos, *Ephemeris Archaeologike* (1937) 278 ff., Plts. 1-2. G. Karo, *op. cit.,* Pl. XXVII, 27-28; The Goddesses hold their hands in front of their breasts and in one example doves are attached on the elbows also.

19a. Marinatos, *op. cit.,* 228, Fig. 1 and Plts. 1-2.

20. In the palace of Mallia was found a unique stone table of offer-ings, 90 cm. in diameter, with 34 cup-like depressions carved around its circumference and a central larger and deeper bowl. Apparently, grains, fruits, and liquids of various kinds were placed in the cups as offerings to the Goddesses. See F. Chapouthier, "Une Table à Offrande au Palais de Mallia," *Bulletin de Correspondance Hellenique* (1928) 1 ff. In other shrines the place of this table was taken by multiple vessels recalling the *kernoi* of the Classical Period.

21. A table with six terra-cotta ewers was found at Phaestos, a silver example was discovered in the IVth shaft grave of Mycenae, and ewers of the same type are represented on works of art between "horns of con-secration" proving their sacral use. See Nilsson, *op. cit.,* 125 ff. A small

libation table was found by Marinatos at Gazi, *Eph. Archaeol.* (1937) 285, Fig. 6.

22. Archaeol. Deltion (1916) App. 1, Pl. I.

23. *Pillar and Tree Cult,* Figs. 4, 52, 53. Nilsson, *op. cit.,* Figs. 72, 73, 77.

24. *Pillar and Tree Cult,* Figs. 1, 12-14, 44-46. Nilsson, *op. cit.,* 307 ff.

25. *Palace of Minos,* II, Pt. II, Fig. 528.

26. Ch. Tsountas, *Ephem. Archaeol.* (1887) Pl. X, 3, and Rodenwaldt, *Ath. Mitt.,* 37 (1912) 129 ff., Pl. VIII.

27. R. S. Seager, *Explorations in the Island of Mochlos,* Fig. 52, and *Palace of Minos,* IV, Pt. II, Fig. 925.

28. *Tree and Pillar Cult,* Figs. 43, 48.

29. *Palace of Minos,* II, 443 ff., *The Earlier Religion of Greece,* 32 ff. and 41.

30. Nilsson, *op. cit.,* 355 ff.

31. *Ibid.,* 515 ff. C. Schuchhardt, *Schliemann's Excavations,* Fig. 142. On altars and bothroi in general see G. P. Oekonomos, *De profusionum receptaculis sepulcralibus* (1921). Palace of Minos, Paribeni, *loc. cit.;* F. v. Duhn, "Sarcophag aus H. Triada," *Archiv f. Religions* (1919) 161 ff.

32. *Palace of Minos,* III, 145 ff. and p. 155, *The Earlier Religion of Greece,* 27 ff., Nilsson, *op. cit.,* 541 ff.

33. Evans, *The Earlier Religion of Greece,* 41. Evans' view has received the weighty support of Dr. Marinatos who favors the conception of one Great Nature Goddess appearing to her worshippers under various aspects, *Eph. Arch.* (1937) 290. See also Persson, *op. cit.* (1924).

BIBLIOGRAPHY

SIR ARTHUR EVANS, *Mycenaean Tree and Pillar Cult* (London, 1901).

————, *Palace of Minos at Knossos,* I-IV (London, 1922-1937).

————, *The Earlier Religion of Greece in the Light of Cretan Discoveries* (London, 1931).

D. FIMMEN, *Die kretisch-mykenische Kultur* (Leipzig, 1924).

GUSTAVE GLOTZ, *La Civilisation Égeènne* (Paris, 1923). (English translation, New York, 1927.)

D. G. HOGARTH, "Aegean Religion," Hasting's *Dictionary of Religion and Ethics* (New York, 1908).

MARTIN P. NILSSON, *The Minoan—Mycenaean Religion and Its Survival in Greek Religion* (Lund, 1927).

J. D. S. PENDLEBURY, *The Archaeology of Crete* (London, 1939).

AXEL W. PERSSON, *The Religion of Greece in Prehistoric Times* (Berkeley, 1942).

CH. TSOUNTAS—J. I. MANATT, *The Mycenaean Age* (Boston, 1897).

MYSTERY RELIGIONS OF GREECE

*The editor's biography of this contributor precedes the previous
article.*

Editor

MYSTERY RELIGIONS OF GREECE

GEORGE EMMANUEL MYLONAS

THE STATE religion of Greece in its origin and substance was pure nature worship. Natural phenomena and elements were transformed into divine beings with which the Olympian pantheon was peopled and which demanded and received the allegiance of the Greeks who were by nature God-fearing. The Olympian Gods were conceived in the image of man, lived in communities similar to those of men, had families, friends, and enemies, and were animated by the same passions as their worshippers. They did not possess the unfathomable mystic qualities of the Gods of the East, but were endowed with virtues and weaknesses and were themselves subject to Fate; they were all powerful but not omnipotent, wise but not omniscient.

The followers of the state religion were born into it and as a rule worshipped the Gods of their choosing not in communal services but in small family groups and in exchange for worldly favors. Those were obtained by rather simple ritual acts and sacrifices that required no special training or divine ordination, acts which had no secret profound meaning but which bore "their meaning on their face." For the state religion of the Greeks had no organized priesthood, no scriptures of any kind, no theology which had to be interpreted by the chosen few who had prepared themselves for the task.

Besides the state religion to which every Greek belonged automatically, however, we find in ancient Greece certain religious rites, which are known as "mystery religions,"[1] and which differed in many important details from the official religion of the state. Membership in them was not automatic and general, but personal and voluntary. It was only open to those who chose to become members, who were willing to undergo the specified purifications and final

171

initiation, and who pledged themselves to keep the secret rites revealed to them. The mystery religions were not concerned with the material welfare of the state, but only with the spiritual welfare of the individual and thus transcended the limits of the tribe, city, and even race and assumed a universal character. They are "cosmic religions," believing in an orderly "cosmos" in the image of God and teaching the unity of life and the unity of God.[2] The relation of the mystes, of an initiate, to his God was not perfunctory, as it was in the official religion, but intimate and close; through initiation the mystes felt that he had attained union with God, and that was the aim and the promise of the mystic rites. Unlike the simple nature creed of the state that never aimed beyond the visible and the material, the mystery religions were made up of symbolic rites whose meaning went beyond the visible action and whose aim was to provoke in the initiate a mystic experience which led him to regeneration (to *palengenesia*) and redemption.

Purifications and processions, blazing lights and fasting, sacramental acts and a passion play, the exhibit of sacred relics and mystic liturgies, were some of the means employed to quicken the imagination, to stir deep emotions, and to bring about the communion with the deity. In the course of his initiation, the mystes felt that his estrangement with God was removed, that bonds of unity between them were forged, that a knowledge of God, γνῶσις Θεοῦ, the gift of God's grace, was imparted to him, that regeneration and redemption were his; and so he felt superior to all the trials of life and secure against the uncertainties of the future and even of death. For the mystery religions were eschatological religions delving into the problem of life and death and even immortality. They were religions which assured the initiates of a continued communion with the patron God even after death, of a blissful existence in the realm of Hades because of that communion, and of a triumph over death and its ills similar to that experienced by the God himself.

Of the members of the Greek Pantheon, two were the special Gods of the mystery cults. "Two chiefest Powers . . . among men there are; divine Demeter-Earth is she, name her which name thou wilt . . . then followeth Semele's Son," states Euripides.[3] And the myths of the life story of Demeter and of Dionysos developed into brilliant passion plays, served as the central theme around which the secret meaning of the rites were woven.

It is generally agreed that the mystery rites were imported into Greece from abroad during the closing centuries of the Prehistoric Era and during the dark ages of its Proto-Historic period. Once established, they experienced a great period in the sixth century, and then again in the Hellenistic Age, when the rise of individualism and the general disrepute into which the worship of the Olympian Gods was held created a vast demand for the spiritual promise held forth by the mystic rites. The closing centuries of the pagan and the opening centuries of the Christian era witnessed their greatest popularity. Perhaps, that popularity will explain the vehemence with which the Early Christian Fathers attacked the mystery religions, because in them they recognized the strongest rival of Christianity. The Eleusinian, the Dionysian, and the Orphic rites were the most important mystery religions of Greece. Of these, the Orphic and the Dionysian seem to have been developed in Thrace and from there were introduced into Greece. Of the two, the Dionysian of a certainty are the older.

THE DIONYSIAN RITES

Our knowledge of the Dionysian rites is derived especially from the many representations of the followers of the God on vases and from various literary sources, chief of which is Euripides' *Bacchae*. Dionysos was the patron God of these rites, and his Theban myth forms their theme. Zeus, the supreme God of the Greeks, the sky and rain God of the Olympian Pantheon, was the father of Dionysos; but his mother was earth-born Semele, the daughter of Cadmus, the founder of Thebes. He was born prematurely when his mother was consumed by the fire and lightnings in the midst of which her lover Zeus appeared to her at her request and at the instigation of Hera. Saved by Zeus from the flames, Dionysos was hidden within "a cleft of the thigh" of the Father of Gods and men. From that hiding place he emerged when his time approached, and when he reached manhood, he set forth in his victorious and irresistible march through all the earth. From Thrace, his worship was introduced to Greece.

173

Dionysos was closely associated with vegetation and especially with the vine and ivy, and was believed to be embodied in various animals, especially the bull. Consequently, he was worshipped as "the incarnation of all natural life and vigor in the fullest and widest sense; as the typical exponent of the most eager enjoyment of life."[4] But life is subject to growth, decay, and death that leads to rebirth; hence, Dionysos was identified with life, death, and immortality. As a matter of fact, it was believed that the God for a time disappeared from among men, to return later and these epiphanies and disappearances of the God correspond to the recurring cycle of birth, death, and rebirth in vegetation life. When away from the circle of the living, the God resided in the world of the dead.

Union with Dionysos, the God of life and the master of death, was the aim and the promise of the Dionysian rites. Both men and women were admitted to those rites, but apparently women were the more ardent worshippers. There was neither a specific time nor an appointed place for the celebration of the mysteries of Dionysos. They were held during the night, for "gloom lends solemnity," and on a mountain top, away from the settlements of men. From the vases and the descriptions of Euripides, we learn that the initiates endeavored to dress like the God. Women, especially, were dressed in long flowing garments, the *bassarae,* over which they wore the sacred "dappled fell of fawn." Ivy leaves crowned their heads, and their hair unfettered was allowed to stream down their shoulders. In the right hand they held the Dionysiac thyrsus, a lance crowned with a pine cone and decked with ivy, and in their left, they held a fawn or serpents. Sometimes even horns were placed over their foreheads, and in Thrace serpents were often entwined in their hair or were used as belts around their waists. Thus dressed like the God, the devotees roamed over the countryside, over mountains and dales, until a suitable mountain top was reached. There in the midst of a wild nature, far from the restrictions of civilized life, in the darkness and by torch light, the worshippers worked themselves up to a high pitch of excitement, to an emotional overflowing which led them to a "divine mania"—"with the God's breath mad," writes Euripides[5]—to the belief that they were possessed by God.

This pitch of emotionalism was developed by night-long wild dances which had nothing in common with the measured movement of the normal Greek dance and of the choral songs. On the vases, we can see the dancers wildly whirling around, tossing and shaking their heads, waving the thyrsus or the torch, striking the ground with it, and jumping wildly in an ecstatic abandon. Thus, they danced to the tune of wild music and to the clashing of bronze cymbals, filling the mountains with their wild shrieks and exultant "Evoes." Gradually as their frenzy mounted, with "foaming lips and eyes that rolled wildly, and reckless madness-clouded soul," they became "maenads", mad ones, believed to be possessed by Dionysos. The magic of that wild revel was felt even by nature: "the hills, the wild things all, were thrilled with ecstasy," writes Euripides.[6]

The belief in their union with Dionysos was further strengthened, and the condition of ecstasy and frenzy was further helped by the drinking of wine. It was not the mere desire of getting drunk that prompted the drinking and the intoxication, but the belief that in taking wine, the devotee was taking in his body the God himself. "He is the God's libation, though a God," explains Euripides. The drinking of wine was indeed a sacramental act which increased the divine "mania" and brought nearer the desired union with the divinity. Even Plato, a bitter foe of drunkenness, condones the Bacchic drinking.[7]

Perhaps, the final stage of the initiation was reached when at the pitch of excitement and divine "mania", the initiates attacked and dismembered with their own hands an animal—a goat, a fawn, or preferably a bull—separated the flesh from the bones and in a frenzy ate particles of raw flesh reeking with blood. The frenzied followers of Dionysos "chased the goat to the death for its blood—for the taste of the feast raw-reeking," and were not considered as fully initiated unless they were able to declare: that they had "fulfilled his red and bleeding feasts."[8] The animal was considered the embodiment of the God, and in eating its live raw flesh, the initiates believed that they were taking in them the God of life. Indeed, it was a sacramental meal which bound Dionysos with his worshipper.

By the excessive stimulation of the senses, the ecstasy of the dance, the sacramental drinking and the partaking of the flesh, the devotee was supposed to attain union with God, to become conscious of a divine contact, to be transformed into a BACCHOS, into a divinized being. In that stage, the worshipper was impervious to pain and capable of performing miracles. "Bacchic maidens," Plato tells us, "draw milk and honey from rivers when they are under the influence of Dionysos but not when they are in their right mind." In a similar fashion, Euripides' Bacchanals performed miracles.[9]

Whether or not these were all the rites celebrated by the followers of Dionysos, it is not possible to determine. But from a passage in the *Bacchae,* we may infer that other ritual acts were added to those known to us, acts which have remained a secret. When Pentheus asked Dionysos "what fashion be these mysteries," the answer of the God was " 'Tis secret, save to the initiates." However, the meaning of the rather primitive ritual, as we know it today, is entirely clear. By means of fasting, roaming in the wilds in darkness and in torch light, even by chewing ivy leaves, the initiates were brought to the proper mood. Through dancing and sacramental drinking, a pitch of emotional excitement was reached that brought about ecstasy, a divine mania, the liberation of the subject from the restraints of normal life, a return to the primitive natural stage, and his possession by the vital urge of life. Through the sacramental meal, a very primitive ritual indeed, Dionysos himself was incorporated into the existence of the devotee, who thus experienced a new spiritual rebirth and became united with his patron God forever.

The divine union, the contact with the divinity, marked the beginning of a new life for the initiate. He became a superior human being, God's own, who, thereafter, lived a dynamic, a Dionysian life. And since Dionysos was not only the Lord of Life but also of Death, the devotee believed that his union with God would continue even after death, that even immortality was within his grasp, since his patron God had attained it, that the joy and exaltation he experienced during his initiation was but a foretaste of the bliss to be experienced both in this life and after death.

As far as we know it, this seems to be the Dionysian doctrine, as it was developed in Thrace, and as it was imported into Greece, where it was established in a modified form. A doctrine and a ritual that appealed strongly to the imagination and the senses of man. It is not possible to determine when the Dionysian rites were introduced into Greece. Homer is acquainted with the orgiastic worship of Dionysos, but at the time of the homeric poems, Dionysos does not seem to belong, as yet, to the Olympian group.[10] The stories of the opposition to his worship belong to the heroic cycle and to the heroic period. Perhaps, we shall be within reasonable grounds if we assumed that in the seventh century the cult began to make itself felt in Greece proper. In spite of the original opposition which the cult met, illustrated by the stories of Lycourgos and Pentheus, it soon became popular; so popular, indeed, that the officials were forced to make room for it in a number of important places. Thus Dionysos was placed at the side of Apollo and was worshipped at Delphi; as Iacchos, he became the third member of the Eleusinian trinity; as the annual spouse of the Basilinna, he was admitted into the state religion of Athens; modified and purged of its orgiastic nature, the worship of Dionysos became the central theme of the Orphics. In the later periods the Dionysian rites spread far and wide and merged with many a mystery cult celebrated all over the Roman Imperial world. Thus the Dionysian rites must be classed among the most dynamic and popular mystery cults of the ancient world.

ORPHIC MYSTERIES

Whether or not Orpheus was a historic figure who charmed man and beast with his music is very difficult, if not impossible, to determine and, fortunately, is beyond the scope of our study. What is of importance to us is the fact that he was accepted by the Greeks to have been the leader of a mystery cult which, after him, was called Orphic, and of a group of devotees who called themselves the Orphics. To them, Orpheus was not a God or his chosen prophet, not a founder of a new religion, but only a reformer, who modified the Dionysian rites by purging away their orgiastic elements, who revealed to his followers the real meaning of those rites, who composed hymns and prayers, and who introduced the celebration of the *"telete"* (initiation) to mankind. The Orphic rites were set forth in a voluminous sacred literature made up of hymns, reputed to have been composed by Orpheus, precepts directed toward the eradication of the original impurity, dogmas and quasi-philosophical speculations dealing with the genesis of Gods and of man and pointing out the way of the latter's redemption. Fortunately, enough of this body of literature has survived to make possible the understanding of the Orphic doctrine.[11]

Dionysos was the great God of the Orphics, but the story of the life of Dionysos Zagreus and not that of the son of Semele formed the sacred theme around which their rites were developed. Zagreus, the horned son of Zeus and of his daughter, Persephone, even as a child, was given to rule the world, was allowed to play with thunderbolts and lightning and to sit on the throne of the supreme deity. The jealousy of Hera brought an end to that happy existence. At her suggestion, and while Zeus was away, the Titans, the personifications of evil in the world, lured the child away from his throne and assaulted him. In vain, Zagreus changed his form to foil their intentions, the pre-ordained had to happen; the Titans killed and dismembered the God and devoured most of his body. Athena managed to save the heart of the child and returned it to Zeus. The Father of Gods and Men was enraged and with his thunderbolts destroyed the impious Titans. Preserving the heart of his beloved son, Zeus gave it to Semele, dissolved in a potion, and so later Zagreus came back to life through Semele in the form of Dionysos. From the ashes of the thunderstruck Titans mankind was created. According to the Orphics, Zagreus was at the end of a cosmogonical development, the story of which explained the formation of the universe, of the life that is to be found in it, and of the Gods who control its destiny. His birth, death, and rebirth, in the form of Dionysos, the son of Semele, reflected the same recurrent fact of growth, decay, and rebirth to be seen in nature and sanctified the belief in reincarnation. The story of Zagreus and of the Titans, furthermore, could be and was developed into an anthropogonic teaching that explained the dualism which the Orphic perceived in the world, the dualism of good and evil, of the body and the soul, of the many and the one in the Greek pantheon, and besides pointed out the means of redemption.

According to the Orphics, man was created from the ashes of the Titans, equated with the evil in this world; therefore, his body is formed of the evil contained in the Titans. But the evil Titans had eaten up Zagreus, whose divine essence is indestructible and immortal; the ashes, therefore, of the Titans, out of which man's body was formed, contained also the divine essence that is immortal and the source of good. Consequently, a tiny particle of

178

that divine essence is contained in every man; it is his soul burdened with the original impurity—corresponding to the original sin—and buried deeply in a body of evil nature. Thus man's nature is dual; it is made up of the Titanic element, responsible for everything that is evil and associated with the body, and of the Dionysian element, the cause of all good, identified with the soul. Between these two elements in man a constant battle is waged. It is the duty of every man to repress the Titanic element in him and give a chance to the Dionysian to assert itself until its final release is obtained. That release of the divine essence, the redemption of the soul, is the utmost and final aim. It can be obtained gradually, and as a result of a series of associations of the soul with a number of different bodies. Thus the Orphic reached his teaching of reincarnation which became an essential part of his dogma and which brought him near the Pythagorean. The belief in the transmigration of the soul was not the invention of the Orphics; it is a belief common to many people. But the Orphics introduced the view that through reincarnation, through its association with a number of bodies and consequently through suffering, the soul is gradually purified from an original impurity.

Life with the body is but a penance which little by little purifies the soul; the descent to Hades but a brief period of freedom for the soul that can be pleasant or very sad; the return to life a continuation of the process of purification. A single life span, even a great many life spans are not adequate for this purification. Plato suggests that three periods of a thousand years each may be required for the process.[12] The alternations of imprisonment in a body and of freedom occur constantly and form the "Great Circle of Necessity." "The wheel of birth," the Orphic believed, "returns ever upon itself in hopeless repetition." The fate of man is indeed hopeless. But there is a way out of this weary process. A release of the soul—an escape from the wheel of physical rebirth—is possible; it could be accomplished not by human means alone but through a divine act of grace. Thus the conception of an original sin, of personal sin, and divine redemption were introduced into the world of beliefs.

To obtain divine assistance, man must become familiar with the writings, the ritual acts and precepts of Orpheus, and finally must be initiated into the Bacchic mysteries revealed by the great leader. What those mysteries were, what were the different stages of initiation are questions that cannot be fully answered in spite of the copious sacred Orphic writings that have been preserved. We may assume that fasting and purifications, sacrifices accompanied by the recital of hymns and prayers, formed the preliminary stages of initiation. According to Nonnus the initiates had to cover their faces with white clay, as the Titans had done when they dismembered Zagreus.[13] This would seem to indicate that a passion play in which the initiates took an active part and which depicted the life, death, and resurrection of Zagreus formed part of the initiation exercises. That the dismemberment of Zagreus was enacted, that a bull, the embodiment of the "horned" God, was torn asunder, that a sacramental feast of raw flesh took place is indicated by Euripides when he makes the members of his chorus in the *Cretans* declare: "Pure has my life been since the day when I became an initiate of Idaean Zeus and herdsman of night-wandering Zagreus, and *having accomplished the raw feasts* and held torches aloft to the Mountain Mother, yea torches of the Kuretes, was raised to the holy estate and called Bacchos."[14] The initiate of the Orphic rites, like his counterpart of the Dionysian, believed that the partaking of the flesh brought him in closer union with God and strengthened the divine essence in himself. After this, the Orphic abstained from the eating of meat.

Perhaps those acts, the most important part of the rites, were followed by the exegesis of sacred formulae which enabled the soul in its descent to Hades to avoid the dangers lurking in the dark domain of Persephone and thus to find its way to the place where it could enjoy a blissful stay.[15] The uninitiated, ignorant of those dangers and lacking proper instruction, met with an unhappy existence in Hades, his soul staying in deep pools of mire. It is interesting to remark that the Orphics developed even rites that could be performed by the living on behalf of the dead and which were supposed to ease the difficulties of departed relatives. The ritualistic acts of the Orphics became so important that they were exploited by shrewd mystery mongers known as *Orpheotelestai*, who traveled from place to place claiming the ability to secure redemption of all those who could pay by simply repeating certain ritualistic acts and by reciting the mysterious formulae. Those mystery mongers, of course, had no relation to the Orphics and were despised and condemned by all.[16]

Important as the Orphic literature, the hymns, the rites, the knowledge of the sacred formulae, and the initiation were, they were not considered sufficient to bring about redemption. This belief is concisely expressed in the famous passage of Plato's *Phaedon* (69C) : "Many are those who bear the wand, but few are those who become Bacchoi." Those who take part in the initiation ceremonies and bear the emblematic thyrsus are indeed many, but few are those who obtain communion with God, who find redemption. Unlike any other mystery religion that promised redemption through initiation alone, the Orphic taught that initiation had to be followed by a "complete Orphic life," a life of asceticism, of self denial, and of purity. Strict precepts were formulated and had to be followed: "Clothed in raiment all white, I shun the birth of men nor touch the coffins of the dead, and keep myself from the eating of food which has had life," repeats the chorus of Euripides' *Cretans*.[17] And so, through purification and ritual, through sacred literature and initiation into the mysteries, through the Orphic life and asceticism, man could hope that the divine essence in him, his soul, by the intervention of divine grace would free itself of the original impurity, would escape the Great Circle of Necessity and the ever recurring weary cycle of rebirth, would attain redemption, and become "God from man." That was the supreme aim of life.

It is impossible to determine where Orphism appeared for the first time, but it seems probable that it started its career in Thrace. In the sixth century, through the instrumentality of Onomakritos, Athens became a great Orphic center. But even before the days of Peisistratos, it was established at Croton in Magna Graecia where it came in contact and perhaps influenced the Pythagoreans. Its followers were banded in Orphic *thiasoi* or brotherhoods unlike the initiates of other mysteries who had no formal ties after the initiation was over. Because of the strictures imposed on its followers, Orphism did not draw as many mystae as the other popular mystery rites, nevertheless, it remained powerful and influential to the end. It seems that in some ways it influenced even Christian ritual, and one wonders whether the many representations of Orpheus in the symbolic Early Christian Art were not the result of an effort to draw

181

Orphics to Christianity. It is interesting to recall that Alexander Severus (222-235) placed in his *lararium* a statue of Christ next to the figures of Orpheus and Abraham.

THE MYSTERIES OF DEMETER AT ELEUSIS

Unlike the Dionysian and the Orphic rites, which could be held at all times and in any place, the mysteries of Demeter were held at a fixed time, in the early fall, and at Eleusis, a small town fourteen miles to the west of Athens. The excavations conducted in 1931 by Dr. K. Kourouniotes, of the Greek Archaeological Society, within the sacred precinct of Eleusis, brought to light an early temple dating from the 15th century B.C., i.e., from the times in which according to tradition, Demeter visited Eleusis and established her rites there.[18] The archaeological evidence seems to prove that in the second half of the Mycenaean Age the rites of Demeter were celebrated at Eleusis. Consequently, those rites appear to be the most ancient of the major mysteries of ancient Greece.

The well-known story of Demeter and Persephone, told in detail by the so-called Homeric Hymn to Demeter,[19] formed the central theme of the mysteries held at Eleusis. Demeter, an earth Goddess and the patron of agriculture and ordered life, in her quest for Persephone, her daughter carried away by Plouto, the God of the nether regions, wandered to Eleusis, accepted the hospitality of the ruler of Eleusis, and undertook the bringing up of Damophoon, his infant son. When her efforts to make the child immortal were interrupted by the curiosity and the fright of the Queen, the Goddess revealed her identity and ordered the Eleusinians to build a temple and an altar for her below their steep citadel. In her sorrow, the Goddess refused to allow the earth to bear fruit and as a result, both men and Gods were threatened with extinction. Zeus was forced to recall Persephone from Hades; but since she had already tasted the seeds of a pomegranate, it was decreed that Persephone was to spend part of the year in Hades with her husband Plouto and the other part with her mother in the upper world. Filled with joy by her reunion with Persephone, Demeter allowed the earth to bear fruit again, commissioned the young Prince Triptolemos to go all over the world and teach humanity how to cultivate the earth, and finally, instructed the leaders of Eleusis into the performance of her rites. Thus, the mysteries of Demeter were introduced to Eleusis by the Goddess herself.

A local cult originally the secret worship of Demeter gradually spread beyond the narrow confines of Eleusis and in historic times, when the village became part of the Athenian Commonwealth, it became a Panhellenic institution. When later on the rites were adopted by the Romans they enjoyed a universal reverence. Throughout the centuries it seems that the rites of Demeter changed but little, the most important innovation being the introduction of Dionysos-Iacchos to the worship in the sixth century.

In contrast to the voluminous literature available for the Orphic rites very few references to the Eleusinian mysteries have been preserved. And the many objects of art and extensive ruins which the work of the Greek archaeologists has brought to light add but little to our knowledge of the rites. The teachings of Demeter were transmitted orally and those entrusted with them and the initiates were pledged to strict secrecy. Dire punishment was meted out to the indiscreet, as the fate of Alcibiades proves.[20] In spite of the many hundreds who in the course of the century were initiated into the Eleusinian mysteries, the secret was well kept and only vague references have been allowed to come down to us. However, we seem to know enough to reconstruct at least the preliminary stages of the rites.

The main celebration was held at Eleusis in the month of Boedromion (September), after the seeds were entrusted to the folds of the cultivated fields. However, candidates for those rites had to take part in the lesser mysteries of Agrae, a suburb of Athens, held six months in advance and in the spring, as a preparatory stage for their initiation. Men, women, and children, even slaves were eligible for candidacy; but it seems that certain strictures were followed in the choice of the neophytes and some were excluded from the rites.[21] When the time for the greater mysteries approached, candidates had to choose sponsors, known as *mystagogoi*, who were supposed to guide them in their preparations. The rites began on the 14th day of Boedromion and continued for nine days. On the 13th day of Boedromion the statue of Iacchos and the sacred relics of Eleusis were brought to Athens by the priests and priestesses of Demeter and were deposited in the Eleusinion below the Acropolis. On the 14th, the ceremonies were officially started by the reading

183

of the "proclamation" (Prorrhesis) by the Hierophant, the great priest of Eleusis, in the famous Painted Stoa of Athens where the neophytes were collected. "Everyone who has clean hands and intelligible speech," "he who is pure from all pollution and whose soul is conscious of no evil and who has lived well and justly," could proceed with the initiation, the rest should abstain.[22] The proclamation was followed by the "katharsis"—by lustrations and purifications of the mystae and their sacrificial pigs in the sea of Phaleron,[23] by the sacrifice of the sucking pig whose blood was sprinkled on the candidates purifying them further, by fasting and consecration.

In the forenoon of the 19th the initiates were started on their famous procession to Eleusis. That procession was one of the most spectacular religious events of the ancient world and in many ways it resembled the processions held through the streets of modern Athens on the night of Good Friday. It was led by the priests of Eleusis, the statue of Iacchos, and the sacred relics of Demeter guarded by her priestesses. Dressed in festal garments, crowned with wreaths of myrtle, holding torches and the bacchos (branches entwined together into a thick club) the initiates rejoicing, singing sacred songs, and calling on Iacchos to lead them on, left Athens and, following the Sacred Way, marched to Eleusis. The outer court of the sanctuary of Demeter at Eleusis was reached around midnight because many a stop had to be made on the way before the altars, shrines, and sanctuaries which flanked the Sacred Way. In the outer court of the sanctuary under a brilliant sky resplendent with ever smiling stars and in the magic of the torch light Iacchos was welcomed back to Eleusis, the sacred relics were replaced in their shrine, and the mystae by the Kallichoron well, consecrated by the dances to Demeter, took part in a celebration of singing and rejoicing whose brilliance is reflected in the verses of Aristophanes.[24]

Our knowledge of the preliminary stages of the Eleusinian mysteries is almost complete; equally complete is our ignorance of the nature of the *"telete"*, of the initiation, which took place during the last two nights of the celebration. It was during those nights that the mystae were allowed into the temple of Demeter, into the Telesterion as it was called, where they were initiated into the famous mysteries of the Goddess. We have the remains of that temple, of the Telesterion of Eleusis. It is a large almost square hall
184

(54 meters in length) whose roof was supported by 42 sturdy columns, and around the sides of which are still to be seen rows of steps on which the mystae stood to follow the rites. We can stand on those steps today, we can people with our imagination the vast space of the hall, we can picture the innermost shrine or the *"anaktoron"* of the Goddess and the upper story as it extended around the central lantern open to the sky; we may even feel the mysticism and imagine the splendor of the place, but we cannot determine the details of the events that took place within the ruined hall, we cannot know what actually transpired within the sanctuary during the nights of the 20th and the 21st of Boedromion.

A great many theories and speculations have been advanced, many a story has been told from Early Christian times to date, but the inescapable fact remains that our knowledge of the mysteries of Demeter remains sadly incomplete. We know that there existed two degrees of initiation, the second and more advanced of which was called the *"epopteia"* and was conferred a year after the first initiation. We know that the officials of Eleusis belonged to certain families who carried their sacred duties from time immemorial and who were called the *hierophant,* the *dadouchos,* or the torch bearer, and the *hierokeryx;* that priestesses of Demeter also lived in the precinct of the Goddess. Finally, we know that the mysteries consisted of three parts: the *"dromena"*—the things that were enacted —the *"deiknymena"*—the things that were shown—and the *"legomena"*—the things which were explained or spoken.

The pageant of the wanderings of Demeter, the story of Persephone, the arrival of Demeter at Eleusis and her experiences there, the reunion of mother and daughter, certainly formed part of the *"dromena."* We may assume that the life story of the Goddess so enacted formed the passion play which aimed not only to repeat the story to the initiates but also to help them participate in the experiences of the Goddess, to give them a share in the distress, the travail, the exaltation, and the joy which attended the loss of Persephone and her reunion with the Mother. "With burning torches Proserpina is sought, and when she is found, the rite is closed with general thanksgiving and a waving of torches," writes Lactantius.[25] The initiates, perhaps, roamed over the precinct looking for the lost Persephone, reached the Parthenion well, where the Goddess was found by the daughters of the ruler of Eleusis, watched the God-

185

dess seated on the "Mirthless stone" sorrowing and in anguish, partook of the potion by which the Goddess was made to break her fast, and finally rejoiced with her for the return of Persephone.

On the red-figured tablet of Niinnion, now sheltered in the Museum of Eleusis, we can see the initiate led by her *"mystagogoi"* to the presence of Demeter and of Persephone seated in their temple. Based on that tablet we may assume that the initiates felt the presence of the Goddesses and even experienced communion with them; that their contact with divinity brought about a spiritual regeneration and filled them with new hope for a blissful existence both in the world of the living and in the domain of Persephone and Plouto. We may further interpret the fortunes of Demeter and Persephone as symbolizing life, death, rebirth and even immortality. But beyond these general facts and assumptions we cannot proceed either in the interpretation or in the establishment of further details of the rites.

Whether or not the passion play as outlined above concluded the *"dromena"* cannot be definitely established. We have seen that the drinking of the sacred potion of Demeter, of the *"Kykeon"* as it was called, formed part of the *"dromena."* And it seems reasonable to assume that a sacramental meal was part of the passion play also; because no other explanation could be offered to the "password of the Eleusinian mysteries" as repeated by Clement of Alexandria: "I have fasted, I have drunk of the barley drink, I have taken things from the sacred chest, having tasted thereof I have placed them into the basket and again from the basket into the chest."[26] As a matter of fact, Foucart and others after him, have assumed that the *"dromena"* were concluded by a holy marriage and even the iconical birth of a child. That assumption is based in the main on the evidence of Asterius, a bishop of the fourth century, who with insinuations was trying to cast discredit on the mysteries. It was Asterius who mentions "the underground chamber and the solemn meeting of the hierophant and the priestess, each with the other alone, when the torches are extinguished, and the vast crowd believes that its salvation depends on what goes on there."[27] However, the latest excavations at Eleusis, in the course of which the sanctuary of Demeter was cleared to the rock level, have proved that no subterranean chambers existed in the temple area. Such chambers were conjured by the biased minds of the

Early Christian writers. It is reasonable therefore to conclude that the purported acts which occurred in those imaginary chambers are equally imaginary. Nor is it known the connection in which was made the statement quoted by Hippolytos, "Brimo, our Lady has born a Holy Child, Brimos,"[28] on which is based the assumption of the birth of a child from the union of the priest and the priestess of Eleusis. In view of the high spiritual level on which the great mysteries were held and the lack of corroborating evidence, we are inclined to believe that a "holy marriage" and the "birth of a child" were foreign to the rites of Demeter.

We are in greater difficulty when we try to determine the nature of the *"deiknymena"* and of the *"legomena."* How important those elements might have been can be inferred from the fact that the advanced degree of initiation, the *"epopteia,"* was attained solely by the revelation—followed by contemplation—of the Eleusinian *sacra,* exhibited to the candidates by the hierophant in a striking manner.[29] As a matter of fact, the title of this high dignitary of Eleusis, hierophant, means he who displays the *hiera.* Apparently those sacred objects were kept in the private shrine of Demeter, known as the *"anaktoron"* and perhaps located in the center of the great Telesterion.

From a rhetorical fragment preserved under the name of Sopatros, we can glimpse the importance of the *"legomena."*[30] In that fragment we read that a youth in his dream was initiated into the mysteries; he had followed the passion play with care but was unable to hear the *"legomena,"* or the *"hieroi logoi,"* recited by the hierophant, and because of that, he could not be considered as properly initiated. The importance of the *"deiknymena"* and of the *"legomena"* may further be inferred from the ritual acts, revelations, and doctrines of the Greek Orthodox and the Roman Catholic churches of our day. It is highly possible, indeed, that acts such as the elevation of the sacred host and others were borrowed by the Christians from the Eleusinian rites.

Perhaps we should add that the *"telete"* was characterized by a dazzling splendor. The Eleusinian inscriptions speak of the "holy night, clearer than the light of the sun." On the vases we see the priests of Eleusis resplendent in their ceremonial vestments. Plutarch has given us the impression made on the initiates by the opening of the shrines when he stated, "He who once enters into philosophy and sees the great light, as when shrines are open to view, is silent and awestruck."[31]

However uncertain we may be as to the nature of the mysteries, of one thing we must be and are very certain: the initiates returned from their pilgrimmage to Eleusis full of joy and happiness, with the fear of death diminished and with the hope of a better life in the world of shadows strengthened. "Thrice happy are they of mortals who have looked upon these rites ere they go to Hades' home; for over there these alone have life; the rest have naught but ill," exclaims Sophocles; and to these words Pindar responds with equal exaltation.[32]

When we read these and other similar statements written by the great or nearly great of the ancient world, by the dramatists and the thinkers, when we picture the magnificent buildings and monuments constructed at Eleusis by great political figures like Peisistratos, Kimon, Pericles, Hadrian, Antoninus Pius and others we cannot help but feel that the mysteries at Eleusis were not an empty, childish affair devised by shrewd priests to fool the peasant and the ignorant, but a philosophy of life which possessed a deep and great meaning and which perhaps imparted a modicum of truth to the yearning human soul. And that feeling is strengthened when we read in Cicero that Athens had given nothing to the world more excellent or divine than the Eleusinian mysteries![33]

The rites at Eleusis were held for more than *two thousand* years; for two thousand years, therefore, civilized humanity was sustained and ennobled by those rites. When Christianity conquered the Mediterranean world, the rites of Demeter, having perhaps fulfilled their mission to humanity, came to an end. The "bubbling spring" of hope and inspiration that once existed by the Kallichoron Well became dry and the world has turned to other living sources for sustenance. The doctrine which inspired the world for so long was gradually forgotten, and its secrets were buried with its last hierophant.

NOTES

1. The term is not so appropriate and is somewhat misleading since those rites as a rule did not demand the exclusive allegiance of their adherents nor did they exclude the simultaneous acceptance by them of

other Gods and religious practices. However, the term has become so well established that we are using it in the present discussion with the understanding that it does not exactly fit our need.

2. S. Angus, *The Mystery Religions and Christianity* (1925) 39 ff.

3. *Bacchae*, vv. 274-275. The quotations are taken from A. S. Way's translation of the tragedy in the Loeb edition.

4. E. Rohde, *Psyche*, English translation by W. B. Hillis (1925) Vol. II, 285.

5. *Bacchae*, V. 1094.

6. *Ibid.*, V. 726.

7. *Ibid.*, V. 284. Plato, *Laws*, 775: drunkenness was excusable "on the occasions of the festivals of the God of Wine."

8. Euripides' *Bacchae*, vv. 141-142, 736-747. *Fragmenta*, 475, quoted from Porphyry, *De Abstinentia*, IV, 19.

9. *Ion*, 534A. *Bacchae*, vv. 704-711.

10. Cf. *Iliad*, VI, 132 ff.; XIV, 323 ff.

11. For the Orphic Literature see Bibliography, Abel, Kern, Lobeck, Taylor. For the Orphic tablets see A. Dietrich, *Nekyia* (1913).[2]

12. *Phaedros*, 249. ch. *Republic*, X, 614 ff.

13. *Dionysiaca*, XXVII, 204, 228.

14. *Cretans*, in Porphyry, *De Abstin.*, IV, 19.

15. For instance we read on the gold Orphic plate from Petelia, dating from the end of the fourth century B. C.:

"Thou shalt find to the left of the House of Hades a spring,
And by the side thereof standing a white cypress.
To this spring approach not near.
But thou shalt find another, from the Lake of Memory
Cold water flowing forth, and there are guardians before it."

These guardians would give the soul to drink refreshing water and dispatch it to the proper place "and thereafter among the other heroes thou shalt have lordship." (W. K. Guthrie, *Orpheus and Greek Religion*, 172-173.)

16. *Republic*, II, 364e.

17. *Cretans, loc. cit.*, IV, 19.

18. For the excavations see K. Kourouniotes, *Eleusis* (1934); *Deltion* (1930-1931, 1931-1932); *Archiv fuer Religionswiss*, XXXII, 52 ff. Kourouniotes-Travlos, *Deltion* (1934-1935) 54 ff. Kourouniotes-Mylonas, *Amer. Journ. of Archaeol.*, XXXVII (1933) 271 ff. F. Noack, *Eleusis* (1927). G. Mylonas, *The Hymn to Demeter and Her Sanctuary at Eleusis* (1942).

19. See T. W. Allen, W. R. Halliday, E. E. Sikes, *The Homeric Hymns* (1936, 2nd edit.).

20. Plutarch, *Alcibiades*, XIX-XXII.

21. For the admission of slaves see *Fragmenta Comicorum Graecorum*,

III, 626 (Meinecke); *Ephemeris Archaeologike* (1883) Pl. 10, l. 71. For the rejection of Apollonius of Tyana, see Philostratus, *Vita Apoll.*, IV, 18.

22. Origen, *Contra Celsum*, III, 59.

23. The call of the hierokeryx, of a minor official of the Eleusinian Demeter, "Halade Mystae—to the Sea O, Mystae" became emblematic of the Eleusinian rites.

24. *Frogs*, 324 ff.

25. *Institutiones Divinae, Epitome*, 23.

26. *Protrepticus*, II, 21.

27. Foucart, *Les Mystères d'Éleusis*, 475 ff. Asterius *Encomium in Sanctos Martyres*, 113 B.

28. Hippolytus, *Philosophoumena*, V. 1, 8.

29. According to Hippolytus, *loc. cit.*, the "great, marvellous, and most perfect mystery" revealed to the epoptae was a "reaped corn-stalk."

30. *Rhetores Graeci*, VIII, 110 (Walz).

31. *Ephemeris Archaeologike* (1883) 79. Plutarch, *De profectus in virtute*, 10.

32. Sophocles, *Fragmenta*, 719; Pindar, *Fragmenta*, 121 (Oxford ed.). Cf. also Isocrates, *Panegyricus*, 28; Plato, *Phaedo*, 69C., etc. Farnell, *Cult of the Greek States*, III, 197.

33. *De Legibus*, II, 14.

BIBLIOGRAPHY

E. ABEL, *Orphica* (Leipzig, 1885).

SAMUEL ANGUS, *The Mystery Religions and Christianity* (New York, 1925).

M. BRILLANT, *Les Mystères d'Éleusis* (Paris, 1920).

F. CUMONT, *Religions Orientales Dans Le Paganisme Romain* (Paris, 1909²).

K. H. E. DE JONG, *Das Antike Mysterienwesen* (Leiden, 1919²).

ROBERT EISLER, *Orphisch-Dionysische Mysterien-Gedanken* (Leipzig, 1925).

EURIPIDES, *Bacchae*, Loeb Classical Library, Translated by Arthur S. Way (New York, 1912).

LEWIS R. FARNELL, *Cults of the Greek States* (Oxford, 1907).

PAUL FOUCART, *Les Mystères d'Eleusis* (Paris, 1914).

W. K. C. GUTHRIE, *Orpheus and Greek Religion* (London, 1935).

JANE ELLEN HARRISON, *Prolegomena to the Study of Greek Religion* (Cambridge, 1903).

O. KERN, *Orphicorum Fragmenta* (Berlin, 1922).

C. A. LOBECK, *Aglaophamus* (Leipzig, 1829).

R. MACCHIORO, *Zagreus* (Bari, 1920).

VICTOR MAGNIEN, *Les Mystères d'Éleusis* (Paris, 1938²).

G. E. MYLONAS, *The Hymn of Demeter and Her Sanctuary at Eleusis* (St. Louis, 1942).

MARTIN P. NILSSON, *A History of Greek Religion* (Oxford, 1925).

FERDINAND NOACK, *Eleusis, die Baugeschichthiche Entwicklung des Heiligtumes* (Leipzig, 1927).

D. PHILIOS, *Eleusis, ses Mystères, ses Ruines, et son Musée* (Paris, 1896).

ERWIN ROHDE, *Psyche,* English translation by W. B. HILLIS (New York & London, 1925).

T. TAYLOR, *The Mystical Hymns of Orpheus* (London, 1896).

HAROLD R. WILLOUGHBY, *Pagan Regeneration* (Chicago, 1929).

THE INHABITED WORLD

Charles Robinson is professor of Classics in Brown University, Providence, R. I., and professor of Greek Literature and Archaeology in the American School of Classical Studies at Athens (1934-35 and 1948). As this essay is being prepared for the press he is in Athens where he is a member of the commission supervising the excavations of the Athenian Agora and a member of the committee which is now engaged in the erection of the museum (a project underwritten by the Rockefeller Foundation). He has also carried on work of excavations with the American School at Corinth, Nemea, Phlius and Prosymma. A member of many learned societies and committees, he is in contact with the most recent findings in the field of the ancient classics.

His publications include: "The Ephemerides of Alexander's Expedition" (1932); "Hellenic History" (with G. W. Botsford, 3rd ed., 1948); "Alexander the Great" (1947); "A Report on Greece", for the U. S. War Dept. (1943); and contributor to "Corinth", vol. 1 (1932), to "Classical Studies Presented to Edward Capps" (1936), to "The Greek Political Experience" (1941) and to encyclopedias and philological and archaeological journals.

He was born in Princeton, New Jersey, in 1900. His education began at Phillips Andover Academy and then a B.A. from Princeton in 1922. He was awarded an M.A. as graduate-scholar in classics by Princeton in 1923. He has held fellowships with the Academy in Rome and at Princeton and has taught at Brown University since 1928. In 1945 Brown honored him with an M.A. degree.

Editor

THE INHABITED WORLD*

CHARLES ALEXANDER ROBINSON, JR.

IT IS an arresting fact that the first person in European history to dream of the brotherhood of man was brought up in Plato's belief that all barbarians (non-Greeks) were enemies of the Greeks by nature, and was actually taught by Aristotle that all barbarians were slaves by nature, especially those of Asia. It was the monumental triumph of Alexander of Macedon, later called the Great, to outgrow this background while still young—and he was never more than young—and at the same time to transform the world both physically and mentally. Alexander's challenge to posterity is not that he created a new religion which has long since been forgotten and to which, perhaps, we should now return, for he founded neither a church nor a dogma nor a school of philosophy; it is rather that, by uniting great dreams with great acts, he produced a new world and a new conception of the world, the world of common interests.

The centuries which culminated in Alexander had divided the world into a few Greeks, on the one hand, and, on the other, into myriads of barbarians; and yet, Alexander's life made it possible for the Cynics, not long afterward, to say, "Make the world your city." Or as Isocrates, in speaking of Athens, once put it: "So far has our city left the rest of mankind behind her in thought and expression that her citizens have become the teachers of others, and have made the name Hellenes a mark no longer of birth but of intellect, and have caused those to be called Hellenes who share in our culture rather than in our descent."

This revolution in the intellectual history of mankind—the most momentous since Thales had displaced the gods by natural causa-

* The author thanks E. P. Dutton and Company for permission to base some of his remarks on his *Alexander the Great* (1947).

195

tion—was not begotten, unaided, by one individual; Alexander simply determined its form and character and channel, and thereby prepared a congenial climate in which the Roman Empire and the Christian Church were to grow. His revolutionary life and ideas sprang, as must always be the case, from the social and political atmosphere of his day, from the very fact that the central idea in Hellenism—the idea of the city-state with all its traditional associations and responsibilities, religious, social and civic—had been undermined by the Peloponnesian War and the fall of Athens. Then, when Sparta in turn failed to unite the Greeks, and when this failure was followed by that of Thebes under Epaminondas, men began to question the fundamental structure of society. There appeared, as a result, two new, central ideas in Hellenism, the individual and the human race, which were now in conflict, now in sympathy. The city-state had made possible boundless versatility in literature, art and philosophy and, through the republican form of government which the Greeks devised in endless variety, had assured to the citizens of many states liberty and democracy; but the need now, in the fourth century B.C., with storm clouds gathering on the Macedonian horizon to the north, was to merge narrow ideas of sovereignty in a broader union before an outsider brought it about by force.

The literature and art attest the vitality of the fourth century— this was the time of Plato, Aristotle and Praxiteles—but nevertheless society as a whole presents the picture of apparent disintegration. Henceforth, wider group loyalties seem to be subordinated to narrower ones; and the individual, who through sophistic training had learned to question all authority, was in revolt against the group. An economic depression, the growing attractiveness of a mercenary career, the interference of the Persian king in Greek affairs, the birth of class consciousness, engendered by the growth of culture and luxury and the concentration of people in cities, further aggravated the situation. In Athens and elsewhere it was felt by many that inequality of property was the root of all evil, for which the only remedy was communism. What was needed more than anything else was emigration, a resumption of the colonization of the archaic period. At the same time, however, the broadening humanity of the day, the waning interest in local politics, and the aversion of cultured citizens to military life meant the decline

ot tne city-state and the development of a larger and more liberal
state-system, the preparation of a transition from regional to world
politics, from racial to cosmopolitan culture.

The fourth century accordingly saw a recrudescence of old
leagues and the birth of new ones, which in the issue proved but
half-hearted answers to the irresistible forces of the day. Plato and
Aristotle, though they lived in the midst of one of the deepest crises
in human history, continued to preach the need of reforming the
city-state and refused to explore the possibilities of a new system
such as federalism. Demosthenes, the implacable foe of Macedon
and champion of Greek freedom, stood for the self-government and
self-sufficiency of the city-state and harked back to a supposed
Golden Age. Against him were arrayed the propertied classes, led by
Aeschines, who were now ready to accept the arbitrary rule of an
alien state, if that was necessary to stop social revolution. Still others
agreed with Isocrates that the Greeks, instead of continuing their
fratricidal strife, should make war upon a common foe. These confusing and confused ideas merged in the popular thinking of the
day and developed into a conviction that the Greeks should unite
under a king for a foreign war. It was understood that Persia was
the common enemy, while the Macedonian monarchy appealed to
some as the ideal instrument of union.

Here, then, was a world full of brilliant men, but a world nonetheless divided and at war, for which Philip and his son, Alexander,
were to find unsuspected and greater opportunity. So accustomed
have we ourselves become to the perpetuation of evil and the piling
of one mistake on top of its familiar predecessor—to the very fact,
that is to say, of the apparent impossibility of thinking our burning issues through from a new standpoint to a really new conclusion—that, did we not know the answer, we would assert that
Philip's conquest of the Greeks meant no more than an increase
in the size of his own dynastic state. How dared he, when it had
never been done before, to unite the Greeks in a Panhellenic union
which can only be described as a constitutional monarchy with a
representative assembly? And in like vein we would declare that the
son, after his conquest of the Persian Empire (essentially the known
civilized world), could do no more than substitute Hellenic for
Oriental despotism!

Alexander's early death, before the age of thirty-three, was a

197

tragedy, for it robbed him of the opportunity of developing his ideas of world government. No doubt he intended that the peoples of his empire should assume their share in working out the pattern; the measure of freedom and the details of government would vary from area to area and depend in part upon the condition of civilization of the individual peoples. This variety would have been but the reflection of his own position in the state, for, somewhat in the fashion of the British monarch of a later day, he was at once the constitutional king of Macedon and commander-in-chief of the League of Corinth, the suzerain of Indian rajahs and the adopted son of a Carian queen, the Great King of the former Persian Empire and the "ally" of the Greek cities of Asia Minor, a god in Greece and Egypt.

Still, the outline of Alexander's chief thoughts was there. He planned a world state, as he had settled his own relation to that state; from the beginning he had used barbarians in administration and army; he had proclaimed universal brotherhood, and had advocated one common, Greek culture and the fusion of races. As Plutarch so passionately remarked of the mass marriages with barbarians: "At the sight of these marriages I should have cried out for joy, 'O dullard Xerxes, stupid fool that spent so much fruitless toil to bridge the Hellespont! This is the way that wise kings join Asia with Europe; it is not by beams nor rafts, nor by lifeless and unfeeling bonds, but by the ties of lawful love and chaste nuptials and mutual joy in children that they join the nations together.' " And, finally, Alexander had arranged personal deification: a meaningless convention in Egypt, but a convenient, *political* device in Greece—a divided land long accustomed to many and various gods— if other, more normal methods of rule failed. His aim clearly was to unify the empire and bind it together as a social, political and economic whole—or, as he expressed it, he bade all men to consider as their fatherland the whole inhabited earth, where they would have concord and peace and community of interests, and he further pledged himself to render all upon earth subject to one law of reason and one form of government, that of justice.

Although Alexander's developing belief in the essential sameness of all people dates from his first year in Asia, it is not till a decade later, in the year before his death (323 B.C.), that our sources first reveal a ringing and vivid public statement by him.

THE INHABITED WORLD

The occasion was a misunderstanding between himself and his troops, and he sealed the reconciliation by a banquet for 9,000 persons. At his own table sat Macedonians, Persians, Greek seers, Median Magi, and distinguished representatives of the other peoples of the empire and, after dinner, they all drew wine from a great *krater*, or mixing bowl, the Greek seers and the Magi commencing the ceremony, and then the whole 9,000 together made one libation at the sound of a trumpet. It was this *krater* that Alexander had in mind when he said that he had a kingly mission from the deity to be the harmonizer and reconciler of the world, uniting and mixing men's lives and customs and marriages as in a loving cup. Then Alexander prayed for partnership in the empire and for unity and concord (in the Greek, *Homonoia*, a union of hearts) in a joint commonwealth where all peoples were to be partners rather than subjects—a prayer that marks a revolution in human thought. Alexander's dream of the brotherhood of man, a dream of peace and union between Greek and barbarian, was a clear and ennobling restatement of his considered policy these many years, that mankind should contemplate not exclusive, "national" societies, but universalism, the idea of the *oecumene,* or "inhabited world," where all men are indeed sons of one Father.

If Alexander's dream of the brotherhood of man took root but slowly after his death, his idea of the "inhabited world" found immediate acceptance. In the new Hellenistic Age man thought of himself more and more as a member of a world society, a society in which there might be (and were) sharp differences, but in which a common, Greek culture nonetheless acted as a natural bond. This culture was different from that of Periclean days, for it was affected both by the rapid rise of the ordinary man and by close contact with Orientalism. The world was new, and it is often said that, because Alexander's empire fell into three large pieces on his death, his conquests had gone for naught. But the great fact of history is that for three centuries, until the coming of Rome, this world was ruled along western Hellenic lines. The new conception of the world, no less than the Hellenization of Western Asia, are the greatest results of Alexander's life; he is, without question, the most important European in history, for he set the course which Western man has followed ever since.

In the vast new world, man emerged as an individual; he could

199

live anywhere, and, with the development of mass production and far-flung trade routes, new lands came within his orbit—Egypt, India, Turkestan, Iran, China, Arabia, Central Africa, Western Africa and Western Europe. We are particularly struck by the complexities and contradictions, in fact by the very modernity, of the Hellenistic Age. The scientific spirit and a keen desire to understand the universe flourished at this time; much labor was spent on editing the writers of the past; but superstition and ignorance remained, and the literature and art, while often interesting and sometimes pleasing, frequently strove for mere effect. Side by side with luxury and sophistication existed poverty and slavery. The huge new cities of the Age and the widening horizon meant both wealth and social revolution.

The Hellenistic Age was a period of experiment, novelties and individualism. Something had to be found to take the place of the city-state of old, with all its obligations and privileges; clubs and associations might be a poor substitute, but they satisfied man's longing in part. The clubs were generally of a social and religious nature and were usually small, though the societies of Dionysiac artists were as large as they were popular. But the Greek found the study of philosophy particularly congenial, because the gods of Olympus no longer satisfied intellectuals. Any generalization, however, would be dangerous, for Fortune was worshipped by many persons of modest education, and the masses still clung to their ancestral religion. Kings and cities paid at least lip-service to the old religion, and it is fair to say that all Greeks, in one way or another, associated themselves with it, for it served to set them apart from the barbarian world. But the new forces of the day were weakening the traditional religion, as is amply proved by the growth of king-worship and the increasing appeal of mystery cults, the cult of Eleusis, Orphic cults, astrology and magic. The eastern religions, too, made some progress among the Greeks, especially among the offspring of mixed marriages, and in particular two Egyptian cults appealed to many Greeks: that of Serapis, the guardian of sailors as he became, whose worship was carried far and wide; and that of Isis, who was very popular because of her promises of future bliss. Among Orientals, however, the Olympic religion made no headway —except among those who, hoping for personal advancement, took over the externals of Hellenism—for the eastern religions were of great antiquity and as a rule were given complete tolerance by Alexander's successors.

But of course Alexander's ideas were never wholly lost. His dream of the brotherhood of man, for example, found its natural fruition and finest expression as much in St. Paul's stirring vision of a world in which there shall be "neither Greek nor Jew, barbarian nor Scythian, bond nor free," as in the realization of a Universal Church comprising Jews, Greeks and Latins, "Parthians and Medes and Elamites and the dwellers in Mesopotamia." The pity of it all is, and this may be one of the great tragedies in the history of man, that world rule was finally given to the Romans rather than to the Greeks, with their sensitiveness and imagination and insistence on the primacy of reason, for, had not Rome intervened, the Greeks might ultimately have given the Mediterranean not only a common culture, but also a form of government ensuring unity, freedom and permanence. Still, it was the new culture of the Hellenistic Age that civilized Rome and facilitated her creation of a world state and Christianity's conquest of that state. As such, it is Alexander's monument, while his dreams have been, and still are, a challenge to humanity to substitute the idea of the solidarity of the world, and with it the dignity of the individual and his labor, for Aristotelian narrowness and strife.

BIBLIOGRAPHY

H. Berve, *Das Alexanderreich auf prosopographischer Grundlage,* 2 vols. (Munich, 1926).

V. Ehrenberg, *Alexander and the Greeks.* Trans. by R. F. von Velsen (Oxford, 1938).

W. S. Ferguson, *Greek Imperialism* (New York, 1913).

W. Jaeger, *Demosthenes* (Berkeley, 1938).

W. Kolbe, *Die Weltreichsidee Alexanders des Grossen* (Freiburg im Breisgau, 1936).

A. D. Nock, *Hellenistic Religion—The Two Phases* (Aberdeen, 1939).

G. Radet, *Alexandre le Grand* (Paris, 1931).

C. A. Robinson, Jr., *Alexander the Great* (New York, 1947).

————, *Alexander the Great and the Oecumene.* Hesperia, Supplement VIII (1949).

M. Rostovtzeff, *The Social and Economic History of the Hellenistic World,* 3 vols. (Oxford, 1941).

FORGOTTEN RELIGIONS

W. W. TARN, *Alexander the Great,* 2 vols. (Cambridge, 1948).

————, *Alexander the Great and the Unity of Mankind.* Proceedings of the British Academy XIX (1933).

————, *Hellenistic Civilisation,* 2nd ed. (London, 1930).

U. WILCKEN, *Alexander the Great.* Trans. by G. C. RICHARDS (New York, 1932).

————, *Die letzten Pläne Alexanders des Grossen* (Berlin, 1937).

MITHRAISM

The essays on Mithraism, Manichaeism and Mazdakism which appear here are placed together to show a connected religious history of Iran. Dr. Taraporewala, author of these essays, is a singularly resourceful scholar in that he is at home in so many ancient languages and thus possesses an intimate acquaintance with the religious literature expressed by them. Only recently, he has translated the Gathas (Songs) of Zarathushtra (Bombay, 1947) and given breath to them by his own faith in and understanding of Zoroastrianism.

He was born in 1884 at Haiderabad, Deccan. In 1903 he won his B.A. at the University of Bombay; from 1904 to 1909 he studied in London and then was called to the bar at Gray's Inn. He was awarded the Government of India Sanskrit scholarship in 1911 which brought him to the University of Cambridge and then to Germany where he later won his Ph.D. degree at the University of Würzburg. After a period of teaching in India he became, in 1917, professor of comparative philology at the University of Calcutta. In 1930 and for ten years he was principal of the M. F. Cama Athornan Institute, Andheri and the following two years director of Deccan College Post-Graduate and Research Institute, Poona, until his retirement in 1942.

His many published papers and books have dealt with a wide range of subjects: Indian Ideals of Education, the Parsis, Sanskrit Dipthongs, ancient philology, the religion of Zarathushtra. American readers have become acquainted with him through his recent contribution on "Zoroastrianism" in the book "Religion in the Twentieth Century" (New York, The Philosophical Library) published in 1948.

Editor

MITHRAISM

IRACH J. S. TARAPOREWALA

IN CONSIDERING the history of any religion we get, first of all, either authenticated Scriptures compiled by the followers of that Faith or else descriptions left by contemporary outsiders narrating how these doctrines and beliefs affected them. In the second place, there is a certain amount of what might be called "floating tradition" and folklore embodied in the varied rites and ceremonies practised by the believers in that Faith. And thirdly, there is a certain amount of "sacred" or "mystic" tradition and teaching known to only a few, and which was jealously guarded from the "profane" who were likely to scoff at it. This "sacred," and therefore secret, lore was known only to a few initiates, but in order that the memory of these may not be completely lost most of this secret teaching was embodied in some sort of symbolic ritual which could be performed openly before the public. This open ceremonial exhibited symbolically some fundamental truths of human life, such as the progress of the soul toward God, the ultimate defeat of evil and untruth, etc. Long after the religion to which these ceremonies belonged had passed away these mysteries persisted in surviving and even attached themselves to some newer Faith that had replaced the older one.

The history of the religion of Mithra illustrates these points. Here we find a very ancient "mystic" tradition attaching itself successively to various Faiths in various lands and adapting itself to the needs of the people who had made it their own.

Mithra was an ancient Aryan Deity, closely associated with the Supreme Being—Asura Varuna. Varuna implied the all-embracing Heavens and Mithra was the Heavenly Light, and so Mithra was invoked together with the all-embracing Father of All, Varuna. Both in the Zoroastrian Avesta and in the Hindu Vedic Hymns

205

Mithra* is invoked as the Lord of Heavenly Light. He is the Light, *not* the Sun; the Sun is his physical vehicle. In Zoroastrian ritual the Litany to Mithra is always recited after the Litany addressed to Khurshed (who is the physical Sun). Mithra is ever awake and on the watch. He has a thousand ears and ten thousand eyes. With these he watches over all creatures, hearing all, seeing all. None can deceive him. Hence he is Lord of truth and loyalty. And he is invoked whenever oaths are taken. He guarantees all contracts and promises and punishes all who violate their bond or break their plighted word. In Iran such offenders were called *Mithro-Druj* (sinners against Mithra), and they were regarded as among the worst sinners. Being light he also represents heat and life, and so he is also called "the Lord of wide pastures" and he is "the Lord of Fecundity". He giveth increase, he giveth abundance, he giveth herds, he giveth progeny and life. He poureth forth the waters and causeth plants to grow. He bestoweth upon his worshippers health of body, wealth and well-dowered offspring. And besides these material comforts he also bestows peace, wisdom and glory. As Lord of Light he is the foe of darkness and of vice and impurity. He leads the hosts of Heaven against the hordes of the Abyss. In a sense Mithra is the prototype of the Archangel Michael.

In India, Mitra is always associated with Varuna. These are the Great Twin Brothers, and here too these two are clearly regarded as two aspects of the ETERNAL LIGHT, and all through the Vedic Hymns while Varuna is worshipped as the Supreme Head of the Aryan pantheon, Mitra has retained his position beside him as his Twin Brother.

In Iran, however, Zoroaster emphasized particularly the complete and absolute supremacy of the Aryan Asura-Varuna under the name of Ahura. So naturally his Twin Brother Mithra could not be regarded as his co-equal. In fact Mithra is not mentioned even once in the Gathas of Zoroaster, because his Twin Brother, Ahura, has concentrated within himself all the attributes of both. But in later Avesta Literature Mithra is again associated with Ahura, the two being invoked together as two Lords, imperishable, exalted and holy. Still on the whole in later Zoroastrian theology, Khurshed (the Sun) is the closest associate of Mithra. An important

---

* It may be noted that the name is spelled *Mitra* in the Vedas, but *Mithra* in the Avesta.

function of Mithra in later Zoroastrian theology is as a Judge of the departed souls in which office he is associated with Rashnu (Justice). And as "Lord of wide pastures" he is associated with Aredvi-sura Anahita, the Deity who presides over Waters.

From a very early period the Iranian people came into intimate contact with both the Babylonians and the Egyptians. So naturally there came into the Aryan Religion of Iran "foreign influences" from both these nations. Both these countries—Babylon and Egypt —depended for their prosperity and their well-being upon the great rivers, Euphrates-Tigris and the Nile. The annual floods of these rivers at the beginning of each spring would naturally give rise to the spring-festival which would be closely associated with the worship of the Waters and of the Deity of Fecundity. In Babylon we thus see the Ishtar-cult established and in Egypt the Isis-cult. In Babylon the Ishtar-cult was early united with astrology and magic, while in Egypt the Isis-cult got amalgamated with the mysteries of the "Perfect Man", Osiris. We thus find in Achaemenian Iran the cult of the Lord of Fecundity amalgamating with the worship of Anahita the Deity of the Waters. The former also represents the Father-aspect of Nature while Anahita represents the Mother-aspect of Nature, which was regarded as purifying the seeds of all males and the wombs of all females so as to ensure a strong progeny.

The Hittites, who too had close contacts with Babylon and Egypt, also worshipped Mitra together with other Aryan Deities. There is reason to believe that the Hittites served as a connecting link in the development of the Mithra-cult in Achaemenian Iran.

There was also a cross-current flowing from Greece, where we find a closely similar spring-cult of Dionysios and Demeter. This cult seems to have been actually practised in prehistoric Crete also. In Greece this cult of Dionysios-Demeter also got connected with the spring festivities, which were celebrated every year with great rejoicings and were often accompanied by a considerable amount of lewdness, loose talk and sexual orgies.

India too had the festival of Love (the Madanotsava), which is the spring-festival described in Classical Sanskrit works. It was closely associated with the worship of the Lord of Love and Fecundity (Madana) and his spouse, the Spirit of Fertility (Rati). In later times this cult united itself with the cult of the Divine Cowherd, Krishna, and his milkmaids, particularly Radha. This last has continued down to the present day and is celebrated each year all over India as the Holi festival, on the first full-moon day in spring. The lewd songs and coarse gestures and the foul language used on these occasions are all relics of the ancient festival of the Lord of Fecundity and Love.

So in Iran in the later Achaemenian days we find the worship of Mithra steadily growing up. In the earlier Achaemenian Inscriptions only Ahura-Mazda is invoked as "the greatest of the Deities", but in later Inscriptions the names of Mithra and Anahita are also invoked in addition to Ahura-Mazda. All three are invoked that they may bless the imperial family and the realm. We are told by Herodotus and other historians that there was a magnificent temple of Anahita in Iran, where her image had been installed. In one of the later Avesta texts (Yasht v) we find a detailed description of the personal appearance of Anahita, and of her superb dress and ornaments, all of which go to support the statement of the historians.

At the end of the Achaemenian period in Iran the religion of the imperial family as well as that of the masses was certainly Zoroastrianism. There was, however, a considerable admixture of Babylonian magic and star-cult and also of the various cults of Greece and Egypt. And the Mithra-Anahita cult was a very strong influence among the masses. During the days of Achaemenian supremacy Iranian Zoroastrians had settled in every corner of the vast empire and even beyond its limits. And wherever they went their beliefs and their customs were carried with them. The conquest of Alexander strengthened still further the Greek influences which had come over Iranian culture. And we find among the Greek writers of that period a clear tendency to see the close resemblances between their own Deities and those of Iran. In fact the Greeks give to the Iranian Deities the corresponding Greek names.

The memories of Achaemenian greatness continued undimmed for many years. The various dynasties that arose in Pontus and elsewhere after the break up of Alexander's Empire all claimed their descent from the ancient line of Cyrus and Darius and tried to keep alive the ancient Achaemenian beliefs and customs. The Mithra-cult was thus kept up in all the kingdoms that were then founded in Asia Minor. As a proof of this we may mention the fact that a large number of the rulers of these new kingdoms, as also of the

208

Arsacid dynasty that followed, bore the name of Mithradates (Mihrdad). At one period (about 130 B.C.) all the rulers in Iran bore this one name.

Rome now comes upon the world-stage as a great power in the West. And at one period she and Iran shared the whole of the known world between them. An ambassador of Iran at the court of Galerius was quite correct when he declared that these two Empires were as "the two eyes of the human race". As the Roman power began to extend eastward the influence of the West upon Iran became more and more pronounced, and similarly the influence of Iran upon Rome began to be felt in greater measure. At first Rome came into touch with merely the fringe of Iranian culture, through the Iranians who had settled down in Asia Minor, but by the first century of the Christian era the contact between the two had become very close and intimate. The petty Iranian dynasties in Anatolia and Commogene disappeared before the advancing Romans. And wherever the Romans penetrated they constructed a network of roads joining the remoter towns with the headquarters. So we find that by the time of Trajan (98-117 A.D.) Rome and Parthia were facing each other across the Euphrates and Roman legions were scattered from the Euphrates to Armenia and the whole of Pontus and Cappadocia had come into intimate contact with the Latin world. In their turn the Roman legions were influenced by Iranian ideas and culture and when they were transferred from Asia Minor to other provinces of the Roman Empire these legionnaries carried Iranian ideas with them to every corner of Europe.

The spread of Mithraism through the Roman Empire began definitely with the conquest of Cilicia by Pompey in 67 B.C. Plutarch has recorded that Pompey "performed strange sacrifices on Olympus, a volcano of Lycia, and practised occult rites, among others those of Mithra". The lands conquered by Pompey resembled the original homeland of the Persians—the land of Pars or Persis—both in its climate and its soil. Hence the majority of both the peasants as well as the nobility of that region (Cilicia) were almost pure Persians by blood as well as by culture. Among these Persians the cult of Mithra, "the invincible Lord of Battles" was definitely practised. The religion of these Persians was that of Mazda-worship as taught by Zoroaster, but it had been modified a good deal in course of time and had come nearer to the pre-Zoroastrian

209

religion of "Nature-worship". The written language of that region was a variety of the Semitic Aramaic. In the Greek inscriptions of that period the priesthood of these Persians has been named the *Magousaioi,* which is clearly a transcription of the original name of these priests. This religion practised by the Iranians of Cilicia was a sort of amalgamation of Mazda-worship and Babylonian beliefs. Ahura-Mazda was assimilated to Bel (-Merodach), Anahita to Ishtar, and Mithra to Shamash (the Sun). And doubtless owing to this, Mithra was always known among the Romans as SOL INVICTUS

In Anatolia, near the small town of Doliche, a Deity was worshipped whose name was recorded by later Roman writers as *Jupiter Dolichenus.* His special weapon was a double-edged axe, an ancient symbol venerated in both Crete and in Egypt. This Deity was later syncretised (assimilated) with the Semitic Baal-Shamin and became completely Semitic in character. But when Cyrus conquered this region this ancient Deity was assimilated to Ahura-Mazda, for Herodotus tells us that this Deity represented "the full circle of heaven and was worshipped on tops of mountains". In post-Achaemenian days this region was ruled over by a petty local dynasty—half Iranian, half Greek—and under them this ancient Deity of Doliche was named *Zeus Oromasdes* and this Deity was reputed to reside in sublime ethereal regions. This same Deity was the *Jupiter Caelus* of the Romans. The Romans also recognized this particular Jupiter as the Head of the pantheon of Mazda-worshippers. And later on this same Zeus Oromasdes was closely associated with the cult of Mithra.

The Mithra-cult with which the Romans came into contact was "a combination of Persian beliefs with Semitic theology, incidentally including certain elements from the native cults of Asia Minor". There seem to have been some influences from the religion of the Hittites. Just before the Roman conquest of this region the Greeks had been the supreme power there, and they had consequently looked upon this cult in their own way and had imposed upon it some of the ritual from their own mysteries. In spite of all these "foreign" influences Mithraism remains in its essence Zoroastrian Mazdaism blended with a certain amount of Chaldean (Babylonian) theology.

It seems strange that the Greeks never took to Mithra-worship. The reasons for this may only be guessed. Some of these might have been (i) the hereditary dislike of the Greeks for anything Iranian, (ii) their own racial pride and consequent narrow outlook and probably also (iii) their spiritual inability to respond to the mystic symbolism and (iv) their inability to submit to the discipline inculcated by the Mithra-cult. Nevertheless the Macedonian conquest of Iran led to the final and definite formulation of Mithraism. "It is certainly during the period of moral and religious fermentation promoted by the Macedonian conquest that Mithraism received its more or less definitive form".

Once accepted by the Romans the cult spread with great rapidity. We can trace it along the banks of the Danube and the Rhine. We find its traces along the Roman walls in Britain, on the borders of the Sahara and also in the valleys of the Asturias in Spain. The Roman Empire and the commerce of the Mediterranean (which was mainly in the hands of Asiatic merchants from the Levant) helped considerably in the spread of this cult. A very large proportion of the missionaries of Mithraism were the slaves and menial workers in the families of the Roman aristocracy. The cult spread so fast that in 307 A.D. a sanctuary to Mithra was solemnly dedicated on the Danube as to "the Protector of their Empire" (*fautori imperii sui*).

Besides this stream of Mithraism flowing from Iran, there was yet another stream of Iranian culture which spread southward and westward from Iran. This appealed specially to three classes of men (i) those who were attracted by ceremonial, (ii) those who had ascetic and mystic tendencies and (iii) those who were intellectually minded. The great library at Alexandria had its share in the spread of this aspect of Iranian culture. The cult of Mithra, however, impressed especially the Roman warriors for it appealed particularly to their sense of discipline and to their valour. By the third century of Christ both these streams of Iranian culture seem to have united. We find, for example, Porphyry deeply versed in the mysteries of Mithra as well as in the "Chaldean lore" of Zoroaster. From that time all the later Platonists were both initiates in the mysteries of Mithra as well as deep students of the *Oracles of Zoroaster.*

In spite of its wide-spread influence all over the Roman Empire, Mithraism was not destined to be the Faith of the West. It almost succeeded in becoming the Religion of the Roman Empire, and in achieving this it prepared, in a manner of speaking, the way for the ultimate triumph of Christianity over Roman paganism. In fact just before the accession of Constantine, Mithraism had all but triumphed. This religion was finally defeated because "Christianity ascended the throne of the Caesars and Christianity became Caesarised". The transition from Mithraism to Christianity, however, was not altogether abrupt, because the Christ-mystery, which replaced the Mithra-mystery also dealt with the same supreme theme, viz., the Perfecting of Man.

There was one last attempt made by Julian the Apostate (360-363 A.D.) to reinstate Mithraism, but it was unsuccessful; and after the death of Julian this religion gradually faded out in the West. In Iran, the land of its birth, the worship of Mithra, "the Invincible Lord" was replaced by the worship of the "Lord of Battles and Victory", the Aryan Verethraghna, the Sasanian Behram, and thus the ancient cult of Mithra faded out in the East as well. But before it disappeared finally it had another recrudescence, veiled as the eclectic cult of Mani, which was the ancient Mazda-worship blended with the best elements of Christianity and of Buddhism. Mani's religion also laid great stress on absolute purity of life, on discipline and on the perfectibility of man. The final disappearance of Mithraism from Iran was certainly due to the Islamic conquest, and to the blending of the ancient mystic lore of Mazda-worship with Islamic doctrines. No doubt the image worship in Mithraism was utterly repugnant to Islamic ideas and this must have hastened the final departure of Mithraism from Iran. Still, the ancient mysteries of the merging of man into the Divine have continued in another garb in the wonderful Sufi poetry about the blending of the Lover and the Beloved.

We may now consider why Mithraism had such wide-spread influence. We have seen that the cult began to crystallize in the days of the mental and moral ferment which followed the break up of the greatest empire of antiquity. The Roman mind which loved law and order and discipline—especially the warrior mind of Rome—was particularly struck by the importance which the Persians attached to their peculiar religious discipline and the rigor with which they enforced it. These Persians had themselves been world-conquerors and as such they had realized the value of self-control and discipline, and the practical Roman mind clearly recognized

212

the value of this virtue for the administration and control of their vast empire. Roman religion had been so far orderly and decorous and dignified; their ritual was such as would befit the elderly self-important patricians of Rome. But just for this reason the pagan religion of Rome failed to impress the masses. These latter were at first carried away by the primitive and more emotional cults imported from Syria; but when they were brought into direct contact with Mithra-worship they at once realized that it was something they had been thirsting for and groping after for years. Here was the cult of a nation as imperial in its outlook as they themselves, and it inculcated order and discipline so dear to the Roman heart. Above all it satisfied "the desire for a *practical* religion that would subject the individual to a rule of conduct and contribute to the welfare of the state". Mithraism infused life into Roman religion by introducing in it the imperative ethics of Persia—a thing deeply appreciated by a military nation.

Mithra being the Lord of Light and the God of Truth and Justice was ever opposed to the Evil One. Hence he was the Guarantor of faith and Maintainer of the plighted word. Thus Mithraism exacted loyalty and fidelity from its followers and imposed upon its adherents a code of virtue similar to what is now understood by the word *honor*. In addition to this, there was engendered an *esprit de corps* and true brotherhood which was a real binding force in such an extensive and heterogeneous empire like the Roman.

Then there was the ideal of Purity. Mithra as the enemy of every kind of impurity stood forth as an ideal and perfect man. The ceremonies and the various degrees imparted to the initiates all tended to emphasize grade by grade the ideal of purity. One trait pre-eminently distinguishes the ideal of Mithra as accepted in the Roman Empire, and that is his absolute Purity. Osiris had his Isis, Bel-Merodach also had his spouse but Mithra was ever single, a celibate. Anahita, his companion from the later Achaemenian days, had dropped out completely. The excesses of the cult of Fecundity imported from foreign lands seem to have caused a natural revulsion in favor of complete chastity. Hence Mithra is *Sanctus* in the true sense of the term. Instead of the orgies of the spring-festival we now had a reverence for chastity in the Mithraism which Rome had accepted.

The Zoroastrian teaching of the Twin Spirits made each individual a soldier in the battle of life and hence Mithraism was "peculiarly favorable for the development of individual effort and human energy". This it was that appealed in Rome to all, slave and master alike. Resistance to temptations and to the promptings of flesh were looked upon as great exploits in the eternal war of Good and Evil, and everyone felt proud to be soldier in the army of the "Invincible" Mithra.

Above all, Mithraism taught the secret of regeneration, of being born anew in the Spirit. It showed the path of attaining the full stature of Man's Divinity and the whole of its ritual was deliberately planned to explain this goal and to indicate the steps by which the individual finally became one with his Father.

BIBLIOGRAPHY

Franz Cumont, *The Oriental Religions in Roman Paganism* (Open Court Publishing Co., Chicago, 1911).

G. R. S. Mead, *Echoes from the Gnosis*, Vol. v, *The Mysteries of Mithra* (London, 1907). The quotations in this essay are mainly from these two works.

M. N. Dhalla, *The History of Zoroastrianism* (Oxford University Press, 1938) pp. 302-308.

H. Stuart Jones, article on "Mithraism" in Hastings' *Encyclopaedia of Religion and Ethics* (Edinburgh, 1915) Vol. 8, pp. 752-759.

I. J. S. Taraporewala, "Some Aspects of the History of Zoroastrianism," contributed to *The Journal of the K. R. Cama Oriental Institute*, No. 11 (Bombay, 1928). In this essay I have followed the general arrangement of section iv (pp. 36-47) of this contribution which deals with Mithraism.

MANICHAEISM

The editor's biography of this contributor precedes the previous article.

Editor

215

MANICHAEISM

IRACH J. S. TARAPOREWALA

THE SASANIAN DYNASTY ruled over Iran for more than four centuries (226-642 A.D.) to all outward appearance with great splendor and glory. Yet when the Sasanian Empire came to grips with the desert Arabs, inspired with the new Gospel of Islam, the whole of this vast and splendid fabric crumbled to pieces within a short time. There was something essentially wrong in the body-politic of Iran from the very commencement of Sasanian rule. Hidden underneath the outward splendor and the vast military achievements of the Sasanians there lurked the germs of decay. All through the four centuries of Sasanian rule Zoroastrianism continued to be the "official state religion", but historians have also spoken of several "heretical sects". Apparently these were suppressed, but "we lack here the material necessary for forming a judgment because the triumph of the orthodox doctrine doomed to oblivion most of the views that deviated from it". In spite of this outward triumph of Zoroastrian orthodoxy, the fact remains that quite a number of "heresies" were formulated from time to time and two of them actually found a very considerable response among the masses. One such heresy was promulgated by Mani at the very beginning of the Sasanian era, and another was the "heresy" preached by Mazdak almost at the end of the rule of the Sasanians. "It may be suggested that the simple fact of the existence of such heretical movements as Manichaeism and Mazdakism is an indication of the presence of those germs of decay which foreshadowed the final downfall of the national faith in Persia".

The Sasanian Dynasty was established by Ardashir Papakan of the house of Sasan in the year 226 A.D. Ardashir headed the national revolt against the fratricidal struggles and the irreligious misrule of the Arsacid (Parthian) rulers of Iran. The Arsacid rulers

217

were Zoroastrians in name, but they thought more of their own power and position than of their country or their religion. Politically the nation had suffered in the eyes of all the world, for the national capital had been taken and sacked by the Romans no less than three times within the course of one hundred years. Added to this shame were the "irreligious" and unorthodox ways of the Arsacid rulers, which gave mortal offence to Ardashir and his zealous followers. Ardashir headed the national movement against the Arsacids, who, the people believed, had led the country to the brink of utter ruin. The province of Pars (Persis) over which Ardashir had been ruling was the center and rallying point of whatever was left alive of the ancient Zoroastrian Faith. Ardashir and his followers believed that it was only by the restoration of the ancient religion that a stable rule could be established and the people made content. Fired by this enthusiasm Ardashir led the double movement for the restoration of the ancient Faith of Zoroaster and for the establishment of the pure Aryan form of government in the land. Ardashir himself was a priest, and his priesthood had been inherited from a long line of ancestors. The whole nation rose to his call, and Ardashir was wholly successful in both his objects. And when he died in 242 A.D. he left his newly founded empire to his son Shapur I. And with it he left the following "testament" for his son to follow:*

> "When monarchs honour
> "The Faith then it and royalty are brothers,
> "For they are mingled so that thou wouldst say:—
> " 'They wear one cloak'. The Faith endureth not
> "Without the throne nor can kingship stand
> "Without the faith; two pieces of brocade
> "Are they all intertwined set up
> "Before the wise. . . .
> "Each needeth other, and we see the pair
> "United in beneficence."

Believing in this Ardashir had established a full-fledged theocracy in Iran. Himself a priest, he followed strictly all the complicated ceremonial prescribed by his Faith, and like an enthusiastic

---

* The *Shah-nama*, the National Epic of Iran has given this in beautiful Persian verses. The English rendering is by the brothers Warner (London, 1912) Vol. vi, pp. 286-287.

and sincere believer he built up his empire upon the solid foundations of religion. This is clearly depicted on his coins, as also on
all the coins minted throughout the Sasanian period. On the re-
verse of each coin we see a fire-altar flanked on either side by a
human figure fully armed. One of these represented royalty, the
secular power; and the other represents the *Dasturan-Dastur* (the
High-Priest of the Empire), representing the spiritual might. These
are the "two brothers".

In this theocratic state established by Ardashir I there lurked
already concealed the germs of decay. Such a theocratic constitution would naturally give special weight to the priesthood of one
particular religion, and give special importance to one particular
set of beliefs and dogmas. The Achaemenians had ruled over an
empire much more extensive than that of the Sasanians, but their
religious policy had been throughout one of tolerance toward all
the various faiths of their subjects. The Sasanians, on the other
hand, sought to achieve solidarity and unity through uniformity of
belief (at least for the majority of their subjects) and in definitely
assigning a higher position in the state to one particular Faith and
to one set of religious practices and dogmas. This favored position
granted to Zoroastrianism naturally led the Zoroastrian clergy to
think themselves as a sort of "chosen people" of God and slowly
but surely worked into them a spirit of intolerance for all other
beliefs.

It is indeed quite significant that the very first announcement of
the new eclectic Faith of Mani should have been made on the very
day that Shapur I, the son and successor of the founder of the
Sasanian house, was crowned at Ctesiphon (20th March, 242 A.D.).

In Mani's own lifetime and in the country of its origin this new
faith was "combated and execrated as violently by orthodox Zoroastrianism as it was by orthodox Christianity when it spread westward into the imperial domains of Rome." Until the beginning of
the present (20th) century of Christ all the information we possessed about Mani and his teaching was from these two sources and
we had nothing more. The Zoroastrian priesthood called him "the
fiend incarnate" and "the crippled devil" (for he was lame), and
Christian writers were equally abusive.

In 1902-1903 the first expedition to the Turfan region in
Central Asia was sent from Berlin and it was led by Grün-

wedel and Huth. This was followed by the second one in 1904 led by Le Coq, and by a third one led by Le Coq and Grünwedel. This last carried on the work from 1905 to 1907 and it resulted in bringing "a veritable treasure trove" of Manichaean Fragments to Berlin. These documents from Turfan include fragments from the original works of the Manichaean Faith, and considerable portions of a once extensive Manichaean literature. These are in a dialect of Pahlavi, in Soghdian, in old Turkish and in Chinese. All these have been deciphered and skilfully edited and translated, and they have shed considerable light on Mani's life and teachings. From these we can conclude that "Manichaeism was not only an offshoot of Zoroastrianism in a way, and the parent of various heretical movements in Christianity, but was also a factor for centuries in the religious life of Central and Eastern Asia".

Mani was a Persian by birth and was probably also brought up as a Zoroastrian. His father was a well-to-do man of considerable learning and with distinctly eclectic tendencies in matters of religion. Mani was born about 216 A.D. At the age of about twenty he had a spiritual vision and inspired by divine revelation he came forward as a new prophet. His endeavor was to make "a synthesis of elements from various existing religions, to form a new religion, eclectic in character, and inspired by the fervor of his own idealistic enthusiasm, one that should not be confined by national borders but be universally adopted. In other words, Mani's aspiration was to bring the world, Orient and Occident, into closer union through a combined faith, based upon the creeds known in his day".

Mani's teaching is designedly a synthesis. He has specially acknowledged his indebtedness to Zoroaster, Buddha and Jesus, whom he regarded as "pioneer revealers of truth which he came to fulfil". From Zoroastrianism he took the doctrine of the fundamental struggle between Spirit and Matter as the basis for the solution of the problem of Good and Evil. In the teachings of the Buddha he found the essential lessons for the conduct of life which should be accepted by all men everywhere. And in Jesus he recognized "the verified ideal of Life". He supplemented his teaching by incorporating the doctrines of Hinduism, and the old Babylonian beliefs which had survived to his days. And in his teaching we may also trace a strong admixture of Gnostic, Neo-platonic doctrines. This eclectic character of Mani's teaching made it easier to be adopted by any person professing any faith, for they would pass themselves off as a sect of their original creed. As it was Mani's teaching was received kindly at first, and even King Shapur I became his friend and protector.

But this new teaching did not quite suit the orthodox and narrow-minded Zoroastrian priesthood. Opposition to Mani's views grew stronger daily and at last Shapur I had to advise Mani to leave the country and to go into exile. Mani thereupon left Iran and for many years wandered about all over Central Asia, penetrating as far east as China. It was during these years of wandering that he gave final shape to his teachings, which were then committed to writing. His creed spread rapidly throughout Central Asia and he had a considerable number of followers among the Chinese. His faith continued in the East till about the 17th century of Christ.

Mani remained in exile till the death of Shapur I in 272 A.D. He came back to Iran and was well-received by Shapur's successor Hormazd I. But when Hormazd I died after a very short reign (272-273 A.D.) his successor, Behram I, showed his strong dislike for Mani by putting him to a horrible death. His followers were cruelly persecuted and the Faith of Mani was banned throughout the whole Iranian Empire. So his followers migrated westward and southward. Passing through Egypt the religion spread all along the northern coast of Africa and from there it penetrated to Sicily and to Spain and thus spread all over Europe. For several centuries it continued active all over Europe disguised as various "heretical" sects of Christianity. One very notable Manichaean was St. Augustine, who was brought up in this Faith in his youth before he took up his active work for the Church of Christ. In Bulgaria Manichaeism appears as the sect of the Bogomil (beloved of God), in Italy it appeared as the Cathari, another "heretical" sect. The last record of this religion is found among the Albigensis in southern France, who were ruthlessly massacred by the orthodox Catholics there.

In the East the stronghold of the Manichaeans was the kingdom of the Uigurs, and there they flourished in peace until the Uigurs themselves lost their kingdom. In China they seem to have faded out gradually.

The main teaching of Mani concerned the struggle between Good and Evil. This is due, according to him, to the existence of the Twin Principles from the beginning and the struggle is to go on to

221

all eternity. Mani taught that Light was Spirit and hence "good" and that Darkness was Matter and consequently "evil". Mani recognized three principal "Ages". The first "Age" was before this visible universe came into being, when the Two Principles were entirely separated. In the second "Age", our present age, Darkness burst through the dividing partition into the region of Light, and this resulted in universal conflict. The third "Age", which will see the final consummation, will bring the final triumph of Truth and Light and the complete separation, as in the first "Age", of the Realm of Light and the Realm of Darkness.

Mani's cosmology is complex and highly imaginative. When the powers of Darkness first broke through into the realm of Light, all our worldly ills began. To repel this incursion of Darkness the Supreme Godhead "evoked" three great Powers. The third of these great Powers seems to possess the traits of Mithra.

Mani regarded the separation of sexes as being especially the work of the Evil One. "His fiendish aim was by this means to incarcerate the light perpetually in the bonds of the carnal body". And so he emphasized the need for complete chastity and celibacy. Only through a life of renunciation, ascetic in its rigor, can one attain to perfection. Mani taught that there is a spark of Light in every human being, and therein lay the hope of our ultimate salvation.

Mani arranged his followers into various graded "orders". Women were admitted freely into these. These "orders" were modelled upon the orders found in Buddhism. Mani strove to arrange his followers in such a manner that they would be the representatives of "an unwalled monasticism".

Mani also gave out "commandments" for his followers. These were very similar to those found in the Old Testament, in the Sermon on the Mount and in Buddhism. The main commandments to be observed were love for the Supreme Godhead, reverence for the Divine element in every human being, and recognition of the Divine inspiration of the great Teachers of Humanity. Added to these Mani insisted on purity of thought, word and deed. Mani categorically opposed all warfare.

Mani was a firm believer in the perfectibility of man. He taught that by following the precepts all "will steadily advance towards perfection and that all the imprisoned luminary particles, separated ultimately from dark matter, will at last be restored to the Realm of Light".

Manichaeism is now "dead", but "it was a veritable religion and exercised an influence for more than a thousand years, upon the lives of countless numbers of devoted followers, inspired by the ideals and high principles of its founder, whom they accounted as divine".

BIBLIOGRAPHY

A. V. W. Jackson, *Researches in Manichaeism with special reference to the Turfan Fragments* (Columbia University, New York, 1932). This book contains an excellent and exhaustive bibliography.

The same author's *Zoroastrian Studies* (Columbia University, New York, 1928) contains a shorter account of Manichaeism (pp. 174-177 and 183-193). The quotations given in this essay are from both these books.

M. N. Dhalla, *Zoroastrian Civilisation* (Oxford University Press, 1922) pp. 339-348.

A. A. Bevan, article on "Manichaeism" in Hastings' *Encyclopaedia of Religion and Ethics* (Edinburgh, 1915) Vol. 8, pp. 394-402.

M. Sprengling, "Mani and Manichaeism" in *Encyclopedia of Religion* (1945) edited by Vergilius Ferm.

MAZDAKISM

The editor's biography of this contributor precedes the previous articles.

Editor

MAZDAKISM

IRACH J. S. TARAPOREWALA

JUST AS Mani's eclectic Faith was a pointer at the germs of decay in the Sasanian body-politic, so also Mazdak's teaching was a pointer at the inevitable downfall towards which the Sasanian Empire was heading. Mani came within one generation of the establishment of Sasanian rule in Iran; Mazdak came towards the end of that rule, about a century before the Empire was overthrown by the Arabs. Both these movements were fiercely and ruthlessly uprooted in the land of their origin, and to all outward appearance it seemed as if the authority of the theocratic state was amply vindicated. But the triumph over Mazdakism was shortlived. There is another similarity between these two movements: Zoroastrian, Christian and Islamic writers have poured unbounded vituperation against both. These unfriendly writings are our only sources of information regarding the teachings of Mazdak. As regards Mani a great deal of new and valuable information has come to light since the Turfan discoveries in 1902. These have shown Mani to have been a really great personage and the founder of a new Faith. But no such finds have yet been discovered to rehabilitate Mazdak.

Still Mazdakism may be viewed as a symptom which indicated a deep-seated cancer in the body-politic of Sasanian Iran. Therefore we should judge this movement after accepting the principle embodied in the saying, "By their fruits shall ye know them".

The founder of the Sasanian dynasty was one of the supermen of history. He was a born leader of men and he led his country and his people to a renovated existence. A man of great fixity of purpose, he carried out to the full the task he had set before himself, and he left to his son a newly established empire, a renovated religion and hundreds of well-trained and enthusiastic men and women ready to carry on the work to its fulfilment. Shapur I, the

227

son of the founder, Ardashir I., was worthy of his father, for he also was a great leader, far above the average. He established the new empire and completed the task of the revival of Zoroastrianism to the satisfaction of all concerned. He loyally carried out his father's admonition, regarding Faith and Royalty as brothers. He fixed firmly and finally the theocratic constitution of the newly estab- lished Sasanian empire. By this the Zoroastrian clergy acquired powers second only to those possessed by the king himself. And naturally also the landed aristocracy of Iran came in for a good share of political power and emoluments.

Of course, it was never the intention of either Ardashir I or of Shapur I that these two great sections of Iranian society—the Zo- roastrian clergy and the landowners—should become the oppressors of the masses. As long as the king at the top was a strong man he could hold both these sections in check and could stand between them and the masses. Both Ardashir I and Shapur I understood that the masses would give full support and would be loyal to the state provided they got justice from their king, and so both these rulers were eager to see that justice was done to the meanest of their subjects.

But once the strong hand of the king at the top was removed the two powerful sections would naturally try to consolidate their own power over the masses and to gain new privileges. In justice, however, to the Zoroastrian clergy it must be mentioned that the spread of Christianity throughout Iran was a constant and growing menace to the newly-revived Zoroastrian religion. To add to these difficulties the Christian Roman empire was steadily growing more and more menacing and truculent. Rome was always trying to find some pretext to make war on Iran, nor was Iran at all behind to find excuses for a fight. Armenia, which held a strategic position between the two empires, was itself torn by the religious strife of the Armenian Zoroastrians and Christians; and Rome and Iran being both theocratic, the affairs in Armenia almost always kindled the flames of war. And in these wars the landholders were ever an important factor for they ensured the victories of Iran. And so we find the power of both the Zoroastrian clergy and of the Iranian landholding aristocracy daily growing stronger and more firmly es- tablished. When the king was a man of easy-going and pliable temperament both these sections consolidated their gains and tried to acquire yet more. And all this was at the expense of the masses.

Ardashir I and Shapur I did all they could to ensure that the masses got a fair deal. But when they were gone a succession of weaker men ruled the empire from 272 to 309 A.D., which gave time enough to the vested interests to work their will in the state.

Then came Shapur II (the Great), a unique figure in history. He was a posthumous son, and he succeeded to the empire *before* he was born. The vested interests naturally looked forward to a fairly long period of minority (at least fifteen years) and they had hopes of moulding the baby king's character to suit their own purposes. But Shapur was a superman, even greater than the first two rulers of his line and at a very early age he gave clear indications that he had a mind of his own and a will also to get whatever he wanted, and that he was a true-born ruler of men. Shapur II wished to curb the powers of the Zoroastrian clergy and of his landholders, for he was wise enough to appreciate the dangers if these were left unchecked. But other events outside Iran forced him to side with his clergy and his aristocracy. Constantine, the Roman Emperor, carried away by his zeal for Christianity, proclaimed himself to be the spiritual head of all the Christians in the world (including, of course, the Christians of Iran). This was more than Shapur II, the proudest of the Sasanians, could tolerate. The poor Christians of Iran found themselves placed in a very false position, torn between two loyalties, to the king of their own country and to the head of their faith, the Roman emperor. Whenever there was war between Iran and Rome (which was practically always) the Christians of Iran were looked upon as foes and "fifth columnists" and had to pay the penalty. This gave the vested interests good opportunities to launch fierce persecutions against the Christians, to which Shapur II, with his offended pride, was not unwilling to lend his support. So on the whole during the long reign of Shapur II (lasting for seventy years) the vested interests had their own way more or less in spite of the strong king.

After Shapur II came a long succession of very ordinary kings and during over one hundred years (379-487 A.D.) there was only one king who was really well above the average. That was Behram V (Behramgore, the Hunter of the Wild Ass), but he was busy most of the time with wars with the Huns. One important event happened in the days of Behram V and that was the final separation of the Iranian Christian Church from the Orthodox Church of Byzantium. The fratricidal strife between the Christians and the Zoroastrians had been going on with ever-increasing ferocity and bitterness ever since the days of Shapur II. Thousands had lost their lives; the manhood of Iran was slowly but surely being bled to death. But after the separation of the Iranian Christian Church from Byzantium the Christians found comparative peace. Still the religious hatred and fanaticism on both sides were of too long a growth to die out completely. Violent polemical writings continued on both sides.

Meanwhile the masses were being ground down relentlessly by the vested interests and seem to have sunk to the deepest depths of poverty and misery. The unsuccessful wars of Firuz I (459-483) against the Huns added to the prevailing discontent. The conditions in Iran soon after the death of Firuz I were almost exactly the same as those prevailing in France on the eve of the French Revolution or in Russia at the end of the First World War. The fruits of these centuries of oppression were soon to be visible in the revolutionary and communistic preaching of Mazdak, who began his work about 488 A.D.

We can but make a guess at the social conditions of Iranian masses by observing the extra violent language in the preaching of Mazdak and in the extremes to which his doctrines went. Even more significant was the extreme rapidity with which Mazdak's teaching was accepted by the masses. Within the course of a few months his followers could be counted by the hundred thousand; and in every part of the vast empire they were drawn from every stratum of society from the king downwards. The king at that time was Kawadh (488-531 A.D.), and in the beginning he openly declared his sympathies with the new preaching. But the vested interests were seriously perturbed and so strongly were they entrenched that the king was forced to leave his throne for a few years (499-501).

Charles Dickens has given a wonderful passage in the last chapter of his *A Tale of Two Cities,* in which he indicates the connection between revolutions and their causes. Describing the rolling of six tumbrils through the streets of Paris bearing the unhappy victims of the guillotine he says:

"Six tumbrils roll along the streets. Change these back to what they were thou powerful enchanter, Time, and they shall be seen to be the carriages of absolute monarchs, the equipages of feudal nobles, the toilettes of flaring Jezebels, the churches that are not my Father's house, but dens of thieves, the huts of millions of starving peasants. No; the great magician who works out the appointed order of the Creator, never reverses his transformation". Further on he adds:

"Crush humanity out of shape under similar hammers, and it will twist itself into the same tortured forms. Sow the seed of rapacious license and oppression over again and it will yield the same fruit according to its kind". By their fruits, indeed shall ye know them. We do not have any historical records of the seeds sown in Iran, but we possess ample evidence of the hideous fruit, from which we may infer the nature of the seed if the Laws of God have any meaning.

Mazdak might well be termed the first Bolshevik in history. Indeed, in some respects Bolsheviks might be regarded as lukewarm compared to Mazdak; he not only preached communism in worldly possessions but he also advocated an equal division of women among men.

When Kawadh was restored to the throne in 501 A.D. he was made wiser by experience and he withdrew his open support of the Mazdakites. He clearly recognized the seed from which this terrible tree of Mazdakism had grown, and he tried his best during the remaining thirty years of his reign to see that the conditions of the masses were made more tolerable. But he was not strong enough to remove the root causes of Mazdakism. That was reserved for a far greater man than Kawadh. It was his son Khusrav I, known to all Orient by his title Noshirwan, who freed Iran from the Mazdak frenzy.

Khusrav was the favorite son of Kawadh and he had been his father's closest friend and counsellor during the closing years of Kawadh's reign. Khusrav was easily the greatest ruler Iran ever had. Indeed, he may rank among the six greatest kings in the history of the world. He clearly saw the imminent danger to both the state and the religion from Mazdak's teaching and the first thing he did was to suppress the movement with an iron hand. But at the same time he saw justice done to the masses. Like a good physician he removed not merely the symptoms of the disease but he removed the disease itself. With equal firmness he brought under control the oppressors of the masses. Quite early he won the title of *'Adl* (the Just), for Justice was his watchword. Under his strong and just rule peace and prosperity returned to Iran, and the masses were satisfied. For this achievement his grateful subjects with one voice called him *Anushak-Ruban* or *Noshirwan* (he of the immortal soul). To posterity he is known as Noshirwan alone, the most glorious name ever bestowed upon an earthly ruler.

Mazdak was certainly a successor of Mani, because his movement was not merely social but was essentially religious. His extreme ideas were certainly a menace both to society and to religion. They certainly threatened the very existence of Zoroastrian priesthood, and so very naturally he was violently abused by Zoroastrian writers. He has been called *Ashemaogha* (a distorter of truth) and one commentator on a religious text explains this epithet by adding, "like Mazdak, the son of Bamdad". The mildest epithet used for him by Zoroastrians is "accursed".

Mazdak's ideas are a natural corollary to the state of Iran in his days, and to the condition of the masses that he had seen with his own eyes. He felt himself obliged to preach extreme communism and an absolute community of possessions, including women. Very likely he was moved by the idea that desperate diseases need desperate remedies. At the same time he also preached a higher ideal of life. He pointed out the value of self-restraint and renunciation of all sense-pleasures including animal food. For this last teaching he has been called "the devil who would not eat". He asserted that the desire for pleasure and possessions constituted the universal cause of all hatred and strife. He also like Mani laid stress on Zoroaster's teaching of the two essential Principles of Good and Evil which pervade our life on earth. He also enjoined the strict purity of God's "elements", fire, water and earth. But we have very scanty positive knowledge of what he actually taught.

Mazdak was treacherously murdered and many of his closest adherents lost their lives at the same time. Then followed a systematic suppression of all Mazdakites, often with much bloodshed. But though outwardly uprooted and completely destroyed the teachings of Mazdak continued to flourish for several centuries after his murder. Under the rule of the Islamic caliphs of Bagdad several "heretical sects" have been noted by historians. They all seemed to get their inspiration from the teachings of Mazdak, for they cite him as their authority. But what is more surprising and very significant is that many of these "heretical sects" have coupled the name of Mazdak with that of Zoroaster, the Prophet of ancient Iran.

BIBLIOGRAPHY

A. V. W. JACKSON, *Zoroastrian Studies* (Columbia University, New York, 1928). Some pages in this work (pp. 175-177) are devoted to Mazdak. But he has given an exhaustive bibliography.

Notices of Mazdak are few and scattered. Special mention might be made of:

R. A. NICHOLSON's article on "Mazdak" in HASTINGS' *Encyclopaedia of Religion and Ethics* (Edinburgh, 1915) Vol. 8, pp. 508-510.

A. CHRISTENSEN, *Le Règne du Roi Kawadh et le communism Mazdakite* (Copenhagen, 1915).

A considerable portion of this essay (particularly the historical background) has been taken from an article contributed by me to the weekly paper of Bombay—*the Kaisar-i-Hind*—dated September 5th, 1937).

OLD NORSE RELIGION

Professor Fowler was born in Cape Town, South Africa, in 1905. He was educated at the Virginia Military Institute, the University of Minnesota, the University of Oregon, the University of Vienna, the University of Chicago and Harvard University.

He is now Associate Professor of Classics and Comparative Philology in the University of Wisconsin.

His doctor's thesis at Harvard (1940) is entitled "Expressions for Immortality in the early Indo-European Languages, with especial reference to the Rig-Veda, Homer, and the Poetic Edda." This thesis is summarized in "Harvard Studies in Classical Philology" (1941).

He has published articles dealing with his special field of research, in such journals as "Classical Philology," "The Harvard Theological Review," the "American Journal of Philology," the "Journal of the American Oriental Society," "The Review of Religion," "Artibus Asiae" and has contributed to the Coomaraswamy Festschrift "Art and Thought" (1947) and to the "Dictionary of Literary and Dramatic Criticism."

Editor

OLD NORSE RELIGION

MURRAY FOWLER

FOR THE investigation of that religion which may properly be called Old Norse, the two collections of prose and verse known as the Eddas are the prime source.[1] The rock-drawings of Sweden, however closely connected in spirit, seem to belong to an earlier stratum of culture—to one which extends both in breadth and in depth beyond the limits of even a common Germanic tradition. The Eddas, on the other hand, although sprung from the same seed, are Scandinavian and Icelandic in spirit as in language.

The Prose Edda, or The Younger Edda, is the work of Snorri Sturluson, an ambitious, wealthy, powerful, and unscrupulous thirteenth-century Icelander who was evidently a scholar, a wit, an artist, and a poet. His Edda consists of two parts: *Gylfaginning*, a compendium of mythology in the form of questions and answers; and *Skáldskaparmál* and *Háttatal*, books of directions for poets, which contain examples of meters, modes of address, accepted figures of speech, and the like.

The Poetic Edda, or The Elder Edda, is traditionally assigned to Saemundr the Wise (1056-1133) ; but although it is possible that he made some collection of early verse, only part of the thirty-four poems now extant were probably saved from oblivion by his industry. The date of the first writing of these verses has been subject to scholarly dispute for three centuries. Reasonably wide termini may be placed at the years 800 and 1200 A.D. The poems are the works of different authors, none of whom is known; the subjects are the myths of the gods and the legends of heroes, for the greater part kept clearly separate. When or where they were composed is likewise unknown; the language is that of Norway and of Iceland. The relation of many of the myths to the great body of common Germanic mythology is, however, certain; and the lean vigor, the

237

hard fire, the dark, almost secretive intensity of the pagan poetry is convincing evidence of its authenticity. Christian influence has been suspected in some of the poems; but it is not unquestionably there at all, and even the suspected influence is slight.

From these two sources much can be learned about Old Norse religion. The one is a collection of sincere, natural, profound religious poetry; the other is an artificial, even skeptical, review of the same material. The Poetic Edda, the better of the two sources, is, it must be said, impossible to exhaust; and it is therefore impossible to understand it completely. Like Homer and the early dramas of Aeschylus, it exceeds the comprehension of modern man, whose world is no longer peopled by immanent pagan gods. By an effort of imagination it may be possible to discern the meaning of parts; but a knowledge of the parts is certainly not that of the whole, and the complete theology of the North—if it existed as a system at all—is not thus lightly to be grasped, as Snorri, in his sophisticated way, seems occasionally to be saying.

If, therefore, Old Norse religion is mentioned in this essay as if it were a clear and certain concept or a body of defined theology, the warning must be given that the term is thus used for convenience only, and that the sole reliable source of information on Old Norse religion is these documents which have been mentioned— no matter how greatly comparative studies of other religions may help to elucidate them; and that the way, therefore, to attempt an understanding of this pagan faith of the cold North is to enter into it by a reading of the magnificent poems themselves, preferably in the pagan tongue.

Creation in Old Norse religion is *ex nihilo,* the primeval chaos (*Ginnunga Gap*) [2] from which all things issued being described in *Volospá* as a vast, gaping void without earth or sea or sky, or sand, or growth of any kind.

This cosmogony, preserved in almost identical form in the Old High German language in the prayer of Wessobrunn (*ms.* of the ninth century) and, with certain striking similarities, in Vedic Sanskrit in the opening stanza of Rig-Veda X, 129, (*circa* 2000-1500 B.C.) is part of the tradition of Indo-European speech and culture. Its affiliation to any other hypothesis of creation is not certainly demonstrable, and its ultimate origin remains, therefore, as yet unknown.

According to Snorri Sturluson's version of the primal act,[3] the cosmic giant Ymir was generated in Ginnungagap by the mutual attraction and opposition of cold from Niflheim and heat from Muspellsheim.[4] In the Volospá it is said only that Ymir existed "early in the ages".[5] From Ymir's flesh, Odin and his brothers made the earth, from his hair the trees, from his bones the mountains, from his blood the sea, from his skull the vault of the heavens.[6] In poetic symbols is thus expressed the ultimate identity of all created things. As Snorri explains,[7] men had observed certain similarities, such as that blood is found throughout the human body, as water is in the earth even on mountain-tops, and they therefore concluded that in some respects all things must be alike. The cosmic horse in Vedic religion is of precisely similar significance. Crude though the iconography may now appear, it yet is legible; and it is certain that Ymir symbolizes in Norse religion the principle of identity in the micro- and the macrocosm.

The word *iotunn*, however, usually translated "giant", which is used of Ymir,[8] seems actually to mean "devourer" or simply "eater"[9]; and the gaping void or gullet, the Ginnunga Gap, or χάος in which the Norse cosmos is established, is, therefore, the very stuff of which, as well as in which, the ordered universe of time and space is later to be constituted, since in the first age there is nothing at all other than the primeval substance.[10] It is the spinning out of this tale of what is utterly incomprehensible, of the origin of life itself, which we find in the dismemberment of Ymir by the "gods", themselves the second generation away from "giants" (as in the Rig-Veda), for there appears to be no actual Creator in Norse religion, but rather a primal act, presumably eternal and without position in time, by which, in which, and out of which all life proceeds.

Of Ymir all giants come, says the *Hyndloljód*,[11] and Snorri repeats the statement. From the fact of their auto-generation (under the hand, and from the feet, of Ymir) the inference may properly be drawn that of Ymir likewise come all the gods, for Odin, the All-father, the supreme among the Aesir, or "gods", is himself descended from a *iotunn* family.

The genealogy of Odin tells a great deal. Although he is the protean thread upon which everything is supported, the All-Father, the God of Gods, the Many-Shaped, the Lord of Hosts—these and

239

fifty other names are used of him—yet his mother is Bestla, the daughter of Bolthorr, a giant,[12] and his father is Borr, or Burr, the son of Buri (or perhaps Burr himself), a man[13] licked out of ice by the cow Audumla which had come into being to provide food for Ymir. It is important to note, then, that Odin, who, as Snorri says,[14] is to be regarded as the ruler of heaven and earth, is in no sense the *creator* thereof excepting only that he divides up the body of Ymir, for he is himself descended, on one side, from the race of Ymir, and, on the other, from a man, whose origin in nature precedes his own. While hardly capable of proof, the guess may be made that this involved genealogy but reflects the involutionary process of eternal creation.

Odin has two brothers, Vili and Ve, of whom little is known[15] beyond their participation with Odin in the shaping on earth of men and women from Askr and Embla.[16]

From Odin, it is generally said, all the gods are descended; and the father of the gods he is, in fact, called[17]; yet an examination of each of the Aesir in turn shows that the descent of none from Odin is completely certain (except, possibly, in the case of Thor), and that they seem, every one, to have a semi-independent existence, participating in the nature of the All-Father, but being different from him in function and existence. Snorri understood this problem thoroughly (it is essentially a theological one and not confined at all to Norse religion) : certainly when he tells the poets[18] that the correct way to write of the Aesir is to call each one by the name of another, and then to distinguish the one meant by his peculiar function and his attributes, he is more than a mere rhetorician: he is enunciating the basic thesis of all apparently polytheistic religions.

To recapitulate, then, the Norse cosmogony assumes creation to have been spontaneous or, at most, the result, or product, of opposed forces (called *heat* and *cold*) ; no creator is mentioned. If a creative principle is implied in this primal act, then this creative principle is not identical with the Aesir, or gods, although its power may be transmitted in and through them, as in the "creation" of Ask and Embla by Odin and his brothers. The first product of creation is not a κόσμος, but the giant Ymir, whom it may be better not to define in terms of *universal* or *cosmic*, but only to regard as a symbol of coalescence.[19] From Ymir's body, when it is dismembered, the ordered world of time and space is made by Odin. From Ymir are descended all the giants; and from him, likewise, on the maternal side, Odin, the All-Father, springs.

Into this complex image, the Norse cosmography (never to be confused with geography) fits precisely. It is Odin and his brothers who, slaying and dismembering Ymir in the first great conflict, make of his head a dwelling for the gods, of his body the earth, of his blood the all-encompassing endless ocean (probably to be equated with the atmosphere); and it is they who then—but only then—by establishing the sun, moon, and stars, bring into existence an orderly universe. To borrow the terminology, both more explicit and more precise, of Hinduism, the battleground is then established for the eternal conflict which is life.

The cosmos thus takes shape. The giants are banished to dwell on the outer edges of the world ocean, in Utgard; Midgard, the earth, lies midway between Asgard, "heaven", and Niflheim, now the misty kingdom of Hel, the home of the dead.[20] Bifrost, the rainbow bridge, joins heaven and earth, Asgard and Midgard. On this Jacob's ladder, the gods have free passage, but a guard, Heimdallr, who dwells near it, stands constant watch lest any giant cross. There is a special dwelling place for the dwarfs. The Midgard serpent lies in the ocean coiled round the earth. The sun moves across the sky, ever pursued by a wolf; the moon at night is followed by another. Outside this world of order lurk the Fenriswolf and the hosts of Surtr in Muspellsheim.[21] The worlds are separated, so, and joined, by Bifrost, the rainbow, the bridge which breaks at last, the unreal symbol of the tragic tension and the temporary peace in the midst of everlasting war. And this, then, is the cosmos, the ordered world of time and temporal relations, a world from which giants are banned, in which the wolf is fettered, and where the fear of chaos and the dark may be forgotten for the moment in the pleasures of a regulated world.

But the threat of disorder and dissolution is always there: when the time of the gods is nearing its end, then the rule of law, the world of order, this tension of opposites, begins to break up. The wolf snaps his chain and runs wild[22]; the forces of Hel come out of Niflheim; Surtr drives from Muspellsheim[23]; Bifrost breaks[24]; the Midgardserpent rises to fight Thor[25]; one wolf catches the sun, and the other the moon. Darkness and chaos return.

Into this hypothesis, to a large degree credible, of a world, or universe, in delicate balance and continual peril, it is hard to fit neatly the clearly comparable image of a world-tree. To be sure, the ash Yggdrasill is the unifying element which connects the world of the gods (made of Ymir's skull) with the world of men (made of Ymir's body); and its roots, furthermore, precisely like those of the oak in Virgil,[26] go down to the realm of Hel. It is possible, therefore, to understand something of Yggdrasill if it be considered alone: by etymology, Yggdrasill is the horse of Odin[27]: it is the means, or the vehicle, by which the All-Father descends and ascends, transmigrates, makes his varying avatars. All this seems clear enough; and the meaning can hardly be other than that of world-trees everywhere—it is the latent invisible fire in the living wood which is the perfect symbol of eternal spirit trapped in matter; and it is on this "tree of life", therefore, that Odin is suspended, sacrificing—the phrase is both explicit and almost infinitely profound—*himself* to *himself*[28]; yet the linkage between this symbol of life and that of Ymir is by no means clear, and the precise articulation of these two certainly distinct yet apparently compatible images in one intelligible symbol is correspondingly difficult to comprehend. Even though they exist side by side and are used together,[29] it is necessary, therefore, to separate them for examination, and to consider Yggdrasill alone.

Under Yggdrasill's three roots are respectively the worlds of Hel, of the giants, and of men. To these three regions correspond Niflheim, Utgard, and Midgard. Yggdrasill is eternally green, yet it eternally decays; deer nibble its leaves, snakes attack its branches, and the dragon Nidhoggr bites at its roots.[30] The symbolism here seems to be quite certain: it is, as Plato said of the figure of Oceanus in the Greek poets,[31] a disguise for the doctrine of eternal change. At Yggdrasill's roots is also found the well of Mimir. Mimir is a mysterious figure whose head[32] speaks wisdom, and to whom in pledge at some previous time Odin had given his eye and Heimdallr his horn.[33] Yggdrasill too figures in the end of the world. At the doom of the gods, when the wolf breaks his fetter, then the shaking and groaning of the old tree[34] symbolize strife, war, confusion, collapse, disintegration, and ultimate return to chaos.

That is the cosmos, viewed through the media of two separate symbols, in which the Norse gods play a part. The number of these

gods varies. Snorri implies that they were twelve,[35] but he elsewhere remarks that Odin has twelve names.[36] Other accounts,
moreover, give names of other gods. Certain it is that they are not
absolutely or always distinct from one another, and it is more than
likely that they are only different aspects of one deity. Nevertheless, it is convenient, if nothing more, to keep them apart, as it is
confusing to merge them too rapidly into one. The gods, therefore,
may be listed as follows: Odin, Thor, Njordr, Tyr, Bragi, Heimdallr, Hodr, Vidarr, Vali (or Ali), Ullr, Loki, Hoenir, Baldr,
Kvasir, Freyr. The goddesses are less clearly defined and are greater
in number: Frigg, Freyja, Jord, Saga, Sigyn, Fir, Nanna, Gefja,
Fulla, Sjofn, Lofn, Var, Vor, Syn, Sith, Idunn, Hlin, Snotra, Gna,
Sol, Byl, Gerdr, Rindr. Of some of these divinities the attributes
are certain; of a few, such as Jord, "earth", the names are trans-
parent. Of most, however, little is known except their isolated actions; and on these few acts, unless exact parallels exist in other
religions, it is hazardous to erect too high or imposing a structure.
Of some few, however, a great deal is known, as even a cursory
reading of the Elder Edda will show. Of others, of whom equally
much is known, even the strictly divine origin may be questioned.
Njordr, for instance, the father of Freyr and Freyja, certainly a
most ancient figure, since he is connected with the sea, is not of
the race of the Aesir at all,[37] but is a hostage given them by the
Vanir, another family (of demi-gods) whose struggle with the Aesir
ended in an armed truce. In exchange for Njordr, the Aesir gave
in return "the one that men call Hoenir" (a paraclete?) ; but although Hoenir, therefore, presumably lives among the Vanir, he
yet figures in more than one instance as a member of a Norse
trinity, the other members of which are Loki and Odin, and the
whole significance of which, like that of divine trinities everywhere,
is not precisely clear.[38]

Similarly, Loki, the crafty, witty, and often evil-spirited god,
although numbered by Snorri among the Aesir,[39] and even mentioned as a brother of Helblindi,[40] who is Odin,[41] is yet the son
of Farbauti, a giant, and Laufey, "leaf-island", or Nal, "needle".[42]
His maternal origin thus allies him with other leaf-born or island-
born deities elsewhere—Agni in India, with whom the parallel is
most precise, and Apollo in Greece; but his giant ancestry requires
that he be virtually adopted[43] into the company of the Aesir be-

243

fore he can be recognized as one of them. But Loki's many meta-morphoses show, as clearly as any evidence possibly can, that no single name of any single personification, or avatar, can ever be more than partially satisfactory in explaining the whole complex intellectual concept. The roots and branches of Loki's genealogy spread out over and around the earth; but in another country "Loki" will have changed his name, lost some of his functions, assumed the costume and manners of the foreign land—and even, in a final transmutation, have quite forfeited his own individuality, ap-pearing here as half of one new god, and there as half of another. The parallel is clear, for example, in the transformation of Sara-nyu, the mother of the As'vins in Vedic mythology, into a mare in order to bear her twin sons, and the similar metamorphosis of Loki into a mare when he gives birth to the eight-footed horse Sleipnir[44]; yet no one would therefore directly identify Saranyu and Loki, even though the whole conception be in each instance demonstrably the same. All the gods of the Norse pantheon, like-wise, it may be surmised, have parallels elsewhere—first, no doubt, or at least most easily to be recognized, among people of Indo-European speech; but not exclusively there, for, if all myth be, in the end, psychological, or if—and this is the same postulate—the cosmos is really and precisely the same whether viewed from the inside, as man imperfectly sees it, or from the outside—and that man cannot see—then, certainly, all myths are merely different views of the same essential, they can differ only in details, and even in these details they will overlap one another. This point of view, this perception of identity, the Norsemen appear to have had in common with the Ayrans in India, and, as it may perhaps be conjectured, with the earliest Greeks. To say, then, that Loki is the god of fire is but to utter a meagre bit of the whole truth: Loki is a Mephistophelean figure of chameleon-like changes; and, like his Faustian counterpart, he has in his spirit a part of the darkness which first gave birth to light.

A word must be said of Baldr and his death.[45] Much has been made of the Christian-like aspects of the good god Baldr; but it is certainly unnecessary to posit Christian influence—and, indeed, if one be looking for such influence, it is easier to find a similarity to the crucifixion in the self-sacrifice of Odin[46] than in any single action of Baldr. Nevertheless, Baldr is certainly the one of the

Aesir in whom moral qualities are most conspicuous: in him there appears to be no intermingling of craft, or guile, or evil of any kind. He has, therefore, been taken to represent the moral side of Norse religion. To a certain extent that may be true; but a more certain clue to his nature would appear to be the fact that after Ragnarok, the end of the gods, Hodr and Baldr return together to dwell with Odin and to discuss the things of the past.[47] Baldr, if he represent only the good, requires, nevertheless, his polar opposite for continued existence: this seems to be given him in Hodr, his slayer. Now Hodr is not representative of complete evil: quite to the contrary, he is merely blind; but his hand is guided by the spirit of evil—in this case, Loki, who, however, is himself, in turn, not mere badness unrelieved. The possibilities of interpretation are limitless; but what is certain is that both good and evil are thought of as existent even after the end of the gods.

In the return of others of the gods after the end of this world there appears to be something superficially similar to the view of the Vedas, almost appallingly impersonal, with its plunging aeons of repeated cycles of time extending far beyond the limits even of human imagining. Baldr does not return alone to found a more perfect world; besides Hodr, who returns with him, come Vidarr and Vali and Hoenir,[48] and the sons of Odin's mysterious brothers[49] Vili and Ve. All these return to dwell in the new world; and if it be in part a better world because it is, at least, a new one, yet destructive forces are there, as in the person of the dragon Nidhoggr,[50] to complete the necessary tension of existence.

This somewhat cold impersonalism is the most typical quality of Old Norse religion. To read Christian ethics into the Baldr myth is, therefore, to be guilty of an error in historical judgment and even in imaginative interpretation. It is hard, indeed, to find what is the ethic of Norse religion, so strictly metaphysical is it. The world of duration is seen as the constant battle-ground of conflicting forces, both of which are necessary for existence. The armed truce is characteristic. One of the finest qualities of this religion, therefore, is the natural result of its most typical one—that is, the sense of tense alertness everywhere: the gods preserve themselves only by constant watchfulness; the universe exists only in a perilous balance between growth and decay; and all things that are—gods, giants, men, animals, plants, rocks—are doomed to eventual disintegration and return to chaos. And from this chaos the cycle of creation once again begins. This is the stark view which the theology of the North seems to present.

It is wholly consistent with this cold, uncompromising view of things as they are, that what there is of explicit ethical teaching in Norse religion should be so worldly as almost to be profanely jocular. The highest counsels are those of prudence:

> Praise a day at evening,
> a sword when tried,
> ice when crossed,
> a wife on funeral pyre,
> a maid when married,
> and ale when drunk.[51]

The highest virtues, likewise, are those of all heroic ages: valor, and pride therein; courage, and the fame it brings; loyalty to friends, and a united spirit against the foe.[52] The gentler graces are almost entirely lacking: non-resistance to evil, or the return of good for evil, is quite unknown, either in the Platonic or in the Christian sense.

Passing over the magnificent poetry in which it is often expressed, what can be found in Old Norse Religion, once the symbols can be read, is a credible hypothesis. And if this hypothesis be once accepted, then there are just as great bottomless profundities in Norse religion as in any other. It is only the strangeness that needs to be overcome; and the setting need never be taken too literally. The Norse riddles are not essentially different from the Brahmodya of Hinduism and the perplexing obliquities of Zen Buddhism; and they are quite as much worth pondering.

Old Norse religion is strictly theological, strictly, indeed, traditional and metaphysical: from it may be abstracted, therefore, fragments of a creed answerable with a *yea* on many levels of thought. It is also capable of posing in poetical guise the unanswerable problems of eternity. Of these eternal problems, the first stanza of *Reginsmál* phrases one thus:

> What is the fish that runs in the flood
> And itself from ill cannot save?

The thought is alien, and the words are strange; but it is the central mystery that is thus expressed.

NOTES

1. There are other original sources. The sagas abound in religious references from which much can be learned. The Poetic Edda, however, contains the myths of the gods in what seems to be the purest form, unadulterated by history or heroic legend.

2. The name has been variously interpreted. It may mean "yawning gap"; or, if *ginnunga* be the genitive singular of a proper noun, then it is the gap, or gaping void, or yawning open mouth, or gullet, of the being prior even to chaos. There are Vedic parallels, such as the source of all life in hunger.

3. *Gylfaginning* V and VI. References to *Gylfaginning, Skáldskaparmál,* and *Háttatal* are to the Prose Edda; all others, unless specially identified, are to the Poetic Edda, with the numbering of stanzas according to the edition of Gustav Neckel (Heidelberg, 1936). A variation will be observed in Neckel's arrangement and that adopted in the excellent English translation by Henry Adams Bellows (American Scandinavian Foundation; Princeton University Press, 1936); but the differences are not numerous, and the corresponding passages can be easily found in the text and the translation.

4. Niflheim (ON *nifl;* German *Nebel,* "cloud") is known later as the home of the dead; and Muspellsheim is later the home of Surtr, who, in the end, destroys the ordered cosmos. *Muspell*— (the word occurs in ON, OS, OE, and OHG) may mean "fire"; but it may also mean something like "the end of the world". For an excellent brief discussion and a useful bibliography see the notes to the Bavarian poem *Muspilli* (c. 830 a.d.) in W. Braune, *Althochdeutsches Lesebuch* (Max Niemeyer, Halle, 1928) p. 200.

5. *Volospá,* 3: *A'r var alda that er Ymir byggdi.*

6. *Volospá,* 3, 4, 5; *Vafthrúdnismál* 20, 21; *Gylfaginning* VI, VII, VIII.

7. *Gylfaginning,* Prologue.

8. *Vafthrúdnismál* 21; *Hyndlolióð* 33.

9. The *iotunar,* or "giants", are, to be sure, the destructive powers against which the gods are required always to be on guard, and the gigantomachy of the Eddas is presumably the same as other gigantomachies everywhere; yet the *iotunn* Ymir, in whom all things potentially are, is neither good nor bad, is neither a sustaining nor a destroying power, is not even—to put it in the most general terms—hot or cold, for these dis-

tinctions remain dormant until his dismemberment: only then is the cosmos established.

10. The polar opposites of hot and cold are mentioned in Snorri's account of Ymir's generation, and in any world of duration some such pair of opposed principles must necessarily be posited; but the Younger Edda's change of the *Volospá* quotation from *Á'r var aldi that er Ymir byggdi* to the birth of Ymir from cold and heat may mean either of two things: a different tradition; or a deliberate interpretation.

11. Stanza 33.

12. *Gylfaginning* VI; *Skáldskaparmál* II.

13. *Gylfaginning* VI. The word is *mathr:* definitely "man".

14. *Gylfaginning* VI.

15. In *Lokasenna* 26 they are accused by Loki of intercourse with Odin's wife, Frigg. Nothing more is known of the episode.

16. *Gylfaginning* IX. The names presumably mean "ash" and "elm". In *Volospá* 18 the same story is told of Askr and Embla, with the important difference that Odin, Hoenir, and Lodurr (=Loki), rather than Odin, Vili, and Ve, give spirit, sense, and heat to Askr and Embla. It is likely that the *Volospá* version is correct, and that the Old Norse trinity is really composed of Odin, Hoenir, and Loki.

17. *Gylfaginning* XX.

18. *Skáldskaparmál* XX, XXII.

19. The solution of this particular problem in the Vedas (*e.g.* RV X, 129) makes an interesting comparison.

20. *Cf.* note 4 above.

21. *Cf.* note 4 above.

22. *Volospá* 49. The wolf Fenrir is fettered by the chain Gleipnir, made (Gylfaginning XXXIV) of six things: the noise of a cat's footstep; the beard of a woman; the roots of a rock; the sinews of a bear; the breath of a fish; the spittle of a bird. As a pledge that the trying-on of this fetter should not be a trap, the god Tyr laid his hand in the wolf's mouth. Once bound, and the world, for a time, safe, he was not again released; but Tyr lost his hand. Tyr's opponent in the final struggle is the dog Garmr; each is slain by the other.

23. *Volospá* 50; *Gylfaginning* IV.

24. *Gylfaginning* XIII.

25. *Volospá* 55, 56; *Gylfaginning* LI contains the whole account of the end of this world.

26. *Georgics* II, 291-2.

27. Yggr is one of the names of Odin; *drasill* is a rare word for "horse". For the complete evidence, and for Vedic parallels, see the *Journal of the American Oriental Society*, Vol. 67, No. 4 (1947), where the

OLD NORSE RELIGION

subject has been discussed under the heading of *RV 10, 27, 14*.

28. *Hávamál* 138: *"... siðlfr siðlfom mér"*. The hypothesis of Christian influence in this crucifixion is quite unnecessary. See Herman Güntert, *Arische Welt-könig und Heiland*, p. 151.

29. *Cf. Volospá* 2 and 3; *Grímnismál* 44; and (on the other hand) *Svipdagsmál*, throughout which the tree is the leading symbol.

30. *Grímnismál* 31; *Volospá* 19 and 66; *Gylfaginning* XVI.

31. *Thaeatetus* 180d.

32. *Sigrdrífomál* 14; *Volospá* 46.

33. *Volospá* 27; *Gylfaginning* 15. F. Detter and R. Heinzel, *Saemundar Edda* (Leipzig, 1903) II, p. 36, point out that it is probably the hearing *(hliod)*, not the horn, of Heimdallr, and the sight of Odin that are hidden in Mimr's well. Since Heimdallr hears everything (even the sound of the grass's growing), and since Odin possesses equally all-encompassing sight, it may perhaps be guessed that the depositing of these senses at the foot of the cosmic tree signifies the limiting of even the deities in a circumscribed world of space and time.

34. *Volospá* 47.

35. *Gylfaginning* XIV, XX.

36. *Gylfaginning* III.

37. *Gylfaginning* XXIII.

38. For Hoenir see *Gylfaginning* XXXIII; *Skáldskaparmál* I, XV, XXXIX; *Volospá* 18, 63.

39. *Gylfaginning* XLIV.

40. *Gylfaginning* XXXIII.

41. *Grímnismál* 46; *Gylfaginning* XX.

42. *Gylfaginning* XXXIII; *Skáldskaparmál* XVI. The "needle" and the "leaf" are presumably equivalent.

43. *Lokasenna* XVI.

44. *Gylfaginning* XLII; *Hyndloliód* 40.

45. Baldr was slain by the blind Hodr with a mistletoe arrow, the aim being given him by Loki. The mistletoe was the only living thing which had taken no oath not to harm Baldr. See *Gylfaginning* XXI, XXII, XLIX; *Volospá* 31.

46. See note 28 above.

47. *Gylfaginning* LIII; *Volospá* 62.

48. *Gylfaginning* LIII.

49. *Volospá* 62, 63; *Gylfaginning* LIII.

50. *Volospá* 66.

51. *Hávamál* 81.

52. *Hávamál* 42, 43, 77, 78.

BIBLIOGRAPHY

Corpus Poeticum Boreale, ed., G. Vigfusson and F. York Powell, 2 Vols. (Oxford, 1883).

Edda, die Lieder des Codex Regius nebst verwandten Denkmälern, ed. Gustav Neckel, 2 vols. (Heidelberg, 1936).

Saemundar Edda, ed., F. Detter and R. Heinzel, 2 vols. (Leipzig, 1903).

The Poetic Edda, trans., Henry Adams Bellows, American Scandinavian Foundation (Princeton University Press, 1936).

Die Prosaische Edda, ed., Ernst Wilken, 2 vols. (Paderborn, 1913).

The Prose Edda, trans., Arthur Gilchrist Brodeur, American Scandinavian Foundation (Oxford University Press, 1929).

Arische Religion, Leopold von Schroeder (Leipzig, 1914).

Grundriss der germanischen Philologie, ed., Hermann Paul, 2 ed. (Trübner, Strassburg, 1900), Vol. III, XI *Abschnitt: Mythologie* (Eugen Mogk).

Lehrbuch der Religionsgeschichte, ed., Chantapie de la Saussaye (Tübingen, 1925), Vol. II, pp. 540-597: *Die Germanen* (Vilhelm Grönbeck).

Studier over de nordiske Gude- og Heltesagns Oprindelse, Sophus Bugge, (Christiania, 1881-89).

TIBETAN RELIGION

*Born in 1900 in Ch'ien-an, a mountainous district east of Pei-
ping (near the Great Wall), Li An-che received his formal education at Yenching University, Peiping, taking his B.S. degree there
in 1929. He was awarded a fellowship by the Rockefeller Foundation, 1934-36, to pursue post-graduate studies in anthropology at
the University of California (Berkeley) and at Yale. He did field
work at Zuni, New Mexico and in Yucatan, Mexico. From 1926 to
1927 he served as assistant in the department of sociology, Yenching
University. Then followed a research-fellowship at Harvard-Yench-
ing Institute, Yenching and a lectureship at the National University of Peiping.*

*From 1936 to 1938 he was lecturer in anthropology at Yenching,
managing editor of the Yenching Journal of Social Studies and a
member of the graduate school. He did field work in the ethnic
province of the Tibetan speaking peoples of Amdo from 1938 until
1941. In 1941 he was made professor of anthropology and chairman of the department of sociology and director of the West China
Frontier Research Institute, West China Union University, Chengtu,
Szechwan, China, from which Institute he was granted a sabbatical,
1947-48. Since 1944 he has been a member of the Committee on
Frontier Education, Ministry of Education, China.*

*He is now lecturer (1947-48) with the rank of professor in the
department of anthropology in the Yale Graduate School.*

*Many of his publications are in Chinese, e.g., "A Cultural Ap-
proach to the Study of the Chinese Books of Li" (1930); "Logic of
Meaning" (1934); "Aesthetics" (1934); translations of Frazer's Sympathetic Magic (1930), of Malinowski's Sex and Repression (1934);
etc. He has contributed many articles to journals, to the "American
Anthropologist", the "Yenching Journal of Social Studies"—articles dealing with Tibetan culture and religion.*

Editor

TIBETAN RELIGION

LI AN-CHE

THE ADJECTIVE "Tibetan" covers a wider range in connection with the Tibetan-speaking peoples than the substantive "Tibet," which is a political unit. For political Tibet is only one of the three provinces occupied by people of Tibetan language and culture, the other two being Kham (Sikang) and Amdo. Political Tibet is subdivided into Tsang, Ü (Dbus) and Ari (Ngari). Kham is east of Tibet, and Amdo is northeast of Kham. Kham is a regular province under Chinese government, while Amdo covers the borders of the Chinese provinces of Szechwan, Kansu and Tsinghai (Kokonor). It is Tibet proper that has been ruled by the Dalai Lama, the priest-king, whose seat is Lhasa, Ü.

The Tibetan religion, popularly known as Lamaism, prevails not only over Tibet, but also over Kham and Amdo. Actually it has been the religion of all the Mongols. *Lama* being the Tibetan term for Buddhist priests, their religion or Buddhism is called by non-believers Lamaism. To follow the logic of calling a religion by the name of its priests, Chinese Buddhism might have been called *Hoshangism*. But to the Tibetan and Mongolian believers, their religion is simply *the* religion. No other name is recognized.

Tibetan religion, however, also includes *Bon*. This is based on the magico-religious beliefs of the Tibetan-speaking peoples before the introduction of Buddhism, but has been so much influenced by the latter that it now has little to distinguish it except externals and names. Furthermore, Bonist priests are also called *lamas*. Here we propose to treat both Bonism and the manin sects of Tibetan Buddhism or Lamaism.

Lamaism and Chinese Buddhism differ in certain respects. First, while Chinese Buddhists are vegetarians, lamas eat meat, a necessity for people at an altitude of 10,000 feet and more, and also

253

inevitable in a nomadic culture. The Chinese are often shocked by this departure from Buddhist practice; but the lamas' defence is that they do not themselves kill animals. Therefore they do not violate the Buddhist rule against life-taking. Second, Lamaism embodies esoteric Buddhism which has very fearful images in sexual embrace, while Chinese Buddhism has lost its esoteric lore, retaining only philosophical doctrines and serene type of images. Because of these two factors, many Chinese Buddhists do not realize that they and the lamas are co-religionists. Reserving esoteric Buddhism for later explanation, it may be pointed out that Chinese Buddhism from the fourth century A.D. included this form and it was formally taught in the eighth century A.D. But it was communicated only from person to person and the tradition was interrupted in China. It was carried, however, to Japan by a Japanese monk.

Third, Chinese monks leave their family entirely behind on entering the life of renunciation. Lamaic priests never lose their family ties, but are supported by their relatives as college students are. In fact, it gives a more accurate picture to consider them Tibetan scholars rather than monks. Some Tibetan priests of the older sects may even have wives in accordance with their esoteric theories and practices. Fourth, Lamaism as an institution, religiously, educationally, politically, economically and socially, has no equivalent in Chinese Buddhism. Its nearest parallel can be found only in mediaeval Catholic monasteries.

The scope of the present essay does not allow any elaboration of these contrasts or their origins, but these brief indications clarify the Tibetan religion.

The Culture Hero of the Tibetans was King Songtsangampo (569-650 A.D.) who in 641 married the Chinese Princess Wench'eng. She and her co-wife, a princess from Nepal, were ardent Buddhists and were instrumental in erecting the first temples in Tibet for worship and to house the images brought from China and Nepal. Thus originated the name Lhasa, "place of the gods." Songtsangampo sent people to India to study, and they invented the Tibetan alphabet modelled on Sanskrit. Having then a written language, Tibetan scholars were able to translate Indian Buddhist texts into Tibetan.

Four generations after this hero, King Khridetsutan married in 710 another Chinese princess, Chinch'eng. During his reign,
254

many Buddhist temples were built, but no monk had yet been properly ordained. It was Princess Chinch'eng's son, King Khrisongdetsan, who, despite opposition from the Bonists, invited from India such famous masters as Çantarakshita (Shi-ba-mtsho) and Lotus-born (Padma-bhyun-gnas), and in 762-766 had the first monastery, Samye, built. The first seven monks were also ordained by this time.

The Buddhism then prevailing belonged to the Yogacarya Mahayana School, which was opposed both by the native Bonists and by the Chinese missionary monks—by the former, because Budhism represented a foreign culture; by the latter, because it was too much colored with image-worship and wonder-working, for the Chinese monks preferred philosophical meditation. But when both opposition parties had been defeated in open debates, the Chinese monks left the field and the Bonists undertook to assimilate Buddhism to Bonism.

Khrisongdetsan's grandson Khriralpacan was even more vigorous in promoting Buddhism of this type. Besides establishing more temples and monasteries, he gave State support to them. He organized his subjects into groups each composed of seven families and ordered each group to support one monk. But his zeal cost him his life, and his brother Langdarma ascended the throne in 836. Although Langdarma did not live long, he was able to wipe out whatever Buddhism there was in Tibet by persecution. Later Buddhism was revived by refugee lamas from Amdo, cooperating with Chinese monks, and in commemoration of the Chinese contribution, Tibetan lamas still wear a badge of the monks' garments. As we shall see later, Amdo has been the base of reinforcement for Tibetan Buddhism up to the present day.

The Buddhism which immediately followed Bonism but was prior to Langdarma is called Ningma, the ancient. Later revivals and reformations are successively known as Sakya, Kagyud, and Gelug. Beginning with Bon, the different orders are popularly designated by colors, respectively the Black, the Red, the Multiple, the White and the Yellow. Of course, the colors have no theoretical significance at all except that in Buddhism "black" is a derogatory description in contradistinction with "white," the pure, in the same way as we speak of "black magic" and "white magic." The so-called "Black-Hats" have nothing to do with the Bonists. In the sacred dances of the lamaseries today, they represent monks of the Red Sect. As an official badge, the White Sect has both red and black hats. The Red Sect is generally called the Unreformed Church in contrast with the Yellow Sect as the Reformed. The Multiple-colored and the White Sects are the semi-reformed. It is the Reformed or Yellow Sect which has also become the Orthodox or Established Church, because its representative, the Dalai Lama, has also a temporal rule over Tibet.

BON OR PRE-BUDDHISTIC TIBETAN FAITH[1]

Since Bonism, though pre-Buddhistic, has become so syncretised with Tibetan Buddhism, it may for practical purposes be taken as one of the sects of Lamaism. Of course, the Buddhist lamas do not take the *Bonpo* or Bonists into the fold of their fellow-believers. But the difference between the two is simply a matter of form. For example, Bonpo keep the sacred objects to their left in circum-ambulation (walk counter-clockwise), while lamas of all denominations keep them to their right (walk clockwise). Names of the deities and scriptures in Bonism are different from those in Lamaism, but their functions and ideologies correspond.

Quoting a Bon scripture, a Buddhist Tibetan historian[2] says: "In the present Kalpa (a fabulous period of time) when the life-span of human beings gradually changes from infinity to ten years, eighteen Masters will be born to enlighten the world." Cenrabs was one of these Masters. He was born in Shangshung, the ancient name for Ngari Khorsum in western Tibet. He founded the Bon faith in contradistinction to *Chos, the* religion of Buddhism. Some make him an incarnation of Buddha Sakyamuni (c. 557-477 B.C.) or contemporaneous with him, while others ascribe to him an earlier date than Sakyamuni's.

Çenrabs' birth was recorded with the same signs as ascribed to Sakyamuni and he was responsible for the subjugation of demons who bothered the Tibetans.

The development of Bon may be divided into three stages: two, (1) Dolbon and (2) Khyarbon, before the time of the Culture Hero Songtsangampo; and one, (3) Gyurbon, since his reign.

During the first stage, there was a lad of the Çen family in Ü who, at the age of thirteen, was possessed by a demon. This lasted for thirteen years, while he moved round all over Kham and Tibet. By the age of twenty-six, he came to himself with the power to identify demons wherever they happened to be. He originated the practice of propitiating and subjugating them for the benefit of the people. This primitive form of Dolbon is otherwise known as the "black sect," being most removed from Buddhism. Dolbon is also the name of a monastery in Kongpo, western Kham.

The second stage of Bon was reinforced by three powerful magicians from, respectively, Kashmir, Bruça (northwest of Tibet), and Shangshung. One was able to fly in the sky on a drum and to cut iron into pieces with a feather. The second could perform divination by miraculous means. And the third could drive away the evil following the death of anyone. At this stage, Bonism developed theories comparable to the Maheśvara School of Hinduism.

The third stage of Bon is divided into three sub-stages: the earliest Gyurnbon, the middle Gyurbon and the latest Gyurbon. Blue-apron Savant is credited with having originated the earliest sub-stage. Having buried some texts of an unorthodox sort by himself, he pretended to excavate them as a secret treasure to be embodied into Bonism. He was also known as having invented texts for carnal knowledge and emancipation by killing.

The middle sub-stage occurred in the reign of Khrisongdetsan, son of Princess Chinch'eng. It was the king's original policy to allow both Bon and Buddhism to propagate their teachings and practices side by side. But later, the conflict came to the point where he had to organize an open contest, in which the Bonists were defeated. Thus driven underground, Bonism assimilated Buddhism into itself.

The latest Gyurbon stage embodied another wave of disguised borrowing from Buddhism on a still larger scale after King Langdarma's suppression of Buddhism in 837-842. This stage comprises the accumulations of all the previous stages, and virtually the whole of Buddhistic literature had been assimilated into Bonism by this time. The last stage of Bonism is generally known as the "white sect," being nearest to Buddhism.

To judge by the Bonist monastery of Tengchen, the most important center of Bon in Kham and Amdo, it has all the appearance of any lamaic monastery elsewhere, and its inmates look exactly like the ordinary lamas. The images look very familiar too, only much more grotesque. Even pure Buddhistic images such as the Buddha, the Coming Buddha, the White Umbrella Goddess, etc., are worshipped side by side with other Bonistic forms.

The Grand Living Buddha and the Abbot bear the same generic names as in Lamaism. The fully-ordained monks are called Drangsrong in contrast with the Lamaic Gelong; the novice keeping thirty-six vows is called Tsangtsul, while the Lamaic name is Getshul. These and other names are either identical with or similar to those in Lamaism.

Furthermore, Bonist monasteries have the same sort of spheres of influence as other Lamaic monasteries as far as the enrollment of student-monks is concerned. Inter-monastic feuds are often the result of one's enrolling students from the area properly belonging to another. While larger monasteries offer scholastic degrees, minor ones only give instruction. Whether the number of annual festivities is large or small also depends upon the size and wealth of the particular monastery in comparison with others.

The Bonists also cause huge piles of stones to be heaped up as objects for circumambulations, and likewise have invented magic formulae to be constantly recited by the laity. While the standard Buddhist phrase is the six-syllable *"Om Mani Padme Hum,"* the Bonists use the eight-syllable phrase *"Om Madri Muye Sale-hdu."* Attempts at explaining these formulae are often futile, for their sound rather their meaning is intrinsically powerful. Finally, as has been pointed out above, Bonist circumambulation is counter-clockwise, and the Buddhist clockwise.

NINGMA OR THE RED SECT OF LAMAISM[3]

The teachings of Ningmapa, the ancient form of Tibetan Buddhism before its destruction by Langdarma, may be divided into nine categories: (1) for those who, hearing the doctrine, understand it; (2) for the perfection of those who attain enlightenment through their own exertions without being concerned with the welfare of others; (3) for those whose enlightenment results from efforts in promoting the welfare of others; (4) esoteric practices concerning external conduct; (5) esoteric practices concerning internal as well as external conduct; (6) esoteric practices aiming at the union with the Universal Spirit in meditation; (7) the Great Yoga; (8) the Anu Yoga; and (9) the Ati Yoga.

The first two (1-2) are of the Lesser Vehicle of Buddhism, while all the rest are of the Greater Vehicle. The former class serves only for the deliverance of the aspirant himself, but the latter is useful for the salvation of the many. Again, the first three (1-3) are exoteric in the sense that everybody who wants to hear them is permitted to do so. All the others are esoteric because they are accessible only to the properly initiated. The first three (1-3) are said to have been delivered by the Incarnate Buddha or Transformed Body, i.e., Sakyamuni himself. The second three (4-6) are esoteric externally, delivered by the Compensation Body or Vajrasattva. The last three (7-9) are esoteric internally, delivered by the Law Body or Samantabhadra.

Of the six categories of esoteric Buddhism, three are classed as external because they are shared by other sects of Lamaism, while the other three are internal because they are particularly characteristic of the Ningma School. The essence of esoteric Buddhism is the utilization of what is otherwise generally discarded, such as anger, lust, and what belongs to the material body. In exoteric Buddhism, the material body is considered a shackle, a source of evil, or something to be dreaded by the spirit. But in the case of esoteric Buddhism, the apparently undesirable is taken as a profitable means to help the spirit in its enriched life of perfection. In order to do this, there are three classes of teaching.

First, the "Transformed" class equivalent to the Great Yoga. It is believed that everyone has within himself what is identified with the Buddha (Enlightenment). But because of ignorance and prejudice, one becomes embedded in entanglements. By means of mentally creating the images of the tutelaries, however, one may become identified with them (union or Yoga), so that the impure are purified, and in the state of meditation thus resulting, the arteries and other parts of the body are relaxed to such an extent that there arise happiness, light and disinterestedness.

Of the eight tutelaries characteristic of this school, Excellent Merit, a manifestation of Manjuçri (God of Wisdom), is the chief. He has twenty-one heads in seven stories, each story with three heads. The number twenty-one indicates so many stages on the

259

path of perfection, and seven so many members of the Bodhisattva road. The faces are of different colors, with the red symbolizing warm-heartedness; the white, purity; the blue, constancy; the green, the four qualities of serenity, fierceness, growth and power; the yellow, completeness in all merits; and the mixed, the comprehensive nature of all phenomena.

His forty-two arms signify so many serene modes. Hence each hand holds an image of the serene type. There are two wings on the shoulders, with the left signifying expediency, and the right, wisdom. This symbolism corresponds also to that of a deity and his consort. There are eight legs, each foot treading on a *deva* king and a dragon. The eight legs indicate eight roads to salvation; the eight kings, the eight senses; and the eight dragons, the eight states of mind. Finally, embracing him, there is a consort, whose name indicates that she is the destroyer of the three arch-enemies, Greed, Anger and Ignorance.

The second class of teaching of the three internally esoteric scripture is the "Assembled," equivalent to Anu Yoga. Here in the process of creation of, and identification with the tutelaries, identification or union is emphasized. This is made possible by primarily using one's own arteries and the semen virile to produce happiness, light and disinterestedness.

The third class deals with the "Mind" alone, equivalent to Ati Yoga. It dispenses with the images and internal energies, which are characteristic of the first two classes, but is concerned with the realization of the true nature of the mind. The Ch'an School of Chinese Buddhism or what is called Zen Buddhism in Japan is quite similar in this respect. But what is unique with the Ningma School is the method of attainment in "the surpassing of the uppermost," whereby self-illumination is maintained so that the material body may vanish in the rainbow as a way of salvation.

The most important Ningma monasteries are Mingrolling and Dorjebrag of Tibet on the one hand, and Kathog, Palyul, Dsogchen and Shichen of Kham on the other; the first monastery of this Sect, Samye, was established in 762-766 in Tibet.

A boy of six or seven may be sent to the monastery to study with a tutor, first the Tibetan alphabet, second spelling, and third sentence formation. Then he will study with a lecturer the necessary formulae in chanting religious hymns. It is not until he is sixteen that his hair is shaven, when he is called a novice-to-be. When about twenty years old, he is formally initiated into thirty-six vows, and is called a novice or a regular student. From this time on, he may attend the Teaching College as auditor. His attendance is only counted when fully ordained as a monk, by taking two hundred fifty-three vows. He is examined then each time after a chapter of religious work has been explained by his teacher. Having advanced far enough by such examinations, he is called a student assistant, and he will help to guide the studies of his fellow-students. After a final examination he graduates from the Teaching College. Should he prove to be the best of all, he is entitled to a Rabbyampa degree, equivalent to the Ph.D., and three gifts, namely, a scepter (Indra's thunderbolt), a Dorje bell, and a suit of monastic garments. The few next best are given gifts of lesser importance accordingly, until the ordinary graduates are named without gifts. Those who fail in the final examination are punished by being tied to the flag-post before the chanting hall to be publicly humiliated.

A graduate of the Teaching College is qualified to enter the Training College. In accordance with the distinctions which he wins in different degrees, he may acquire the titles of "Self-perfecting lama" and "perfection-instructing lama." The former indicates self-training, while the latter, the training of others. In this College one is taught initiation ceremonies, injunctions and instructions for self-development. According to a popular saying, "One stays three years in the open and again three years in the dark." For private religious practice takes place in dark cells.

After graduation from these two colleges, a monk is entitled to the rank of a professor, which carries with it both academic and spiritual distinctions. He may either remain in the monastery to instruct students or become an abbot of some smaller one under the jurisdiction of the mother monastery. In case he aspires to further self-development, he may also travel around to visit more advanced masters for more enlightened guidance.

SAKYA OR THE MULTIPLE-COLORED SECT OF LAMAISM[4]

The originators of the Sakya Sect trace their ancestry to Khonpalboche, who was a minister to King Khrisongdetsan (born in

261

742 A.D.), son of Princess Chingch'eng. Khonpalboche's son Khon-luwangposrungba was one of the first seven monks in the monastery of Samye. Counting from the first monk, the Khon family, for ten generations produced famous monks or married lamas of the Ningma School.

In the eleventh generation, however, there were two brothers, both of whom were learned in exoteric as well as esoteric Buddhism, but one of whom saw a disturbing scene, a public dance on the street by the lamas impersonating certain deities. Khonton Konchog Gyalpo, the younger, reported this to his elder brother, who said: "The esoteric lore has become corrupted. No precious sage will now arise in Tibet. I am old, but you are young. Go to country of Mugu where betake yourself to the Chomi Translator Shihkya Yeshe [993-1078]. Learn from him the new esoteric doctrine."

Konchog Gyalpo (1034-1102) followed this course and became the founder of the Sakya Sect, establishing a monastery of that name in 1073. One explanation of the name was that the monastery was built in the middle of white sandy ground. Ground or earth in Tibetan being *sa* and white or colorless being *dkar* or *skya,* Sakya got established. The popular name "Multiple-colored" comes from the fact that on the wall of the Sakya monasteries there are usually parallel stripes of three colors, namely, red, blue, white, representing respectively the Bodhisattvas Manjuçri, Vajrapani and Avalokitesvara.

Of the seven noted Sakya lamas, the fifth became most famous, Phagspa (1235-1280). It was he who was entitled "Teacher of the Emperor" Khubilai Khan. He was able in 1258 to defeat, in a contest in the Khan's court, both Chinese Taoists and Western Nestorians, and to give a Mongolian script to the Emperor in 1269. And Tibet having been conquered by Chengis Khan in 1205, Phagspa was made sovereign ruler of the territory. Khubilai Khan would like to order all the Tibetans to join the Sakya School of faith, but Phagspa allowed them the freedom to choose their own form of religion. As time went on, Sakya influence gave place to that of Kagyud and Gelug respectively. Nevertheless, even today, it remains one of the most respected sects.

In addition to the old seat of Sakya, there gradually developed three sub-sects. First, the Ngorpa, deriving its name from its founder

Ngorpa Kungah Sangpo (1382-1456), who built Ewam Chosdan. Second, there are followers of Kungah Namgyal who founded the monastery of Gangkah Dorjedan in 1464. Third, the Tsharpas are followers of Tshachen Losel Gyamtsho, born in 1499, whose seat is the monastery of Warlung.

The Sakya priests are noted for their seven stages of study, five academic degrees, five ritualistic practices, ten rules of worship, seven ways of daily observance, and eight annual festivities. Due to limitation of space, we may summarize only the third, ritualistic practices to attain one's own psycho-physical development in process.

Having become acquainted with all religious works and instructions, one rejects from one's mind the dichotomy of things as existing outside the mind and things of mental construction. In other words, one must realize that the thinker, the thing thought about, and the thinking are but one. Such a realization is the first attainment. One's second attainment comes when one is able to create freely mental images of the tutelary deity, on whom one meditates and with whom one identifies oneself. Third, the aspirant's attainments start with the first saintly stage of perfection and proceed successively to the tenth, when finally the Buddha's wisdom is born in his mind. He will then be the Buddha in flesh.

KAGYUD OR THE WHITE SECT OF LAMAISM[5]

While some may ascribe the name of this sect to the white robes of Yogi ascetics, Ka (bkah) is generally taken to mean in Tibetan, "utterance," direct word of mouth from the Buddha, and Gyud (brgyud), the lineage of succession from master to disciple to pass on this word of mouth. There are two original lines of Kagyud and both have branched out into sub-sects and sub-sub-sects. The first transmits the various doctrines which the Dakinis (Mother Fairies) imparted to Khyungpo (1002-1064), which became known as Çangpa Kagyud; the second, the teachings which Tilopa, a Bengali ascetic about 975, passed to Naropa, janitor of the famous Indian monastery of Nalanda. From the latter the teachings were transmitted to his Tibetan disciple Marpa (1012-96). It is Marpa's line that is most powerful. Marpa's outstanding disciple was Milarepa (1040-1123), whose biography has been translated into English.[6] The life of a contemplative anchorite led by Milarepa gave a peculiar characteristic to the Kagyud School. Of Milarepa's innumerable pupils, the "sun-like" Dwagspo (1079-1161) was the founder of the main sect, Dwagspo Kagyud. His pupil, Karma Dussumkhyenpa (1110-93) founded the sub-sect, Karma Kagyud. Karma used to wear a black hat, and his second incarnation, Karma II (1204-83), was given by the Mongol emperor also a black hat, which gave rise to the "Black-hat Ones." Karma II was also the originator of the institution of reincarnated lamas. Karma III (1284-1339) had a disciple who was given by a Mongol Emperor a red hat, thus giving rise to the "Red-hat Ones." Karma IV (1340-87) initiated Tsongkhapa (1354-1419), founder of the Gelug or Yellow Sect, into the vow to renounce the five cardinal sins (murder, theft, fornication, lying, and drunkenness). Karma V, a friend of Emperor Yunglo (1403-24), had a disciple by the name of Maselogrosrinchen, who originated the institution of the Sacred Dance to dramatize the deities.

Besides Karma Kagyud, other disciples of Dwagspo's founded three other sub-sects: Tshalpa, Bahram, and Phagmo. The founder of the last sub-sect, Phagmo Grubpa (1110-70), was a native of Kham and gave rise to a dynasty and eight sub-sects. The dynasty lasted from 1349 to 1618, displaced in 1618-42 by a Karma family, which was in turn displaced in 1642 by Dalai V, whose successive incarnations have been ruling Tibet to the present day. Brugpa Kagyud, one of the eight sub-sects of Phagmo Kagyud, was once so famous as to justify a Tibetan saying: "Half of the Tibetan people are Brugpas; half of the Brugpas are begging ascetics; half of the begging ascetics are saints." For following the example of Milarepa, ascetic life is essential even for those who live in monasteries.

So far as exoteric Buddhism is concerned, Kagyud has nothing to differ from any other sect. But in esoteric Buddhism its peculiarities are associated with the art of generating internal heat and the worship of the Diamond Sow. Her shrine Samding was established by the disciples of Khyungpo, founder of Çangpa Kagyud. It does not belong to the Ningma Sect as often thought by outsiders.[7] The manifestations of this goddess are the famous Lady Living Buddhas in Tibet and elsewhere.

GELUG OR THE YELLOW SECT OF LAMAISM⁸

Both the Sakya and Kagyud Sects of Lamaism were influenced by Atiça (982-1054), whose function as a master from India in helping restore Buddhism in Tibet after its destruction by Langdarma was comparable with its first introduction by Lotus-born and Çantarakshita. But it was Tsongkhapa (1354-1419), founder of the Gelug Sect, who traced direct lineage to him. A native of Amdo, Tsongkhapa had the benefit of studying with many of the masters of the above two sects. Seeing the degenerating tendency of the Order due to conflicts between the sects because each was striving for power, he established a monastery of his own, namely the famous Geldan, in 1409, to keep "the virtuous" manner, which is the meaning of the sect. The popular name "Yellow" came from an accident, Tsongkhapa's inability to get the proper garnet color to his garments. But yellow hats and garments today are no longer characteristic of this sect, being shared by others, and anything in this color is only official with the Gelug lamas, using garnet color for ordinary wear.

Tsongkhapa's followers established more monasteries, the more famous being Chepung (Braspung) in 1416, Sera in 1419, and Kraçilhunpo in 1447. Two of his many disciples became better known through later reincarnations: Dalai who assumed temporal power in 1642, when the Mongol Prince Kusri Khan having put an end to the Karma dynasty gave it to him; and Panchen whose seat has been at Kraçilhunpo in Tsang. Dalai's power was confirmed by the Manchu emperor in 1652. The present Dalai XIV is a Chinese boy from Amdo, who on being discovered as the proper reincarnation was not yet able to speak any Tibetan. The discovery of Panchen X is still not yet decided upon, though three candidates have been competing with one another. It was due to the support from the Manchu emperors and later from the National Government of the Republic of China that the Yellow Sect of Lamaism has been the Orthodox or Established Church.

While the four monasteries of Tibet are large centers of learning, none of them has component colleges of different characters to make them comparable with modern universities. In Amdo, however, there is the monastery of Labrang, 140 miles southwest of Lanchow, provincial capital of Kansu, which does compare favorably in this respect. It was founded in 1709 by a native who had been the Abbot of a large college at Chepung. It accommodates some 3,600 inmates, including 500 Living Buddhas. These are divided into six colleges: a College of Letters, the largest of all, specializing in exoteric Buddhism; two Colleges of Theology, two Colleges of Astronomy, and one College of Medicine, all specializing in esoteric Buddhism.

The curriculum of exoteric teaching includes five classics divided into thirteen classes; Indian Logic graded in five, Transcendental Wisdom in four, Doctrine of the Mean in two, the Treatise on Reality (Abhidarma Kosa) and Monastic Discipline in two. To finish all these requires at least fifteen years of attendance. And there are two academic degrees conferred on successful candidates, equivalent to B.A. and M.A. When one completes in addition the courses of one of the esoteric colleges, something like a D.D. is granted. For those who join the colleges of esoteric Buddhism directly without training in the first college, there is no degree and the courses are grouped into only three grades, without definite years of attendance, to suit individual progress. One may transfer from the College of Letters to any of the esoteric colleges at any stage. But none from any of the latter is allowed to step into the former. The idea is that one with a liberal education may any time indulge in technical skill, but a mere technician cannot be qualified for philosophical discussion.

Public festivities consisting of sacred dances, academic and administrative officers, and stages of monastic discipline are similar in nature to those in the monasteries of older sects. Names and particular deities may be different for any particular occasion. But the pantheon is essentially the same in all denominations, being principally introduced from India. As each sect has its own deified saints, their worship may have varied emphasis on the part of sectarian believers. Even here, however, the principal ones of all sects are worshipped by all.

It is a misconception, then, to say that Tsongkhap has purged Lamaism of magical performances. In so far as esoteric Buddhism includes magic, the founder of the Yellow Sect is far from keeping away from it. Esotericism is as important to him as philosophical Buddhism. It is in comparison with the older sects that philo-

266

sophical discussion is more emphasized by him. It may also be easily understood that the common conception of Lamaism as a debased form of Buddhism, particularly due to the influence of Bonism, is unfounded. It is Bonism that was particularly influenced by Buddhism. If Tibetan Buddhism is debased in any sense, it is the difference between the later Buddhism of India, which the Tibetans borrowed, and its primitive form immediately following the Buddha. So far as Tibetan Buddhists are concerned, there are all gradations of mental response, from animatism through nihilism to condescending pity-taking on the ignorance of the masses who are entangled by verbalism. In fact, there are Lamas, who being Living Buddhas themselves would announce that they will not come back again, being fully aware of the artificiality of the institution, but at the same time refraining from doing any damage to the vested interest of their colleagues.

"What constitutes a Living Buddha?" some may ask. He is supposed to be a reincarnation of a previous deity or saint. Any important personage may find a reincarnation after his death, due to the interest of his followers in deifying him. Once recognized as a deity incarnate, he will prophesy before his death as to where and in what manner he is to be born again. Following his instructions, his followers make a search a few years after his death. A few brilliant boys may qualify for the requirements and become candidates. Selection is based on more tests and divination, including political pressure and the recognition on the part of more advanced Lamaic dignitaries. The successful candidate then becomes a Living Buddha. In accordance with vested interest in self-perpetuation, once a Living Buddha, there will surely be successive reincarnations. As new ones may come up, the number of Living Buddhas is always increasing. Previously, the Manchu Government put a limit to this number. But popular demand would make it possible for self-perpetuation on an increasing scale. The institution of the Golden Vase to help identify the reincarnations of Dalai and Panchen was adopted in 1792 by the Manchu Imperial Court as the result of a false prophecy, wherein the expected candidate turned out to be a female infant. Names of the candidates, according to this institution, were written in Manchu, Chinese and Tibetan languages together with their respective hours and dates of their births. They were put in the Golden Vases, one in Lhasa and another in Peking. After proper ceremony, lots were drawn simultaneously in these places. Identical lots as coming first out of the Vases would show the names of the successful candidates. But this institution ended with the end of the Manchu regime.

As a political mechanism, however the institution of reincarnate lamas assures Lamaism a better choice of leadership than pure aristocracy where hereditary heirs do not invariably show the proper quality. Strict discipline of the young Living Buddhas in the hands of their former incarnations' associates also eliminates the danger of having them spoiled. Even when they have full control of monastic affairs, councils of elders and assemblies of the whole congregation may be able to check their individual fancies at the expense of communal welfare. This mechanism, together with the prestige of the monastery through controlling social standards, monopolizing educational facilities, and through serving as the largest unit of economics, gives the monastery always an advantage in competing with other forces.

For it should be remembered, the Tibet-speaking peoples are organized into semi-independent groups, either under a chieftain or a monastery or a combination of the two. This is true not only in Kham and Amdo, where Dalai never had any direct control, but also even in Tibet proper where he rules indirectly through many such autonomous entities supervised by his appointees. Whenever there is any conflict between the monastery and a chieftain, it is always the former that comes out better in the long run, irrespective of denominational differences, including Bonism itself.

A last word may conclude our discussion of Tibetan religion. Each wave of reformation resulted from a revolt against previous abuses. Each aspiring denomination had something to contribute, but within each there was a tendency such that once it was dominant, abuses crept into its own system. Nowadays, the Established Church has scholastic distinction, but the highest spiritual attainments are more often found amongst those in older denominations. Considering Tibetan religion as a whole, unless there is a change in its curriculum of training to include modern science and unless the priests become interested in teaching the masses instead of merely performing rituals for them, their place in world civilization may be challenged. However, there are already signs of change.

TIBETAN RELIGION

When these become fully manifest, in addition to its direct benefit to the Tibetans, Tibetan religion will no doubt have distinctive contributions to make to the future civilization of the world.

NOTES

1. Li, An-che "Bon: the Magic-religious Belief of the Tibetan-speaking Peoples," *Southwestern Journal of Anthropology* (1948).
2. Lozang Choskyi Nima: *Mirror of the Sects* (brub-mthah-çel-me), pp. 164-169 (1801).
3. Li, An-che "Nigmapa: the Early Form of Lamaism," *Journal of the Royal Asiatic Society* (1948).
4. ————: "The Sakya Sect of Lamaism," *Journal of the West China Border Research Society*, Vol. XVI, Series A (1946).
5. ————: "The BKah-brgyud Sect of Lamaism," *Journal of American Oriental Society* (1948).
6. W. Y. Evans-Wents: *Tibet's Great Yogi, Milarepa,* Oxford University Press (1928).
7. L. A. Waddell: *Buddhism of Tibet,* p. 276 (2nd ed., 1934).
8. Li, An-che: "A Lamasery in Outline," *Journal of the West China Border Research Society,* Vol. XIV, Series A (1942).

BIBLIOGRAPHY

Without attempting any iconographical treatment and because of the amount of confusion and misconception in the current literature on Tibetan religion, a very limited reference is made as follows, in addition to those made in the notes:

W. Y. Evans-Wents: *The Tibetan Book of the Dead* (1928).
————, *Tibetan Yoga and Secret Doctrines* (1935).
Lama Yongdon: *Mipam: Lama of the Five Wisdoms* (1945).
Alexandra David-Neel: *My Journey to Lhasa* (1927).
————, *Magic and Mystery in Tibet* (1932).
————, *Superhuman Life of Gesar of Ling* (1934).
Marco Pallis: *Peaks and Lamas* (1940).

THE RELIGION OF THE
AUSTRALIAN ABORIGINES

Dr. Elkin, since 1934, has been professor of anthropology in the University of Sydney, Australia. Prior to this, he held fellowships for field work in north-west, central and south Australia and has conducted repeated researches on the religious life of the people of New Guinea as well as of the Australian aborigines. This chapter was written soon after his visit to Arnhem Land where he was associated again with the people about whose religion he writes.

He was born in West Maitland, N.S., Wales. He holds an M.A. degree from St. Paul's College, University of Sydney and a Ph.D. from the University of London. Since 1933 he has been chairman of the Committee on Anthropology of the Australian National Research Council, and now is chairman of the N.S.W. division of the Council, vice-chairman of the Aborigines' Welfare Board (N.S.W. Government) and a trustee of The Australian Museum in Sydney. Since 1933 he has been an honorary editor of "Oceania".

Besides the two volumes mentioned in the bibliography of his article he has written: "Studies in Australian Totemism", No. 2, "Oceanic Monograph" (Sydney, 1933); "Studies in Australian Linguistics" (ed.), No. 3, "Oceanic Monograph" (Sydney, 1938); "Society, the Individual and Change" (Sydney, 1941); "Our Opinions and the National Effort" (Sydney, 1941); "Wanted—A Charter for the Native Peoples of the South-West Pacific" (Sydney, 1943) and "Citizenship for the Aborigines" (Sydney, 1944).

Editor

THE RELIGION OF THE
AUSTRALIAN ABORIGINES

A. P. ELKIN

THE PEOPLE AND THEIR ENVIRONMENT

THE AUSTRALIAN Aborigines are a chocolate-brown people of average height, with broad noses, deep-set eyes, wavy hair and thick skull bones. Their culture is based on food-gathering, not on food-production. Inhabiting a country about the size of the United States of America, they numbered less than 500,000 in 1788, when its settlement by Europeans began. They were divided into about 500 tribes, each having its own territory, language or dialect, and name, and its own heritage of myths, rites and sacred sites. Groups of tribes shared social customs and some rites and beliefs, forming loose cultural communities of tribes. At present there are only about 60,000 full-bloods, many tribes having completely disappeared. In northern Australia, some groups, especially on missions, show signs of increase. In addition, there are 30,000 or more persons of mixed aboriginal and white descent. Their future lies in assimilation into the white social and economic life.

Broadly speaking, Australia presents three environments: the non-tropical east and south-eastern coastal strip from Rockhampton to the mouth of the Murray and also the small south-western corner of the continent—areas of rivers and good rainfall; the tropical northern coastal regions extending from Cape York Peninsula west to Broome, together with a hinterland up to 200 miles in depth; and the dry to desert region, west of the Great Dividing Range—a region which reaches the coast at the Great Australian Bight and also on the tropical coast south of Broome. This dry major portion of the continent is relieved, however, by two fairly

273

reliable river systems, the Darling-Murray and the Cooper Diamantina, and one unreliable—the Finke in Central Australia.

These differences of environment are reflected in life-bearing capacity. Today, all but an insignificant proportion of the white population and of its stock and crops is found within 200 miles of the eastern, south-eastern, and south-western coasts. And these same belts were comparatively thickly populated by Aborigines. Good rivers, coasts and inlets provided a regular and assured source of food within small areas. This reduced nomadism and the size of tribal territories. The many rivers, divides and inlets provided natural boundaries, within which the various groups, mostly self-contained economically, developed differences in language and custom, and became distinct tribes, many in number.

Similar conditions led to a thick multi-tribal native population in the tropical coastal region, but except in a short strip from Rockhampton to Cooktown, the white population is very sparse. The swamp-lands, valleys difficult of access, tropical wet season, and distance from the temperate centers of population and from markets, have proved an insuperable obstacle to successful European settlement. It is, however, "good blackfellow country".

The dry third region has been unfavorable to both white and black. In the great desert areas, tribal territories are very large and the population sparse. In some cases, different tribes are really widely separated sections of one tribe. Along the great river systems, however, tribes were numerous and population fairly dense, especially the lower Cooper-Diamantina which is usually flooded every year as the result of rains in north-central Queensland, and the Murray fed by the snow-capped Kosciusko mountain. The Darling River system at times almost fails while the Finke frequently does so.

The Aborigines have almost disappeared from the first region. In the second, they live in good conditions, which are usually constant and reliable. But in the third, they were and are subject to a very hard environment, in most of which rain falls only occasionally. Half of this region receives less than 10 inches of rain a year, and the rest, from 10 to 20 inches, and is everywhere subject to severe droughts.

ADAPTATION

The climatic and general geographical conditions which control the distribution of civilized man, in spite of his scientific and mechanical advances, exert a similar control on a food-gathering people. Moreover, in the latter case, at least, this control is not only economic and distributional; it is also formative in social and religious life.

A people which neither tills nor sows, and which does not breed and pasture animals, but only collects and kills, must divide the inhabitable territory into food-gathering areas, and for the most part live in separated groups, each in its own country.

The size of the local or sub-tribal group and of its domain depends, of course, on the type of country. But the constitution of the group is founded on the biological fact of male, female and children, and consists of an association of families, in Australia closely related in the male line. It seldom, if ever, happens that any one such subdivision of the tribal territory, contains all the types of foods and other useful materials, known to exist in that territory and in the surrounding tribal territories. Indiscriminate hunting and food-gathering, however, might cause depletion of food sources and certainly would cause strife. Rules were, therefore "laid down" governing food-gathering, visiting, trespassing, and co-operation. Associated with this is the "law" that the women of one local group marry the men of other groups and go to live with them. Thus, the hunting groups visit each other not only to obtain food, but also wives, and through intermarriage are linked together. The food-gatherer's existence depends on reciprocity, and this principle is applied not only to hunting and food-collecting, but also in marriage rules (e.g., exchange of sisters and nieces, own or "tribal") and, as we shall see, to ceremonial life. In each case, the unit is the local group, whose exogamy is an expression of this reciprocity and mutual inter-dependence.

Ritual

In addition to this social adaptation, the Aborigines have worked out a ritual adjustment to nature. This ritual expresses the food-gatherers' dependence on nature—on the coming of rain and the increase of animals and plants in due season. But further, through it, they maintain continuity with the past, with the cult-heroes and ancestors; and by participation in it strengthen and revivify those social and moral sentiments, on which social unity depends. Behind this is a philosophy of life—of man and nature—which may be summed up as totemistic, animistic and historical.

TOTEMISM

The basic fact or premise is the Aborigines' complete unaided parasitical dependence on nature—a dependence which is not made indirect in any way—such as by gardening, clothing, flooring or any form of housing (except occasionally in some parts). On this basis they have developed a dogma that man and nature share a common life and belong to one moral order. Geographical and economic exigencies have caused human beings to be organized into groups; but it is obvious that the natural species and phenomena on which the former depend and with which they are ever associated, are also organized in groups—namely, species and related phenomena. In accordance with the same principles of segmentation (or group organization), mutual dependence and reciprocity which operate in social and economic life, specific segments of nature, that is species and objects belonging to the tribal environment are linked with specific human segments. Thus, one human group is linked to a particular species, say, the plains kangaroo, and possibly also to several other natural species and objects. The next human group may be linked with the emu and some other species and objects; and so on. Such species are the totems of the groups concerned.

This link, it must be remembered, is not a hook which can be unfastened; it cannot be "melted" or "cut off", nor can a new one be "forged". The segment of nature to which any individual is linked was determined by this conception on birth, that is, by his membership of a related human segment. It is not a matter of choice, but of "determinism", of history, of dogma. This being so, we are not surprised to learn that the link is more than nominal: it is one of life, not merely of name.

Such is totemism in Australia. It has several forms, however, varying according to the different types of human groups linked with natural species and objects. These may be local groups, membership of which is determined by being born or conceived in a locality associated with a particular totem (animal, plant, object), clans or other social and ceremonial sub-divisions of the tribe, such as moieties, sections, or the sex-grouping, each of which frequently has its own totem or set of totems.

The important aspect of totemism, however, is its function. This is of two main types. The first is social: the group of human beings who say that a certain species is their totem or "flesh", regard it as the symbol of that common inheritance of flesh and blood which they have received through their mothers, mothers' mothers', and so on back to one matrilineal source. They, therefore, respect their totem as the flesh of their own mother, sister, brother, and mother's "uncle". They neither kill nor eat it, unless on occasions of dire distress, and then with prescribed ritual. On the other hand, the natural species acts as guardian of the totemites, warning them of danger by appearing in the flesh or in dreams, and strengthening them in illness. In addition, so real is this symbolism of common flesh that persons possessing the same social totem do not marry, never mind how distantly related they may be. Indeed in some tribes, a man does not even marry a woman whose father's social totem was the same as his own. It is "too close in religion". But there are, as far as we know, no ceremonies designed to increase the matrilineal social totems, and no sacred places connected with them, though there are myths explaining "historically" how the human groups came to be so named. Social totemism is confined to south- and central-east Australia.

This symbolic function of totemism is associated with the doctrine of pre-existence of spirits, and with a corollary that the father contributes nothing physiologically to the child, although the latter is socially and spiritually his. According to the most widely accepted doctrine, the "child-spirits" sojourn in known spirit-homes, where they were left by totemic cult-heroes or by the sky-hero in the period when these heroes walked on earth. In some regions the sky-being still creates them and puts them in the spirit-places ready for incarnation. From such places the spirits issue and directly, or sometimes indirectly in a particular vegetable or flesh food, enter the womb of the selected mother. The husband

277

usually learns through a dream or a vision what is about to happen, or has happened. The spirit-child becomes flesh through its mother, the father contributing to this process, or "growing it up", by providing the mother with food. When born, the child belongs to its father's local group and country, and will share his ritual and mythological heritage.

Incidentally, the location in his "country" of the spirit-home from which he came, and to which he will return after death, binds a person indissolubly to his "country". The bond is spiritual; it is one of life.

Cult-Totemism

The other fundamental function of totemism is to group men, according to various rules of birth, conception and locality, into "lodges" or "societies," for the observance of specific cults, each with a totemic aspect. The members of such a "lodge" will say that their totem is kangaroo, iguana, rain, emu, *etc.*, but this totem is not their "flesh" or "meat"; it is their "Dreaming". If we ask a man for his Dreaming, he might say kangaroo or iguana, or give the name of a hero; or he might commence the recital of a long myth, and even suggest organizing a rite to represent it. If he does not do so, a question about the travels, deeds and (sacred) place of the kangaroo or hero will bring reference to the myth. For cult-totemism is concerned with ritual myths which record the doings of heroes and ancestors, with sanctuaries (mostly rocks) associated with these, and with totemic groups or lodges. The heroes are (and were) human beings of heightened powers, thought of as having totems, and referred to by animal or bird names; in some cases they were great animals or birds.

The period in which these heroic beings traveled and hunted and made natural phenomena (the hills, valleys and rivers) is called the Dream-Time, while the hero or his totemic symbol is "Dreaming". The Dream-Time partakes of the nature of a dream in that the limitations of time are transcended. It is not merely past; it is present, and even the future becomes real in the present. It is a condition or state as well as a period. It includes both continuity with a creative past time, and participation in a present creative power. And man is a channel and a sacramental expres-
278

sion of, not merely a link with, the "Eternal Dream" in both its aspects—of time present and of present power.

The significance of the Dreaming is manifold. It explains through the myths how things came to be as they are. It enshrines sanctions for social rules in the examples and incidents "recorded" in the myths, and sets the patterns for the rites on which faith, hope and charity (social cohesion) depend. If through disintegration, following on the advance of white settlement, individuals have no Dreaming, they become aimless, like corks bobbing about in a ruffled stream. "He who has no Dreaming is lost".

This form of totemism, which is fundamentally an heroic cult, is found with some variations over most of Australia, except perhaps in the south-east and south-west. In the former there was a cult of sky-hero, who was one time on earth, forming its natural features, organizing social totemic groups and instituting rites and laws. He was the center of a cult, with myths and ritual, but this cult was tribal and even inter-tribal in extent. It thus differed from the Dreaming cults, each of which belongs to a sub-division of a tribe, though frequently linked with a similar sub-division or lodge in another tribe, through whose country the same hero had traveled. Indeed, the whole continent is crossed and criss-crossed with the paths traversed by the Dream-Time or sky-heroes, and to be born in, or to belong by patrilineal descent to a path, or the country crossed by it, confers on males eligibility for admission to knowledge of the heroic myths connected with that path and country.

THE RELIGIOUS MYSTERY

Initiation

Birth and descent bestow eligibility, and that only. Knowledge of the secrets, of the mystery, is imparted and gained only through initiation—a ritual death and a "rising" or re-birth, which all males must undergo. The general pattern of the initiation is the same all over the continent, but the symbol of killing varies from the knocking out of a tooth or cicatrisation, or simply the pulling out of facial and pubic hair in the east and south-west, to circumcision in the center and north-west, where some of the former operations are also practised. The new life which is gained is symbolized in the east by quartz, a substance closely associated with the sky-hero and with the rainbow, by being "painted" with red-ochre or human blood, especially in the western two-thirds of the continent, and by the gift of a pearl-shell pendant in the north-west in particular—pearl-shell, the symbol of the rainbow-serpent.

However, the chief objects revealed everywhere are the bull-roarer, the symbol and voice of the sky-hero or of the totemic Dream-Time heroes, and other sacred symbols, usually of stone; these are often transformed parts of the heroes. In addition, knowledge of myths, rites, and dogmas is imparted though only gradually and as the individual grows in strength—that is, in fitness to be the custodian of the esoteric, to be a channel of the Dreaming.

Totemic Rites

The rites revealed are of two chief kinds. In the desert and near-desert region of the continent, the most important series of rites is connected with centers associated with the totemic cult-heroes. At these places certain natural objects, mostly of rock, are said to be transformed bodies or parts of heroes or of totemic species which appear in the cult-myths. Myths in chant-form are sung, actors represent the heroic scenes, and as a rule, human blood (or else red ochre) is applied to the stone symbol. As a result the natural species increases, pre-existent "spirits" of the species going forth to be reincarnated. In some regions these "spirits" are thought of as emanations from a totemic hero or from the ancestral spirit of the species which are to be "incarnated".

In the east, west, far north-east (Cape York Peninsula) and the far north-west (the Northern Kimberley), the head man of the local country cleans the mythological totemic stone or heap of stones associated with a species; in some cases he merely rubs or hits the stone; in others he puts blood on it or mixes this with scrapings from the stone; but in all cases he "tells" the spirits of the species to go forth and increase in various named "countries" where this should normally occur. The ceremonies are less pretentious and less esoteric, and less the prerogative of secret totemic cult-societies, as we pass from the desert regions to the regular rainfall areas of the tropical and the eastern coasts and hinterlands. There is the same mythological background and the same animistic
280

doctrine of "spirit" centers of natural species, but the ritual al-most becomes a formality in the hands of the local headman and those interested.

In the desert regions, however, the performance of increase-rites is a very stern and serious business in which the whole tribe is con-cerned, for existence depends on the efficacy of the ritual. Cult-societies perform the rites, "commanded" and watched in each case by prescribed "associate-members" of the particular cult-society concerned. The preparations for the rites, the circumspection sur-rounding them, the concentration of thought, the expenditure of energy, and the use of human blood, express the importance at-tached to the rites. And what is very striking is that in most cases the members of the totemic group do not eat, except once and sacramentally, the species which has increased as a result of the rites. Members of other totems do so. In this way reciprocity oper-ates in ritual and in the results which are believed to ensue. Each group denies itself one food, and depends on the other groups for the ritual increase of the foods it does eat.

There is a second series of totemic rites, including myth-chants, action and symbols. These are usually performed at temporary sacred places, and not at sanctuaries set apart by Dream-Time heroes. Moreover, they are seldom believed to result in the increase of the species which is symbolized in the totem or in parts of the rites. These ceremonies are historical, being a re-enactment of the revered creative past and of the heroic type-life, from which all must learn. In them, singers and onlookers become carried away. They often cut themselves and they dance with all their vigor in time-ordained style, as they realize the presence of the Dreaming and, indeed, are enveloped by it, even as they are by the dust which is raised by the stamp of feet and by beating the time with sticks on the ground. The energy expended and the abandon must be seen to be realized. But an important effect is the maintenance of continuity with the past, the enhancing of the feeling of social unity in the present, and the renewal of the social sentiments, ideals and sanctions on which faith, hope and social cohesion de-pend.

In Arnhem Land, there are no increase-rituals for particular species are absent, but there is an important series of inter-tribal ceremonies representing the great serpent, which is associated with the rainbow, and another related to the "Old Woman", the "Earth Mother". The two series with their myths coalesce in some tribes. Moreover, they represent the parts played by the sky-rain and the earth, the male and female elements, in the maintenance of the normal succession of the wet season and the dry, which is essential for existence. These ceremonies, however, not only ensure this succession; they are themselves also means by which the various local clans rid themselves ritually of "uncleanliness" and the unsocial, so that the living and reciprocal relationship of each group with its totem or segment of nature will not be disrupted. For if this occurs, the seasons will be abnormal and man will suffer. Obedience to the moral and social laws, and observance of the rituals and taboos are fundamental. He who breaks or scorns these must be killed actually, or else ritually, by being thrown into the "Big Sunday", as some of the natives now term these great ceremonies. In this way the individual is made new and society is purged, the Dreaming is respected and the co-operation of nature ensured.

THE HIGHEST DEGREE

Medicine-Men

While all men are initiated into the secret life of myths, ritual, and symbol, a few selected or gifted ones proceed further, entering the mysteries of the sky-world, and become through a "Second ritual death" endowed with psychic power. These "men of high degree", or "medicine-men" as they are generally called, practise meditation, telepathy and hypnotism, claim to know what is happening at a distance, and act as coroners and seers. They also heal the sick by physical and psychological means. In south-eastern Australia they played the leading part in initiation ceremonies, for there the latter introduced the novice to the sky-hero and his world, the special province of the "men of high degree". But everywhere they were and are the tribes' link and medium with the unseen world of spirits of the dead and of other types. They deal with the apparently contingent and unexpected, especially in the sphere of sickness and death, the causes of which are deemed animistic and personal. They protect revenge-parties from the magical dangers of the way, as these go forth to exact retribution for sor-
282

cery. They are the preservers of the tribes' psychological health, and perform at least part of the rôle of the priest.

DEATH AND THE PATH OF LIFE

Burial rites vary. Internment is widespread, but the grave is usually not filled in until prescribed preliminaries have been complied with. In eastern Australia a form of "mummification" is practised, at least in the case of important men; in this the body is dried, carried about and mourned over for months, but is finally exposed or cremated. In the north-west quarter of the continent, the corpse (of important persons at least) is placed on a tree-stage until the bones are free of all flesh. These are then painted and become the center of a final "burial" ceremony, after which they are put in a sacred heroic cave, enclosed in a standing totemic coffin, or buried in totemically "dedicated" ground. An inquest to determine by various divinatory means who caused the death by sorcery, and a revenge expedition to kill "the right man" unless compensation be decided upon, have to be carried out before the final "burial". Only then too, does the soul depart to its totemic or Dream-Time home, or to the sky.

Doctrines differ regarding the fate of the soul. But extinction is seldom suggested. For the soul which pre-existed independently of human flesh before its incarnation, does not necessarily cease to exist after the instrument of its temporary embodiment is of no more use—or as the Aborigines would say, after the soul, the "shade", has finally left the body, not merely temporarily as in a dream or in a severe illness.

Thus, the child comes from the sacred Dreaming and spirit-world, and if a male, after a few years on the "outside" in the profane world, he is re-admitted through initiation to that same sacred world of the Dreaming or of the Sky, or at least to a knowledge of it in myth, rite and symbol. Finally, through the transition-rite of burial, he enters again the spirit-world—perhaps after being tested, to remain in a state of "plenty", or according to the doctrine of many tribes, to return to his spirit-home on earth, and eventually to be reincarnated. A female, however, does not travel the middle part of this path or cycle, though she does learn something of the fundamental doctrines and myths, especially as she

283

grows old. And, of course, she is the means through which the pre-existing spirits are incarnated. She is not altogether profane, and her lot, in the other world or through reincarnation, is similar to that of the male.

CONCLUSION

I have not attempted to define religion, and then to describe those beliefs and practices which fit the definition. I have preferred to describe in a necessarily summary way the Aborigines' non-material adjustment to the unseen, to the normal, and to the contingent, the doctrinal solutions he gives to the problems of life and death, and the way in which he establishes himself in his world. Therefore, I have been concerned with the environment and totemism, with pre-existence and the Dreaming, with myth and ritual. I have stressed the moral relationship of man and nature, for to the Aborigines this is the basis on which they, as food-gatherers, can understand and cope with nature's changes and chances. And I have drawn attention to the experience of unity and strength, of "faith, hope and charity" which is gained in the great ceremonies.

I have not discussed the distinction between the religious, the magico-religious, and the magical. I have been satisfied simply to convey an impression of that "world" of the Dreaming and of the cult-heroes, which is the source of life, the inspiration of social behavior and the pattern of ritual performance—a world which is ever present, and of which it is the Aborigines' earnest endeavor never to lose hold.

BIBLIOGRAPHY

A. P. ELKIN: *The Australian Aborigines: How to Understand Them.* (Sydney, 1938; 4th Reprinting 1948).

——, *Aboriginal Men of High Degree* (Sydney, 1946).

W. L. WARNER: *A Black Civilization* (New York, 1937).

B. SPENCER AND F. J. GILLEN: *The Native Tribes of Central Australia* (London, 1899).

VARIOUS AUTHORS: Articles on field-research among the Australian Aborigines, in *Oceania*, published quarterly by the Australian National Research Council; now in its XVIIIth volume.

SOUTH AMERICAN
INDIAN RELIGIONS

Dr. Julian Steward is professor of anthropology in Columbia University (since 1946). His positions have included an instructorship in anthropology in the University of Michigan, 1928-30; associate professor in the same field at the University of Utah, 1930-33; lecturer in the University of California, 1934-35; anthropologist with the Bureau of American Ethnology, 1935-42; director of the Institute of Social Anthropology, Smithsonian Institution, 1942-46.

Born in Washington, D. C., in 1902, Dr. Steward took his bachelor's degree in 1925 at Cornell University, his master's and doctor of philosophy degrees at the University of California, in 1926 and 1929 respectively.

He has published various articles and monographs on the ethnology of the Shoshonean tribes of the Great Basin, on southwestern archaeology and ethnology, on the anthropology of South America, the ethnology of British Columbia, with particular attention to the theory of culture, acculturation and area studies of contemporary peoples.

The editorship of the "Handbook of South American Indians" has been committed to him, a publication of the Bureau of American Ethnology in six volumes, of which the first two appeared in 1946.

Editor

SOUTH AMERICAN
INDIAN RELIGIONS

JULIAN H. STEWARD

THE RELIGIOUS concepts, practices, and values of the aboriginal Indian tribes of South America were as varied as those of the peoples in any other continent. The primitive Ona of Tierra del Fuego differed from the Inca of Peru no less than the Bushmen of Africa differed from the ancient Egyptians or the Malayan Negritoes from the Chinese. Despite the infinite variation of its local patterning, ritual detail, and social function among the hundreds of tribes, native South American religions may be grouped roughly into two types, one being found among the more primitive tribes and the other among the civilized peoples. These must be understood in terms not only of the more formal aspects of religious concepts and practices but of the deeper sociological patterns and values, which religion expressed and implemented.

Among the hunting and gathering tribes, who occupied eastern Brazil, the Gran Chaco, Patagonia and the Chilean archipelago, and among the simple farming tribes, who dwelled in small villages in the rain forests of the Amazon-Orinoco area and in the Lesser Antilles, religion was a matter of personal concern more than of collective or tribal interest. Its principal manifestations came in crisis situations—birth, puberty, death, sickness, and at other times when malevolent influences threatened the individual. These primitive tribes had little group worship, or cult religion, because economic and social activities provided few occasions for communal or collective projects that were of concern to the group. A corollary of the absence of group ritual was the general absence of true tribal gods and of a priesthood to mediate between man and his gods. Supernatural beings were conceptualized as various nature spirits,

287

which might threaten individuals but which were not supplicated for tribal needs, and to mythological characters.

A very different kind of religion served the needs of the more civilized peoples of the Andes and of the Circum-Caribbean area, which includes Central America, Colombia, Venezuela, and the Greater Antilles. These people were intensive farmers, they lived in large, permanent communities, and they were organized in multi-community states. Their socio-economic patterns required the construction of irrigation works, public buildings, religious centers, and forts. Empires were extended through national warfare, and civil administration necessitated strong centralized government.

Archaeological evidence indicates that religion was the principal factor that integrated society in the early phases of these cultures. The ritual aspects of agriculture placed a priestly class in a superordinate position, for it was the priesthood which reckoned planting seasons and which insured the benevolent intervention of the gods in successful cultivation, which was the most important activity of the mass of people. Later, in the periods of militarism and conquest, gods of war appear alongside the gods of farming. But in all periods, the more personal or domestic forms of religion, which characterized the primitive hunting and gathering tribes and the peoples of the Amazon, did not entirely disappear. Birth, puberty, and death rites, fear of witchcraft, practice of magic, and reliance upon the shaman for personal needs survived the cults of the local states and of the empires, and they persist in some degree even today. As controls tightened over local life, village or local gods appeared, each having its shrine or place of worship, its priests, and its public ceremonies. As states were enlarged, superior gods were added to the national hierarchical pantheon, ceremonialism ᵇ ᵉcame more complex, and a stratified priesthood developed. At each level of social integration there was an appropriate priest-temple-idol cult that implemented state purposes while reflecting its cultural values. These patterns, like those of ancient Egypt, Mesopotamia, and China, were dependent upon developed economic, social, and political institutions. They could not have occurred among the smaller, simpler societies.

We shall consider each of these two types of religion, analyzing concepts about the supernatural, describing ritual procedures, and

288

relating the purposes of religion to the cultural needs of the different tribes.

The hunting and gathering tribes of South America had extremely primitive cultures, which were very similar to those of the tribes of other marginal areas, for example, the Bushmen of South Africa, the Australians, and the aboriginal tribes of western and northern North America. All of these tribes inherited their basic religious patterns from a very old, world-wide, pre-agricultural, or palaeolithic, culture, for the principal features of their religion, were similar. Crisis rites, shamanism, witchcraft, and magic were the means by which man contended with a universe that was largely beyond his control, with a life that was extremely precarious, and with hunger, suffering, and sickness that were his daily companions. Physical survival was the primary interest of these tribes, for their dependence on hunting sparse game, gathering wild seeds, and fishing left a small margin of safety. Life was extremely insecure, infant mortality was high, famines were frequent, and the hazards of existence were great. Religious practices reflected the needs for individual survival. There were few activities, which might occasion collective ceremonialism designed to enlicit supernatural assistance for group ends.

From birth on, the precarious nature of existence required special observance to ward off evil influences. The hazards of childbirth and infancy caused the parents to observe innumerable tabus and ritual precautions. The expectant mother was subject to dietary and other restrictions. After the infant was born, both parents had to be very circumspect in their behavior. In parts of the Amazon area, it was believed that the child's welfare depended more upon what the father did than upon what the mother did, and for some days after birth, the father had to repose safely in his hammock lest his behavior bring evil to the infant, while the mother went about her business—a custom known as the couvade.

While growing up, children were variously scarified, painted, whipped, their hair cut, and the like in order to help them reach adulthood and to prepare them for marriage. Some tribes formally initiated pubescent boys into a men's secret tribal society—one of the few occurrences among these primitive peoples of a kind of cult religion. These societies had sociological as well as religious

289

significance, for they expressed male solidarity in rather extreme form. This solidarity was reinforced by the use of sacred masks and musical instruments to impersonate supernatural beings and by the practice of certain secret ritual, all of which women and uninitiated children might witness only on pain of death. Among the Tucanoan tribes of the north-west Amazon, the society was organized around a cult of the dead. The men of each local, patrilineal kin group used bark cloth masks to impersonate their ancestors and secret trumpets to imitate their voices. Young men were initiated into these secrets in a special ceremony in which they were whipped.

In Tierra del Fuego, the Ona had a similar men's organization, but, instead of centering in a cult of the dead, it involved a somewhat otiose supreme being, a religious concept that is very rare among primitive peoples. Among the Ona, young initiates were ceremonially "killed", as evidence of which they lay naked out-of-doors, sometimes in the snow, for 24 hours. After this, they were "restored", given lectures on tribal customs, and subjected to further rites.

Death was accepted without great ceremony, and there were even many instances of parenticide, or mercy-killing, when the aged, feeble, or sick became so helpless as to endanger the entire group. Among some tribes of the western Amazon a son might regretfully kill his ailing parent, cremate the corpse, mix the ashes with chicha (a kind of native beer), and reverently drink the mixture. Cremation, however, was unusual; most tribes merely buried the deceased in a simple grave. Beliefs about the soul (or souls) of the dead and its fate in the afterworld were extremely varied. Ghosts were usually regarded with some apprehension, but a cult of the dead, like that of the north-west Amazon, was not common.

Supernatural beings were not always clearly conceptualized, except as a great variety of nature spirits were thought to populate the universe. Tales of celestial beings were recounted in mythology, but these beings had little interest in the affairs of men. Bush spirits were of greater concern to people, for they were potentially malevolent, especially at night. General forces for evil could be avoided by observing tabus and by using charms and magic. Witchcraft was the most feared of all supernatural forces, and it was usually manifest in sickness. When ill, a person called upon the shaman, or medicine man, whose special contact with and control of spirit helpers enabled him to counteract witchcraft.

Among the simpler tribes, for example, some of those of Tierra del Fuego and eastern Brazil, the shaman's power came from a dead person, or ghost. Among other tribes, it came from some special nature spirit, such as an animal or bird. Treatment of disease was usually dictated by the belief that sickness was caused by a spirit object which a malevolent practitioner had shot into the patient's body. Singing, smoking, blowing on the body, and massaging, the shaman then proceeded to suck out the object and perhaps even exhibit it to his audience.

The shaman was also able to predict weather, forecast the outcome of hunting and warfare, and perhaps to control the movements of wild game. In short, he was the specialist in dealing with the supernatural, and he was called upon in times of great need. Consequently, he had very great influence over his fellow tribesmen and very often was in effect the chief.

Public ritual was not characteristic of these tribes, but some of the farming groups in the tropical rain forests held a few community ceremonies in connection with crop-growing, harvesting, fishing, and hunting. The shaman took charge of these, thus serving somewhat in the capacity of priest. Frequently, the shaman also served as oracle, calling upon his spirit-helper to furnish answers to questions asked by his clients.

The Civilized Tribes

The more personal forms of religion just described were not absent among the more civilized tribes, but they were heavily overlaid by a priest-temple-idol cult, which developed in response to the needs of complex, agricultural societies.

The principal steps in the development of national religious cults can be traced in Andean pre-history. The very early agricultural communities, though small, were grouped around ceremonial centers, which consisted of temples placed upon earth mounds. Realistic ceramic decorations from these early periods portray feline deities and gods of the mountain peaks, the earth, the ocean, and the like, and they show tribal rulers, who had attributes of divinity. In subsequent periods, as warfare increased in importance and states were enlarged through conquest, war gods become more prominent in the pantheon and human sacrifice seems to have been practiced. By the time of the Inca conquest of the Andes, a conquest which started only 100 years before the arrival of the Spaniards, human sacrifice was infrequent, though it survived in great force in the Northern Andes and around the Caribbean Sea. In the Central Andes, the Spaniards found a well-organized state religion, which was dedicated to a hierarchical pantheon of gods, ranging from the Creator and the Inca Sun God down to minor, local deities, and which was served by a comparable hierarchy of priests.

As religion developed in the Andes and in the Circum-Caribbean area, state cults were added, period by period as empires expanded, to the local or folk religion, but the latter was not eliminated. Ritual observances at birth, puberty and death, shamanistic curing, divining, and forecasting continued in force through all periods and survive among the less acculturated Indians to the present day. Each household had its shrine and fetishes, each kin group had its sacred ground where the revered male heads of lineages were buried, and each village or valley had its shrines, place gods, and local ceremonialism. The rise of the national temple cults superimposed a better organized religion on but did not replace local worship. When the Inca conquered the entire Andean area from southern Colombia to northern Chile, they required principally that the Inca emperor, who was considered to be the son of the Sun, be acknowledged as the divine ruler and as the superior of all local rulers, that the empire cult of the Creator, Sun, Moon and other gods take precedence over local gods, that priests of the national temples rank above those of the lesser temples, and that the common folk supply food, goods, and various services to the state religion. A member of the Inca empire thus found himself involved in religious spheres of increasing magnitude: personal, household, kingroup, village, local state, and empire.

Inca state religion reflected the extraordinary organizing ability of these people. The national temple cult was of such magnitude that all farmers had to provide a large portion of their produce—Garcillaso says one-third—for its support. In addition, the church drafted large numbers of craftsmen and artisans to make its religious objects and thousands of laborers to construct its temples.
292

In the pantheon of national gods, the Creator, who was really nameless but is now generally known as Viracocha, was supreme, and his image, usually in solid gold, was the principal one in all temples. Viracocha created men, and, in the rôle of Culture Hero, he taught them how to live. He created the other gods, who became his servants. Among these, the most important was the Sun, who protected and matured crops. The Sun was believed to be the divine ancestor of the Inca royal family, which, prior to their conquest of Peru, had been a small, local group, possibly a lineage. Other sky gods ranked below the Sun. Thunder was the Weather God, to whom prayers for rain were addressed, and Moon, wife of Sun, provided a basis for reckoning the calendar of agricultural ceremonies. There were several star gods, which were variously associated with agriculture, with llama herding, and with wild animals. The Earth and Sea also ranked among the major deities.

Other objects of worship, generally known as huacas, which really means "shrines", were so strictly localized that there is some question as to whether they were regarded merely as sacred places or whether they were believed to be the residing places of spirits. These included a great variety of things, such as hills, caves, springs, palaces, meeting places, bridges, tombs of ancestors, temples, and even prisons. To judge from ancient ceramic paintings, place-worship, especially of mountain peaks, has long been extremely important.

The priesthood was a complex hierarchy, which was headed by the Inca emperor, who was so divine that his sister alone was sufficiently sacred to be his wife. Principal positions under the emperor were held by members of the royal Inca family. The more important temples had a staff of diviners, sacrificers, caretakers and other assistants. The Sun temples also had a kind of nunnery, or group of women known as Virgins of the Sun, who wove sacred textiles and prepared chicha. Lesser temples and shrines were under the charge of inferior members of the priestly class.

Inca temples were built to house the priesthood and the religious equipment, but they were not places of worship. Public ceremonials were held out-of-doors and were attended by thousands of people, who enjoyed the dancing, singing, and chicha-drinking no less than the more sacred performances.

The major public ceremonials were agricultural rites, which followed a fixed cycle, but special ceremonials might be held in times of crisis or when an Inca emperor was buried or coronated. God images, mummy bundles of deceased Incas, and other religious gear were brought into the public plaza. Dances and recitations were interspersed with offerings of coca, sea shells, chicha, and sacrificial victims. Human beings were sacrificed only on important occasions, and human sacrifice, though evidently of much greater importance in earlier periods, did not compare with the gory rites of the Circum-Caribbean and Mexican tribes. Instead of human beings, llamas were generally used for blood sacrifice in major ceremonies and guinea pigs in minor ones.

The common people of the Inca empire not only participated in the national religion, but they made sacrifices to their local shrines, consulted oracles, practiced divination, and patronized sorcerers and shamans. Sorcerers were known principally as practitioners of black magic, though some of them furnished love charms. Shamans were engaged to heal sickness. As among the simpler tribes, they enlisted the assistance of their spirit-helpers when administering to a patient. Disease was believed to be caused by a spirit-object having entered the body, by the soul having strayed away by winds, and by evil forces generally, especially those attributed to witchcraft. The cause of disease was divined by examination of the entrails of a guinea pig or of spitel from coca. The shaman then sucked out the disease-object or found and restored the patient's soul, after which offerings, prayers, and sacrifices were made.

In contrast to the more primitive tribes, the Andean peoples believed that the cure of disease might also require that the patient confess any violation of the state-imposed code of behavior and do penance, both under a priest. This socialization of what, among other tribes, was a matter of private concern and involved only a shaman, reflected the highly regimented Inca society and helped implement it.

Among the Circum-Caribbean tribes, religion was integrated with a distinctive socio-political organization. Most of these tribes were extremely warlike, but they fought less to conquer empires than to take captives. Warfare was important to religion in that male captives were used as sacrificial victims. This religious expres-
294

sion, however, was but part of a deeper lust for bloodshed. Social prestige was acquired through war exploits, and a successful warrior advertised his feats by displaying the skull, arms, legs, and even the entire stuffed skin of his victims. Moreover, many of these tribes had a genuine taste for human flesh, so that a captive not only supplied the temple with a sacrificial victim and a warrior with human trophies but he supplied a substantial amount of food. Some tribes went so far as to trade in human captives, buying, selling, and fattening them, like so many animals, for the primary purpose of eating them.

The Circum-Caribbean tribes, like those of the Andes, had national deities, which were worshipped by the members of small states, or realms, and which were served by priests. These tribes, however, never achieved huge empires, comparable to that of the Inca, and they consequently lacked a standardized pantheon of deities and hierarchy of priests that dominated worship over wide areas. Instead, there was much local variation in religious organization and in conceptualization of the supernatural. Some of the less developed tribes had little more than household shrines, which were served by a member of the family. Others had true temples that were placed on mounds and that housed god images. Among such tribes, there was a true priesthood, which officiated at public ceremonies. Elsewhere, the shaman rather than the true priest was the religious leader, though he might consult oracles and preside over group ritual.

Concepts of supernatural beings among the Circum-Caribbean tribes are not well understood, for the culture of these people, particularly their state religion, rapidly disintegrated after the Spanish Conquest. It is clear, however, that celestial deities and sacred places were revered. It is also certain that there was a distinction between national and domestic religion—that the worship of state gods in various kinds of priest-temple-idol cults was superimposed on an older stratum of religion, which included offerings to local shrines and spirits, ritual observances at birth, puberty, and death, belief in witchcraft, and shamanism.

The domestic or local religious beliefs and practices had such vitality that they not only survived the imposition of national cults among the civilized tribes but they also persisted after Catholicism replaced the national religions. The early Spanish fathers, finding that witchcraft, shamanism, and other features of local supernaturalism survived along with a genuine acceptance of Christianity, decided to tolerate them so long as they did not constitute "idolatry". After all, many similar folk beliefs and practices had survived in Spain. These more personal forms of religion are very old among mankind, and they continue to flourish in many parts of the world despite an overlay of national religion. Even assimilation to modern civilization does not stamp them out entirely.

BIBLIOGRAPHY

South American Indian religions are treated in hundreds of books and articles. The few general works on the subject are not very satisfactory. The reader is therefore referred to the *Handbook of South American Indians,* each volume of which contains a fairly complete bibliography of the tribes described therein. The *Handbook* is Bulletin 143, Bureau of American Ethnology (Julian H. Steward, editor). Volumes to be consulted are:

The Marginal Tribes, vol. 1 (1946).
The Andean Civilizations, vol. 2 (1946).
Tribes of the Tropical Forests and Savannas, vol. 3 (1948).
The Circum-Caribbean Cultures, vol. 4 (1948).

SHAMANISM

Born in Bucharest in 1907, Dr. Eliade studied for the "licence ès lettres" in Bucharest, Rome and Geneva. His B.A. degree was awarded by Bucharest in 1928. His preparation for the doctorate lay in the fields of philosophy and Orientalism, and was pursued in Calcutta, Benares, Rishikesh (Himalayas) from 1928 until 1932 and awarded in 1933 upon the presentation of his thesis "Yoga, Essai sur les origines de la mystique indienne" and published in Paris in 1936.

He has been lecturer at the University of Bucharest, from 1933 until 1939, in charge of courses in the comparative history of religions, the history of Oriental philosophies and the history of logic. During these years he travelled extensively for study, in Berlin, Berne, London and Oxford. The Rumanian government sent him on a cultural mission to London during 1940-41 and for a period of years he became cultural adviser for the Rumanian legation in Portugal.

Dr. Eliade has lectured at the Sorbonne, the Ecole des Hautes Etudes, Religious Sciences section, during 1946-48. He holds membership in the Society of Men of Letters (Bucharest), the Asiatic Society (Paris), the Bengal branch of the Royal Asiatic Society (Calcutta), the Institute of Ethnography and Archaeology (Lisbon), the Academy of History and Belles Lettres (Cordova) and others. His contributions have appeared in many journals, Rumanian, French, Italian, Portuguese, Spanish, Indian and English.

Mention can be made of only a few of his publications: "Le problème de la philosophie indienne" (Buc., 1929); "L'Alchimie asiatique" (Buc., 1935); "Cosmologie et alchimie babilonienne" (Buc., 1937); "Techniques du Yoga" (Paris, 1948); and "Manuel d'histoire des religions" (Paris, 1948).

Editor

SHAMANISM

MIRCEA ELIADE

SHAMANISM* IS a religious phenomenon peculiar to Siberian
peoples. The word shaman itself is of Tungus origin (*saman*) and
it has passed, by way of Russian, into European scientific terminology. But Shamanism, although its most complete expression is
found in the Arctic and North-Asiatic regions, must not be considered as limited to those countries. It is encountered, for example,
in Indonesia, among certain North American tribes, among the
Munda peoples of southern India, etc. Likewise, traces of Shamanism could be found in ancient India, China, old Persia, and
among the Scythians. But right away an important distinction is
to be made between the religions which are dominated by Shamanic ideology and techniques (as is the case of Siberian and Indonesian religions) and those where Shamanism constitutes rather an
isolated phenomenon, limited to certain peripheral groups (India
and ancient China, etc., for instance). In the limited number of
pages at our disposal we shall have to be content to give a very
succinct account of Arctic, Siberian, and Central-Asiatic Shamanism, i.e., in localities where the religious life of the community is,
if not appropriated by the shaman, at least centered around him.

Certain writers have been accustomed to confuse the shaman
with the medicine men, magicians, and sorcerers known to every
primitive society. This confusion is improper and may give rise to
misunderstanding. For, although he may have many traits in common with the medicine man and sorcerer, the shaman is distinguished from them by a magico-religious technique which is in a
way exclusive to him and which may be called: the ecstatic trip to
Heaven, to the Lower World, or to the depths of the ocean.

---

* This essay is translated from the French by Professor Pauline Ihrig,
Ph.D. of The College of Wooster.—Ed.

Among the Siberians the shaman is not necessarily the only magician-priest, but he is the only one who can undertake this ecstatic voyage, which takes place either for the purpose of curing a sick person or to accompany the souls of the dead to Hell, or, finally— as a part of periodic collective ceremonies—to present the soul of the sacrificial horse to the Celestial Deity. It is not always the same shaman or the same class of shaman which carries out the three kinds of ecstatic voyages. Sometimes, as for example among the Yakuts, Buriats, and Tatars of Altai, two classes of shaman exist: the first "white", having relations with the God of Heaven and his sons; the others "black", concerning themselves exclusively with "spirits" (Eliade, *Le Problème du chamanisme*, p. 21), and the same dichotomy is observed also in Indonesian Shamanism (*ibid.*, p. 15). But it is always a shaman who accomplishes the ecstatic voyage, of whatever class he may be.

Shamanism is a complex religious phenomenon whose morphological and historical study has scarcely been begun. In its present form it presents several elements which are distinct although integrated into a whole: animism and ancestral worship; faith in a God of Heaven; and especially a cosmological "theory" concerning the various celestial and infernal regions through which the shaman may pass on his trips. Each of its elements plays an important rôle in the ideology and magico-religious technique of Shamanism. Indeed, if the Altaic shaman can rise to highest Heaven to bring to Bai Ülgen the soul of the sacrificial horse, he can do it because he is well acquainted with celestial topography and because he is aided in his ascent by protecting spirits. Similarly, the shaman descends into the lower regions armed with his topographical knowledge of them and protected by the friendliness of certain "guides" (guardian animals). All these ecstatic voyages are made possible by the fact that the shaman knows, on the one hand, the itinerary of the dead and of the souls of the ailing, and on the other hand, he knows how to follow these souls and capture them and reinstate them in the bodies which they have just left.

All shamans are healers and conductors of souls; they descend into the lower regions to capture the fugitive soul of the patient and also to accompany the soul of the deceased into the realm of the shades. Let us cite an example of each of these two voyages. Among the Yukaghirs, after conjuring up the spirits of the ancestors, the shaman announces: "The soul of the patient, it seems, has travelled along the road to the kingdom of Shadows". Accompanied by his protecting spirits, the shaman, too, descends into the domain of the dead and arrives in front of a small house where he meets a dog and an old woman. The latter asks him if he has come for good or temporarily. Without replying, the shaman continues his way to a river which he crosses in a small boat, still accompanied by his protecting spirits. On the opposite bank he meets, among the crowd of the dead, the relatives of the patient, who refuse to give him the latter's soul. The shaman, through his magic power, steals the soul by breathing it in. Once back on earth he succeeds in replacing it in the patient's body (Cf. V. J. Jochelson, *The Yukaghir and the Yukaghirized Tungus* [Leiden and New York, 1910–1926] pp. 196 ff.).

As for the voyage which the shaman undertakes in accompanying the soul of the dead to the kingdom of Erlik, here is the description Radlov has given of it. It concerns a séance organized to conduct the soul of a woman who has been dead forty days. The ceremonial takes place during the night, inside the *yurta,* around the fire, and begins with an invocation to the dead woman. She speaks through the shaman—who attempts to imitate her voice. She complains of not knowing the way, of being afraid to go far away from her people, etc., but she finally agrees to be conducted by the shaman, and the two of them set out together for the realm beneath the earth. On arriving there the newcomer is denied entrance by the souls of the dead. Prayers are of no avail, so brandy is then offered. The séance gradually becomes more animated, to the point of being grotesque, for the souls of the dead, through the shaman's voice, begin to quarrel among themselves and to chant all together. At last, they agree to receive the dead woman. The second part of the ceremony represents the return trip; the shaman dances and shouts until he falls to the ground, unconscious (Cf. V. V Radlov, *Aus Sibirien* [Leipzig, 1884] pp. 52 ff.).

The two voyages follow the same route through the lower regions. But it is necessary to observe that the descent sometimes reveals a submarine aspect. Thus, for example, the Tungus, Chukchees, and Lapps speak of the shamanic trance as an "immersion" (Uno Harva, *Relig. Vorstell,* p. 552). Among the Iglulik Eskimos, the shaman directs his way towards the "great mother of the seal,

Takánakapsâluk, at the bottom of the sea (K. Rasmussen, *Intellectual Culture of the Iglulik Eskimos* [Copenhagen, 1929] pp. 124 ff.). On the other hand the shamanic voyage in search of the soul of a sick person sometimes takes a heavenly direction. Thus, among the Dolgans and Yakuts the cure includes, among other magico-religious actions, a symbolic ascension of the shaman to Heaven, accomplished by means of three or nine trees which represent the three or nine heavens (Harva, *op. cit.*, pp. 545 ff.).

Consequently, there are three possible routes one may follow to bring back the soul of a patient: the subterranean descent into Hell, immersion to the bottom of the ocean, and the ascent to Heaven. The shaman's trance, although having the same ecstatic intensity, nevertheless differs in regard to its morphology; by imitating the flight of a bird one mimics the ascent to Heaven, by imitating submersion one suggests the submarine voyage, by riding a horse one descends into Hell, etc. The same ecstatic itineraries are likewise found in Indonesian Shamanism. The soul of the patient, like that of the deceased, moves towards the sea and submarine depths, or towards Heaven. And the Indonesian shaman, exactly like his Siberian colleague, follows these souls in a bark (evidently a "spirit-bark", see A. Steinmann, *Das Kultische Schiff*, pp. 182 ff.) or flies away by aid of a bird (E. M. Loeb, *Shaman and Seer*, p. 78), or magically climbs a "Tree of Life" which takes him to Heaven (Steinmann, pp. 162 ff.). This plurality of ecstatic funereal itineraries is due either to a plurality originating in religious traditions in the heart of the same people, or to the fact that different religious traditions, belonging to different cultures, met and joined within one culture. Nevertheless, one must note that the technique specifically shamanic is the ascent to Heaven. We shall see presently that there are reasons to believe that it is also the most ancient.

Among the numerous descriptions of shamanic ascents given by ethnographers, let us cite only one Altaic ritual and one ceremony of initiation among the Buryats. On the occasion of the sacrifice of the horse among the Altaics, the shaman undertakes his ecstatic voyage to the highest heaven to present the horse's soul before Bai Ülgen. After fumigating his drum, after putting on his shaman's garments and invoking Merkyut, the bird of Heaven, to "come singing" and to "sit upon his right shoulder", the officiating shaman begins the ascent. Climbing easily by means of notches in the ceremonial tree, the shaman penetrates successively the "nine heavens" and describes to his listeners, with infinite detail, everything he sees and all that is happening in each one of these heavens. In the sixth heaven he venerates the moon, in the seventh, the sun. Finally, in the ninth, he prostrates himself before Bai Ülgen and offers him the soul of the sacrificial horse. This episode marks the culminating point of the shaman's ecstatic ascent. He finds out from Bai Ülgen whether the sacrifice has been accepted and he receives weather forecasts; then the shaman tumbles down, exhausted, and after a moment of silence, awakens as from a deep sleep (Radlov, *Aus Sibirien*, II, pp. 19-51; cf. Harva, pp. 553 ff.).

The Buryat ritual of shamanic initiation also includes an ascension. Nine trees are placed in a row and the candidate climbs all the way up the ninth one, then passes over the tops of all the others. Also a birch tree is placed in the *yurta*, its top sticking out of an opening; the neophyte climbs the tree, with a sabre in his hand, until he gets above the tent, thus accomplishing passage into the farthest Heaven (cf. Harva, pp. 487 ff.). The birch is named *udesi-burkhan*, "the guardian of the door", for it opens to the shaman the entrance to Heaven (Harva, *ibid.*), but it is also called "ladder" (*sita*) or "step" (*geskigür;* cf. Partanen, *A Description of Buriat Shamanism*, p. 16).

The symmetry between these two shamanic ascents is perfect. Several factors are to be noted: (1) going up to Heaven is symbolized by ceremonial climbing; (2) the tree (the birch) represents the Cosmic Tree and the notches symbolize the heavens; (3) therefore, the shamanic birch tree is assimilated by the Cosmic Tree which is supposed to be in the "Center of the World". Let us leave to one side the Oriental influences which we have already had occasion to study in *Problèm du chamanisme* (pp. 39 ff.). The important fact is the relationship between the shaman and the Tree of the World; the ecstatic trance (= the celestial voyage) is accomplished during the ritual scaling of a birch tree which represents the Cosmic Tree. This relationship is confirmed by additional facts. The capital rôle played by the shamanic drum in preparation for the trance is well known. Now, among the Samoyedes, Ostyaks, Yakuts, Tunguses, Dolgans, and Golds, the frame of the drum is supposed to be made of the very wood of the Tree of the World (cf. E. Emsheimer, *Schamanentrommel und Trommelbaum,* "Ethnos" [1946] pp. 166-181, esp. pp. 173-174, 177). That means that the manipulation of this drum is already the equivalent, in a certain sense, of the symbolical ascension of the Tree of the World. Just as the shaman, in climbing the birch tree, is really climbing the Tree of the World, so the shaman who beats his drum finds himself very close to that Tree of the World. But the Tree always represents an *Axis Mundi,* i.e., the point at which communication between Heaven, Earth, and Hell is made. The idea of an axis linking the three cosmic zones is frequent among the Arctic, Siberian, and Central-Asiatic peoples (Eliade, pp. 143 ff.) and it is found also in other archaic cultures, a fact which makes one believe that it is very ancient *(ibid.,* pp. 36 ff.).

The thing that is peculiar to Shamanism is not this "theory" of an *Axis Mundi* connecting the three cosmic zones, *but the ecstatic technique which permits the shaman to fly up to the Heavens or to descend to Hell.* It has just been seen that the ecstatic trance always includes a symbol of the Tree of the World (birch tree, pillar, drum). That is why the shamanic drum (= the Tree of the World) is called by the Yakuts the "shaman's horse", and by the Altaics "the whip" (Harva, p. 536); for it is with the "horse" that the shaman carries out his ecstatic voyage. (Other Siberian and Altaic peoples call the drum "bow", or use in place of a drum, a bow, Harva, pp. 537 ff.; it is the same idea of "flight", "rapid ascension" and "magic voyage".)

Let us recall that the Tree of the World plays an important rôle also in Indonesian shamanism. Indeed, the so-called "spirit-barks" in which the Indonesian shaman is supposed to undertake the (ecstatic) voyage in pursuit of souls of the sick, sometimes bear a symbol of the Tree of the World (Steinmann, pp. 163 ff.). As elsewhere the Tree, for the Indonesians, links Earth to Heaven, i.e., it is an *Axis Mundi.* But a symbol of this Tree of the World is found in every village and even in every house (cf. H. Schärer, *Die Gottesidee der Ngadju Dajak in Süd-Borneo* [Leiden, 1946] plates I-II and pp. 76 ff.), for each house is a "Center of the World" (a notion universally widespread, cf. Eliade, pp. 43 ff.). However, the possibility of ecstatic ascent to Heaven by means of a Tree of the World, is exclusive to the shaman; what is called the

Indonesian "Tree of the shaman" is considered as a ladder leading to Heaven (Steinmann, p. 163).

On the other hand one notes a perfect symmetry in the *symbolism of flight* among the Indonesians and the Siberians and Altaics. The Siberian shaman is costumed as a bird (Harva, pp. 506 ff.) ; he imitates the movements of a flying bird (Eliade, p. 24), and he frequently counts a bird as his "ancestor" or protecting spirit (Harva, pp. 466 ff.). Likewise, in Indonesia, the shaman is supposed to be transformed into a bird (Eliade, p. 26) and he possesses magic means of flying into the air like a bird (Steinmann, pp. 162 ff.).

All these magico-religious facts prove the truth of an ecstatic structure or origin, and it is precisely this ecstatic character that bestows upon them the "shamanic" appearance. But—as we have already noted in regard to the "theory" of the *Axis Mundi* implied in the shamanic ideology of the ascent—the symbolism and the main lines of the cosmological and religious system revealed by these various shamanic rituals surpass the domain of Shamanism properly so called. The ceremonial ascent to Heaven by scaling the sacrificial post is found, for example, in the Brahman sacrifice which is a *dûrohana,* a "difficult mounting". The sacrificer climbs by means of steps the sacrificial post and on reaching the summit, stretches out his arms (like the wings of a bird) and cries: "We have come to Heaven, to the Devas; we have become immortal" (*Taittirya Samhita,* I, 7, 9; cf. Eliade, *Dûrohana and the "waking dream"* in *Coomaraswamy Volume* [London, 1947]). In Egypt, Mesopotamia, and China the ritual mounting of temple stairs, of a sacred tower, of the platforms of a palace, etc., was the equivalent of an ascension through the heavens (Eliade, *Problème du chamanisme,* pp. 40 ff.). The symbolism of flying and of the bird is diffused almost everywhere throughout the world (*ibid.,* pp. 34 ff.). Along with a great number of myths and symbols (for instance, the Celestial Mountain, the "chain of arrows", the descent of the "ancestor" from heaven on a spider's thread, a vine, etc., which bound Heaven to Earth), this symbolism is in its turn inclosed in a universal and old magico-religious ensemble which can be called: the ideology and technique of the ascension (or elevation) of the human soul to the heavens (or to God). The countless symbols, myths, and rites which constitute this ensemble reveal, more or

305

less explicitly, faith in the possibility of a concrete communication between Earth and Heaven. The myths speak of a distant epoch when man (or the mythical ancestor) could pass at will between Heaven and Earth, and, consequently, direct relationship between the human race and divinity was within reach of everyone. As the result of a ritual sin or of some other mythical event, communication between Heaven and Earth was forbidden to the majority of humans and became reserved for a few persons only: kings, magicians, heroes, shamans, etc.

The shamanic ascension is an experience which includes—as an ideological infrastructure—a "theory" analogous to the myths and symbols just reviewed. This "theory" can be summed up as follows: the Tree of the World links the three cosmic zones and it is by means of such a "tree" (birch, drum) that the shaman ascends to the last Heaven or descends to Hell (drum). It is exclusively the shaman who can have the *experience* of this ascent, an experience which always equals an ecstatic trance. For the rest of the community, communication between the three cosmic zones is only a "theory" implied in their magico-religious beliefs and kept alive by various symbols (the central pillar of the house, identified with the "Pillar of the World", etc.; cf. Eliade, *Problème*, p. 43). So, the categorical difference between, on the one hand, the shaman and the rest of the community, and, on the other hand, between Shamanism and the magico-religious theories and practices of everywhere else (for example, the Brahman sacrifice, etc.) —this difference is constituted by the *intensity* of the shaman's ecstatic experience. The trance is peculiar to Shamanism to such a degree that people have even tried to explain this religious phenomenon by psychopathology (see for example the book by A. Ohlmarks; but see also Eliade, *Problème*, pp. 9 ff.). Of course, the majority of shamans are (or have been) psychopaths. But what matters is not this pathological predisposition, but on the contrary, the fact that the shaman, although generally a former psychopath, has succeeded in *curing himself*. In spite of his "trances", the shaman presents a reintegrated conscience.

Whatever the origin or pathological structure of the shamanic trance may have been, religious psychology and the history of religions are interested in other facts: the *images* and *symbols* which express and give a consistent signification to this trance. Now, the
306

SHAMANISM

same *images* and the same *symbols*, organized and articulated into one general cosmo-theological "theory", are found almost everywhere; they constitute, in truth, an important sector of the history of religions. It is true that the shaman manifests a tendency to *experiment in a concrete manner* with this cosmo-theological "theory". The resulting shamanic "trance" proves to be most of the time abnormal. As for the question of knowing whether the abnormal character of this trance is due to the fact of having tried to experiment *in concreto* with certain symbolisms which, by their very nature, refuse to lend themselves to such "experimentation"— that is another problem beyond the limits of this study.

BIBLIOGRAPHY

Ouvrages Genéraux: (General Works)
MIRCEA ELIADE: "Le problème du chamanisme" *(Revue de l'Histoire des Religions,* t. CXXXI, Janvier-Juin, 1946, pp. 5-52).
ÅKE OHLMARKS: *Studien zum Problem des Schamanismus* (Lund-Kopenhagen, 1939).
J. W. LAYARD: "Shamanism. An analysis based on comparison with the flying tricksters of Malekula *(Journal of the Royal Anthropological Institute,* vol. 60, 1930, pp. 525-550).

Sur le chamanisme sibérien, matériaux et interprétation dans:
V. M. MIKHAILOWSKI: "Shamanism in Siberia and European Russia *(Journal of the Royal Anthropological Institute,* vol. 24, 1894, pp. 62-100, 126-158).
G. NIORADZE: *Der Schamanismus bei den sibirischen Völkern* (Stuttgart, 1925).
CASANOWICZ: *Shamanism of the natives of Siberia* (Smithsonian Report for 1924).
N. R. CHADWICK: "Shamanism among the tartars of central Asia" *(Journal of the Royal Anthr. Inst.,* vol. 66, 1936, pp. 75-112).
UNO HARVA: *Die religiösen Vorstellungen der altaischen Völker,* (Helsinki, 1938), spéc. pp. 449-561.
JORMA PARTANEN: "A description of Buriat Shamanism" (translation of text N° VIII, in Pozdneyev's Mongolian Chrestomathy, *(Journal de la Société Finno-Ougrienne,* vol. LI, 1941-1942, 34 p.).

Bibliographie des publications russes concernant le chamanisme:
A. A. POPOV: *Materialy dlja bibliografii ruskoj literatury po izuceniju samanstva Severo-Aziatskich narodov,* (Leningrad, 1932).

FORGOTTEN RELIGIONS

Bibliographie générale sur le chamanisme arctique, sibérien et central-asiatique, Å. Ohlmarks, pp. 356-374; Mircea Eliade, pp. 6-7.

Sur le chamanisme indonésien et polynësien:

G. A. WILKEN: *Het Shamanisme bij de volken van den indischen Archipel*, (Gravenhage, 1887).

E. M. LOEB: "The Shaman of Niue" (*American Anthropologist*, vol. 26, 1924, pp. 393-402) ; *id.* "Shaman and Seer" (*ibid.* vol. 31, 1929, pp. 60-84).

ALFRED STEINMAN: "Das Kultische Schiff in Indonesien" (*"IREK,"* 1939-1940, pp. 149-206, sp. 182 sq.).

Indications bibliographiques sur le chamanisme américain, munda, indien, iranien, chinois et germanique, Eliade, pp. 5-6.

Sur les influences indiennes sur le chamanisme central-asiatique et la controverse provoque par les travaux de S. Shirokogorov, voir Eliade, pp. 46 sq.

Concernant l'origine du mot shaman, voir B. Laufer, "Origin of the word shaman" (*American Anthropologist*, vol. 19, 1917, pp. 361-371) .

THE RELIGION OF THE ESKIMOS

Dr. Lantis has made field studies of the native cultures in Alaska; under the auspices of the U. S. Bureau of Indian Affairs in the Aleutian Islands, 1933-34; under the auspices of the American Philosophical Society and the University of California in the North Bering Sea, particularly Nunivak Island, in 1939-40; and under the auspices of the Arctic Institute of North America in the Lower Kuskokwim River area and Nunivak Island in 1946. She has also held grants for library research and writing on Alaska from the University of California (1940-41) and the Viking Fund (1947-48).

Her publications on Eskimo life and culture have appeared in the "American Ethnological Society Monographs", the "American Anthropologist", the "Journal of American Folk-Lore", the "American Philosophical Society Transactions" and in other journals. Several of her articles will appear in the forthcoming "Encyclopedia Arctica".

Born in Ohio in 1906, she holds her bachelor's degree from the University of Minnesota (1930), attended the University of Chicago and won her Ph.D. degree from the University of California at Berkeley (1939) and has taught in Reed College and at the Universities of Minnesota and California. During and after World War II she conducted social studies for the Bureau of Agricultural Economics and for the Bureau of the Census.

Editor

THE RELIGION OF THE ESKIMOS

MARGARET LANTIS

INTRODUCTION

THE ESKIMOS live in a great coastal area extending from the southeast shore of Greenland to the western shore of Bering Strait, that is, to the eastern tip of Siberia. Despite the extensive geographic range and the isolation of some groups, there is a surprising degree of uniformity of language and culture. The largest divisions are (1) the Eastern Eskimos, including those in Greenland, Baffin Land, Labrador, and the Central Region, explained below, (2) the Western Eskimos, comprising those from the mouth of the Mackenzie River to Siberia and St. Lawrence Island, and south to Kodiak Island and (formerly) Prince William Sound on the Pacific Ocean side of Alaska, and (3) the Aleuts of Alaska Peninsula and the Aleutian Islands. Because the Aleuts had become linguistically so different and because so little is known about their aboriginal religion, they are excluded from this discussion. The Central Eskimos include those northwest of Hudson Bay: inland on the Barren Ground and on Melville Peninsula, Franklin Isthmus, Boothia Peninsula, King William Island, and around Coronation Gulf. The most northerly group are the Polar Eskimos of Smith Sound at the northwest corner of Greenland, living close to lat. 80° N. By comparison, the Eskimos of southern Labrador and those around Bristol Bay in Alaska live in mild sub-arctic regions.

SHAMANISM

Becoming a Shaman. At Ammassalik, in East Greenland, when the youth Ajukutoq sought to become a shaman, he went to a solitary spot on a rocky hillside and sat for three days rubbing a small

311

stone around and around on a large rock. He thought always of the power he wished to possess and anxiously awaited some great event that would give it to him. He entered a trance, during which a great bear rose out of a lake, swallowed him, and he died (lost consciousness). Then it spit out his bones; gradually his body took form again; and he returned to consciousness, with his garments rushing onto him one by one. The experience was terrifying, yet exalting. Every summer for three or four years, he fasted and concentrated thus until he had acquired various strong spirit-helpers who had first shown themselves to him in his visions but which later he could call at will. These were pledged to help him and no others.

Even when a young boy, he had begun to receive instruction from an older angakok (shaman) who had selected him as a likely candidate. He was taught about the deities and local spirits, regarding tabus and chants and a shaman language substituting certain nouns for other common ones. In fact, most shamans had several paid teachers. Ajukutoq and his tutor kept the whole instruction secret until he was sufficiently sure of his power to demonstrate it publicly.[1]

At Pt. Hope on the northwest coast of Alaska, Umigluk when a young man and a fast runner was sent on a long errand. On the way he heard paddles dipping slowly in water, a boat came circling down as from the moon and stopped by him. A shaman who had died some time before stood up in the boat and asked about his family. Umigluk replied that they were fine. The man sank down and another rose, wearing fine clothes, and mittens with pieces of metal on them. He seemed to have one big eye instead of two. He danced, his mittens rattling. A white ermine, then a brown ermine appeared, and one chased the other around the gunwhale, which entertained Umigluk. The shaman spirit reappeared and spoke of the broken tabus that had caused his death. Then the boat disappeared and Umigluk continued on his way.

Although by the time he reached home he had forgotten the vision, during the next four days Umigluk did strange things that he could not account for. He was "crazy" (delirious?) but gradually recovered. Thereafter, the spirit in the fancy clothing took possession of Umigluk when he drummed and went into a trance in the men's ceremonial house. In this state, he learned eight songs

312

and the spirit's name, and with this assistance became a great shaman.[2]

On Nunivak Island in Bering Sea, Kangalik, who was a cripple and had had an unhappy lonely childhood and who was the son of a powerful shaman, started "dreaming" when he was eleven or twelve years old. When he told his father that he was seeing strange things in his dreams at night, his father told him not to mention this to anyone. Kangalik was very afraid at first, then came to accept his strange dreams, even felt happy because of them. Later he not only saw spirits in dreams, he might see them anywhere when awake. Any object might seem to be moving, its spirit making it move. Or tiny people and even their dogs would come out from the twigs when he looked at shrubs dreamily through nearly-closed eyes. Or at night when everyone in the men's house was asleep, Kangalik would wake up and see many people moving around on the ceiling. During such visions or after he heard a loud noise, he would tremble as shamans usually did. Because Kangalik did not talk about these experiences, he did not know for a long time that others were not having similar visions.

He tried hard to follow the instructions of his father and older men regarding tabus, regarding not sleeping much and sweeping out the ceremonial house entrance—to please the spirits—but it was difficult for him to gain sureness of his power. However, when others, having noticed that Kangalik looked ill and emaciated and having thus become aware of his peculiar reactions, asked him to cure a sick man, he undertook to do it. He found then that he heard songs coming right out of things, perhaps the lamp or the rim of his drum.[3]

There was always the belief that the novice shaman dies or nearly dies and recovers and always the idea of spiritual appointment even though the appointment was secured differently. Eastern and Western Eskimo shamans differed in that the former deliberately sought power through solitude, concentration, and physical self-mortification, while the latter were un-selfconscious—although equally suggestible—in undergoing the same conditions. The spiritual beings of their locality just came to them out of their normal solitude. At the same time, both were trained in certain earthly techniques, better demonstrated in performances by skilled mature shamans. And in both regions there was a tendency for shamanism to be carried on in certain families. This does not contradict the idea of spiritual election.

The Shamanistic Performance. A shaman in an Iglulik settlement, of the Central Eskimos, prepares to journey to the bottom of the sea. The people urge him to this, so that he can tame and conciliate the Sea Goddess, Sedna, who is withholding the sea animals that they must have for food.[4] The communion with the spirits occurs, then, in an atmosphere of great anxiety. The shaman, wearing nothing but boots and mittens, sits behind a curtain way back on the sleeping-platform in the snow house. He remains for a while in silence, breathing deeply and concentrating. He begins to call upon his helping spirits, repeating over and over, "The way is made ready for me; the way opens before me," and the people answer, "Let it be so." The spirits begin to arrive but the angakok still must struggle for a long time until he can cry that the way is open. Then "Halala—he—he—he" is heard from under the sleeping-bench, then from under the entrance passage, and recedes farther and farther, finally disappearing. Meanwhile the other people, sitting with closed eyes, sing spirit-songs in chorus. Sometimes the shaman's discarded clothes come alive and fly about the room. The people hear deep sighs and the breathing of ghost spirits who are also the shaman's helping spirits. The sounds of seals and other animals splashing and coming up to breathe also are heard. At last the angakok is heard a long way off and he shoots up from the deep to his place behind the curtain.

The shaman has learned that individuals' breaches of tabu have offended Sedna, hence she withholds the animals. People hasten to confess, under emotional stress, their most serious offenses, thereafter feeling greatly relieved. Others are grateful to them for the self-punishing confession, and all experience reassurance and joy because now there is certainty that seals will be available.[5]

In East Greenland, the shaman is placed on the floor near the house entrance with his drum and drumstick on a flat stone beside him.[6] His feet rest on the lower edge of the dry skin hanging in front of the entrance. With his hands behind him and his head forced down between his knees, he is bound tightly. A thong is bound around his head, which helps him to see clearly when all the lamps have been extinguished. He becomes stiff and uncon-

314

scious though his feet move convulsively, rattling the dry skins at the door, which sound as if caught in a rushing wind. His spirit-helper appears and sets the drum dancing around the shaman's head.

Holm described such a seance in which he participated in 1884.

> "The drum now started into motion, dancing first slowly, then with ever increasing speed, and mounted slowly up to the ceiling. Now ensued a veritable pandemonium of noises, a rattling, a blustering, and a clattering," sounding now like a machine factory, now like great winged creatures. "At one moment it was the angakok one heard, succumbing to a power mightier than himself, groaning, wailing, shrieking, whining, whispering; now came the sound of spirit-voices, some deep, some feeble, others lisping or piping. At frequent intervals a harsh, demoniacal, mocking laughter made itself heard."

> "The drum was manipulated with extraordinary dexterity, frequently making the round of the house, and particularly often floating above my head. The beating of the drum was often accompanied by singing, which ever and anon was subdued, as if it proceeded from the nether world. Lovely women's voices were sometimes heard from the background. Then once more that deafening chorus of clattering, rattling and blustering noises—the drum fell to the ground with a crash and all was still. This was the signal for the entrance of the dreaded monster, *Amortortok* . . . it has black arms and anyone whom it may happen to touch turns black and is bound to die. It walked with a heavy tread round the house and on the platform and roared out crying 'a—mo! a—mo!' All cowered into the furthest recesses of the platform for fear that the monster might touch them. It dinned in my ears and tried to tear away from me the skin on which I sat, in order to get me up in a corner with the other people, but only succeeded in tearing the skin."

After this and other supernatural creatures had gone, a man asked Sanimuinak, the shaman, whether the lamp could be relighted. Sanimuinak replied in his natural voice that his spirit helper was present and the lamps could not be lighted just yet. But finally it retreated.[7]

On such an occasion, the shaman perhaps is journeying to the moon to get a child for a barren woman, a service for which he is paid later, as for all other services. When, after such a journey, he finally returns to himself and the lamps are lighted, his hands are free of lashings, and he is perspiring and limp from exhaustion.

From one Eskimo group to another and even within the same group, opinions differed as to whether the angakok flew bodily through the air and dived under the sea or whether only his soul traveled to the home of the winds, to the moon, and elsewhere. But the reality of the journeys was not questioned.[8]

Some of the shaman's acts verged on simple magic (in the technical sense in which ethnologists define magic). Clear across the top of the continent, but possibly not on the south side of Alaska, an important step in the shaman's performance was divination by weighing, that is, by lifting a patient's head or some object. According to the usual system, the answer to a question was "yes" if the object was heavy. Such divination was more important among the Central Eskimos than in Greenland and Alaska.[9]

Nature of the Shamanistic Experience. There is no doubt of the shaman's sincerity even though he used ventriloquism, sleight-of-hand tricks, and the elation, exhaustion or other abnormal states of his spectators to assist him. In most Alaskan seances there used to be also prolonged dancing, drumming and chanting to the point of frenzy, at which the shaman would be contorted and would make the cries of all kinds of animals and birds or speak in some strange language. In Alaska, the shaman might be killed, after elaborate preparations, and return to life. This was pure trickery. Yet the initiative, strength, and reassurance to others that these unusual people—men and women—could demonstrate is impressive.

The condition of the shaman in his novitiate and to some extent in his mature performance resembles the progress of schizophrenia: a panic state at first when he or she has auditory or other hallucinations and realizes that there is something strange about him. He has a period of profound perplexity, withdrawal, unsureness of himself. He may be catatonic or hebephrenic, or each successively. Then his beliefs regarding the beings that he has seen, his relationship to them, his powers to do remarkable things, as well as his fears, autistic speech and other abnormal behavior become organized into a system. This is so real and coherent to him
316

that songs, masks and other carvings, and specific tabus are accepted as logical products of experience. If this really is a kind of schizophrenia, we can assume that the self-induced ecstasy or hypnotism, disturbing and exhausting as it is, nevertheless is far more satisfying than the original anxieties from which these experiences grew. In many of the cases for which there is biographical information, there does seem to have been some unusual difficulty in early life, although not enough is known so that this can be asserted for every case.

´ Once the nature of the experience becomes unquestionable, no matter how bizarre, then the portrayals of it are acceptable. The visual image is so clear and forceful that the shaman can not only carve a mask with one-half the face looking like a wolf and the other half like a man, but he can tell another man exactly how to carve it. He henceforth lives two kinds of lives, in two different systems of relationship, and convinces others that he does.

This leads to two conclusions: (1) If indeed the shaman's experience is schizophrenic, it is nevertheless controlled, and the sufferer recovers. He does not become irretrievably disorganized or so paranoid that he cannot be tolerated by his fellowmen. (2) The remainder of the community accepts the possibility of such dual functioning, that is, in relationship to the social environment and to the natural-supernatural environment.

On the first point, it has been suggested regarding Yurok Indian women of northern California that those who could organize and control their abnormal behavior became medicine women while others who showed similar early behavior but who could not direct it in a way that the community understood became merely neurotic or "crazy."[10] The same appears to be true of the Eskimos.[11]

In regard to the second point, not only shamans can see ghosts, little people who live in crevices, or animals that can take human form. Probably every Eskimo at some time will see, hear, or feel awesome things, even outside the angakok's seance. But he escapes from the encounter unharmed, may even acquire some special gift of his own, if he is unafraid and does what is proper for that kind of Being. Here shows up the suggestion (emotional preparation) from myths, organized religious belief, and stories of others' personal experiences. He who has seen the vision himself cannot deny that it is possible for another man.

317

Also, it is noticeable to those who know Eskimos intimately that they all, to some extent, are living a dual life. The Eskimo's "good humor is a conspicuous characteristic." People have referred to his highly buoyant nature, optimism, volatile laughter, his "effort to get the maximum joy possible out of the passing moment."

> "But sound the depths of his mind, and this joviality and good nature appear as but a defensive veneer. At bottom his thoughts revolve about the misfortunes that are unpredictable and inescapable; . . . . Thus, there are two opposite sides to the Eskimo's nature: one a deep, sober, fearful reverence for the awesome mysteries of life, the other a mobile lightheartedness. . . . ."[12]

Functions of the Shaman. His greatest services to the community, in the Eskimo view, were given by providing food (animals and fish) and by curing illness. He also helped to change the weather, prevent or repair injuries, bring personal success of various kinds, divine the cause of present difficulties or prophesy the future, and combat sorcerers. Anyone with so much greater knowledge and power than ordinary people might do great evil as well as great good. Not infrequently, especially in Alaska, there was an uneasy suspicion and antagonism between shamans and the remainder of the community.[13] An angakok might send a spirit-helper to put a pain in the victim or to steal his soul. If such was suspected, another shaman would be hired to fight the sorceror, and a terrifying contest of supernatural powers would occur. The practice of sorcery was most elaborate, so far as we can tell now, in Greenland and Baffin Land where a special type of practitioner could make an animal figure of bones, parts of infants' corpses, and miscellaneous material, endowing it with supernatural powers of flight and injury. This creature would be sent out against the victim.

Among the Western Eskimos where there were elaborate ceremonials, highly developed art, and a larger population than in the Central Region at least, the shaman had greater opportunity for leadership, and used it, sometimes overbearingly. If he was considered a great shaman, he might become wealthy even if he could not cure every patient. He was admired and a little feared because he had conquered the forces that laymen were afraid of; and he

318

was respected if he used his power in order to secure food but not to harm others.

COSMOLOGY

General Attitudes. Eskimos are not much interested in origins or ends of existence, rather, concentrating their attention on the present. An occasional individual does speculate and try to find philosophical explanation of life, but most people try to account only for today's illness or shortage of food, and account for it as due to specific acts of people, living or dead, or of evil beings. As Essene says, the lack of cosmological cycles of myths (though they do have separate myths) shows that Eskimos have not tried to systematize their world, either natural or social. They do not intellectualize the religion, do not talk in abstractions or personify abstractions such as Love, Gluttony, Tragedy. The beings of their universe are as personal and unpredictable as people. Eskimos see Life as a very personal struggle.[14]

Though the Eskimo view of the world is remarkably concrete in its visual and auditory imagery, there is no fixed canon. As Birket-Smith says, they lay no claim to a revealed religion, stated once and for all time. To them, their view of life is a series of rational conclusions based on observation and experience. It can be modified, added to by new experience, hence is relative. The only difference from modern scientific views of the world is that the Eskimos and many people like them have not been able to observe and test enough. So they fill in the gaps with imagination and careful reasoning from wrong primary assumptions.[15] These processes tend to make the religion highly personal.

An Eskimo generally meets the exigencies of his life with remarkable practical skill and realistic acceptance of its results, successful or unsuccessful. But perhaps he is too often unsuccessful. Despite skill, use of many amulets, observance of innumerable tabus, and the special efforts of shamans, misfortune still occurs. His belief in the unreliable whimsicality of Nature and Supernature and his fatalistic acceptance of that whimsicality explain and make acceptable to him the uncertainties of a difficult, ungenerous environment. His beliefs regarding the world perhaps are symbolizations of such uncertainties. His fatalistic attitude may have developed as an emotional relief—a "way out"—from the bur-

FORGOTTEN RELIGIONS

den of guilt he would have had from extending rigorously and systematically his belief that misfortune can come from broken tabus.

It is actually more reassuring to a woman to think that her husband has been crushed by the Clapping Mountains when he paddled between those two mythical islands, rather than suspect that a walrus pulled him under the sea because she had carelessly given salt-water instead of a fresh-water drink to the last walrus killed by her husband. And sometimes it is better to think that one's illness is due to a sorceror rather than due to one's own offense to the great Spirit of the Air. Either alternative is possible according to Eskimo belief. What actually is believed in a given situation depends on personalities and material circumstances. In any case, (paraphrasing Marshall) there is little worry for the unpredictable future or remorse for the unalterable past.[16]

Belief: Spirits. Eskimo cosmology is an almost complete animism. Everything seems to have a soul-spirit. Geographical features, all the animals (except the dog, in some areas), lamp, entranceway and other items of structures and furnishings, tools, clothing, all have souls. A mussel or a little pond may seem weak and insignificant items of the natural world, yet the mussel's spirit may guard a child against drowning, hence be worn as a protective amulet, and the pond may be inhabited by a dragon-like creature, hence be avoided.

Because of the variety of souls and other spiritual beings and because of slight variations of concept from group to group, one cannot easily organize and characterize them. Thalbitzer says that *inuat* (sing., *inua*), often mentioned in literature on Eskimo religion, are not souls of the dead, do not live in the abode of the dead. They are spirits in human form or that can take human form, however.[17] This probably is true among Eastern Eskimos, but among Western Eskimos the *inua* is or can be, among other things, the human soul. The *inua* concept is basic and universal, as summarized by Weyer (paraphrased):

> The key to the subject lies in the nature of the human soul; the word *inua*, which designates the soul even of an inanimate object, means "its man," being the possessive of *inuk*, "man" or "person." The nominative plural, *inuit*, is the

320

term by which some Eskimos refer to themselves as a people. In the Bering Strait region, hunters at sea and elsewhere in lonely places cast down food and water as offerings to the inua of the place before eating or drinking, often adding propitiatory words. These spirits are believed to have the forms of men and women but their faces are curiously distorted and grotesque. Shamans who may have seen them will carve, therefore, fantastic masks.[18] Some of the dance masks are made double, so hinged that the outer portion showing the animal form can be opened, revealing the human face of the spirit underneath. (Or the center of the mask will be a human face, surrounded by disjointed, carved appendages of the bird or animal, e.g., head, wings, feet, and tail feathers.) Alaskan mythology contains the correlative idea that animals can change from their own to human form by the simple expedient of pushing up their beaks or muzzles.

Possibly the root word *inua* might better be translated "individual" (or better still, "its owner") rather than "man", since the soul of an animal or object is not always envisaged as a homunculus, especially in the Central and Eastern areas. Sometimes it is imagined as a miniature of the thing itself. Thus, among the Iglulik Eskimos, the souls of animals are miniatures of themselves even though the word for soul, *inusia*, means literally "appearance as a human being." The Labrador Eskimo's conception of the souls of inanimate objects is illustrated in their belief that if a small model of a soapstone lamp or kettle is made as well as the large one, the latter will last until the little model is cracked or broken. In Greenland, an animal's *inua* is not its soul but its vitality and here also resembles the animal itself.[19]

At Pt. Hope (northwest Alaska) and to some extent through southwest Alaska, the *inyua* (*chua* and other variants) is conceived of as the "owner" of the river, cooking pot, or what-not, while the souls of men and animals are given a different but related name, such as *inyusaq* or *chuchik*.[20] We can conclude that, no matter what its etymology or appearance, the *inua* is modeled on the human soul and functions much like one.[21]

In Greenland, the *tornait* (equivalents: *torngrat, tartat, tungat,* etc.) are spirits of all kinds that become shamans' helpers, Thalbitzer says.[22] This seems to be a special Greenland usage of a term that elsewhere, most clearly in Alaska, applies to Beings that are not souls of visible things but have strange forms of their own. Often the word is used particularly for the Beings that are evil and harmful if not treated just right, for example, Half-people (as if split lengthwise) and thirsty little dried-up Wanderers and mountain Giants. They are races or groups which some Eskimos think are controlled by chief spirits.[23] In Alaska and the Central Region, they may or may not be shamans' supernatural helpers, and they are not the only familiar spirits of shamans, who may have animal spirit-helpers as well. The Central Eskimos believe that there are evil *tornrait* and helping *tornrait*.[24]

> For example, to the Copper Eskimos (Coronation Gulf, in the Central culture-province), *tornrait* are nearly human in form, but never have lived as human beings. They are of a different order from the shades of men and animals. They are divided into male and female. At times they are distinguished from human beings only by some peculiarity such as extraordinarily long hair. They can change form and appear or disappear at will. Some have definite homes in hillocks or tide-cracks or old stone houses, but are not confined to such places. Generally they live in isolation and are especially dangerous in solitary places and in the dark. In Bathurst Inlet the opening of the sealing season is marked by a battle beween the shamans and the many little tornrait that live on the ice. The shamans fight the spirits with snow-dusters as if fighting dogs, so vigorously that sometimes the shamans' mouth and snow-duster show blood. If the tornrait were not got rid of, they would drive away all the seals and the people would starve. Usually the soul of a dead person or an animal is the shaman's familiar-spirit, even though it also is called *tornrak* (sing.) The Copper Eskimos do not make such sharp distinctions as some others between the various kinds of spirits.[25]

It can be seen that Eskimo religion contained animism in the Tylorian sense.[26] (It need not be assumed, however, that Eskimo religion developed exactly in the manner postulated by Edward Tylor.) But this religion was not limited to such animism. It had great deities, as well.

Belief: Deities. In Labrador and Greenland, the idea of a ruler of the spirits was developed, to the point that the Labrador people assigned supreme control of all *tornrait* to Torngarsoak. He, as husband of the Sea Goddess, became one of the two principal deities and was thought to preside over the sea animals.[27] In most places, however, Sedna the Sea Goddess herself or the Moon-man controlled the sea animals, hence held power of life or death for the Eskimos.

Central Eskimos tell the origin and life of Sedna essentially as follows, despite many local variations of detail:

> A girl who had married a sea-bird was brought home from the bird's place of abode by her irate father. On the way home in a skin-boat, the bird husband aroused a storm. To placate him, the father threw Sedna overboard. When she clutched the gunwhale, he cut off the first joints of her fingers, then when she rose again, the second joints, and so on until she could no longer hang on and sank to the bottom of the sea. The ends of her fingers became whales; the next joints, seals; the last, walrus. She lives under the sea, with a dog (or a dwarf or her father) guarding the entrance of her house. Her hair hangs over one side of her face, unkempt and full of vermin, supposedly because with her mutilated hands she cannot comb it. The dirt in her hair, which irritates and angers her exceedingly, consists of people's broken tabus and evil deeds. She therefore withholds the sea animals, which lie on the floor of her house or in a pool beside it.[28]

When a group feared starvation, it implored the shaman to visit Sedna and prevail upon her to release some animals for the penitent people. He undertook the hazardous journey, overcoming several obstacles, and finally by cajoling Sedna and by combing her hair reduced her antagonism to man and got her to send out some of her offspring, the sea animals. Upon the angakok's return home, he would call upon individuals to confess their sins, or he would make specific accusations, and people at the seance hurriedly confessed their infractions of tabus, as we have seen. If the animals still did not appear, further explanation was necessary, for example that Sedna still was not sufficiently placated. Her relationship to men and animals was not questioned any more than the relations of great deities in other religions.

The Moon-man came into his own in the Norton Sound and Kotzebue Sound areas of Alaska (at least as far north as Pt. Hope) where he was thought to provide the animals that man needed. Here also, the shaman had to go begging—to the Moon— in order to bring animals in a time of scarcity. Although the Moon-man might become angered and vengeful, he was on the whole a benevolent being. Throughout southwest Alaska there are tales of Moon-man noticing that some woman on earth was being mistreated and his coming down to rescue her, usually taking her to the moon and marrying her.[29] An eclipse of the moon naturally was much feared, but the shaman usually could set things right. While the Eastern Eskimos did not think that the Moon-spirit controlled the sea-animals, they did believe that it was a man, that he would befriend orphans or others, and that he could make women pregnant. It is strange that the Moon-man was not more feared, since he was thought to have committed a great sin long ago.

> A girl was visited on several successive nights by some man who wooed her and had intercourse with her. Seeking to find out his identity, she put soot on her hands, touched his face, and next morning scrutinized all the men of the village. When she found that her lover was her brother, she became very angry, taunted him, caught up her lamp and started to run away, with her brother following her. She rose into the sky and became the sun, while her brother became the moon, always trying to catch her.[30]

Light and sun were surprisingly unimportant in Eskimo religion and mythology. The far Arctic tribes naturally were aware of the sun as the sub-Arctic tribes could not be. The former would hold a little new-fire or purification ceremony at the reappearance of the sun after the winter solstice.[31] Only in southwest Alaska (as far north as Seward Peninsula) was there anything that might be called a Rite to the Sun, which took the form of saluting the light with a song, ritual bathing in sea or stream, or other acts, on first going outdoors every morning. In most cases this was done by the men only and apparently was done to obtain success in hunting. In fact, in some places it may have been more of a supplication to Sila than to the Sun-spirit.[32]

Sila is the most remote, most pervasive, most impersonal, ab-

324

stract of all *inuat*. *Silap inua* is the Spirit of the Air, almost the Spirit of Heaven or the Universe. Sila also seems to mean, in Greenland and Alaska, spiritual power or understanding. Unlike Sea Goddess, Sun, and Moon, no earthly origin is presupposed for Sila. Nearly all groups speak of this deity as masculine, yet he never is seen—only heard occasionally in the wind. He is a great and stern supporter of the system of tabus, seeing transgressions and punishing them with bad weather, dearth of game, and sickness. Although Sila can be kind—just as we say that the weather is kind—Sila can be terrifying also, especially if an Eskimo has not treated the food-animals properly. Among the Iglulirmiut and neighboring peoples who have developed most highly the cult of the Sea Goddess, *Silap inua's* powers evidently are not so inclusive in this regard. Sila is not a Supreme Being, able to control Sun, Moon, monsters, and all other independent spirits, but he is the most intellectualized of the deities, with a consistent awesomeness and none of the human-like vagaries that other Eskimo deities are subject to.[33]

Belief: Human Souls. It is doubtful whether most Eskimos believe in multiple souls as has been claimed. Holm said specifically that the East Greenlanders told of small souls in different parts of the body, yet he spoke also of "the soul" of a person.[34] This much can be said of Eskimos generally, they believe in:

1. A soul-being that can become a soul-spirit like other supernatural beings. Occasionally the shadow is identified with it. In different places it takes other forms: a ball of fire or a light, steam, a skeleton.
2. The name, which has personal qualities but has no form, no lasting existence as a separate entity. It does not go to the afterworld.
3. The life essence, warmth, breath.

Because of the special importance of his name to a person, several devices to avoid saying the name are used (nicknames, teknonymy, etc.), and quite widely a child is named for the most recently deceased in the community, regardless of sex. "The implications of this naming custom differ widely among the various groups of Eskimos. In some the practice carries very little suggestion of a transfer of the soul, while in others this idea is so strong that the namesake is treated as though he were actually the dead person, living again on earth."[35] Perhaps all Eskimos formerly believed in reincarnation although it usually was not the name-soul that was reborn. In regard to reincarnation, as in many other respects, Eskimo belief is full of contradictions which cannot be detailed here. In any case, the reincarnation concept appears most clearly in south-central Alaska.

Miscellaneous beliefs regarding other worlds appeared sporadically: the earth rests on four pillars or on a central pillar; there is an entrance to the underworld in the west, or one can go down to it through any crevice, or through the sea; there are one, two, three, or five skyworlds. Despite these differences of belief, all groups agreed that the particular destination of each soul was primarily dependent upon the person's manner of death. It did not depend solely on his morals in life on earth although there occasionally was differential recognition for good people and for murderers. This conforms with the Eskimo philosophy mentioned above, with its emphasis on the accidental, the personal variable in misfortune.

While all Eskimos believed in both skyworld and underworld, they did not agree as to who went to each. For example, Greenlanders thought that the good and those dying a violent death went to the land under the sea, which was more desirable than the upper world where the souls of ordinary people went. But in Labrador, it was thought that those dying a violent death went to a heaven in the aurora borealis while those dying a "natural" death went to the underworld. Without reference to the aurora, the general belief of Central and Western Eskimos was that the skyworld was the pleasant one in which lived those who had been murdered, committed suicide, starved, died in childbirth, or been killed in an accident.

Perhaps people recognized a need for compensation to those who died violently, a compensation often required. Perhaps the belief was an expression of esteem for those who lived vigorously and were most likely to die by accident, such as hunters of whale and polar bear.

No matter what form the soul was thought to have usually, it could take other forms. Even a magic change of form of the body could occur: animal-into-human, human-into-object, etc. Tales of such transformation that sound to us like fairy-tales were really stories demonstrating the great power of amulets, songs, totemic animals, and spirit-helpers, by means of which transformations could be made.

From the basic concept that animals have souls came widespread practices relating to animals:[36]

1. Giving a drink of fresh water to recently slain sea-mammals and giving fat to land animals. It was thought that, denied these because of their respective habitats, the animals craved them.

2. Funeral and mourning customs for the animals like those for human beings. In the Norton Sound area of Alaska, properly despatching the souls of seals back to their homes under the sea, to be reincarnated and caught again by man, required days of elaborate ceremonial.

3. Avoidance of injury, contamination, or affront to particular food-animals, by tabus on dogs gnawing sea-mammal bones, tabus on putting together or handling at the same time the skins or other parts of land animals and sea animals; tabus on "unclean" women going near hunting gear, boats, men's food bowls, etc.

4. Delighting the spirits of animals by giving masked dances, feasts, games, and other things proper for a festival.

Whether these are done with a kind of desperate negativism— the acts carried out in a precarious resistance to all the probable harm to the food supply—or whether done with positive reassurance that thus the animals are pleased and allow themselves to be taken by man, evidently has depended very much on actual amount of uncertainty of securing food. There is always some uncertainty and corresponding anxiety, but the amount of anxiety varies greatly from group to group even though ritual acts and tabus may be identical. Also, while (in the past) ceremonial satisfied the routine demands of animal spirits, in extremity there was need for the shaman's journey to the great Beings controlling the animals; and in the far Arctic we find more frequent shaman-seances to obtain food. In contrast, in southwest Alaska apparently the angakok more often was bent on curing illness or on overcoming some other shaman. In sum, emotion and relative emphasis are as important as "custom" or "practice" and "belief" in studying religion.

Morality in Relation to Cosmology. Let us see first what is regarded as good behavior and what is bad. Eskimos esteem hard work, alertness and awareness, consideration for the feelings of others (tactfulness), generosity, skill (hunting, for a man; sewing, for a woman), and physical courage, demonstrated in suffering violence. They disapprove quarrelsomeness, stinginess, theft, tabu-breaking, and murder. Aside from incest prohibition (which does not extend to cousins) and observance of sex tabus in certain ritual periods, sex has not been part of the tabu system. It can be seen that the traits listed combine in support of strong community life. Hard work in some cultures means working hard to achieve more than others, but here combined with generosity, it means working to get subsistence for the village. Religion supports this system.

Sin here, as elsewhere, is any offense to the Supernatural, a transgression of divine law. In the Eskimo system, what is thus offensive and deserving of punishment appears somewhat more materialistic and non-social than in many systems. Let us look at an example quoted by Weyer:

> A girl in northern Labrador was banished from her village, even though it was winter, because she had persisted in eating caribou and seal together. She was regarded as a threat to her community not because she had directly injured their life or property but because, by repeatedly transgressing a fundamental tabu, she had exposed her people to punishment from supernatural powers, that is, she was indirectly but certainly endangering them.[36]

This treatment may seem barbaric, and the particular punishment undoubtedly was. That the girl was punished at all cannot be so quickly censured. People in other societies may believe that murder is a sin as well as a crime (i.e. offense against society) and that it will surely receive divine retribution. Yet they do not leave the punishment to supernatural agencies but assign it to agencies of society. In other words, they anticipate divine justice, as the Eskimos do, thus protecting society. Also, having seen what are the spiritual premises, notably the idea that animals have souls, we cannot easily condemn these people for their apparently particularistic and materialistic tabus. We have seen, too, that punishment and reward do not come after death but are given right now.

328

And finally, Eskimos know that everyone may suffer for the sin of one—a concept with no mean proportions.

There is, however, almost no conceptualization of Good and Evil, or of divine law or natural order, except possibly in Sila. Just as punishment is seldom a torture of the soul but takes easily-observed somatic forms, so also tabus are of a physical nature. (Eskimos do not go to the extreme of physical torture, however.) The most common ones are temporary food tabus and other use-tabus. For example, at Pt. Hope, Alaska, in times past, after a whale-hunter and his crew had gone out in their big skin-boat, the hunter's wife returned to her house from the ritual boat-launching.

> "She refrained from any work during . . . their absence. She could neither wash nor comb her hair, change her clothes, nor scrub the floor (if she scrubbed the floor, the skin of a slain whale would be thin). She must remain tranquil and act like a sick person so that the harpooned whale would also be quiet and easy to kill. She must never use a knife (her food must be cut for her), because she might sever the harpoon line holding the whale."[37]

Besides the imitative magic which is obviously the basis of tabus here, there is a general idea of contagious magic. The hunter's wife was intimately associated with him in the ritual aspects of that greatest of all efforts: whaling. Not only did she symbolize the whale—this idea was more clearly developed around Bering Strait—but also anything that she did might be a kind of contagion or contamination of her husband and all his gear. She could communicate purity and religious strength, or uncleanness, faltering, and injury. A moral woman was one who did not endanger her menfolk's lives and success in hunting.

The theories of contamination and purification show more clearly in funeral observances. Generally Eskimos are not afraid to die, unless they have been frightened by over-emphasis of certain Christian teachings. But they do fear the soul-spirit of the recently deceased person. That is, they do not fear death for themselves but fear the death of another person. For example, in the Bering Sea area, to prevent contamination from or to sever the former contact with the deceased, mourners might stuff moss in their nostrils or tie herbs under the nose, make cutting motions under the corpse as it was held aloft or throw firebrands behind it as the funeral procession left the village and would refrain from going hunting or even walking out on the ice or looking up to the sky. This tabu on any unclean people looking up, enforced especially on girls at puberty, was required to prevent affront and contamination to Beings in the heavens.

Yet the widower or widow might remarry after only a few days' observance of such tabus (whatever was thought adequate so that he or she would not harm others) although, of course, many individuals, from grief, did not want to remarry immediately. The point is that many interpersonal relationships in the community were not regulated by tabus as were man's personal contacts with the Supernatural. (Remarrying would not be inherently harmful to the community, which seems to have been the real, although unstated criterion of moral judgment.) Marital separation, extramarital sex relations, adoption, and most other social relations and changes of status were merely matters of personal adjustment. Although there were some that might be called social tabus, for example the name tabu previously mentioned, incest tabus, prohibitions on speech familiarity between in-laws and between brother and sister (observed especially in southwest Alaska), most others were stated in terms of physical relationship and welfare. This really applies even to these "social" tabus. Seemingly, principally physical condition and change of physical status, such as puberty, were thought important in relations with the Supernatural, a characteristic even of religions that supposedly have advanced much farther.

Fear of the dead seems to increase as we go north. Possibly the anxiety regarding subsistence spreads until it covers all relations with the natural-supernatural world. For example, an illness usually is assumed to indicate that the Spirits have been offended; if they are offended, they may send even greater danger such as storm or epidemic. Illness and death then may induce greater anxiety than that to be expected for the sickness of one person. Morality thus is maintained by the most basic fears.

Illness in Relation to Cosmology. If spirits or sorcerers cause sickness, just how can they accomplish this? How can the illness be cured? The Polar Eskimos and apparently most others of Greenland and Canada believe that sickness is due only to loss of the soul, which either has been stolen or has been frightened or tormented out of the patient. The shaman then goes on a spirit-flight to recover the soul, having "diagnosed" the case by deciding the probable means of losing the soul. In Labrador, the Coronation Gulf area (Copper Eskimos), and Alaska—probably elsewhere—there is an alternative explanation, especially in cases of pain rather than general debility: a sickness has been implanted in the patient. The shaman, male or female, then may sing, dance, exhort, and contort, to drive out the sickness, finally sucking or pulling it out triumphantly. He may even show it to the patient in the form of a bit of blood, a worm, or something else. This is not possession by a spirit in the Christian sense, being more like the "pain theory" of the Indians of northwest California.[38]

Conclusion: (1) There was no basic male-female dichotomy of Supernatural Beings or even of the greatest Powers. A large proportion of the myths deal with interpersonal relations, especially male-female relations, but this probably is attributable more to the very personal, here-and-now character of the religion. (2) There was no clear human-animal dichotomy. Any person's soul could travel away even while he was still living and could encounter animals' soul-spirits. Animals could take human form and live among people—at least, this had occurred in the past. (3) There was no preoccupation with the dead, indicated by the very meager funeral, little concern regarding after-life, no ancestor-worship or other cult of the dead, no personification of death, and the willingness to use an infant's body or parts of an adult corpse as an amulet or magic agent. On the Pacific coast of Alaska this went to an extreme of making a human "poison" used in whaling, a practice undertaken by only the powerful whalers, however. (4) Religion had a physical orientation, indicated by the following: (a) most tabus related to the food supply; (b) in the myths, the savior characters saved people from physical dangers rather than from sin (this was visualized as a personal contest, with the protagonist pictured as a strong, clever person, not a pure, meek one); (c) a human origin or physical identity was attributed to most supernatural powers, Sila being the only completely disembodied one.[39]

SOCIETY AND RELIGION

The Family. Among most Alaskan Eskimos, animal protectors or helpers were inherited from the father; masks representing these animals (usually birds) were worn; and people observed certain tabus on killing or eating the totemic animals. This was not, however, a fully developed totemism. Apparently there was no thought of descent from or other kinship with such animals and no naming of lineages according to their protectors. The "totems" were either spirit-helpers or else amulets—and sometimes both, the amulet representing the animal.

Patrilineally inherited were the designs, representing not only these animals but also mythical creatures such as the large worm with a human face, which were painted or etched on wooden dishes, skin-boats, hunting implements and other things. In Alaska could be inherited also songs referring to personal encounters with beings that had become guardian spirits. Finally, many of the innumerable amulets that Eskimos wore and tied on their boats, hunting gear, etc., were used especially by particular families. Apparently nowhere were all such songs and amulets owned or controlled exclusively by families. They always were acquired originally by personal spiritual experience, with greater tendency to subsequent inheritance in some areas than in others.

Let us stop to look at those amulets, so intimately a part of the individual and usually of the family, also. Occasionally a child's body and clothing were weighted with, literally, dozens of amulets, comprising small carved ivory figures, parts of animal bodies, and small shell-fish, insects, pebbles or other things sewed up in little bags. Each could confer on the user a specific power.[40] While some of the other symbols and conveyors of spiritual and magical power were more highly developed in Alaska, for example masks, these little amulets proliferated among the Central Eskimos.[41] Because of the encompassing animism (the belief in spirits in things), possibly these should be called fetishes rather than amulets. The shamans' "dolls"—large wooden figures possessed of a spirit—undoubtedly can be designated fetishes; but the bear's teeth and similar objects are best designated merely as amulets. Such objects have power as one of a class rather than as individual spirit-powers. This is characteristic of totems also, distinct from the guardian-

332

spirit concept. In totemism, not a particular individual eagle but all eagles of a given variety become sacred to a group of people, as in Alaska.[42]

Returning to the family: The mythology does not validate the social position or even the religious power of families, although purely local legends recount the power of great hunters and shamans. Unlike much of the ceremonial of North Pacific Coast Indians, Eskimo religious festivals, which have now almost disappeared, did not primarily or avowedly validate status or prerogatives. Yet most ceremonials were occasions for feast-giving, exchange of gifts, and display of fine clothing and other possessions—all of which established the superior abilities, wealth, and prestige of some families far beyond others. The more secure was life materially, the more these traits were recognized in accounting for individual differences of fortune, instead of erratic fate.

The Community. Anciently, almost all Eskimos had a meeting-house. In the high Arctic where settlements were small, where driftwood was scarce, and life migratory and difficult, the "men's ceremonial house" was given up or was just another snow-house. In Greenland there are now only hints of its former use. In Alaska it still may be seen in isolated villages. Here men worked, ate, slept (southwest Alaska chiefly), entertained visitors, instructed the boys, held games and contests, rehearsed new songs and dances for the festivals, watched the shamans' seances, and carried out the rituals essential to maintain their universe. While some aspects of religion seem anything but reassuring, in contrast ceremonial was constructive and gave confidence. (Similarly, the myths often are grim, showing the constant threats to life. Yet they usually end with a conquest of difficulties.)

Personal events—the "life crisis" so prominent in many religions—were minor in Eskimo public ritual except those events involving food-getting, notably a young man's first catch of a major food animal. Ritual was directed largely toward assuring current food supply, and second, toward assuring both spiritual and physical continuity, for example by symbolization of reincarnation (chiefly Lower Yukon area) and by exchange of sex partners during certain ceremonial periods. In general, ceremonial provided release of many tensions, by giving the shaman opportunity to prove his skill, by lifting most food tabus, by encouraging people to dance the Eskimos' wonderful mimetic and muscular dances or to beat the drums until exhausted, by singing to the spirits and making everything right with them. Even though in large villages there were three or even more meeting houses, usually as many people came together as could possibly crowd into one of these half-underground log houses. The result was a strong feeling of community solidarity. The people who crowded into a snow-house up in Baffin Land, even though the group was much smaller, the performance much shorter, felt nearly the same reassurance after the angakok's "drum dance" as the Alaskan Eskimos felt after one of their Messenger Festivals, in which one village entertained one or more other whole villages with mask dances for several days. Thus constructively they coerced with magic, supplicated, propitiated, in a sense paid in advance for spiritual assistance, with not much thanksgiving afterward. The Eskimos' contest with the world provided little place for thanksgiving.

Eskimos had virtually no political organization, and social and economic organizations were simple. Hence religious participation was one of the principal means of instructing the young and achieving cooperation and conformity.

SUMMARY

Despite the great distances covered, there is remarkable uniformity in Eskimo religion. It evidently was strong and satisfying, to last through long migrations and subsequent isolation. Regional differences were principally differences of emphasis and elaboration. For example, the tabus to enforce rigid separation of land and sea animals were more numerous and inclusive among Central Eskimos, while in Alaska such tabus might differ from family to family.[43] The following generalizations are given, therefore, with the reservation that there are such local differences.

First, symbolism of fluidity, changeability of life, even of unreliability, and a lack of symbolism indicating attachment to the land are noticeable. There is a Sky Deity but no Earth Deity except dwarfs and other local trolls.[44] The prominence of bird guardian-spirits in Alaska and of bird characters in the myths of all regions seems especially typical. This fluidity probably reflects the ancient as well as modern mobility of the Eskimos, who must be continu-

334

ally moving about in search of food and who most often seek that food from the sea.

Second, there is much individualism in the religion: (1) The shaman gains his power in solitude and in highly personal experience rather than by elaborate initiation given by community or priesthood. (2) There is little chanting in unison and apparently no dancing in unison east of the Copper Eskimos, and even in the Western Region the individual usually sings and dances his own composition. (3) Man's relation to the supernatural most often is symbolized as a personal struggle, both in myth and in the shaman dramas. There is noticeable lack of myths concerning migration, war, daily life and the origin of daily customs, or other examples of community effort.[45]

Third, some aggression is shown in the religious experience, but evidently there is not so much as might be expected from the amount of individualism. Although shamans formerly had to enter contests, it was not essential for the layman to wrestle with evils in order to have religious experience and obtain supernatural aid. The person who starved, nearly drowned, or died (became unconscious), the child who was sickly or mistreated saw the spirits whether he sought to or not. The aggressor, the one who showed violence toward his people, was a wrongdoer, while the sufferer of violence was thought to be rewarded in after-life. As for aggression characterizing the religion as a whole, religion to the Eskimos was not a militant cause and not enforced on others. The Eskimo in religion, as in many of his social relations, was passive—he did as the Spirits directed him to do and assumed that others must do the same.

Fourth, a here-and-now orientation characterizes the religion and even the mythology more than most other bodies of belief. Although etiological and teleological beliefs and tales are not lacking, they are not elaborated or organized into a cosmogony. Because in the past their expectations of punishment for tabu-breaking were so immediate and vivid, and not relegated to the after-world, Eskimos' attention to details of behavior, especially toward the game animals, and their anxiety regarding broken tabus were great. We must not be condescending or condemnatory of those tabus, ludicrous as they may seem to us. The little Eskimo settlement could not know what conditions of ice 500 miles away were keeping the walrus and whales from appearing as usual. There was so little of a practical nature that they could do even though scarcity of oil for light and heat, of skins, rawhide line, bone, ivory, baleen for tools, as well as of meat, was immediately threatening. It is unimportant whether they thought that things of the land and sea should be kept separate or that they should always be matched and put together. The true value of the religious requirement was that it gave opportunity to do something specifically directed to the source of the anxiety, unequivocally directed to reducing uncertainty. A vital religion is not an agglomeration of unadaptive rites, lagging superstitions, and tabus without meaning. It is a functional whole, the functions relating to basic spiritual needs—in modern words, emotional needs. In terms of daily life, Eskimo tabus had meaning, and the religion was vital.

Fifth, the factor of abnormality in Eskimo religion undoubtedly has been over-emphasized in several accounts of it. The religious leaders did go through periods characterized by behavior that could be called abnormal in almost any culture's standard of normal behavior. The important point regarding Eskimo shamans is that they did pass through their difficulties, gain self-assurance, and learn to control and organize their peculiarities so that they could assure others also.

Thus, in considering the fuctions of Eskimo religion, we see that for many individuals, regarded as individual personalities (notably the shamans), religion redirected, channeled, and formalized their aberrant behavior, which probably had arisen from social causes. It substituted supernatural guardians for human guardians who too often were lacking, and it gave opportunity for emotional release that some people could not get adequately in everyday life. For the community, religion mitigated the physical threats to existence, which most people normally feared much more than their social threats, and it consolidated the community by making each person's relations with the Supernatural important for the welfare of all.

NOTES

1. Weyer, 429-431.
2. Rainey, 275-276.
3. Unpublished information from Nunivak Island.
4. The Iglulik people call this deity Takanakapsaluk, but as she is

generally referred to in literature on the Eskimos as Sedna, a name used by another Eskimo group, the simpler name will be used here.

5. Rasmussen, (1929), 123 ff. Also: Weyer, 356-358.

6. All Eskimos have a one-face tambourine-drum with a short handle. Houses: The south Greenland house, but not the Polar house, is a large well-built structure with stone foundation. Most native Alaskan houses are built of wood and sod. Only in Central and Northeastern Regions are there snow-houses.

7. Holm, 90-97. For additional descriptions of shaman performances, see Rasmussen, (1927), 84-86, 122-123, 275-277.

8. Weyer, 350-355.

9. *Ibid.*, 443-444; Birket-Smith, (1936), 173.

10. Erik Erikson. "Observations on the Yurok: Childhood and World Image." *University of California Publications in American Archaeology and Ethnology*, v. 35, no. 10, (1943), 263.

11. For a good statement of the personal and social significance of the novitiate experience, see Paul Radin, *Primitive Religion*, (1937), chap. 6.

12. Weyer, 253-254. See also: Marshall, 357.

13. *Ibid.*, 442-444; Birket-Smith, (1936), 151.

14. Essene, 31. Birket-Smith says that not only does each thing have its spirit owner but even abstractions like sleep and food have spirit-owners or controllers (1936), 162. This does not seem to be a common or characteristic idea, however.

15. Birket-Smith, (1936), 160.

16. Marshall, 357.

17. Thalbitzer, (1926), 368-369.

18. Alaskan Eskimo masks, because of what appears to be their unusual originality, plus artistic calibre in their proportion, economy of line, etc., have been exhibited in many art museums. The carver does not regard them as original expressions of himself but as portrayals of a real and objective universe.

19. Weyer, 299-300.

20. Rainey, 271-272; Lantis, (1946), 197-198.

21. Birket-Smith agrees with Rainey that *inua* means "its owner" and with Thalbitzer that it is not a soul (1936), 162-163.

22. Thalbitzer, *op. cit.*

23. Weyer, 394, 399. Also: Essene, pt. v, "Tales of Supernatural Beings."

24. *Ibid.*, 395-398. Although old ceremonial has given way to Christian ritual, and to the Eskimo pantheon has been added or substituted the Christian Deity, the belief in the local trolls is still firm.

25. *Ibid.*, quoting Jenness, (1922), 185-191.

26. E. B. Tylor, *Primitive Culture*, 5th ed., v. 1, chaps. 11-15.

27. Hawkes, 124.

28. Weyer, chap. 21.
29. Lantis, (1938) (b), 139-144.
30. Weyer, 381-385; Rainey, 270-271; Lantis, (1946), 197, and (1947), 36-37.
31. Weyer, 385-389.
32. Lantis, (1947), 35-36.
33. Weyer, 389-392. Also: Birket-Smith, (1936), 164; Lantis, (1946), 197.
34. Holm, 80-81.
35. Weyer, 291-292.
36. Weyer, chaps. 20, 22, and figs. 18A, 18B; Lantis, (1938) (a), and (1947), 38-81; Rainey, 245-264.
37. Weyer, 378.
38. Lantis, (1938) (a) ; Rainey, 259.
39. Weyer, chap. 19. See also: Lantis, (1946), 202-203.
40. *Ibid.*, 406-407.
41. The power of most Eskimo amulets is based on the two basic principles of imitation and contagion.
42. Weyer, 311-316.
43. Birket-Smith, (1936), 169. Birket-Smith believes generally Eskimo amulets are fetishes. However, such classification is a matter of definition; and definitions vary.
44. Weyer, 368.
45. The Prince William Sound Eskimos of Alaska (Pacific Eskimos) believed in a land counterpart of Sedna, a woman living in the mountain forests who governed the land animals. This seems to have been the Eskimos' closest approximation of an Earth Deity. Birket-Smith, (1936), 165.
46. Essene, 30-31.

BIBLIOGRAPHY

H. D. ANDERSON AND W. C. EELLS: *Alaska Natives*, (1935).

KAJ BIRKET-SMITH: *The Eskimos*, (1936).

————, "Ethnography of the Egedesminde District, with Aspects of the General Culture of West Greenland." *Meddelelser om Gronland*, v. 66, (1924).

FRANZ BOAS: "The Central Eskimo." *Bureau of American Ethnology, Ann. Rept.*, 6, (1888).

————, "The Eskimo of Baffin Land and Hudson Bay." *American Museum of Natural History Bulletin*, v. 15, pt. 1, (1901); pt. 2, (1907).

W. BOGORAS: "The Eskimo of Siberia." *American Museum of Natural History Memoir*, 12, pt. 3, (1913).

F. J. ESSENE, JR.: *A Comparative Study of Eskimo Mythology.* Ph.D. Thesis, University of California (Berkeley, 1947).

THE RELIGION OF THE ESKIMOS

E. W. Hawkes: "The Labrador Eskimo." *Canadian Geological Survey Memoir* 91, *Anthropology Series*, no. 14, (1916).

G. Holm: "Ethnological Sketch of the Angmagsalik Eskimo." *Meddelelser om Gronland*, v. 39, pt. 1, (1914).

D. Jenness: "The Life of the Copper Eskimos." *Rept. of the Canadian Arctic Expedition, 1913-18*, v. 12a, (1922).

A. L. Kroeber: "The Eskimo of Smith Sound." *American Museum of Natural History Bulletin*, v. 12, art. 21, (1900).

M. Lantis: "Alaskan Eskimo Ceremonialism." *American Ethnological Society Monograph*, 11, (1947).

————, "The Alaskan Whale Cult and Its Affinities." *American Anthropologist*, v. 40, pp. 438-464, (1938).

————, "The Mythology of Kodiak Island, Alaska." *Journal of American Folk-Lore*, v. 51, pp. 123-172, (1938).

————, "The Social Culture of the Nunivak Eskimo." *American Philosophical Society Transactions*, v. 35, pt. 3, (1946).

R. Marshall: *Arctic Village*, (1933).

J. Murdoch: "Ethnological Results of the Point Barrow Expedition." *Bureau of American Ethnology Ann. Rept.* 9, (1892).

E. W. Nelson: "The Eskimo about Bering Strait." *Bureau of American Ethnology Ann. Rept.*, 18, pt. 1, (1899).

F. G. Rainey: "The Whale Hunters of Tigara." *American Museum of Natural History Anthropological Papers*, v. 41, pt. 2, (1947).

Knud Rasmussen: *Across Arctic America*, (1927).

————, *The Eagle's Gift*, (1932).

————, "Intellectual Culture of the Caribou Eskimos." *Rept. of the 5th Thule Expedition 1921-24*, v. 7, no. 2, (1930).

————, "Intellectual Culture of the Copper Eskimos." *Report of the 5th Thule Exped. 1921-24*, v. 9, (1932).

————, "Intellectual Culture of the Iglulik Eskimos." *Rept. of the 5th Thule Exped. 1921-24*, v. 7, no. 1, (1929).

V. Stefansson: "The Stefansson-Anderson Arctic Expedition of the American Museum: Preliminary Ethnological Report." *American Museum of Natural History, Anthropological Papers*, v. 14, pt. 1, (1914).

W. Thalbitzer: "The Ammassalik Eskimo." *Meddelelser om Gronland*, v. 40, (1923).

————, "The Cultic Deities of the Inuit." *International Congress of Americanists*, v. 22, pp. 367-391, (1926).

————, "Cultic Games and Festivals in Greenland." *International Congress of Americanists*, v. 21, pp. 236-255, (1925).

L. M. Turner: "Ethnology of the Ungava District, Hudson Bay Territory." *Bureau of American Ethnology Ann. Rept.*, 11, (1889-90).

E. M. Weyer: *The Eskimos*, (1932).

THE RELIGION OF THE
NAVAHO INDIANS

*The wide range of Dr. Wyman's mind and interests is shown by
the fields of teaching and research in which he is engaged. He
teaches both theoretical and experimental physiology in the Boston
College of Liberal Arts, teaching also Southwestern Indian Cultures in its department of sociology and anthropology and gives
courses in American Indian Art and Asiatic Art in its department
of Fine Arts—both at the undergraduate and graduate levels. From
1942 until 1946 he was chairman of the Division of Medical Sciences at Boston University and since then associate professor of
biology in the College of Liberal Arts. He has done considerable
research work in physiology with some fifty published papers to
his credit.*

*Considerable field work in New Mexico, among the Navahos,
is the basis for the essay contributed to this volume. Dr. Wyman
has lived with a Navaho family (almost as a member), participating
in its activities. He has been an actual patient in one Navaho healing ceremonial. He has directed research work in Navaho ethnology for three summers under the auspices of the University of New
Mexico's department of anthropology. Some thirty papers have
been published by him relating to his studies of the Navaho peoples. Twelve summers, in all, have been spent in this area of research, studying native medicine, ceremonialism and folk-lore.*

*He was born in Livermore Falls, Maine, in 1897. He took his
bachelor's degree in 1918 at Bowdoin College and his Ph.D. at
Harvard in 1922. He has travelled abroad, doing research work in
his professional field in the laboratories of England, Scotland,
France, Germany and Scandinavia. He is an elected fellow of the
American Academy of Arts and Sciences as well as of the American
Anthropological Society, besides holding membership in many
other academic fraternities.*

Editor

THE RELIGION OF THE
NAVAHO INDIANS

LELAND CLIFTON WYMAN

"In another sense, speaking of 'Navaho religion' does violence to the viewpoint of The People. There is no word or phrase in their language which could possibly be translated as 'religion' ".[1]

BUT THE Navaho do have a body of beliefs concerning the dynamics of the universe, their "philosophy" if you will, and a highly organized system of techniques for dealing with those segments of experience which are not subject to rational means of control. Thus, if we accept the frequently quoted anthropological definition of religion as "man's confession of impotence in certain matters" they do have a "religion" in this sense, and a belief in what we would call "the supernatural", although they might not make it a separate category of thought as we do.

The Navaho Indians constitute the largest remaining group of native Americans within the boundaries of the United States. There are nearly sixty thousand of them and they are increasing at the rate of about two per cent a year. They have overflowed the

---

[1] Clyde Kluckhohn and Dorothea Leighton, *The Navaho* (Cambridge, Mass., 1946), p. 122. For practical purposes further documentation will be dispensed with in this paper. A short selected bibliography is given at the end. This does not relieve me, however, of the necessity for acknowledging my great debt to my associations with and to the published and unpublished works of my colleagues in Navaho studies, especially Father Berard Haile, Clyde Kluckhohn, and Gladys A. Reichard. There is hardly a statement here that could not be documented by reference to their works, indeed even the very language is doubtless moulded, albeit unconsciously, by their style.

boundaries of their reservation in Arizona and New Mexico so that the land occupied by them is now in excess of eighteen million acres. This land is a part of the wild, colorful, highly eroded plateau country of the Southwest, beautiful to look at but hard to make a living in, and it is ample evidence of what Kluckhohn has called their "genius for adaptability" and "for making alien ideas congruent with a pre-existent design for living" that they are still able to make a living of sorts (although they have become the government's number one economic Indian problem). Further expression of these same traits is the preservation of their "religion", intact in the face of long and vigorous pressure from European culture, not a "forgotten religion" but a vital, functioning system.

The Navahos view the universe as an orderly unitary system or continuum of interrelated events. Reichard says "Navajo dogma connects all things, natural and experienced, from man's skeleton to universal destiny, which encompasses even inconceivable space, in a closely interlocked unity which omits nothing, no matter how small or how stupendous, and in which each individual has a significant function until, at his final dissolution, he not only becomes one with the ultimate harmony, but he *is* that harmony." This all-inclusive unity must contain, therefore, both good and evil, so the universe is a dangerous place. Evil and danger come most frequently from disturbance of the normal order, harmony, or balance between elements in the universe, and, as Reichard says, from absence of control, which depends upon knowledge. Good and evil, therefore, are not abstract ethical concepts, but complementary components of the universe, or any part of it; the controlled, harmonious, orderly, and the uncontrolled unharmonious, disorderly portions of every unit or complex. Thus every human being, no matter how "good" he is in life, has an "evil" portion which becomes a dangerous "ghost" after death and which may do harm to the living if not controlled.

Man has his place in the universal continuum and if he misbehaves with respect to the traditional restrictions on human behavior in relation to the "supernatural" there is a breakdown in the harmonious balance of things, resulting usually in illness of the transgressor or future illness of his or her unborn child. Occasionally some other disaster may occur, as when a winter of serious blizzards, causing loss of life among humans and livestock, was attributed to Navahos having danced while wearing sacred masks at a traditionally unauthorized place and time of year (the Gallup "Intertribals" of 1931). Ghosts of the dead, and living humans who malevolently misuse certain types of ritual knowledge, that is, witches, may likewise cause disorder and resulting misfortune. Human "misbehavior" may not always be intentional. There are numerous things in the universe which are inherently dangerous, certain animals, lightning, winds, the Holy People themselves, and unwitting contact of an improper nature with them, direct or indirect, may cause disease.

Fortunately there are means for dispelling evil, for bringing the dangerous under control, for restoring harmony in the relationships of an individual or a group with the world, even for rendering an individual immune to further attack by the same "supernatural" influences. These means are the knowledge and application of orderly procedures, that is control by ritual, in which the principles of compulsion by repetition, like cures like, identification with "supernatural" beings, and other well known patterns usually called "white magic" are operative. The ceremonials based upon this ritual are permeated with a colorful system of symbolism, expressed in words, in behavior, in material paraphernalia, including symbols of direction, color, sex, number, sound, and numerous others. The word imagery of the songs, the prayers, and the myths associated with these ceremonials, the music accompanying them, and at least one graphic art, that of the drypaintings, must be reckoned among the great arts of the world.

If knowledge of the ritual procedure and performance of it are correct and complete, then harmony is restored quite mechanically. The divinities of the Navaho may judge only as to the correctness and completeness of performance, and if this is attained they must come and "set things right". Offerings are not made for the purpose of glorifying or thanking the spirits, but to attract their presence. Reichard expresses the situation well as follows. "He does not 'count past blessings,' nor does he give thanks in prayer. Thanks are not compulsive; all the words of a prayer are. Mortification and humility, opposites of gratitude, are similarly absent." "He does not ask for pity, he uses the compulsive technique learned from the gods themselves." ". . . he seeks not pity but correction. Since he does not humiliate himself he does not ask or receive patronage; if he kneels when praying it is not because of lowliness and he need not bow when his wishes have been granted."

From what has been said so far it may be concluded that the main aim of Navaho "religion" is the restoration of universal harmony once it has been disturbed. It is doubtful, however, if the average Navaho would so state his aims if questioned as to why he indulged in ceremonial behavior. Like us, most of them are quite practical minded. It has been amply demonstrated that the type worry of the Navaho is for health, and it is true that there is much disease among them. The great majority of the ceremonials are primarily for curing disease, and it follows that every perform-ance is given for an individual patient. Along with the cure of the individual there may be blessings which extend to the group, the family, the local community, even to the whole tribe. Rain may be secured in time of drought, and other tangible benefits, but heal-ing of the specific patient is always primary. There are a few cere-monials, which will be mentioned below, which are performed for other purposes, for general prosperity and well-being. Our Navaho, therefore, would tell us that the aims of his "religion" are first the restoration and maintenance of health, and secondarily the in-crease of wealth, the well-being of home, flocks, and fields, the security of himself and his relatives. He would speak of acquiring ceremonial property, such as the bead token which protects from lightning and snakes. Although he might not mention it, he would doubtless recognize the prestige value of giving costly ceremonials and the opportunity for social intercourse. Finally, he might sum it all up in a single Navaho word, which actually is untranslatable, but which has been variously rendered, most often as "beauty", but also as "blessing", "perfection", "harmony", "goodness", "nor-mality". It has been said that the meanings of this, and of a few other untranslatable words, contain the key to real understanding of Navaho religion. One other such word has been rendered as "evil" or "ugly", and refers to harm done by ghosts and witches. Another, usually translated as "holy" or "sacred", refers to a class of supernatural beings, a set of ritual techniques, and to anything which has been brought under control by the use of these tech-niques, thus differentiating it from the merely "good". Finally there is the word usually rendered as "dangerous" or "tabooed", which characterizes the dangerous nature of any element in the universe which is traditionally hedged about by ceremonial re-strictions.

The Navahos' interest in health and their use of ritual to cure the individual with the common good seemingly a secondary consideration signalizes a striking difference between their "religion" and that of their neighbors, the Pueblo Indians of Arizona and New Mexico. Pueblo religion is thoroughly integrated with social organization; their ceremonials are primarily for bringing rain and fertility with curing only secondary; they are conducted by highly organized priesthoods, religious societies, or other groups, rather than by individual practitioners; they are carried out in an annual round according to a set religious calendar; and the focus of interest is the common weal with the individual so subordinated that he hardly seems to exist. The Navaho have no organized priesthoods or religious societies, but ceremonials are conducted by individual specialists, social organization touches ceremonial practice in only a few and rather minor ways, and just as their religious system is not socialized so it is not tied in with any sort of calendar (except for a few seasonal restrictions) but ceremonials are carried out whenever they are needed. This "individualism" is more apparent than real, however, for the Navaho have to cooperate closely in their difficult physical environment for mere survival. Carefully maintained reciprocal behavior patterns among relatives, real or classificatory, in a close-knit consumption group is their secret of making a living in the semi-arid Southwest. As Reichard has pointed out, "Between the Pueblo and Navaho there is no difference of purpose, but only a difference of emphasis." "They differ in their interpretation of what well-being consists of and how it is to be achieved." "The Navaho individual is the reason for the coördination of universal phenomena; he therefore directs his ritual from the individual outward. There can be no tribal well-being unless each member enjoys it. The Pueblo, on the other hand, considers world harmony as paramount, and he directs his major effort toward attaining it. If then the individual benefits, so much the better, for his health depends primarily upon the condition of the whole group."

Besides the Earth Surface People and the ghosts of their dead, the Navaho universe contains many personalized powers, conceived as beings something like humans or capable of assuming human form at will. These are the Holy People, not virtuously holy but powerful and therefore "dangerous". They may be said to form the Navaho pantheon but they do not form a hierarchy. They vary with respect to properties and powers, each "having charge of" a given group of things, but like everything else in the universe they are all interdependent, complementary parts of the whole. Reichard has said that she is "convinced that Navaho ritual centers about a Sun cult," and that "in seeking world harmony the Navaho consider Sun as its center." Nevertheless, although Sun may be a dominant deity he cannot dispense with lesser powers for successful operation. Certainly the most beloved deity is Changing Woman. Her twin children sired by the Sun, Monster Slayer and Child of the Water, slew the monsters which were threatening mankind, and thus represent war power. Changing Woman, the Sun, and the Hero Twins, form then a sort of "holy family", prominent in myth and ceremonial, but immediately after the emergence of the Holy People from the underworlds there was a "first family", First Man, First Woman, First Boy, First Girl, and their associates Coyote and *be'gochidi,* who were prominent in early events on the earth surface while it was being made inhabitable for mankind. Another group of Holy People are the *ye'i,* led by Talking God, who are impersonated by masked dancers in the public performances of certain ceremonials. Then there are animals, plants, and natural phenomena, "who used to be people", and who may still assume human form; Big Snake, Cactus People, Thunders, Winds. There are a multitude of these, and finally there are those curious little helpers of deity and man, such as Big Fly and Corn Beetle. Every element in the universe has its power which may be personalized as a member of the pantheon. Some of these beings are dependable or at least may be persuaded or coerced. Changing Woman is always so, but others may be persuaded or controlled only with difficulty, and some are wholly dangerous. It is man's responsibility to maintain harmonious relations between himself and the Holy People, or at least to avoid them, lest he suffer the consequences. Thus an attack from the Holy People is not primarily because they are inimical to man but because man himself has been the transgressor, whereas an attack by a ghost or a witch may be unprovoked (although a ghost has usually had some provo-

348

cation for returning, such as improper burial or disturbance of the grave).

The Navahos group their ceremonials into categories according to various criteria. Two groups are now obsolescent for obvious reasons, the War Ceremonials and the Gameway group (hunting rites), although some of the former were revived by the Navahos during the recent world conflict as a part of their contribution to the war effort. (The suffix "-way" is a translation of the ending of Navaho names for ceremonials.) One of the ancient war ceremonials, Enemyway, which was used to protect warriors from the ghosts of slain enemies, has been preserved as a cure for sickness caused by the ghosts of non-Navahos, and is now classed with the other "ghostway" ceremonials. The remaining song ceremonials may be placed in two groups, which have been called "rites" and "chants" by ethnologists. The first and smaller group comprises the Blessingway rites which are comparatively short (two nights; Navahos reckon time by "nights", i.e., from sundown to sundown, instead of by "days") and simple, but which constitute the cornerstone of the whole ceremonial system. Nearly every ceremonial has its Blessingway part. Blessingway is performed not as a curing ceremonial but as the Navahos say "for good hope", that is to invoke positive blessings and general well-being, for protection of livestock, to consecrate ceremonial paraphernalia, at the installation of a headman, preceding childbirth, or for leaving or returning warriors. The songs sung in the girl's puberty rite, in a marriage ceremony, in the house blessing, and in other minor rites, are from Blessingway. Although not for curing, there is usually "one sung over" who represents the group to be benefited. The rite consists of a few songs the first evening, a ritual bath with songs and prayers the next day, and a final all-night singing. Drypaintings (*v.i.*) of variously colored cornmeal and pollens (actual or pulverized flower petals) may be made on buckskin spread on the ground.

The group of Chantways is by far the largest, and in turn may be divided into three groups, each dominated by a given ritual or pattern of behavior governing procedure, Holyway, Ghostway (Evilway) and Lifeway. The Holyway chants again are the largest group, with some twenty-two separate chant complexes (although five or six of these are extinct or obsolescent), many of which are

349

further divided into male and female or other types of branches. This group contains many well known ceremonials, such as the Shooting Chants, the Mountain Chants, the Beauty Chants, the Night Chants, and the Wind Chants. They are used for diseases which have been traced to such etiological factors as lightning, snakes, bears, winds, and various other Holy People. The Holyway ritual is further subject to several sub-rituals, such as peaceful-way and injury-way, the former being characterized by a preponderance of procedures designed to attract good, to summon the Holy People by means of invocatory offerings, etc., and the latter by procedures for driving out evil, that is, exorcistic in nature. Nearly all Holyway chants have or had two or three and five night forms, and most of them had nine night forms. The five night form may have been basic while the two night form represents a condensation of it and the nine night an elaboration. The Ghostway or Evilway chants are specific for curing sickness caused by native ghosts or witches, and associated with them is the Enemyway rite for dealing with alien ghost sickness (*v.s.*). Evilway ritual is naturally characterized by a predominance of exorcistic techniques, among which blackening of the patient is a prominent feature. All chantways, irrespective of ritual, however, contain both invocatory and exorcistic elements. A given ritual may be dominated by one of these categories but the other is not excluded. Upward-reaching-way is the fundamental Ghostway ceremonial. The third group, the Lifeway chants, are specifically for injuries which have resulted from accidents. They are simpler than the other chantways, and their duration may not be fixed, a ceremonial being continued as long as needed or desired. The common two night form includes a short singing the first night, a bath the next morning, and painting the patient red and an all night singing on the final night. The fundamental Lifeway chant is Flintway. Father Berard prefers a dichotomy of ritual, placing the Lifeway chants under Holyway, but Kluckhohn and I believe that the trichotomy exists. A given chant may be conducted according to one or the other of the three rituals, depending on the purpose involved. Thus the Shooting Chant may be found in all three groups. Today knowledge of all three rituals does not exist for all chantways and we are not sure that it ever did, although there is evidence that certain rituals for some chants are only recently extinct.

350

Within the major groups mentioned above the Navaho make smaller divisions of associated ceremonials which "go together" according to various types of linkage. The names of some fifty-two ceremonials, excluding the various Blessingways and the obsolescent hunting and war rites, have been obtained from Navaho informants. If we subtract, however, the duplications due to male, female, and other branches of the same ceremonial, and those arising from the fact that some chants are conducted according to more than one ritual, we are left with about twenty-six distinct names. About nine of these are now extinct or obsolescent and of the remainder only about ten are commonly performed. Some of the others may be known by only a few individuals.

Besides the song ceremonials there are prayer ceremonials, long prayers being said for four days without singing, and minor rites for trading, salt-gathering, and the like. Some of the prayer ceremonials are valued for treating the victims of witchcraft. Since the singing is all important in most ceremonials, the Navahos call their practitioners "singers". Ceremonials are learned by apprenticeship, and most singers specialize in one, two, or three, and know how to perform parts of several more, sometimes as many as twelve. The largest number of complete chants a singer is likely to know is six or seven although some chanters have claimed to know eight.

Since the most commonly performed ceremonials (save for Blessingway) and certainly the most complicated are those of the Holyway group, a typical five night performance will be outlined. Upon superficial acquaintance the system of chantways seems to be stupendously complex but in fact a Navaho chant is a framework into which are fitted more or less discrete units, each fulfilling a single function, which ethnologists have called "ceremonies" (as distinct from "ceremonial" which refers to a complex of ceremonies forming a unit having a name and an origin legend, and conducted according to a particular set of rules or ritual). Some ceremonies are more or less fixed and others may be modified, inserted or omitted in accord with the practice of the singer, the wishes of the patient or family, the nature of the illness, or other circumstances. Within a ceremony there may also be acts and procedures which are similarly manipulated. The same ceremonies are used over and over again in different chants, with modifications in songs, paraphernalia, procedure, and so on, according to the specific symbolism of

351

the chant being given. Similarly, much of the ceremonial equipment is common to all, or most, chants, but some is specific for a given chant or group of chants. Single ceremonies, or combinations of two or three, may be carried out as a rite lasting only a portion of a day or night, often as a test performance and if the patient seems to be benefited the whole ceremonial may be given. Theoretically a chant which has cured a patient should be given a total of four times, usually in alternate five night and two night forms, but repetition of performances may be delayed over many years. Thus the intricacy of Navaho ceremonialism is not quite so overpowering once it is clearly understood.

In reading the following description it should be kept in mind that there are certain procedures which are found throughout all ceremonies. Most important is the singing, usually accompanied by a rattle, led by the singer but joined by all (usually men) who know how. Singing accompanies nearly every act, indeed in Navaho thought most acts would be meaningless or ineffective without the songs. Knowledge of several hundred songs is required for most full chants. Without the songs there can be no ceremonial, with a few songs if nothing else some good may be done. Medicines, usually herbal, are prepared in special cups of abalone shell or turtle shell and administered at frequent intervals. Occasionally a "bullroarer" is whirled to make a sound like thunder and thus intimidate evil. Ceremonial paraphernalia, especially the contents of the pouch specific for the chant, are laid out in fixed order upon a calico spread at the west in the hogan (Navaho house). These, and other objects, are occasionally applied to the body of the patient by the singer, while voicing a sound symbolic for the chant, in the ceremonial order, that is from the feet upwards. All procedures involving the motion of participants is from left to right or sunwise. Occasional prayers are said by the singer and by other participants. Communal pollen prayer, taking a pinch of corn pollen from a sack with a mumbled or silent prayer by all present, comes at or near the close of ceremonies. Fumigation, inhaling fumes from a concoction sprinkled on two glowing coals, closes most ceremonies. Following each ceremony materials and objects which have served their purpose are disposed of by trusted helpers in stated directions and situations at some distance outside the hogan, sometimes with meal or pollen prayer. During the ceremo-
352

nial and for four days thereafter the patient is subject to numerous restrictions on behavior, and certain ones, such as sexual continence, apply to the singer as well.

The ceremonial is opened at sundown the first evening by *consecration of the hogan.* The modern Navaho house or hogan is a roughly circular or hexagonal structure of logs or stone, chinked with mud, with a central opening in the roof for a smokehole. The family hogan is cleared of its contents for the chant, and consecrated by the singer by placing cornmeal and sprigs of hard oak on or above four roof beams in the cardinal directions, with prayers and Blessingway songs.

Following this after sundown on the first night and on each of the three succeeding evenings there may be an *unraveling ceremony,* lasting about an hour. The essential feature of this is the preparation of a stated number (four to fifteen) of *unravelers,* bundles of herbs and feathers tied together with a wool string by crochet knots so that when the end of the string is pulled it will unravel and come free, and the application and unraveling of them at parts of the patient's body in ceremonial order. This symbolizes release from harm, "untying" and dissipation of evil. (For obvious reasons it is a favorite treatment in cases of difficult labor.)

A *short-singing* for an hour or so follows unraveling if that is performed or occurs after sundown during each of the first four evenings. The singing is sometimes accompanied by basket drumming, beating an inverted basket with a special drumstick made of yucca leaves.

If a sandpainting (*v.i.*) is to be made a *setting-out ceremony* is held just before dawn (on the second to fifth mornings inclusive when four sandpaintings are made). Symbolic objects known as bundle prayersticks are stuck upright in fixed order in a small mound of earth outside and in front of the hogan door. These serve to notify human and supernatural beings alike of the procedures within the hogan.

Just after dawn on each of the first four mornings a *sweat and emetic ceremony,* lasting an hour or two, drives evils away through internal and external purification. On the first morning a fire is kindled with a firedrill, and coals from it are used to kindle the permanent fire which serves throughout the chant. Four small sandpaintings, often of snakes, may be made at the cardinal points

353

around the central fireplace, and another northwest of the fire on which the patient's basket of emetic is placed. Four wooden pokers, ritually prepared, are laid beside the sand paintings. The participants undress outside, men retaining a breechcloth and women a skirt. An enormous fire which induces intensive sweating is built in the fireplace. A large quantity of the emetic decoction containing many kinds of plants is prepared in a pail and dispensed in a basket for the patient and in pans for others. All participants bathe in the warm emetic mixture, feet upwards, and the patient and others who wish drink some and vomit into a basin of sand (which is later disposed of). Other procedures, such as a procession around the fireplace, may occur and finally the singer sprinkles everyone with a cool and fragrant herb lotion by means of an eagle feather brush.

Immediately after breakfast on the first four days an invocatory *offering ceremony* summons the Holy People. A given number of "jewel" offerings, painted reed offerings stuffed with native tobacco and other things ("cigarettes"), and/or prayerstick offerings of small cut and painted wooden sticks, are prepared, held by the patient while a long litany is said by singer and patient, and then ritually deposited by a special helper at some distance from the hogan and in a carefully specified place and manner. Certain phases of some chants are characterized by the large numbers and complication of the offerings.

In the forenoon of the fourth day a *bath ceremony* further purifies the patient. A platform of sand, often covered with herbs, is prepared and a basket is placed upon it. Water and a piece of root from a yucca plant is placed in it and whipped into a stiff mound of suds. Designs of pollens and powdered herb medicines are strewed on the suds, which are then applied to the patient in ceremonial order by the singer. Then the patient kneels, washes his hair and bathes, assisted by helpers, dries himself with cornmeal, and dresses in clean clothes.

After the offerings (or the bath on the fourth day) the *sand-painting* is begun. This is a symbolic picture, often large and complicated, made by strewing pulverized red, yellow, and white sandstone, charcoal, and a few mixtures of these, on a smooth background of clean, tan-colored sand from a nearby field. (See Fig. 1.) The pigments are allowed to trickle between the thumb

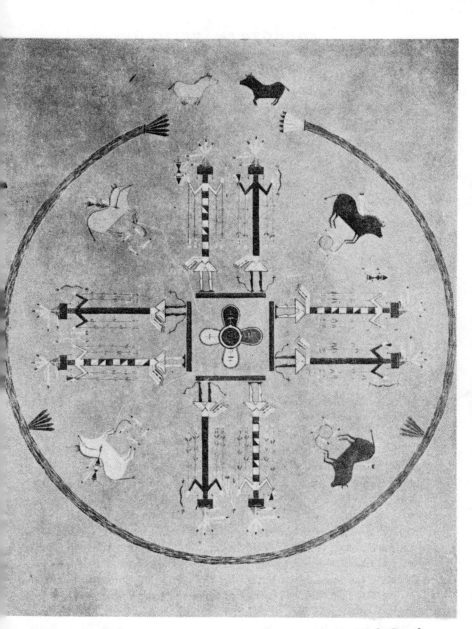

Figure 1. Sandpainting from the Navaho Shooting Chant, "Holy People Overcome Buffalo."
(From the Louisa Wade Wetherill Collection, Arizona State Museum)

and flexed index finger, and anyone who knows how may participate under the direction of the singer. Sandpaintings vary in size from small ones a foot or two in diameter to those twenty feet or more in diameter which must be made in special hogans. The average size is about six feet, requiring the work of four to six men for three to five hours for completion. The designs are handed down in memory from singer to apprentice, and are rigidly prescribed. The number of paintings pertaining to a single chant or chant complex varies from two or four to a very large number (as for the Shooting Chants). For a given ceremonial the singer selects four from his repertoire according to the wishes of the patient, the nature of the illness, or some such factor. Some six hundred different drypaintings have been recorded by investigators or native informants, and it is believed that many others are known. Again, however, the complication is more apparent than real for the same motives may be combined in numerous ways to produce "different" designs. When the painting has been completed the ceremony begins. The bundle prayersticks are brought in from the set-out mound and set upright around the painting. Cornmeal is sprinkled on it by singer and patient. On the last day only, the patient's body is painted from head to foot with symbolic designs, including anthropomorphic figures and snakes or lightnings, by means of mineral pigments, and a bead token and a head plume are tied in his hair. The bead becomes his property, a protection from further danger. The patient then sits on the sandpainting, and the singer applies sand from various parts of the painted figures' bodies to corresponding parts of the patient's body. He may then similarly apply the bundle prayersticks and parts of his own body to the patient. Finally the patient leaves the hogan, the sandpainting is erased, and the sand is ritually disposed of. The chief symbolism of this ceremony is the identification of the patient with the supernatural beings represented in the painting, powers that can cure him; he becomes "strong like the Holy People", immune to further harm. For this reason he must observe the four day post-ceremonial period of restrictions, lest he harm others through his newly acquired power.

The ceremony of the fifth and final night is an *all night singing*, continuous until after the dawn songs when the patient is allowed to go outside, face the east, and breathe in the dawn four times.

A final prayer and a Blessingway song closes the ceremonial.

Certain optional ceremonies, such as ritual eating of cornmeal mush or a meat decoction, may be added to the final day at extra expense. Large numbers of visitors attend the final day and night, sometimes a hundred or more, and all must be fed by the patient's family. The singer must be paid, in advance, and numerous articles and materials must be furnished. A five night ceremonial, therefore, may cost the equivalent of a hundred dollars or more. A two night form is less expensive, perhaps twenty-five dollars, but a nine night chant, which may be attended by a thousand or more spectators may cost well over five hundred dollars. Some of these, which may be given only between the first frost and the first thunder storm, present public performances by teams of masked dancers who impersonate certain Holy People ("Yeibichai"), or other exhibitions like a huge sacred vaudeville show (the Dark Circle of Branches, "Corral Dance", or "Fire Dance"), throughout the final night, and numerous other ceremonies not described above. The expense of such a great ceremonial is huge indeed.

From the preceding description it may be seen that in a five night chant there are usually ten or a dozen ceremonies. The consecration of the hogan, bath, body painting and token tying, all night singing, and the dawn procedures, occur only once, while the other ceremonies are repeated four times. In a nine night chant the short singings, setting out, and sandpainting ceremonies are moved ahead to the fifth, sixth, seventh, and eighth days, and of course the bath and final night are on the eighth and ninth, so spacing of ceremonies rather than the addition of new ones achieves the nine night form. In the two night condensation the sweat and emetic ceremony is omitted for it must be repeated four times, and of course only a single unraveling, short singing, setting out, offering, and sandpainting ceremony may be performed.

The genesis of a chant is somewhat as follows. A Navaho makes known to members of his family group that he is troubled by illness, bad dreams, recollection of violation of some restriction, fear of witchcraft, or some other indication that he requires ceremonial aid. An informal discussion as to the possible causes follows, and sometimes the family conference decides upon the etiological factors and chooses a ceremonial and a singer. More often a diagnostician is called in. Diagnosis is accomplished through divination

357

by specialists who usually are not singers. There have been several techniques, star-gazing and listening which depended upon the interpretation of things seen or heard, but the commonest type to-day is hand-trembling in which involuntary motions made by the hand while the diviner is in a trance-like state are interpreted. Thus the cause of disease, the ritual to cure it, and often the right practitioner to select, are discovered. Lost or stolen articles, water, and so on, may be found by divination. Diagnosticians come the closest to the shamanistic tradition of anything in Navaho culture, for their ability comes to them suddenly, "like a gift", but even here certain techniques may be learned. Singers, on the other hand, acquire their knowledge and powers solely through learning, for which they pay, so they are strictly within the priestly tradition. Women often are diviners, but there are very few female singers. After the singer has been selected an intermediary goes to make arrangements with him, and to bring his bundle to the home of the patient. Unless there is urgency or prior engagements to interfere a date four days in advance is usually set for beginning the ceremonial.

The ceremonial complex is transmitted orally from singer to apprentice but it is further enshrined and sanctioned in the large body of mythology, commonly told around family firesides in the winter. A singer need not know the myths pertaining to his specialty ceremonials, but it is felt that he should, and the best ones do. The basic myth of Navaho religion, which is their nearest analogue to the Christian Bible, is their emergence story, which tells of pre-emergence events in the underworlds, of the emergence to the present earth surface, of the immediately post-emergence events (setting the earth in order), of the slaying of the monsters by the Hero Twins (Monsterway), and finally of the origin of earth surface people and the growth of the Navaho nation. From this basic myth the origin myths of most ceremonials branch off at various points and are elaborated as more or less separate tales, so the body of mythology forms an interlocking whole. The rite myths tell how the ceremonial started and how it should be carried out. Even the fraction of Navaho mythology which has been recorded fills hundreds of pages, but as in other areas of Navaho religion where limited numbers of ceremonies or sandpainting motives are combined in various ways and with various individual minutiae,

so does the mythology possess a somewhat limited number of episodes and incidents or types thereof which recur over and again
in the origin legends of different chants. Navaho myths are filled
with vivid word imagery, deep emotional feeling, fine ritual poetry,
keen humor, and great imaginative power; it is a pity that space
forbids quoting some passages here.

The functions of myth and ritual have been admirably analyzed
by Dr. Kluckhohn in his various writings. The primary manifest
function, of course, is curing the patient, and cures *are* effected,
partly because some of the procedures are of actual therapeutic
value, but more because a Navaho ceremonial is a potent means of
psychotherapy. The prestige and authority of the singer, the mysticism and power of the ceremonial itself, the rallying of many relatives and friends to aid in his cure, all contribute to a feeling of well-
being. Then there are secondary social functions, opportunities
for visiting or for match-making, and the prestige values from ex-
hibiting skill in drypainting or singing, or from merely sponsoring
a costly chant. Fully as important, however, are the latent functions for the individual and for the group. The Navahos' "religion" like that of any other people is a source of security in a bewildering and changing world. As Kluckhohn says, "In a world
full of hazards, myths affirm that there is a rhyme and reason after
all. They give the future the appearance of safety by affirming the
unbroken continuity of present and past." "Their system of beliefs, then, gives Navahos something to hold to." "Ritual and
myth provide fixed points in an existence of bewildering change
and disappointments." "In the absence of a codified law and of an
authoritarian chief, it is only through the myth-ritual system that
the Navahos can present a unified front to—disintegrating pres-
sures. The all-pervasive configurations of word-symbols (myths)
and of act-symbols (rituals) preserve the cohesion of the society
and sustain the individual, protecting both from intolerable conflict."

Navaho ideas concerning eschatology, except for their frequent
preoccupation with the activities of ghosts, do not loom large in
their "religion", and they are reluctant to discuss the subject because of their morbid fear of the dead and anything connected
with them. Although the concept of the ghost, the evil part of man
which may return to earth and harm the living (*v.s.*), is well

formulated similar beliefs about the "spirit" or the good in an individual are vague, lacking, or much confused and contradictory. The Navahos have no equivalent of the Christian "soul" or of individual "immortality". In summary, man contains evil and good (which may or may not be synonymous with breath and/or life). At death both leave the body. Evil goes to the afterworld in the north and becomes the ghost. If breath is not synonymous with good it may be what becomes the ghost. Good may or may not go to the afterworld. If it does it may live there in a different place than does evil. The afterworld, therefore, is peopled with spirits which may be of one or two kinds, either all capable of return to earth as ghosts, or ghosts and good spirits not capable of return. The afterworld is a place like this earth somewhere far to the north below the level of the earth, possibly one of the underworlds. It is approached by a trail down a sandy hill or cliff, and at the entrance old guardians or deceased relatives apply tests to see if death has really occurred. Existence there is not particularly inviting, but most informants seem to feel that it is at least as pleasant as this earth. There are no generally accepted ideas concerning punishment of the wicked or a separate "hell" for the sinful. Indeed, as Kluckhohn points out a "shame" culture has no notion of "sin" nor can the Navaho easily conceive of "laying up treasures in heaven". Possibly their vagueness and confusion concerning eschatology is the result of lack of opportunity for systematizing the pertinent concepts because of their reluctance to discuss it.

It is appropriate to close this chapter with the Mountain Song from the Night Chant (translated by Washington Matthews) :

> "In a holy place with a god I walk,
> In a holy place with a god I walk,
> On Tsisnadzi'ni with a god I walk,
> On a chief of mountains with a god I walk,
> In old age wandering with a god I walk,
> On a trail of beauty with a god I walk."

BIBLIOGRAPHY

From a host of references the following have been selected to serve as a basis for a more detailed review of the subject. In the not too distant future a definitive work on *Navaho Religion* by Dr. Gladys A. Reichard

THE RELIGION OF THE NAVAHO INDIANS

will appear, and also a paper by Dr. Clyde Kluckhohn on *The Philosophy of the Navaho Indians.*

Franciscan Fathers: *An Ethnologic Dictionary of the Navaho Language* (Saint Michaels, Arizona, 1910).

B. Haile: *Origin Legend of the Navaho Enemy Way, Yale University Publications in Anthropology,* No. 17 (1938).

————, *Navaho Chantways and Ceremonials, American Anthropologist,* Vol. 40 (1938) pp. 639-652.

C. Kluckhohn: *Myths and Rituals: A General Theory, Harvard Theological Review* (1942), Vol. 35, pp. 45-80.

————, *Navaho Witchcraft,* Papers of the Peabody Museum of Harvard University (1944), Vol. 22, No. 2.

C. Kluckhohn and D. Leighton: *The Navaho* (Cambridge, Mass., 1946).

C. Kluckhohn and K. Spencer: *A Bibliography of the Navaho Indians* (New York, 1940).

C. Kluckhohn and L. C. Wyman: *An Introduction to Navaho Chant Practice* in *Memoirs,* American Anthropological Association (1940), No. 53.

W. Matthews: *Navaho Legends* in *Memoirs,* American Folk-Lore Society (1897), Vol. 5.

————, *The Night Chant,* a Navaho Ceremony in *Memoirs,* American Museum of Natural History (1902), Vol. 6.

F. J. Newcomb and G. A. Reichard: *Sandpaintings of the Navaho Shooting Chant* (New York, 1937).

G. A. Reichard: *Navajo Medicine Man; Sandpaintings and Legends of Miguelito* (New York, 1939).

————, *Prayer: the Compulsive Word* in *Monographs,* American Ethnological Society (1944), No. 7.

————, *Distinctive Features of Navaho Religion, Southwestern Journal of Anthropology,* Vol. 1 (1945), pp. 199-220.

L. C. Wyman: *Navaho Diagnosticians, American Anthropologist,* Vol. 38 (1936), pp. 236-246.

L. C. Wyman, W. W. Hill, and I. Osanai: *Navajo Eschatology, University of New Mexico Bulletin,* No. 377 (1942).

L. C. Wyman and C. Kluckhohn: *Navaho Classification of Their Song Ceremonials* in *Memoirs,* American Anthropological Association, No. 50 (1938).

THE RELIGION OF THE
HOPI INDIANS

Mischa Titiev was born in Kremenchug, Russia, in 1901, but was reared and educated in the United States. He attended the Boston Latin School, after which he entered Harvard University where he received the degrees of B.A., M.A. and Ph.D.

Beginning in the summer of 1932, Dr. Titiev undertook an extensive study of the Hopi Indians of Arizona, concentrating particularly on the inhabitants of Third Mesa. Between August of 1933 and March of 1934 he was permitted to live in the old pueblo of Oraibi and to take part in the daily life of the community. Return visits were made in 1937 and 1940. The results of his investigations have been published in numerous articles and in a full-length monograph entitled "Old Oraibi: A Study of the Hopi Indians of Third Mesa."

Dr. Titiev became an instructor at the University of Michigan in 1936 and now holds the rank of associate professor of anthropology. During World War II he was supervisor of the East Asia ASTP unit at Michigan and later became a research analyst and CBI historian for the Office of Strategic Services. His duties included an overseas assignment that took him to various parts of India, Burma, Assam and China.

At the present time Dr. Titiev is about to begin a field trip to Chile where he plans to study the changing pattern of culture among the Araucanian Indians.

Editor

THE RELIGION OF THE
HOPI INDIANS

MISCHA TITIEV

I. BACKGROUND

PERCHED picturesquely on the flat-topped summits of three high mesas in northeastern Arizona are nine Hopi Indian villages. These, together with two communities on the plains nearby, make up the settlements of the entire tribe, which numbers about 3000 individuals. Not all of the villages are of the same antiquity but the oldest one, known as Oraibi, was founded in the middle of the twelfth century* and has been continuously occupied ever since. Each town is politically autonomous, has its own chief and, for the most part, conducts an independent cycle of ceremonies. Nevertheless, in spite of some local variations, all of the Hopi pueblos conform to a single pattern of social and religious behavior.

As far as can be determined the Hopi have lived by agriculture from the time of their first arrival at their present location. Hunting was never more than a secondary pursuit; the arid environment provided little or no chance for fishing; and neither sheep, cattle, nor horses were known to these Indians until after the coming of the Spaniards in 1540. Only by hard and continuous toil have the Hopi successfully sustained themselves as farmers, for they live in a region where the soil contains great amounts of alkali and where rainfall is scant, uneven, and so distributed that very little occurs during the growing season. Over the centuries they

---

* As to the pre-history of the Hopi before 1150, there is no direct evidence. As part of the general Pueblo culture, the record goes back into the so-called Basket Maker times of the early Christian era, but it is impossible to state that the Hopi as a tribe are descendants of any particular Basket Maker people.

have developed hardy strains of plants and clever agricultural techniques which enable them, except in greatly prolonged periods of drought, to raise adequate amounts of corn and other vegetables and fruits. For all their skill in farming, however, the Hopi people live in constant dread of a failure in their food supply.

Another threat to the security and stability of the natives arises from the nature of their social organization. Although they are grouped into communities of several hundred each, they lack centralized governments. The powers of the chiefs are strictly limited and the people are independent and cherish their kin and clan ties more than their village or tribal allegiances. Consequently, each settlement is faced with an ever-present threat of disintegration; and, from time to time, schisms have taken place that have split apart some of their largest towns.

To make matters worse, the residents of the pueblos live in terraced clusters of houses that bring them into close and unhygienic proximity to each other. There is no running water of any sort on the mesa tops, toilet facilities are entirely wanting, flies and other insects are numerous, and during meals all the diners dip into a single dish with their hands. Small wonder if, under such conditions, the introduction of a contagious disease should have terrifying consequences.

Taken together, lack of rain, threats of crop failure, internal strife, and occasional epidemics have combined to make existence highly precarious for the Hopi. To counteract these dangers they have taken whatever practical measures they could, but since their scientific and technological resources are too limited to provide them with a sense of security, they have turned to the supernatural in the hope that it would give them the comforting assurance that they will not be destroyed.

II. "PRIESTS" AND "CHURCHES"

Nearly all of the villages carry out schedules of annual rites, with certain activities recurring at specific times of the year. Two officials, appropriately designated as Sun Watchers, keep track of the seasons and notify the celebrants whenever one of these rituals falls due.

In view of the frequency and magnitude of their ceremonies it is somewhat puzzling to find that the Hopi have no formal priesthood. Even the chiefs who are responsible for the proper performance of major observances can scarcely be termed priests; for not one of them devotes himself exclusively or primarily to religious exercises, none customarily wears distinctive garb, and none is regarded as sanctified or holy. Instead, as the ceremonial cycle progresses, various leaders successively assume responsibility for a set of rites and then revert to lay life for the remainder of the year. At the same time, the sacred and the civil are closely interwoven concepts in the socio-political system of the Hopi, for every town official is in charge of at least one important observance. This is particularly true of village chiefs, each of whom is, *ipso facto*, the head man of an essential ceremony.

Religious leadership is also bound up with the clan system, for each rite is said to belong to a particular clan. This means, primarily, that the care of sacred materials and the selection of officers are the duty and privilege, respectively, of the controlling clan. It also means that in practice the principal man of a clan is pretty certain to be the leader of his group's observances. But ownership in this sense does not imply exclusive possession, so that secondary officials and general participants are likely to be drawn from any clan in the village.

A small number of basic rites are held in the main houses of the clans in charge, but much more commonly ceremonial performances take place in underground chambers called kivas. A Hopi kiva is a rectangular room some 10 feet high, 12 feet wide, and 25 feet long. It is entered through a hatchway cut in the roof, by means of a stout ladder. The floor is built on two levels, with the area behind the ladder being raised several inches higher than the other portion. When ceremonies are in progress the raised portion is given over to spectators and minor activities, while the principal events take place on the lower section.

Whenever a religious observance is being held inside, a kiva is closed to all but qualified participants. At other times men and boys are free to come and go at will, but females may enter these chambers only on a few, carefully stipulated occasions. There are from two to eight kivas in each Hopi town and, instead of resorting to them at random, young men prefer to affiliate themselves with particular ones. There thus come into being a number of kiva groups whose members work and play as units under the leadership of kiva chiefs. Kivas function, therefore, not only as "churches" but also as men's clubrooms.

III. THE RITUAL PATTERN

To facilitate the conduct of rituals the populace of every village is organized into several secret societies, each of which is responsible for the performance of a single ceremony. Any individual of the proper sex and age may seek initiation into as many of these orders as he chooses; usually, by the simple expedient of asking a member of the society in question to serve as his sponsor or ceremonial father. If a person who has thus been approached agrees to accept the responsibility, he takes his "child" into the kiva where the esoteric rites are being held, instructs him in their meaning, sees to it that he abides by such tabus as are in force, and on the fourth day of the observances washes his head in yucca suds and bestows a new name on him. Thereafter the initiate gradually learns the group's secret traditions, prayers, songs, and dances, and prepares to take an increasingly active part in future performances of the rites.

Although it is customary for members of a clan which owns a ceremony to join the associated secret society, there is no compulsion in the matter. Boys of six or eight years of age normally start their religious lives by being initiated into the Katcina cult. Not long after they usually join one of two Flute societies and either the Snake or the Antelope order. Before their twentieth birthdays they are expected to enter any one of the four cooperating fraternities that jointly conduct the Tribal Initiation ceremonies; after which they may climax their careers by being admitted to the Soyal observances.

Compared with the boys, Hopi girls participate only to a limited degree in religious activities. They, too, are admitted to the Katcina cult in early childhood; but only in rare cases are females allowed to join anything additional, other than one or more of three feminine secret societies.

All major rituals, except in special years, last for nine days. The first eight are given over to esoteric exercises held in kivas, and the ninth is featured by a public exhibition, commonly called a dance, during which the celebrants appear in colorful costumes before their fellow villagers.

The greater part of the secret actions that take place in kivas is devoted to the erection of temporary altars, the preparation of a medicinal liquid, the fashioning of dry painting made of colored sands, and the manufacture of prayer offerings to be deposited at shrines dedicated to the society's patron gods. These activities are accompanied by much smoking of native tobacco, singing, praying, and dancing. Sometimes, too, mimetic practices and dramatic performances are carried out.

Those who engage in ceremonial exercises are expected to make certain that they are in good health and have untroubled minds. It is thought best for any who are ill or upset to abstain voluntarily from active participation. Moreover, celebrants must observe tabus that forbid them to eat salt or fats, or to engage in sexual relations, for four days prior to the beginning of the rites, during their progress, and for four days after their conclusion.

IV. THE CEREMONIAL CYCLE

(a) *Introduction.* Perhaps the most fundamental concept of Hopi religion is a belief in the continuity of life after death. As is brought out in their mythology, they believe that in the beginning mankind emerged from an underground home (kiva) to the surface of the earth. Soon after, a witch caused the first death but escaped punishment by pointing out that the deceased had merely gone back into the underground kiva. So insignificant at the outset was the distinction between the quick and the dead that there was freedom of movement between the lower and upper realms until a mischievous Coyote threw a stone over the kiva opening, and thus brought about a permanent separation of the two worlds. Even so, the spirits of the dead are permitted occasionally to visit the living.

Life in the nether world is pictured in Hopi tales as a shadow replica of life on earth. The dead grow the same crops, eat the same foods, wear the same clothes, and observe the same ceremonies. They do not, of course, possess solid bodies, wear material clothes, nor eat anything more than the essence or "smell" of food;

hence they can float in the sky like clouds and, like clouds, they can bring rain.

(b) *Katcina Cult.* Not only are clouds and the spirits of the dead interchangeable according to Hopi belief, but they are also equivalent to the supernatural beings called katcinas. As part of their Emergence story it is said that when the people climbed out of the Underworld they were accompanied by kindly disposed deities, who were named katcinas. Whenever the Hopi settled down and planted crops the katcinas would perform rain-bringing dances. At last the Hopi were attacked by enemies, vaguely identified as Mexicans, who killed all the katcinas. Their souls promptly returned to the Underworld where they mingled with the other spirits; but their masks, costumes, drums, and rattles were, perforce, left behind. The surviving Hopi sadly missed their good friends and, in the hope of retaining some of their benefits, they established the Katcina cult in which men wear the sacred paraphernalia and seek to bring rain by impersonating the gods.

Most of the impersonations take the form of group dances, with a score or two of participants. They meet secretly from time to time in order to rehearse appropriate songs and steps and on the day chosen for a public exhibition, they appear in colorful costumes featured by large masks that cover the face and head. The mask imparts sanctity to an impersonator, and he is regarded as a living god just as long as he wears his mask. In addition, the mask serves to conceal the wearer's identity and, to further the illusion that he is a supernatural visitor, a katcina dancer is forbidden to speak in his natural tone, although he may utter some special cry in a disguised voice.

No fixed limit is set to the number of katcina types that may be portrayed, and a wide range of variations and innovations is permitted. Popular representations include several deities and a host of plants, animals, heavenly bodies, natural phenomena, and men and women of other tribes. Each katcina has distinctive mask and body markings, a particular song and dance pattern, and conventional gestures and cries. As a rule an entire group of performers will represent the same katcina, but on some occasions mixed katcina types perform together.

There is an open and a closed season for katcina events. Masked impersonations are permitted only in the months that fall approximately between the winter and the summer solstices. During the rest of the year the katcinas are supposed to remain in their other world homes.

Annually, at Oraibi, katcina activities begin very late in November with the appearance of a solitary Soyal katcina whose coming announces the start of the open season. During the weeks that follow group katcina dances are staged whenever some enterprising person finds it possible to make the necessary arrangements. Since it is now apt to be cold, the performances are held in kivas. An open fire, carefully tended, provides light and heat; women are admitted as spectators on these occasions; and an atmosphere of joyful excitement prevails.

As soon as the February moon is sighted an announcement is made of the forthcoming Powamu celebration. This is the major ritual pertaining to the katcina cult, but its performance involves many other elements. Most important of these is the secret growing of beans and corn in super-heated kivas. Before the ceremony ends the fresh sprouts are distributed to the populace both as a mimetic device to promote good crops and as a visible token of the Powamu society's supernatural power, which enables it to grow food in the dead of winter.

With the coming of warm weather katcina dances are held at frequent intervals out-of-doors. Some are sponsored by people who have just recovered from illness, and others are staged on request to celebrate such events as a child's birthday. A religious element is invariably present, but it is often overlaid by the sheer pleasure and entertainment derived from the spectacle. Every dance day is a holiday, and in each home guests are freely welcomed. At last the time comes when the katcinas must depart. A final home-going (Niman) dance is held, after which the katcinas are symbolically locked up until the following winter.

A great many factors go to make up the katcina complex, but the details of their integration are of little moment to the Hopi. They make no effort to systematize their beliefs, but are content to regard the katcinas as an indeterminate host of friendly spirits. To impersonate them is a pleasure, to observe them a delight. Quite apart from its formal features the operation of the Katcina cult brings more warmth and color into the lives of the Hopi than any other aspect of their culture.

(c) *Solar Ceremonies.* Like all farming people the Hopi are keenly interested in the passage of the seasons and take careful note of the solstices. At these times the Gray and Blue Flute societies assemble to make offerings and prayers to the sun. Later, in mid-August, the two orders combine again to stage an elaborate nine-day ceremony, which is probably a modified summer solstice celebration. Once more prayers to the sun play an important part, but requests for rain and abundant crops are the dominant themes.

Events during the first eight days conform to the usual pattern, but the ninth day is full of special activities. A cottonwood bower is erected in the village plaza before dawn, and a foot-race is held just at daybreak. In the afternoon the members of the two societies repair to a spring where, to the accompaniment of flutes and rattles, they sing and pray. One of their leaders then plunges into the spring and brings out several gourds full of water that have been previously concealed. There follows a ceremonial procession from the spring to the town's plaza, during which two girls and a boy toss symbolic "ducks" before them as they go. Singers, flute players, and rattlers accompany the youngsters and keep up a constant flow of shrill music. When at last the procession comes to the plaza the water-filled gourds are handed to a waiting official who sits in the cottonwood bower. This action dramatizes the fact that by the power of their ritual the Flute societies have been enabled to bring water to the pueblo.

There are five Hopi villages that currently maintain Flute groups. In each of them the Flute rites alternate in successive years with performances by the Snake and Antelope societies.* A great many detailed resemblances provide evidence that in Hopi ceremonialism the Flute rituals and the Snake-Antelope observances are regarded as equivalent and interchangeable.

Although the Snake and the Antelope orders are independently organized, many of their ceremonial practices are carried out cooperatively. When the members assemble in their respective kivas in mid-August biennially, they follow the customary schedule of religious exercises for the first four days. On the fifth day, however, the Snake men go out to gather all the reptiles they can find to the

---

* By agreement among the pueblos these rites are so scheduled that in even-numbered years three towns hold Snake-Antelope celebrations and two have Flute ceremonies. In odd-numbered years the ratio is reversed.

north; and on the three following days they hunt to the west, south, and east. Snakes of any size or species are collected, "baptized" in the kiva, and saved for use in the public performance on the ninth day which is widely famed as the Snake Dance.

As in the case of the Flute rites the opening acts on the ninth day of the Snake-Antelope ceremony include the erection of a cottonwood bower and a foot-race that is held at daybreak. Late in the afternoon the Antelope men emerge from their kiva and take up positions with their backs to the bower. After a few moments the Snake men come striding into the plaza and line up facing the Antelopes. There is some preliminary singing by both groups, following which the Snake line breaks into pairs, with each couple dancing in a circuit about the plaza. When a pair reaches the bower the front man kneels, receives a live snake, puts it between his lips, and goes on with his dance. This continues until all of the captured snakes have been danced with, whereupon four runners hurry to release the reptiles at designated shrines, with prayers for rain, crops, and good health.

Like all of the main Hopi ceremonies the Snake-Antelope performances are not centered about a single theme. Included in the rites are prayers for rain and bountiful crops, links between the worlds of the living and the dead, several militaristic notions, and a strong element of sun worship.

(d) *Tribal Initiations.* Soon after the attainment of adolescence, but usually prior to his marriage, a young man is expected to go through a Tribal Initiation ceremony. This set of rites, celebrated in November, is practically universal for the male population and marks the transition from boyhood to adulthood. The observance is known as the Wuwutcim, but its performance is shared by four distinct societies called Singers (Tao), Horns (Al), Agaves (Kwan), and Wuwutcim. Membership in the Wuwutcim branch is by far the most common, but adult status may be achieved by joining any one of the four orders. The combined Tribal Initiation rituals are the most complicated and among the most vital of all Hopi ceremonies, and their significance must be appreciated if one wishes to grasp the essential meaning of Hopi religion.

The best clues to an understanding of the Tribal Initiation are to be found in the events that pertain to the induction of novices. Initiates into any of the four cooperating societies are called fledgling chicken hawks and are instructed to behave like immature birds for the first four days. They are also treated in several regards as if they were newly born babies.

A climax occurs on the night of the fourth day. It is a night of mystery and terror, for the spirits of the dead have been invited to return to the village and to participate in the festivities. Patrols of Kwan and Horn men patrol the pueblo's boundaries to make sure that no witches or evil sprites have mingled with the good spirits. Around midnight all the tyros are brought into the Kwan kiva. No white observer has ever seen what transpires there, but it is quite certain that in some way the novices are "killed" as boys and "re-born" as men. In keeping with this idea each initiate receives a new name and discards the name that he has used up to this time.

Various parts of the Tribal Initiation also serve to dramatize portions of the Emergence story. The continuity of life after death is affirmed by the supposed presence of visitors from the realm of the dead, and each candidate is assigned a specific station in the other world.

Of the societies that jointly conduct the Tribal Initiation the Singers and the Wuwutcim are conceptually much alike, and the Horn and the Agaves are closely linked. The former pair carry out numerous activities designed to stimulate fertility and germination, and the latter two are concerned with hunting and war. In addition, all four branches combine to bestow manhood on their initiates, to teach them the story of the tribe's origins, and to introduce them to the secrets of the other world.

(e) *The Soyal Rites.* Any young man who has passed through the Tribal Initiation is eligible to take part in the Soyal, but only those who had gone into the Wuwutcim society at the Chief kiva (see below), are qualified to participate in the full schedule of esoteric rites. These observances occur at the time of the winter solstice in December, and are designed to speed the sun on its northward course.

From many points of view the Soyal is the keystone of Hopi ceremonialism, especially at Oraibi. Its ownership is entrusted to the ruling Bear clan, its leader is the head man of the clan and serves also as Village chief; the chamber in which the secret exercises are held is designated Chief kiva, and the supporting officers

374

comprise the most important body of officials in the pueblo.

The Soyal ceremony is timed to begin sixteen days after the appearance of the Soyal katcina. Nothing unusual happens until late afternoon of the fourth day when a thick war medicine is prepared, the residue of which is carried out of the kiva by Soyal men who smear it on household mates to give them strength. On the sixth day messengers collect bundles of corn from every home. They are stacked next to the altar in the kiva, prayed over, and returned on the morrow to their owners for use as seed corn in the spring. Events on the ninth day commence soon after midnight and reach a climax when a sun symbol is twirled rapidly as a mimetic device to hasten the sun on its journey. At dawn every Soyal man makes the rounds of the village, handing out prayer-sticks to relatives and friends—much in the spirit that Americans distribute Christmas cards. Female villagers then hurry to deposit their offerings at a spot sacred to children, while the males rush to do the same at a hunting shrine. In addition, countless prayer feathers are tied to domestic animals, kiva ladders, fruit trees, chicken houses, and elsewhere.

As befits a ceremony that is conducted by the highest officers of the town, and which permits a measure of participation to virtually the entire populace, the Soyal touches on every important motive of Hopi religion. Expression is given to requests for good luck in connection with war, hunting, plant germination, human and animal fertility, the weather, and relations between the living and the dead. Observers are agreed, however, that the central aim of the Soyal is to induce the sun to begin on its northward journey, in order that warm weather may ultimately arrive and make possible the planting of crops.

(f) *Women's Ceremonies.* Although the operation of the annual cycle of rituals is entrusted primarily to males, the other sex is by no means totally excluded. Girls join the Katcina cult, and certain females take part in the Powamu, Flute, Snake-Antelope, and Soyal performances. In addition, there are three feminine societies called Marau, Lakon, and Oaqöl. As far as their organization is concerned the women's rites parallel the men's. They are owned by particular clans and conducted by secret societies; and their esoteric portions take place in kivas and include the standard practices of Hopi ceremonialism. All three groups hold their major exercises in the fall, and women may join one or more units at their pleasure.

Only slight variations occur in the performances of these ceremonies, but the Marau is the only one that has its own permanent kiva and that shows close ties with the main body of masculine rituals. In all three cases the most distinctive portion of the rites is the performance given in public on the ninth day. On such occasions most of the celebrants arrange themselves into a semicircular formation and begin to sing and move clockwise in unison. They are then joined by two or three special performers who enter the half-circle and throw gifts out to the spectators.

A comparative study of the women's ceremonies leads to the conclusion that they may well be regarded as three manifestations of a single ritualistic pattern. Furthermore, as their songs, prayers, initiation procedures, and religious symbols clearly indicate, the feminine observances are probably little more than a reflection of the men's rites.

V. The Meaning of Hopi Religion

Hopi ceremonialism has been aptly described as a kaleidoscope of ritual functions, with ever the same rites and functions appearing in ever different combinations. Such a situation presents a confused intermingling of repetitive details, but it also holds forth the hope that one may gain an insight into the meaning of Hopi religion by isolating the essential features that serve as common denominators throughout the rites.

As has been stated above, the most fundamental idea is a belief in the continuity of life after death. So strongly rooted is this faith that the demise of an individual is not looked upon as a loss to the society. On the contrary, the Hopi regard a dead person as one who will acquire supernatural power by undergoing a change of status to a cloud or a katcina. In every ceremony, therefore, the cult of the dead plays an important part.

A second basic element is the concept of a dual division of time and space between the upper and lower worlds. The Hopi believe that the sun comes out of an eastern home at dawn and descends into a western residence at dusk. During the night it travels underground from west to east, hence day and night are reversed in the two realms. The same principle applies to the seasons, with the result that when it is summer above it is winter below. In regard to religion these beliefs mean that corresponding ceremonies are being simultaneously performed (with the seasons reversed) in both spheres, and the implication is strong that the living and the dead can and do cooperate for each other's benefit.

Shorn of its elaborate and colorful superstructure of costumes, songs, and dances, the entire complex of Hopi religious behavior appears to be a large-scale attempt to safeguard Hopi society from dissolution. Whether an important figure dies, or a clan faces extinction, or drought threatens the crops, there is little need to worry for people and clans live on in the nether world, and in the guise of clouds or katcinas the spirits of the deceased can be counted on to provide rain. Moreover, the solar ceremonies are designed to win help from the sun, which is recognized as a powerful agent of germination.

Thus reduced to its barest essentials Hopi religion turns out to be a local manifestation of universally held beliefs. Everywhere primitive societies strive to achieve stability and permanence, and when material measures prove insufficient they resort to the supernatural world for help. It is primarily to achieve a guarantee of survival under all conditions that the Hopi religious system has been devised.

BIBLIOGRAPHY

ERNEST AND PEARL BEAGLEHOLE: *Hopi of the Second Mesa* in *Memoirs* of the American Anthropological Association (1935), 44.

F. H. CUSHING: "Origin Myth from Oraibi," *Journal of American Folklore* (1923), 36.

G. A. DORSEY AND H. R. VOTH: *The Oraibi Soyal Ceremony*, Field Columbian Museum, Anthropological Series (1901), 3.

——, *The Mishongnovi Ceremonies of the Snake and Antelope Fraternities, Ibid* (1902), 3.

E. EARLE AND E. A. KENNARD: *Hopi Kachinas* (New York, 1938).

J. W. FEWKES: "The Walpi Flute Observance," *Journal of American Folklore* (1894), 7.

——, "The New-Fire Ceremony at Walpi," *American Anthropologist* (1900), 2.

————, *Hopi Katcinas*, Bureau of American Ethnology, 21st Annual Report (1903).

E. A. KENNARD: "Hopi Reactions to Death," *American Anthropologist* (1937), 39.

E. C. PARSONS: *A Pueblo Indian Journal*, in *Memoirs* of the American Anthropological Association (1925), 32.

————, *Hopi Journal of Alexander M. Stephen*, Columbia University Contributions to Anthropology (1936), 23.

————, *Pueblo Indian Religion* (Chicago, 1939).

A. M. STEPHEN: "Hopi Tales," *Journal of American Folklore* (1929), 42.

M. TITIEV: "Dates of Planting at the Hopi Indian Pueblo of Oraibi," *Museum Notes, Museum of Northern Arizona* (1938), 11.

————, "Notes on Hopi Witchcraft," Papers of the Michigan Academy of Science, Arts, and Letters (1943), 28.

————, "Hopi Snake Handling," *Scientific Monthly* (1943), 57.

————, *Old Oraibi: A Study of the Hopi Indians of Third Mesa*, Papers of the Peabody Museum of Harvard (1944), 22.

H. R. VOTH: *The Oraibi Powamu Ceremony*, Field Columbian Museum, Anthropological Series (1901), 3.

————, *The Traditions of the Hopi, Ibid* (1905), 8.

————, *The Oraibi Marau Ceremony, Ibid* (1912), 11.

INDEX

379

INDEX

INDEX

INDEX

INDEX

Indonesia, 299.
Indra, 94, 261.
initiation, 181, 184, 185, 279ff., 289, 290, 368, 373ff.
inua, 320, 321.
inuat, 325.
inyua, 321.
inyusaq, 321.
iotunn, 239.
Iran, 206-209, 211, 212, 217, 218, 227-230, 232, 233.
Iranians, 48ff.
Ishara, 126.
ishib, 52.
Ishkur, 60.
Ishtar, 9, 52, 61, 68, 70, 71, 87, 91ff., 94, 95, 98, 126, 207.
Isi, 32.
Isimud, 59, 61.
Isis, 9, 28, 31, 33, 37, 41-43, 200, 207, 213.
Islahiye, 89.
Islam, 212, 217, 227, 232. See Moslem.
Isocrates, 195.
Israel, 114, 115, 130-134, 139, 140.
Istanu, 91, 92.

Jacob's ladder, 241.
Japan, 254, 260.
Jeremiah, 130.
Jesus, 220.
Jochelson, V. J., 301.
Jord, 243.
judgment, 36, 37.
Juktas, 150.
Julian, 212.
Jupiter, 43, 87, 94, 210.
justice, 99.

ka, 35, 263.
Kabta, 60.
Kagyud, 255, 262ff.
Kait, 93.
Kallichoron well, 184, 188.
kalpa, 256.
Kamares, 148.
Kamrusepa, 93, 100, 101.
Kanes, 86.
Kangalik, 313.
kangaroo, 276, 278.
Kansu, 253, 266.
Kantuzzili, 99.

Karatepe, 115, 123.
Karma, 264, 265.
Karma Dussumkhyenpa, 264.
Karma Kagyud, 264.
Karzi, 92.
Kashmir, 257.
Kasku, 91, 92.
Kassites, 69.
Kassu, 70.
Katahzipuri, 93.
Katcina cult, 368ff., 370ff, 375-377.
Kathog, 260.
Kattahha, 93.
Kawadh, 230, 231.
Kedesh, 31.
Kesh, 60.
Kham, 253, 257, 260, 264, 268.
Khaybet, 35.
Khepri, 10.
Kherheb, 38.
Khidr, 126.
Khnemu, 6.
Khnum, 30.
Khonluwangposrungba, 262.
Khonpalboche, 262.
Khonsu, 30.
Khonton, 262.
Khu, 35.
Khubilai Khan, 262.
Khurshed, 206.
Khusrav, 231.
Khridetsutan, 254.
Khriralpacan, 255.
Khrisongdetsan, 255, 257, 261.
Khyarbon, 256.
Khyungpo, 263, 264.
Ki, 57, 59.
Kimon, 188.
king, 78, 118, 119, 130, 132. See royalty.
kishar, 12, 14.
kittu, 99.
kivas, 367-369.
Kizzuwatna, 97.
Kluckhohn, C., 343, 344, 350, 359-361.
Knossos, 150, 153-158, 161, 162.
Kodiak Island, 311.
Kohanim, 134.
Kokonor, 253.
Konchog Gyalpo, 262.
Kôshar, 124, 135-137.
kosharat, 125.
Kourounites, K., 182.

385

INDEX

INDEX

Mercer, S. A. B., 25.
Meri, 31.
Merkyut, 302.
Mesopotamia, 48ff., 65ff., 69, 71, 78, 84-86, 88, 94, 96, 97, 103, 104, 114, 305.
Mexicans, 370.
Mexico, 294.
Mezzulla, 90, 92, 99.
Michael, archangel, 206.
Midgard, 241, 242.
midrashim, 116.
Milarepa, 263, 264.
Milky Way, 6-9, 11-17, 23, 24.
Mimir, 242.
Min, 30.
Mineptah, 127.
Mingrolling, 260.
Minoan culture, 147ff.
Minos, 126, 147, 150, 153, 154.
mîšaru, 99.
Mishor, 123.
Mithra, 205-214, 222.
Mithraism, 205ff.
Mithradates, 209.
Mithro-Druj, 206.
Mitra, 94, 206, 207.
Mizar, 8.
Mochlos, 162.
monasteries, 258, 261, 265, 266, 268.
monotheism, 163.
Mons Casius, 89.
Montu, 30.
Moon-man, 323, 324.
morality, see ethics; morality, Egyptian, 41ff.
Moslem, 154. See Islam.
Môt, 122, 136.
mountains, 8, 89, 161, 164, 174.
Mt. Meru, 8.
mtrh, 132.
Multiple-Colored Sect, 261ff.
multiverse, 117.
mummification, 283.
Mummu, 9-11.
Mursili, 98, 99.
Mushadamma, 60.
Muspellsheim, 239, 241.
Mût, 31.
Mycenae, 151, 152; Mycenaean Age, 182; Mycenaean culture, 147.
Mylonas, E. G., 145, 169.

mystagogoi, 183, 186.
mystery cults, 200; mystic rites, 173ff.
Mystery Religions of Greece, 171ff.
myths, 100ff., 118, 119, 135ff., 141, 244, 278, 280, 319, 333, 359; mythology, 237ff.

Nabû, 69.
Nal, 243.
Nalanda, 263.
names, 325.
Nammu, 56, 57.
Namni, 94.
Namni, Mt., 89.
Nanna, 51ff., 57, 58, 68, 243.
Naropa, 263.
Nasatyas, 94.
nature worship, 171, 210.
Navaho Indians, Religion of, 343ff.
Navajo, 24; Navajo mythology, 8; Navajo religion, 4.
Nebo, 69, 70.
Neith, 31.
Neolithic Age, 147ff.
Neo Platonism, 220.
Nepal, 254.
Nephthys, 31, 33, 37.
Nergal, 58, 68, 70, 92, 123.
Nerik, 90, 99.
nesili, 85.
Nesite, 85, 86, 93.
Nestorians, 262.
Nether-World, 12, 68, 77, 102, 120, 122, 123, 128, 129, 136, 157, 158, 300, 369.
New Mexico, 344ff.
Ngari Khorsum, 256.
Ngorpa, 262, 263.
Nidhoggr, 242, 245.
Niflheim, 239, 242.
Niinnion, 186.
Nikkal, 94, 123.
Nile, 6, 33, 34, 207.
Nilsson, M. P., 156, 158, 163.
Niman, 371.
Ninatta, 92, 94.
Ninazu, 58.
Ningal, 52, 94.
Ningirsu, 70.
Ningma, 255, 258ff., 262.
Ninhursag, 59, 60.
Ninive, 91.
Ninkurra, 59.

387

INDEX

Ninlil, 58ff., 70.
Ninmah, 57.
Ninmu, 59.
Ninshubur, 61.
Nintud, 95.
Ninurta, 9, 70.
Nippur, 58, 68.
Niron Khani, 159.
Njordr, 243.
Nonnus, 180.
Norse Religion, Old, 237ff.; editor's preface.
Noshirwan, 231, 232.
Nudimmud, 9, 11-14, 23.
numen, 119, 129, 141.
numina, 121.
Nun, 31, 33.
Nunivak Island, 313.
Nut, 9, 28, 32.

Oaqöl, 375.
ôb, 129.
Oceania, 7.
Oceanus, 242.
Odin, 239, 241-244.
oecumene, 199.
Ogdoad, 33.
Ohlmarks, A., 306.
Old Testament, 114, 116, 123-129, 131, 133, 134, 139, 140, 222.
Olympian Gods, 171.
Olympus, 209.
Om Mani Padme Hum, 258.
Ombos, 29.
omina, 96ff.
Ona, 290.
Ona of Tierra del Fuego, 287.
O'Neill, 7.
Onomakritos, 181.
Ophiōneus, 139.
Oppenheim, A. L., 9, 11-13, 63.
oracles, 95ff.
Oraibi, 365, 371, 374.
Orion, 7, 12, 17, 24, 29, 32, 138, 139.
Orpheotelestai, 180.
Orpheus, 177ff., 182.
Orphic, 126, 200; Orphic mysteries, 40, 173, 177ff.
Orthodox Greek Church, 230.
Osiris, 29-37, 39-43, 207, 213.
Ostyaks, 303.
Ouranos, 14.

388

Padma-bhyun-gnas, 255.
Pahlavi, 220.
paintings, 280, 349, 369, 293; Painted Stoa, 184; Painted Temple, 51ff. See sand-paintings.
Palaic, 93.
Palaumnili, 85.
palengenesia, 172.
Palyul, 260.
Panchen, 265, 267.
Papaver Somniferum, 159.
paprātar, 98.
paraclete, 243.
Paradise Myth, 59ff.
parenticide, 290.
Pars, 209, 218.
Partanen, J., 303.
Parthenion, 185.
Parthenos, 127.
pashes, 52.
Passover, 133.
Paul, St., 201.
Pausanias, 40.
Peisistratos, 181, 188.
Pelagia, St., 126.
Pelasgi Religion, 165; editor's preface.
Pentateuch, 133.
Pentecost, 139.
Pentheus, 176, 177.
Pericles, 188, 199.
Persephone, 136, 178, 180, 182, 185, 186.
Persia, 197, 299.
Persson, A. W., 157.
Peru, 293.
Pesah, 133.
Pessinus, 95.
Petsofa, 150.
Phaestos, 153, 154, 159.
Phagmo, 264.
Phagmo Grubpa, 264.
Phagspa, 262.
phallos, 5, 10, 11, 13, 16, 30; phallic rites, 4.
pharaoh, 32, 37, 42.
Philip, 197.
Philistines, 127, 128.
Philo Byblius, 103.
philosophy, 32.
Phoenicians, 4, 5, 103, 132, 133, 139.
Phrygian, 132.
Pindar, 188.
Plague Prayers, 98, 99.

INDEX

supernaturalism, 290, 295, 318, 319, 328, 330, 331, 336, 344, 345; supernatural beings, 287ff.
Suppiluliuma, 98.
Surtr, 241.
Sutekh, 31.
symbols, 72, 73, 151.
Syn, 243.
Szechwan, 253.

tabu, 277, 290, 323, 328-330, 333, 334, 336, 346, 347.
Takánakapsâluk, 302.
tâkultu, 131.
Talliya, 129.
Tammuz, 71, 95, 101, 119.
Tanis, 128.
Tannin, 139.
Tao, 373.
Taoists, 262.
Taraporewala, I. J. S., 203, 215, 225.
Tarhunt, 88, 93, 95.
tartat, 321.
Taru, 88, 92.
Tatars, 300.
Tefnet, 11.
Tefnut, 30, 32, 33.
Telepinu, 93.
Telesterion, 184.
telete, 177, 184, 187.
Telipinu, 95, 101, 103.
Tell el-Amarna, 30, 114.
Tell Halaf, 89.
temples, 53ff., 133ff., 153ff., 184, 292; Egyptian, 38ff.; Mesopotamian, 73ff.; Sumerian, 51ff.
Tengchen, 257.
tenûphah, 133.
Teshrit, 130.
Teshub, 88-90, 92, 94, 103, 104.
Tethys, 126.
textiles, 2.
Thalbitzer, W., 320, 321.
Thales, 195.
Thamuatz, 9.
Thebes, 35, 39, 196.
theocracy, 228.
theogony, 103, 104.
theology, Sumerian, 54ff.
theoxenia, 131.
thiasoi, 181.
Thor, 240, 241, 243.

Thot, 33, 37, 40.
Thothmes, 127.
Thrace, 173, 176, 181.
Thummim, 134.
Thutmose, 38.
Tiamat, 6, 9, 12-14.
Tibetan Religion, 253ff.
Tierra del Fuego, 291.
Tigris, 67ff., 69, 207.
Tilopa, 263.
Tiryns, 159.
Tishri, 131.
Titans, 178-180.
Titiev, M., 363.
tophet, 141.
tornait, 321.
torngrat, 321.
tornrait, 322, 323.
tornrak, 322.
totemism, 276ff., 283, 327.
trance, 306.
transmigration, 179, 326.
Tree, Cosmic, 303, 304, 306.
trees, 5.
trichotomy, 350.
trilithon, 150.
trinity, 243.
Triptolemos, 182.
Triton, 159.
Tsang, 253.
Tshachen Losel Gyamtsho, 263.
Tshalpa, 264.
Tsharpas, 263.
Tsinghai, 253.
Tsongkhap, 266.
Tsongkhapa, 264, 265.
Tsountas, C., 147, 152.
Tucanoan, 290.
tungat, 321.
Tungus, 301.
Tunguses, 303.
Turin Papyrus, 40.
Tuthaliya, 86, 87.
Tvastri, 124.
Tylor, E. B., 322.
Typhon, 102-104.
Tyr, 243.
Tyre, 127.

U, 253, 256.
udesi-burkhan, 303.
Ugar, 129.

391